KAYLEE MILLER

THE VEIL OF OPPRESSION

REVELATIONS SERIES
PART ONE

Kaylee Miller

The Veil of Oppression, Revelations Series, Part One / Kaylee Miller

ISBN: 979-8-89316-275-2—paperback
ISBN: 979-8-89316-276-9—ebook
ISBN: 979-8-89316-319-3—hardcover

This is a work of fiction. Names, characters, places, and incidents either are the product of the author's imagination or are used fictitiously. Any resemblance to persons living or dead is entirely coincidental.

All brand names and product names used in this book are trademarks, registered trademarks, or trade names of their respective holders. Kaylee Miller is not associated with any product or vendor in this book.

The author does not consent to any Artificial Intelligence (AI), generative AI, large language model, machine learning, chatbot, or other automated analysis, generative process, or replication program to reproduce, mimic, remix, summarize, or otherwise replicate any part of this creative work, via any means: print, graphic, sculpture, multimedia, audio, or other medium. The author supports the right of humans to control their artistic works. No part of this book has been created using AI-generated images or narrative, as known by the author.

The author acknowledges that this work of fiction was crafted on the unceded traditional territories of the xʷməθkʷəy̓əm (Musqueam), Sḵwx̱wú7mesh (Squamish), and səlilwətaɬ (Tsleil-Waututh) First Nations, as well as the territory of the Mississaugas of the Credit First Nation, and the territories of the Anishinabek, Huron-Wendat, Haudenosaunee and Ojibway/Chippewa peoples. The author acknowledges, honours, and respects that she has lived, worked, and thrived on the unceded territories of the peoples listed above, and continues to do so on the traditional territories of the xʷməθkʷəy̓əm (Musqueam), Sḵwx̱wú7mesh (Squamish), and səlilwətaɬ (Tsleil-Waututh) First Nations.

Trigger warning: This book contains depictions of emotional and physical abuse, gore and violence, sexual content, drug and alcohol use, societal discrimination, and strong language that may be sensitive to some readers. Reader discretion is advised. All acts of a sexual nature that have been depicted between the characters are consensual.

Book Cover Design: Miblart

For you, my reader: For always keeping me grounded in my "why," and being my reason to keep typing, and typing, and typing.

Only in learning to stand on your own can you stand for others.

To gain exclusive access to soundtrack guides, deleted scenes, and more, sign up to my author newsletter at:

www.kayleemillerwriter.com

CONTENTS

Part Two – The Snare of Addiction (sneak peek)

PROLOGUE
VANCOUVER

On a typical Wednesday afternoon on the manicured streets of downtown Vancouver, a man in a black jacket shoots a man in a three-piece suit outside a coffee shop. These bullets are not intended to warn or to scare; they're intended to kill, and the man in the trench coat pulls the trigger, three times, at a loss for hesitation. The time has come. The final straw has broken, and there's no other way. Now, the suited man must pay, and he must pay with his life. It has to be him.

People scream, people scatter, their otherwise ordinary day interrupted, but it doesn't matter now. The sidewalk is bathed in blood and so is the sixteen-year-old who watches the man in the suit die. The boy drops to his side in horror as the light leaves his black suited man's eyes. Only then is the shooter aware that the deed is done.

He's dreamt of this moment many times. In fact, it's been running on repeat for days in his head, and now that it's come, he's in pain. He's vindicated, for what it's worth, but he's suffering and choking on his breath. He shakes as he falls to his knees. The blood runs down the sidewalk and seeps into his pants in a sudden reminder of what he's just done. Soon the police will arrive to take him away, but it doesn't matter. He knows he won't get away, but it had to be done. It had to end, and now it has. He had no other choice.

So, on that dreary day at the corner of Georgia and Howe, a man shoots another man until he lies dead in the street. Because he thinks it's the only way that he can save his son.

1

CHAPTER 1
DON'T FORGET TO REMEMBER ME

I saw the first person who would change my life at gate D thirty-eight at Toronto's Pearson International Airport. The one with the electronic sign which declared *Vancouver: 11:00*. I caught sight of her as I glanced around the waiting area; a trim, older woman, probably in her early seventies, sitting near the check-in desk. She had short, grey hair, and was wearing designer clothes. Though she wasn't talking to anyone, she had a *kind* energy. I could feel it. She was reading a book with a worn cover, which looked like it'd had a sleeve before. A Louis Vuitton carry-on with a matching purse was sitting on the floor beside her.

I was interested in her for a reason that I couldn't explain. She was so well dressed that she didn't seem like she belonged on an economy Air Canada flight to Vancouver, but she carried herself like she was meant to be there. Spine straight. Lip curled in a gentle half-smile. Intrigued, I began to run through the scenarios of who she could be. A stuffy woman forced on a cheap business flight? The loving mother of a pilot, too nervous to fly with anyone but her son? A doctor on the edge of retirement, who's on her way to a last-minute medical conference at the Marriott in downtown Vancouver?

She glanced up from her book, and her pale brown eyes met mine with the shock of our souls connecting. I glanced away, pretending that I hadn't been looking. I turned toward the seats with the charging ports.

Now that I was distracted, reality returned, and I drew a heavy breath as I plopped my backpack next to my seat and pulled out my charger. Not half an hour before, I'd left my parents at the airport door, and now the thing was quivering when I tried to plug it in. Trying my best to settle, I put my phone aside and crossed my legs into a lotus pose, pulling my wavy, blonde hair into a messy bun and straining against the tension in my hips. I inhaled and exhaled as I tried to push them further. The yoga session that I'd done in my mum's home studio the night before hadn't done much.

I pictured the sitting room in our early-twentieth-century house that she'd converted into her studio and thought about how I wouldn't step foot in there for a long time. Tears pricked the back of my eyes. Her studio was filled to the brim with love and passion, and she'd covered the walls in all manner of tapestries and artwork that brought her peace. Buddhas, chakras, copper elephants, mandalas of every colour. She'd even hung the misshapen lotus that I'd painted her for Mother's Day when I was six, right above the door so she could look at it during her sessions.

"It fits there, Em," she'd told me when I begged her to take it down. "It's a reminder of the great blessings the Universe has gifted me."

When she'd started teaching yoga, it was just a small group of her friends, but now she welcomed a rotating door of Botox-filled, *Real-Housewives-of-Toronto* types. It'd taken her years, and endless hard work, but she was finally making a good living off her homemade business.

My stomach twisted when I remembered our session the night before and how upset she was that I was leaving.

"I'm in my late twenties," I'd told her, as her cheeks started to dampen. "You're lucky I've been too lazy to leave the house already."

She didn't respond the way I'd wanted. She was a master at controlling her emotions, but there was no joke that was good enough to get her to crack a smile that night. My dad, quiet as he nursed a glass of whisky, had been just as bad. He was a professor of education at York University who literally taught people how to teach, so I'd imagined he'd understand a move across the country to get more education. The glass alone proved me wrong. Apparently, emotion trumped logic when his only daughter was flying the nest. Especially when that daughter was as fragile as I was. Especially when that daughter was *me*.

Surrounded by the bustling energy of the airport, I held the corners of my eyes and tried to control the biting emotions with my mum's breathing techniques. I was lucky—*so* lucky—to have such devoted and supportive parents. That I knew. And I couldn't contain how much it hurt me to leave them too, but I had to. It had been years since I'd finished my undergrad, and if I didn't pull myself out of my stagnant life now, I was afraid I'd never get out.

With my face flushing from holding my breath, I wiped my eyes and focused on the people moving through the airport. Couples held hands as they passed, their bags wheeling along leisurely behind them. Stressed parents pushed trollies filled with carry-ons as their children skipped after them. A group of girls giggled at an inside joke as their travel pillows swung from their backpacks. They all had somewhere to be. Somewhere other than my home city. And now, I did too. I looked down, realizing that I'd been twisting the emerald ring that'd never left my finger.

"Oh, God..." I breathed, turning to my phone for another distraction.

How was I supposed to do this? I'd never been on my own before, let alone moved to the other end of the country. What would I do if something went wrong? Who would help me when I needed it? My parents would be 5000 kilometers away, and I wouldn't be able to depend on them. Who could I run to when it was all too much? And why the fuck was I doing this to myself?

Shivering, I pulled up Facebook for a dopamine hit, but it didn't work. Up popped one of those "On This Day" memories: a bright and cheery photo of my ex-boyfriend Andy and me three years ago. Our faces pressed together as we grinned from ear to ear. The CN Tower looming in the background. It was a photo taken at a different time. A time that had seemed like a dream, but now was a series of painful memories. Back when we were still in love. Or what we hoped was love, anyway.

I scoffed, pressing the lock button on my phone to take the image away.

If they're going to show shit like that, they really need to install a "No happy photos of me and the man that I used to love" button, I thought.

It hurt like a kick in the teeth.

My phone dinged, and a text from Mum appeared to make things worse. *Send me a message when you're boarded and going into airplane mode. I miss you already.*

Pressure built somewhere in the middle of my brain.

Yep, I text back. *Just at the gate. Boarding soon.*

I love you endlessly, Emily Alice, is what came back.

The pressure intensified.

"Fuck." I tossed my phone aside and ran my hand across my head. Though I couldn't feel the ridge of the scar that sat somewhere near the back, the distinct tingle reminded me that it was there. "Fuck, fuck, fuck."

It wasn't too late to turn around. I could snatch my backpack, run back through security, beg the attendant to pull my suitcase back, and call my parents to take me home. We hadn't boarded yet. There was still time to change my mind. I mean, it would *suck*, but I still could if I really, really wanted to.

From across the gate, the older woman was looking at me again.

No, I thought, avoiding her gaze. *I have to do this. I can't cling to my parents for the rest of my life.*

Never mind the fact that I had no friends left in town, I was bored to death with the job I'd held onto after I'd graduated, and my life in Toronto was slowly slipping into numbness. I needed this opportunity to start fresh. There was something waiting for me in Vancouver, and I was sure of it. I refused to be a victim of my comfort zone. But the self-assurance didn't stop the guilt from spreading through my bones. My whole world was changing and, inevitably, so were the worlds of my parents. Was it for better or worse? That was yet to be seen...

The electronic board changed the status of our flight to *Boarding*, and we were called to line up by zone. My heart started to race. I packed my phone and charger into my backpack and made my way to line up with the rest of the crowd. The older woman went back to reading; waiting with the patience of a saint to join the line last.

Minute by minute, the chance to turn back was slipping away.

When I'd settled in my window seat with my backpack tucked at my feet, those minutes were nearly non-existent. I'd boarded in the last zone, and I was very aware that soon we'd be taxiing for takeoff.

"All passengers onboard," a voice on the intercom said, as if to punctuate this. "Flight attendants secure the cabin."

My emerald ring was bound to leave a mark if I kept twisting it so much.

Then, the energy of my neighbouring passenger entered from the aisle. I looked up to find the older woman lifting her Louis Vuitton into the overhead like a frequent-flier pro.

Interesting. Why would the Universe bring us together like this?

There was a sign here. I was sure of it. Otherwise, why would I have picked her out from the crowd at the gate? Why would she be in the seat next to me? Infused with a lifetime of my mum's spiritual beliefs, I was, well, *aware* of things like that. There were messages, signals, direction, and nudges that came from our spiritual protectors. Or even directly from the *Source*. You just had to know where to look for them and pay attention when they came up. That was the hard part. Noticing, listening, and taking the right action. That's what I had trouble with. And, as she slid beside me and started to browse through the inflight magazine, I wondered what kind of role she'd play in my new life. If any. *If* I let her...

She blinked as she looked at me, and I realized I'd been staring. I turned to the window and put way too much attention into watching the last of the bags being loaded instead.

"Good morning, passengers," the intercom said, "this is your captain speaking from the flight deck. The crew's finishing up with the last of the cargo, and then we should be on our way. Time to Vancouver is approximately five hours and eight minutes. We anticipate a bit of bumps over the prairies, but other than that, it should be a smooth flight. Local time upon landing will be just after 1pm. The weather in Vancouver is a beautiful eighteen degrees with sunny skies—"

I tuned out, because I didn't care about the weather in Vancouver. I cared about whether I was making a drastic mistake by choosing it.

Soon, the plane began to move, and the safety video started. My heartbeat picked up a bit. Unlike the older woman, I wasn't much of a frequent flier, and this flight marked the beginning of a new chapter for me. One of the biggest chapters in my life, in fact. I was moving all the way across the country, without any proof that it was safe. *Without* my support system.

Once again, I asked myself what the fuck I was doing.

We stopped at the end of the runway, and the engines began to whir, lurching the plane forward. A hand gripped mine tightly, and I looked over at the woman next to me. Her expression was pinched and not at all what I'd expect from a *frequent-flier* pro. I shot her a questioning look, trying hard not to be rude while I slid my hand away.

"Sorry," she said, clenching her fist around the armrest. "I'm not much good during takeoff."

I smiled tightly, masking my own nervousness as the plane surged forward and lifted off. I closed my eyes as we rose higher into the sky, away from Toronto, and by the time I was brave enough to open them again, my city was falling away. We turned one way, and then the other. I watched the CN Tower and the SkyDome slip out of sight, knowing that I wouldn't see them for another year or so. My stomach clenched. But then we breached the cloud barrier, and the sunlight bathing us filled me with a contrasting hope. It made me feel like I could finally breathe again.

You can do this, Em, I reminded myself. *This is a new adventure. That's all.*

Besides, no one would know me in Vancouver or shoot me sympathy when I passed. I hated the looks I got from the people who knew what happened to me, and why I'd been living with my parents well past the time that most kids fly the nest.

New start, yeah?

And if I didn't like it, I could always go back...

"Excuse me," the older woman said, getting up from her seat.

I nodded in her direction, then glanced back out the window. Outside, the fluffy, white clouds created a cushion underneath us.

This'll be an amazing adventure, I tried to tell myself.

But I couldn't help but long for the safety net of *home.* Being independent was a strange feeling, and I wasn't sure I liked it yet.

Gripping the seat, I pushed the past away and shifted my focus to the future. After all, it was happening whether I liked it or not, so I needed to embrace it. I needed to build my own life, and that started now. No more relying on Mum's interpretation of every little thing that happened to me. No more calling Dad every time I got into the tiniest bit of trouble. I'd do this on my own. I'd been accepted into the University of British Columbia's master's program for Medical Ethics, so someone thought I had what it took.

I drummed my fingers on the armrest, taking several deep breaths as I tried to convince myself that everything would be okay. Frustrated with the buzz of nervousness from my core, I decided to pull out my headphones and browse through the movies on the screen in front of me. The woman returned and huffed when she sat down. I gave her a weak smile, but the memories of my past were still torturing me. Like some sick mental photo reel. And not *sick* in the good way.

After ten years together, my ex-boyfriend Andy and I had gone through a nasty break up two months before. We'd been dating since high school, and I thought one day I'd marry him. Spend the rest of my life happily ever-after, by his side. But it hadn't turned out that way. He'd changed in the past couple of years, and the root of it lay in how *I'd* changed after my accident. The freakish ability I'd been "gifted." The fact that I'd started uncontrollably calling another man's name after waking up from using it. I'd changed and therefore *he'd* changed, but it wasn't my fault. If he couldn't accept me for who I was, then we were no longer aligned with what we wanted for our future. I'd known that our relationship had to end for a while, but I'd never faced it until I was forced to. Oddly enough, it'd ended the day I'd accepted my offer to the UBC...

The flight attendant came by with her cart, offering drinks and snacks. The people surrounding her perked up like little prairie dogs from their dens.

The woman turned to me. "I'm going to order a glass of white wine," she said. "Would you like one?"

"Oh, no." I choked out a laugh and gave a dismissive wave. "I don't wanna pay for expensive airplane wine."

"Nonsense. It's on me. Don't even worry about it."

I hesitated. "Um. Okay. That'd be nice. Thanks very much." I figured it was rude to refuse. And maybe it'd help with my nerves?

She flagged the flight attendant and ordered. The flight attendant made them and passed them one at a time. The woman gave the first to me before setting the other on the tray in front of her. She paid with the tap of a fancy-looking credit card.

"Thank you," I said.

"You're welcome," she replied. "It didn't seem right to leave you in turmoil while I get to relax with some wine."

The laugh I did was *way* more nervous than I wanted it to be. "That obvious, huh?"

"Just a little." She smiled. "So, what brings you out to Vancouver..." she paused expectantly.

"Emily Anderson," I said.

"Carol Hart." She extended a well-manicured hand. "Nice to meet you, Emily."

"You too," I said.

We made idle chit-chat for a bit. I told her about my master's and learned that she'd been in Toronto visiting a few friends. It was nice to have someone to talk to, and it took my mind off the whirlwind of emotions that were smacking around in my head. But eventually the wine started to make me sleepy, and when I mentioned this to Carol, she giggled.

"You have the right idea," she said. "I'm going to do the same."

I smiled and bunched up my sweater, pressing it against the chilled plexiglass window.

What the fuck are you doing here, Em?

I rested my head on the soft fabric and closed my eyes. Everything would be okay. I just had to follow the signs.

I can see through Carol's eyes that she's standing in a massive kitchen with white marble countertops and light grey cabinets. She's placing baking liner on some cookie sheets that are on the countertop. Top of the line appliances deck out the kitchen, and the windows go all the way to the top of the high ceilings. Light floods in above the double sink. To the left of the kitchen is an informal dining area, and at the back of the house there is a set of French doors that lead out onto a patio, pool area, and sprawling gardens that are set dormant in winter.

A young boy with brown hair and light brown eyes that match Carol's is standing on a step stool at the edge of the countertop, removing the six-wire whip paddle from an automatic mixer. A bowl of batter sits below. He must be around seven or eight.

Carol smiles and turns to him, catching his wrist when he goes to lick the paddle. "Travis, I told you not to taste it. The batter has raw eggs in it, which are very bad for you."

He looks up, giving her puppy-dog eyes. "But Grandma, you let me last time. Come on, I've done it before. Nothing bad happened then. Plus, it's my favourite part."

She sighs and I feel her give him a contemplating smile. "Well. I suppose if I turn away for a moment, I won't see if you've done it or not. But you should know that you're not supposed to."

After all, she tells me through her thoughts, *what grandmother doesn't let their grandchildren lick the paddle when they're baking? It could only do his immune system some good.*

Travis grins and she turns away, walking over to the informal dining area where a baby with dark red hair is cuddled in an infant seat, cooing away. Carol smiles down at him, and I notice that his eyes are a beautiful dark brown. So dark, in fact, that they're better described as black. She starts running her fingers through the baby's soft hair, and shimmers of affection tickle her skin. He gives her a toothless smile and reaches out, trying to grip her hand.

"My little Elmo," she says softly.

Then a stern man walks in and joins them. He is undoubtedly handsome and tall, with a strong jawline and symmetrical features, and his copper hair and black eyes match the baby's. He's dressed in a pinstriped suit and a red tie; though his feet move across the floor in simple, black socks. He gives Carol a nod as he makes his way over, kissing her sharply on the cheek. "What's going on in here, then?"

She grips the top of his arm. "Welcome home, John."

"We're baking, Dad!" Travis announces, looking happy now that he's finished cleaning the paddle.

"Baking?" John says, shooting Carol an apprehensive look. But then he goes to the baby, breaking into a contrasting smile when he looks down at him. "Are you having fun?"

"Yes," Travis says, holding the paddle over the sink and watching the batter stretch and drip down to the bottom.

"Well, I am happy to see you're enjoying it, Travis Benjamin," John says. "But I require some father-son time."

Suddenly, there's a tightness in Carol's throat. She swallows, but it doesn't clear.

The paddle droops in Travis's hand, and he watches his father with sudden unease; light brown meeting dark. He sighs as he drops it. It clinks as it lands in the sink.

"Meet me in the lounge when you're cleaned up, son," John says, giving the baby one last glance before turning away from them. "I'm looking forward to the cookies, Carol, but my boys don't need to learn how to bake." His voice echoes harshly from the walls as he goes down the hall.

Travis drops his gaze into the sink before stepping off the stool in a huff. He drags himself over to Carol and wraps his arms around her waist. "Do I have to?" he whispers.

"Yes, honey," Carol says, holding him back. "You can't take the time with your father for granted. Now run along. It's best not to keep him waiting." Her feelings don't match her words. I can tell that she doesn't want to let him go.

Travis lets her go instead, then makes his way over to his baby brother. He flashes him a quick smile before kissing him on the forehead. The baby grins, and Travis says, "I love you," before dropping his arms to his side. He continues sulking as he trudges down the hall, following in his father's footsteps.

Carol watches him with gloom washing over—

I sprung awake and realized my throat was burning. I glanced around cautiously, looking for any sign that I'd been screaming. A couple of people confirmed it with dirty looks, but most were still watching TV.

"Emily?" Carol's voice was soothing from beside me. Her light brown eyes searched mine. "Everything alright?"

I drew a couple of sharp breaths, embarrassment rising as she studied me. She had the look of a grandmother that very much wanted to put the back of her hand to my forehead. "Oh... Yeah... Everything's fine. I must have fallen asleep and had a nightmare, is all."

Tell me I didn't scream it...

But Carol's eyes stayed glued to mine. She seemed shaken, and I felt bad for scaring her.

Oh, fuck. I did, didn't I?

Sweat was starting to bead on my forehead.

"Did I say something?" I asked. "When I woke up?"

Carol searched my face before she slowly lifted an eyebrow. "Yes. You said, 'Barrett.'"

I did a mental facepalm. Of course I had. That name had been haunting me since the accident. It was the massive question mark of my ability and was probably the biggest reason for my breakup with Andy. Every time I saw a memory, I'd wake up screaming for a stranger.

Then Carol gave me a funny look and hit me with something even funnier. "It's just... That's my grandson's name... Do you know him?"

CHAPTER 2
PARADISE

The colour drained from my face.

It's... It's what?

Here we go again with the signs.

"Isn't it Travis?" I sputtered.

"Sorry?"

"Your grandson's name. Isn't it Travis?"

Carol paused. "Did I tell you that?"

Oh my God. How the fuck do I explain this?

I zipped my lips together, and Carol blinked. The stretch of silence that happened after was about as tense as a rubber band about to snap.

How do I cover this without revealing how much of a freak I am?

Luckily, Carol shrugged and solved the problem for me. "I guess I mentioned it somewhere during our chat."

"Yep. That must've been it." There was a bubble in my throat that refused to pop.

She still looked wildly uncomfortable. Like she was searching the plane's ceiling for what to say next. "They own Roth Pharmaceuticals, you know. My grandsons are Travis and Barrett Roth."

Explains the Louis-Vuitton. And why I was so drawn to her...

"Travis—as you've so expertly remembered—is the CEO," Carol explained.

"Oh," was all I said.

She paused. "Are you quite sure you've never met him? Barrett, I mean?"

I shook my head. Of course, I knew about Roth Pharmaceuticals. They were the biggest pharmaceutical company in North America, and their products were all over the pharmacies, grocery stores, and convenience shops. But I'd never heard of the men that owned it. Those kinds of people—really fucking *rich* people—were not what I cared about when my family was struggling to pay our utility bills. Plus, the questionable morals of big pharma were part of the reason why I'd decided to study Medical Ethics. They were shit. A necessary evil, but commonly shit. So... *what?* How could her grandson possibly be *my* Barrett?

After the accident, I *had* Googled the name "Barrett" in a desperate attempt to gain some clarity on why I'd started screaming it. But all I'd got was a list of faceless celebrities and a story about a sixteen-year-old boy whose father had been murdered on the streets of Vancouver. I never imagined in a million years that I'd find the person that belonged to this mysterious name; let alone be nudged toward him on the very first day of my move.

Vancouver. Roth Pharmaceuticals. What did it all mean?

Suddenly, all the horrid memories of my accident came flooding back. The scream of the tires, the pain of impact, the shattering glass. The pavement on Eglinton. The coma. Mum crying at my hospital bed as she slipped the emerald ring on my finger. Grasping it in desperate hope. The way that my parents couldn't let me go after it happened—

"Are you alright, my dear? You look like you've seen a ghost."

I nodded. Vehemently. "Yeah. My mouth. A bit dry, is all."

"Shall I flag them for some water?"

"No, really. I'm okay."

Carol looked confused. "Are you sure I haven't upset you?"

I waved her off. "No, no. Course not. Bad dream is all. But would you excuse me, please? I need to go to the bathroom."

15

"Oh. Yes. Alright."

I stumbled over the feet of the teenager at the end of our aisle, who'd flat-out refused to move out of the way. People stared as I moved toward the back of the plane, and my legs felt like they were made of jelly. Thankfully, the washroom was free, and I stepped inside, closing the door, and sliding the plastic lock to "occupied." I turned to the tiny mirror and stared into the blue of my irises, trying to breathe myself into some sort of calm.

She's a stranger... A complete fucking stranger, and I just saw one of her memories...

I pushed the button and ran the sink, splashing the cold water on my face and spitting it back. My thick hair was bothering me, so I pulled it out, raked my fingers through it, and tied it back up. I looked at my reflection again before sitting down, dropping my head into my hands as I collapsed on the toilet.

Who was I, really? Who was I going to be in my new life? A shivering child, weighed down by the past? A fearless adult, ready to embrace her independence? A haphazard mix of both?

It'd been a while since I'd seen a memory, and I'd hoped that part of my life was over, but now it was clear that I'd been dead wrong. They'd started immediately after my accident, when I'd fallen asleep on the couch with my mum and saw my parents' wedding day straight from her eyes. I could hear what she thought. I could feel what she felt. It was like I'd gone back in time and become her, only to jolt awake screaming, "Oh my God! Barrett! No! Someone please help him!" It was weird. *So* fucking weird. And I had no control over it—except to avoid skin-to-skin contact with other people when I fell asleep. What I saw seemed to be completely random and could range from cheerful to fucking *traumatic*. It was like a mystery bag of memories. I never knew what I was going to get.

"Why does it have to come back now?" I whispered to myself. "What does this have to do with my move?"

I wished the Source could appear in the mirror and tell me what to do with all this.

"Yeah, right. Like it's ever that simple."

I didn't always see memories when I fell asleep touching someone else. In fact, it happened less often than not. But it was something that I'd wanted to leave in Toronto with my old life. Now, right off the fucking *bat*, the Universe seemed to be leading me to this Barrett person—like I'd been asking Them to for years before giving up—and I had no idea what to do with that. All I wanted was a new start, and for the past to screw off and go away. Leaving my parents had been hard enough without all the weirdness that came from my kooky ability being kicked up again.

Somewhere on the other side of the door, I heard the seatbelt sign ding. It sounded like the engines were straining. I was mortified about facing the plane full of people that I'd woken with my screaming. I turned my palms up at the ceiling and shook.

Day one, and you send me his grandmother? Really?

How did I not notice that she'd been touching me?

I finished and washed my hands, taking another moment to wipe my face with the cold water before drawing a deep breath and heading out into the aisle. And, of course, Carol was on the other side, so I nearly fell into her when I stepped out. We did an awkward waltz around each other, and then I went back down the plane to stumble back over the teenager.

Okay. I get it, alright? You don't have to literally shove her in my face.

I plopped into my seat and thought I was going to be sick. This was so hard. So much to deal with in one shot. Why couldn't the change be dripped to me in small increments? Like those fraudulent antibiotics that I'd been given when I was in the hospital.

The owner of a pharmaceutical company.

I shivered harder than I ever had before.

In front of me, the moving map on the screen said we were in Vancouver. We were landing, and the dive had started when I was in the washroom. I glanced out the window, where the mountains and ocean were coming into view. A stunning metropolis was spread across the jagged land below. I perked up and put my forehead to the window, straining to look down. Gawking at the magnificence. Because Vancouver's beauty, even from the air, was indescribable. My blood began to rush.

New start, yeah? I told myself. *Forget the memories and the fact that Barrett's unexpectedly popped up again. Try to go with the flow, Em.*

The seat belt sign started flashing, and the pilot's voice came over the intercom telling the flight attendants to prepare for landing. We'd be on the ground soon. On the ground in my new life. It was almost too weird to think about.

I put on my seatbelt, glancing back to look for Carol. I felt oddly relieved when I saw her coming back down the aisle.

"Just in time, eh?" she said, sinking back into her seat and clicking her seatbelt on. She leaned across me, peering out the window at the city. "I never get tired of the view of Vancouver from the air. As a new person, I'd suggest that you watch this."

I jolted and turned to the window to cover for it. Outside, the mountains grew as the plane dropped, and I was mesmerized. A buzz and thud told me the landing gear was down, and the engines whirred as they controlled the descend. A pit pulsed in my stomach.

Carol held out her hand for mine, and I hesitated before I gripped it. Out the window, my new life rushed up at us. We put our heads back, both clutching our seats as the ground met the plane and the brakes were slammed. In what seemed like a lifetime, the plane slowed from a roaring sprint to a crawl, and Carol and I let out a synchronous breath. My muscles melted into the seat below me. I caught sight of the coniferous forest that surrounded the airport and felt like I was in a foreign land. Even though the sun was out, those trees stayed cloaked in a unique kind of darkness. A subtle mist was rising from between their branches.

"Welcome to your new home," Carol said, which pumped lava into my stomach.

My new home. I repeated. *Welcome home, Em.*

As the plane docked, we stayed in our seats, allowing the passengers ahead to get off first. The teenager got up with a snort and grabbed her bag from the overhead compartment, storming down the aisle without another glance. I helped Carol bring her Louis V down, and once it was our turn, we left the plane together. The pilots were standing at the exit, and I gave them a warm, "Thank you," before following Carol off the plane and down the hallway.

As we stepped onto the forest green carpets, it was immediately clear that this wasn't Ontario. And it felt just like I'd imagined the west coast would feel. All dark wood trim peppered with elements of the sea, and nature incorporated as much as anything manmade. Glancing around the smaller airport, I followed Carol blindly to baggage claim, gawking at everything like a lost orphan.

We tailed a couple of girls in Blundstone boots and passed several totem poles. I caught a glimpse of the distant mountains through the windows and insides flipped.

My new home.

I could almost smell the salty air from within the airport.

We made our way down an escalator to baggage claim, where we had to wait at the conveyor marked with our flight number. Carol and I made small talk, passing the time before it started up with a whirr, the bags sliding down from the conveyor above. She spotted her bigger Louis V first, and I helped her lift it off, grunting. My single bag came along soon after, and I rolled my shoulders in preparation to lift it. When I gripped the handle and heaved, I regretted that I'd packed it so heavily. My ribs tightened when I remembered that my dad was 5000 kilometers away, unable to lift it for me.

There was a moment of stiffness as Carol and me stood there.

"Well," I said, sliding my backpack onto the bag's handle. "I guess I'd better get a taxi."

"Oh. Yes." Carol blinked several times and then smiled. "They're just through those doors there. You can't miss it."

"Great. Thanks."

"You're welcome."

A twinge in my finger told me I was twisting my emerald ring again. "Um. T–Thanks for the company. It was good to meet you." I gave her an awkward wavelike motion and rolled forward. "See you, Carol."

"Yes. See you."

Four or five footsteps were put between us before her voice rose behind me. "Wait, Emily!"

I stopped and turned. "Yeah?"

"Well... It's..." She seemed as unsure about all this as I was. "Look. You seem like a nice girl, and you've only arrived, and you're all alone."

Cheers for the reminder.

She spread her diamond-clad hands. "I wonder if I can be of some help. Barrett is around your age, I think. You're going to need friends. So, I wonder if you might like me to introduce you to him?"

I swallowed. I was supposed to be here for my master's. That was it. How much of the past did I really want to drag into this?

"At least let me offer you a ride home." Her phone pinged, and she glanced down at it. "Travis is outside to pick me up—"

"Carol, I r-really don't want to inconvenience—"

"Nonsense!"

Suddenly, I'd lost the ability to fucking speak. "I..."

Carol took a breath. "Now, don't make a fuss, Emily. There isn't a taxi or Uber driver in town that I'd trust to keep you safe." She raised her chin adamantly and shot past me with her Louis Vuitton collection. "It really is no trouble. So. Right this way."

I sighed before I trailed after her.

Follow the signs, the Universe was saying.

Yeah, but why here? Why now?

CHAPTER 3
LIFE IS A HIGHWAY

Carol and I stepped through the arrivals entrance, which led outside to a pickup area. Cabs and limos lined the curb outside, which proved my original plan wouldn't have been too much of a bust had I'd followed it. It was a lot cooler here than it was in Toronto, but the ocean air was incredibly fresh. I took a deep breath, filling my lungs. Carol grinned, and we walked forward.

Further down, behind the line of cabs, there was a man on the curb leaning up against the passenger side door of a two-door, silver Mercedes convertible. It had red leather seats, and looked like it was worth more than I could ever spend on education, even if I got my PhD. A few other crazy-expensive cars were lined up behind him, and there was an obnoxious number of Teslas around. Did *everyone* in Vancouver have money to burn?

Carol waved—hand fanning widely though the air—and I realized that the man was Travis. But he certainly wasn't an eight-year-old making cookies with his grandmother anymore. As we rolled up, I got a better look at him, I wondered how many people would kill to get him between their thighs, even for a minute or two. Like his dad in the memory, he was tall, with the same symmetrical features. He still had the dark brown hair, and Carol's pale brown eyes. He was dressed in a black suit with a navy tie, flashing a bright white smile as Carol went over. She rushed forward, releasing her Louis-Vs in the process, jumping into his outstretched arms, and squeezing him. Not long after, she peppered his face with grandma's kisses.

"Oh, honey! I've missed you so much."

He chuckled quietly. "How was it?" His voice was as smooth as honey, and exactly the tone you'd expect would come out of a stunning, mid-thirty-something man.

"It was amazing, as always," she said, still beaming at him. "Incredible. I loved it. But I'm happy to be home."

"I trust your domestic flight was satisfactory?"

"It was wonderful."

He rolled his eyes subtly and smiled, his palm resting on the middle of her back. "I would have preferred you to take the jet. Especially when we're not travelling, and it's sitting in the hanger. I cannot fathom why you insist on these ridiculous public flights. But, alas, when have I ever been able to stop you?"

I bit my lip. There were diabetics in this country that were dying because they couldn't afford their insulin, yet here was the owner and CEO and whatever-else-he-was of Roth Pharmaceuticals, worried that his private jet was deteriorating in the hanger. *God*, these weren't my type of people. What was I doing accepting a ride from them?

"Oh, hush!" Carol said, snapping me from my thoughts. "That's your father talking."

Travis looked taken aback in a way I wouldn't have noticed if I hadn't been watching him.

Carol didn't notice. She gave him a soft pat in the middle of his tie. "It's nice to live like a normal person sometimes, my love." She turned to me. "Speaking of my flight—and normal people—this is Emily Anderson. She's from Toronto and has moved out here short term to pursue her studies. This is her first time in Vancouver."

Travis shifted his attention from his grandmother to me, offering his hand. "Welcome to Vancouver, Emily. I'm Travis Roth."

"Nice to meet you, Travis," I said.

As an adult, and not an eight-year-old in memory.

His hand was warm, and his grip was strong.

"I hope my grandmother wasn't too much trouble," he said, beaming at Carol. "You'll have to excuse her. She doesn't have much of a filter when it pertains to friendliness."

Carol clicked her tongue. "Oh, stop."

I shrugged, my gaze trailing the SkyTrain behind him as it pulled up at the station above us. "Actually, she's been a life saver. I would've been lost without her."

Not untrue, for a kid that's only flown the nest at twenty-eight.

Travis nodded, putting an arm around Carol's shoulders, and pulling her close. "I'm pleased to hear this."

She looked up at him. "Actually honey, Emily needs a ride home, so I offered to drop her off before we head back. Is that alright? The poor thing was going to take a cab, and I just couldn't let her do it. She's too new to the city."

"Ah, yes." He shot a quick glance at his watch before he caught himself. "That shouldn't be an issue, but I'll need to make a call on the way. Where are you staying, Emily?"

"Um." I hesitated, pulling out my phone so that I could frantically search for the address. "It's a place called Ladner. The house at the end of Calvert Drive. Let me just pull up the number..."

"Delta?" The annoyance in Travis's voice was unmistakable.

"Nothing like a short road trip, eh?" Carol said. "It's such a nice day for it, too."

He drew a controlled breath. "Yes, yes. Well—"

"I—Is it far?" I threw a glance at the taxis. "Because, really, if it's too much trouble..."

"Nonsense," Travis said, relieving the tension. "It *is* a beautiful day for a drive, and I shall be glad to do it." He took Carol's Louis Vuittons and my suitcase—looking very shabby in comparison—and began to wheel them to his trunk as we followed. "Besides, it gives me a much-needed excuse to spend some time out of the office."

I watched his muscles flex against the fabric of his suit as he lifted the bags and closed the trunk of the Mercedes.

Nothing like spending time with the CEO of Roth Pharmaceuticals on your first day in Vancouver, I thought sarcastically. *Well done, Em.*

"Thanks, Travis. I-I really appreciate it."

He smirked; energy almost overbearing when he touched my shoulder and passed. "Don't mention it. I'm happily obliged." He opened the passenger door, welcoming me inside. "Please. Have a seat."

"Uh. Thanks." I slid into the back. The red leather was warm and smelled good.

"My pleasure."

As Travis opened the door for Carol, she kissed him on the cheek. "I really appreciate you stepping out of the office for me."

"There's no need to thank me, Grandma," he said. "I missed you, and I wanted to see you safe myself."

Hmmm. This was interesting. After the antibiotics issue, I'd began to question the morals of those that ran companies like his. Now Travis Roth had just served me a sliver of doubt... But *just* a sliver.

Carol slid into the seat ahead of me, and Travis closed the door. As he walked around the hood to the driver's side, he took off his suit jacket and loosened his tie, revealing a baby blue dress shirt underneath. He dropped into the driver's seat and pulled the tie from around his neck, turning to set it and his jacket in the back beside me. He was definitely wearing a gold wedding ring. "Excuse me, Emily."

I nodded. Twisting my own ring, I glanced out of the convertible, foot tapping on the flawlessly clean floor. The ocean air sent a sudden shiver down my spine.

Beware of stranger danger. Wasn't that rule number one of being on your own? What would my parents say when they learned I'd gotten into a car with two people I'd just met?

"Alright, Emily. Where to?" Travis rolled up the sleeves of his dress shirt and unbuttoned the top.

"Uh..." I swallowed and pulled out my phone again, finally

fucking finding the address. He programmed it into the built-in GPS. Once the coordinates were set, he asked us to excuse him as he closed the roof of the convertible, which Carol instantly complained about. "Only for a moment, Grandma. Be assured." He shifted the car into drive. "Now. Let's give Mr. Roth a call, shall we?"

He pulled out, the powerful engine letting him put us ahead of the traffic. Then—to my horror—he called Barrett through voice command. Upon hearing his name, I held my breath. I was about to hear his voice for the first time. Oh, fuck. If this Barrett was truly *my* Barrett, I was about to hear his voice for the first. Fucking. Time. Suddenly, I was worried that my heart might pound out of my chest.

Barrett answered quickly. "Yeah, Trav."

Something quivered inside me, but I couldn't pinpoint what chakra it was.

"Brother, I'll be late from picking up Grandma. Much later than I'd planned for. In fact, I may not return to the office at all tonight. I need you to cover the marketing touchpoint at 16:00."

Barrett sounded annoyed. "Well, lucky you. I trust you have good reason to throw another commitment at me?"

"Trust that it's important enough to *require* you to cover. That's all I ask for once, Bear."

"Yes. Alright, *boss*. Calm yourself. I'm merely fucking with you, Trav. So, relax. I was scheduled to attend, anyway."

"Please don't call me *boss*. We're business partners. It's awkward."

Now I could hear the grin in Barrett's voice. "You love it, brother. Besides, from a technical perspective, it's what you are, and I only do it because it bothers you."

Travis sighed. "I have little patience for defiance today, Bear."

Barrett chuckled. "I apologize, oh great leader. And it is noted, though not necessarily observed."

"What else is new?" Travis grumbled.

"Anyway, why are you late? Was her flight delayed? I wish she'd take the jet. It would save a lot of these mundane annoyances."

My lungs burned, and I exhaled.

Not my people.

Then how is he my *Barrett?*

Travis looked at Carol, raising his eyebrows and jerking his head suggestively. "Not a delay. Call it a spontaneous afternoon adventure."

"That sounds like trouble."

"On the contrary, brother." Travis met my gaze in the rearview, and I drew another heavy breath. "It is a much-needed detour."

"Alright. Well. I'm glad some of us are having fun. And I will sleep when I am dead, I suppose."

Travis rolled his eyes. "Drama queen."

"Barrett Roth," Carol cut in.

"Grandma! How are you, old girl? And how was The Six? Did you and the girls do plenty of partying on Ossington? Did you get out to that old women's club like I told you to? Did you climb the CN Tower and do the Edge Walk?"

Oddly, I smiled at the reminders of home.

"It was amazing," she said. "We did lots, and yes, that *old women's club* was incredible. You were right. We went out to the artist collective night. What a group of inspiring women! Helen finally bought a membership in the end."

Huh?

"What can I say?" Barrett said in a pompous tone. "I know what old women want."

Who the hell are *you?*

"Hey, I take offense to that," Carol said. "Who are you to call your grandmother old?"

"I humbly apologize," Barrett said. "Of course, I meant no offense."

Carol sighed. "Anyway, hot shot. I've presently decided that we're going out for dinner tonight as a family. Perhaps *Five Sails* or the *Blue Water Café*. Which do you prefer? Somewhere with a view. I'm sick of dull landscape."

"Tonight?" There was hesitation in his voice, and I imagined him checking a Rolex or something. "Grandma, I'm going to be at the Tower until at least—"

"No excuses!" Carol said. "I've only arrived home, and I want to see *both* grandsons, for once. And that means you. Elusive, little bugger. Do me a favour and call that friend of yours that owns *Five Sails*. What is it? Ryan? Richard? Something? Anyway, would you? Tell him we need a table for tonight. *With a view.* There's a good boy."

"Alright. I can call, but—"

"What did I just say, Barrett Nicholas?"

Travis grinned. "You better shuffle your priorities, Bear. She looks angry with you."

Barrett's exhale whooshed through the speakers of the Mercedes, before he changed his tone. "Yes, Grandmother. That sounds lovely. I shall make it happen. Or, rather, Natalie will make it happen. That's what assistants are for."

"You're darn right," Carol said. "Dinner for your grandmother should be at the top of her to-do list. Seven o'clock, sharp. Have her tell Ryan something. See you then, sweetheart."

"Thank God I took the Ferrari today. I'm going to need it."

Not *my people!*

They had no idea how pretentious they sounded to my lower-middle-class ears.

"Don't be late," Carol said.

"Yes, Grandma," Barrett said. "Welcome home."

"Thank you, sweetheart."

There was a scratchy sound over the phone, and Barrett's voice went all mumbly like he'd started talking to someone else. "I must go," he then said to us. "I love you both."

"Oh, honey," Carol said. "We love you too."

"Ah! Barrett?" Travis interjected.

"Yes, brother?"

"Remember what I want out of Marketing." He shoulder-checked as we merged onto a highway leading south. The road signs were making butterflies tickle my stomach. "Do not let Mauricio leave that room until he meets the deliverables we agreed upon last week."

Once again, I heard the grin in Barrett's voice. "I'll wear my Bad-Roth badge with honour."

Travis pushed the Mercedes forward as we passed the slower traffic on the right, engine roaring. "Be nice."

Barrett laughed, which somehow stirred the butterflies. "Not my forte, Trav. Besides, he owes me some answers as well. I'm going to enjoy the look on his face when he watches me walk into the room without you. I'll see you both tonight."

"Seven o'clock!" Carol reminded him.

"Love you, brother," Travis said.

"I love you, too."

Three beeps over the speakers, and he was gone. My skin broke into goosebumps, and it wasn't from the Mercedes' air conditioning. It'd been my very first encounter with him, and all I'd learned was that he was a bit of a prick that told his family he loved them.

"I apologize for the interjection, Emily," Travis said, jolting me. "I had to make a quick call to my brother."

"Oh, don't worry about me," I said, wrestling the guilt of getting into a car with strangers again. "I just feel bad that you've had to go out of your way for me."

Travis didn't answer. He sighed as we hit more traffic.

"I appreciate it," I added, hoping to prompt him. "Thank you so much."

He looked into the rear view again, and when his light brown eyes met mine, he made me even more unsure about all this.

I watched water droplets streak sideways down the window as we continued south. Tracing them with my index finger, I imagined that it must have rained earlier. I studied the landscape of my new province, as Travis impatiently weaved the Mercedes around the slower traffic. Everything was darker, yet more vibrant. The coniferous trees were a stark contrast to the flowers and foliage that grew wildly, peppering the landscape with bright dots of colour and all shades of green. There was such an abundance of life here, and it gave me hope that this was a good place to live. Maybe I hadn't fucked up...

The traffic forced the Mercedes to a crawl, as we bottlenecked at a tunnel that ducked under what the sign said was the *Fraser River*.

"Top down, honey," Carol said.

"Oh, right," Travis said. "Yes, of course. Apologies. I was stuck in my thoughts." He pressed a button that folded the roof into the back behind me, and the cool wind surrounded us with the scent of the sea.

I inhaled, enjoying the freshness in my lungs after holding my breath earlier. "So, where do you live?" I asked, hoping to ease some of the tension.

A man in the next car over gave the silver convertible a look between envy and disgust.

"Up in West Vancouver," Carol said.

"Um. Isn't that the other way?" I didn't know much about Vancouver, but I knew West Vancouver was *behind* us.

Travis shot me a subtly annoyed look. "Don't fuss, Emily. I welcome a drive over my office chair, occasionally."

I was clearly starting to test his patience, so I shut up.

"Speaking of," Carol said to him, "how come you got hooked into picking me up? Usually, I can't pull you out of the office for anything, and Barrett would have jumped at the chance."

"He's tied up with multiple commitments today," Travis said. "I'm actually a freer man than he is, if you can imagine that."

"You two have been working too hard lately," Carol said, giving the folded baby blue above his elbow a poke. "I've barely seen either of you for weeks, especially Barrett. He's been particularly bad."

"You've been in Toronto for weeks, Grandma," Travis pointed out.

"You know what I mean," she said. "I feel like I'd need to set both your offices on fire to get you out of there."

Travis laughed. "Please don't. That would be very expensive and frivolous for me."

"Oh, Travis," Carol said. "One would think you'd be a master at being CEO after twelve years."

I blinked.

Wait, he's been CEO for twelve years? Isn't he only in his mid-thirties? What about their dad? The one in the memory that totally had big pharma CEO vibes?

Travis glanced over at Carol and smiled. "I'd be a fool to think that there was not more to learn."

"Still. It should warrant a break once in a while!" Carol said. "You're turning into your father."

He suppressed a flinch and shrugged. "Well, you're aware of the reality. Running a well-established yet growing company is a vast commitment of time. We have our sustainability goals due, a facility to open, products to create and acquire, an ever-evolving, world-class team. Plus, we're preparing our presentations for the banquet. It's a particularly busy time, and Barrett and I need to keep up the momentum. I would expect no less from either of us."

Carol propped her elbow on the window frame. "I understand, honey. I really do. I just value my time with you two."

Travis revved the engine at the crawling traffic. "Well, perhaps you'd better spend more time enjoying being stuck in traffic with me." He pulled his grandmother over, kissed her on the forehead, and grinned. She held his arm for a while after.

I sat quietly and thought about how confusing these people were.

CHAPTER 4
HOUSE OF WOLVES

The Roths and I continued through the tunnel, the orange lights harsh on either side. It came out onto a small island, before the highway crossed a short bridge over a river. My breath hitched when I caught the green sign for Ladner. It stood, slightly crooked on the side of the highway in bold, blocky letters, as if to haphazardly welcome me home. I was moments away from discovering my house and meeting my first roommates, but I was much more nervous than excited. What would life without my parents be like? Would I get along with my roommates? Would I struggle?

As we made our way toward what a smaller sign said was River Road, I caught sight of a small harbour to the right. This was river land—there was no doubt about it—and the massive Fraser wound around the area like an artery. The smaller waterways fed into it like veins and capillaries. I watched the boats bob up and down in the gentle waves and managed a smile-slash-grimace at a fisherman steering his toward the sea.

And I was fine. I was *totally* fine.

We turned right onto River Road, where the trees overhung before they broke, giving way to a large marshland. I noticed that Vancouver's North Shore Mountains were visible in the distance. On the left, there was a bit of farmland before the residential area began, and—having grown up in the biggest city in Canada—the area seemed rural to me. I started to worry that I'd picked a place that was further from the university than I'd thought. No wonder the rent on my room had been cheap. And one thing was for sure; I'd need a car.

Finally, we got to the edge of Ladner—which already had total small-town vibes—and followed the side streets before turning onto Calvert Drive. We drove until we reached the end, where the plain, paved driveway led up to a two-story house. It had tan brick and a brown-shingled roof, trimmed with a lighter brown somewhere in between the two. On the left, there was a two-car garage with a room overtop which looked down into the driveway. To the right was the walkway up to the entrance of the house, which trailed the length of the garage before it reached the front door. The front door was chestnut brown and solid, with heavily frosted windows on either side. To the right of the walkway was a small garden with a couple of bushes and not much else. There was a blue Honda Fit, and a grey Mazda3 parked in the driveway when we pulled up.

I twisted to look North again, watching a plane taking off in the distance. Probably going back to Toronto. Probably going back to my *real* home. Across from the driveway, there was a small creek, and next to that, River Road. Beyond River, there was a small field area and more marshland. This place had country living down to a science.

"Is this it?" Travis asked, as he shifted into park. His convertible Mercedes looked out of place among the other cars.

"I think so," I said, unbuckling myself from the back and sliding to the left.

He opened his door and folded his seat forward for me, then stood beside the car, looking up at the house with his hands on his hips.

To the billionaire you probably are, it must not look like much, huh?

Ignoring my snappy thoughts, I studied the brown brick as I stepped onto the driveway myself. My mind ran over it like a dozen little tentacles, trying to get a pulse on the energy here. I couldn't read much yet, but the chirping of the birds in the front garden was a good sign.

Travis made his way to the trunk to get my bags, but Carol stayed seated in the passenger side with her arm resting on the open window. She squinted into the sun as I walked up.

"Thank you so much, Carol," I said, reaching over to give her an awkward side-hug. "I truly mean that."

"It was my pleasure, Emily," she said, smiling. "And, hey. Let's exchange numbers. I'm retired, you know. I get bored, and my two grandsons are far too 'busy' to pay much attention to me. Perhaps I can help you with networking here?" She suggestively handed me her phone.

"Um. Okay..."

"Yes, please call her," Travis said, pulling my suitcase to my side with the wheels scraping across the pavement. "For the love of God, please."

"Oh, I know!" Carol said. "Let's have coffee at The Teahouse in a week's time."

"Uh. Where's that?" I asked, handing her phone back, my number very much inside.

"Stanley Park. It's lovely, and you'll enjoy it. I promise."

My phone pinged with the text she'd typed out while talking. "Uh. Okay."

I still wasn't sure about the Roths. How was I supposed to connect with them and *their people* when there was such a big societal gap between us?

Travis made me stifle a jump by putting a hand on my shoulder. "She makes a great *Gatsby*, Emily. Trust me."

Hmmm. I guess if she'll help me network, at least I'll be less alone...

I slapped on a grin. "Great. Thank you both so much. It was nice to meet you."

"Likewise," Travis said. He gave my shoulder a final pat and made his way over to the driver's side, sliding back into the car.

"Have a good dinner," I said, with a wave. Then, with a heavy swallow, I turned and followed the walkway to the front door of my new home.

The Mercedes had pulled out of the driveway before I'd even reached the chestnut door.

I stood on that doorstep for an unknown amount of time, breathing deliberately and wrestling the urge to turn around and run. My palms were clammy against the handle of my suitcase, and I was having trouble pulling one out of their death grip so I could knock on the door. Who would be behind, and would they keep me safe? I knew next to nothing about my new roommates besides what I'd seen on their Instagram profiles, and I'd only talked to the landlord when I arranged my move in date. Plus, it was difficult to judge someone from a collage of random photos meant to highlight the best parts of their lives. This could have been a house of full of psychos and thieves for all I knew.

If you don't knock on that door, you'll be stuck in the past, living with your parents...

I drew a deep breath and held it for five seconds before letting it out. Okay. So none of this had felt entirely *real* until now. I'd been going through the motions, but not really recognizing the impact of said motions. And now that I was here, that impact was right in front of my face in the form of a chestnut-coloured door. *My* chestnut-coloured door. The door to my new home. There was no going back on that plane. Not if I wanted to move forward with my life.

"Okay. It's gonna be okay. Just knock, Em. Just knock."

Then I realized that it was pointless to knock. There was a doorbell that I hadn't seen before now. Because of course there fucking was. I made myself press it, waiting with my toes tapping on the patterned bricks below. I heard a noise behind the door. A blurred shape of a person appeared through the frosted glass. I thought I might faint.

The chestnut door opened, and on the other side was the second person who changed my life after my move to Vancouver. The man with the dazzling green eyes and the amazing accent and the beautiful smile. He had black hair with loose curls, some of which fell lazily in front of his eyebrows. There was a short beard around his lips, and as he smiled, he revealed the whitest teeth that I've ever seen on someone. A blue tank top hung from his frame, which revealed a large tattoo on his upper right arm. It was a black and grey portrait of a wolf's head. And I wanted to run a finger across it to see if I could feel the detail etched into his skin.

Wolf spirited, I thought.

That was a bit of a relief. My wannabe-hippie mother always told me that we are spirits living in mortal bodies, and that our spirits have multiple forms; one of which includes an animal. In the spirit realm, we switch freely between them. But on Earth, we take one or the other, while our second form remains inside. Every human has a spirit with an animal form, whether they know it or not. The reminders come to us throughout our lives, consciously and subconsciously. It's even reflected in our behaviour. The wolf was mine (I'd done enough guided meditations with Mum over the years to be sure); even though I was presently standing there like a broken pup. And from the careful way that his tattoo was crafted, I could tell this man felt it was his too. Whether he was consciously aware of it was another question. Not many people shared in my family's strange spiritual beliefs.

Is he part of my new pack?

He watched me as I gawked at him like an idiot. "Hello," he said gently. "Are you Emily?"

"Yes," I said, clearing my throat. "I—I am. Emily, I mean."

"Well, what're you saying?" he said, offering his hand. "I'm David. David Mathis."

I had no idea why he'd said, "What're you saying?" but I took his hand and shook it. As soon as our skin connected, a tender energy spread up my arm. A flower petal touched by the sun. "Nice to meet you, David."

"Welcome," he said, swinging an arm inside. "Please, come in."

Wondering if David's accent was *normal* for Vancouver, I stepped into the small lobby of the house, pulling my suitcase along with me. On the main floor was a kitchen and a staircase that led upstairs to the left. There was a circular table in the middle of the kitchen that looked second hand. The appliances spread out on the back of the countertops looked like they'd come from Facebook Marketplace. The curtains that flapped above the sink were that discoloured kind of white that'd probably started out as a light yellow.

"Hey, Avril," David called toward the back of the house. "She's here! Come meet her!"

The person that I assumed was Avril appeared from an area to the left of the kitchen that probably led into the living room. She had straight blonde hair and blue eyes, and looked like the kind of person that should be stuck-up but didn't know it. As she neared, I noticed that freckles peppered her face around her nose. "Hi Emily," she said, extending her hand. "I'm Avril Warner."

"Nice to meet you, Avril," I said.

After our handshake, she put her hands into the front pockets of her jeans and rocked back on her heels. "So, you're going to be our new roommate then?"

"Yeah, I'm afraid you're stuck with me for at least a year," I said, giggling nervously.

"That's a good amount of time!" she said. "Our last roommate stayed for what, David? Three months?"

"Give 'er take," David said.

"Yeah," Avril said. "It'll be good to have some stability again. At least for a while."

"Great," I managed.

There was a heavy pause. I couldn't find something else to say. I just studied the two of them and wondered what kind of support system they'd be for me. Probably not even a quarter of what my parents were. Oh, God...

Avril looked at David and raised an eyebrow.

"Uh," he said. "Do you wanna see your room?"

"Oh. Yeah. Sure." I made an awkward movement toward my bag. My emotions hit me with a painful reminder that my real home was 5000 kilometers on the other side of that chestnut door. I swayed as I reached for it.

"I got it," David said.

"You sure?" I asked.

"'Course." He lifted my suitcase by the handle and started upstairs. The muscles on the back of his shoulder showed through the armhole of his tank top. The suitcase wheels spun in response. I followed, still definitely okay with all of this. The old stairs creaked like they were calling my bluff. Avril giggled in a *not* nervous way and came up behind me.

Upstairs, there were four rooms—one for everyone that lived here—and the tiniest bathroom of all time. Space on the vanity came with a premium. The air was somehow stuffy, yet fresh. The carpet that lined the stairs and hallway smelled like a subtle perfume called *Eau de Dust*.

"You lucked out," David said, opening the door to my room. The stale air that hit me right in the face said it hadn't been used in a while. "You have the biggest room."

"Although it can get cold as it's above the garage," Avril pointed out.

"That's okay," I mumbled. "I'm from Toronto. I'm alright with cold."

My room was rectangular, wider than it was long, and had a good amount of space. On the wall at the front of the house, there were two windows which had a sheer set of curtains, complete with a wine-red set over top. Between the windows was a bed with two nightstands on either side. On the right wall, there was a closet, and on the wall directly across from the bed, there was a dresser with a circular mirror overtop. There was a rug on the floor between the bed and the dresser. All in all, it was *enough*, but would it really be *home?* I looked at the bed and contemplated how I was going to lay my head there with my parents on the other end of the country.

"Whaddya think?" David asked, flashing me his white smile again.

"It's... nice." I stepped into the room and looked around. "Even a little bigger than my room back in Toronto."

"Great!" Avril said. "I'm glad you like it."

"We'll give you some time to unpack," David said, lifting my bag on the bed. My backpack rolled off the handle, but I was relieved when a dust cloud didn't puff up into the air. Someone had taken the time to clean the linens for me. That was nice. "When you're done, jus' come on down to the living room. We're hanging out there."

"Okay," I said, fiddling with my suitcase lock. "Uh. *Cheers.*"

They left me to get settled, and the first thing I did was dart over to the windows, throwing them open to invite fresh air inside. I sighed as I glanced out across River Road at the marshlands and the muted, blue mountains beyond. It was a completely different view than the one I had at home, which was just of the neighbouring townhouse. But somehow the mountains still didn't look real. It was like my mind hadn't accepted the fact that I was here now. In my new home. Having abandoned my old one.

Gulp.

I unlocked the suitcase and started to unpack, throwing a glance out the window each time I passed one. I only got halfway through my suitcase before nausea hit me and I wanted to call my mum.

No, I thought, yanking the nearest sweater from the corner of my bag. *I have to do this on my own. No more crying home to mommy.*

Instead, I texted her and told her that I'd arrived. *Everything's fine,* I added. Even though everything was very much not fine.

She immediately called, but I put my phone on the nightstand and let it ring.

One night. Just try one night without calling them, and we'll go from there.

I needed time to wrap my head around my new home first.

When my suitcase was empty, I took my stuff to the bathroom. Three toothbrushes sat in an old mug beside the sink, and I stuck mine with them before asking myself whether it looked like it belonged there. Bile sat bitter at the back of my throat.

Adamant for distraction, I went back downstairs and looked around the kitchen for a bit. Someone's breakfast crumbs sat in a semicircle around the toaster. A worn dishrag hung limp on the faucet for the sink. The window was lined with succulents that ranged from healthy to on the verge of death. When I opened the fridge, the smell of Thai takeout was strong enough to make my eyes water.

"How you doing, Emily?" Avril's voice made me accidentally slam the fridge shut. Beer bottles rattled from inside.

"Yeah. I'm okay. Just... exploring."

"Awesome. Well, explore away. It's not much, but it keeps us happy." She frowned as she stepped over to touch one of the succulents. "Try as I may, this one doesn't want to be happy."

"You're probably watering it too much."

"Oh, really?"

"Yeah. That or it's not getting enough sun because it's in the corner."

She smiled. "Do you like plants?"

My ribcage was too tight. Like it'd shrunk a couple sizes. "Um, I wouldn't call myself an expert, but my mum is. She, uh, uses them for a lot of medicinal purposes."

She grinned and threw a thumb over her shoulder. "So does David. Though, probably not *quite* in the same way."

A waft of weed smoke from the living room told me it was *exactly* the same way. I laughed. "You'd be surprised."

There was another one of those long pauses, but at least she was beaming at me. "I was going to have some wine," she said, motioning to the fridge. "Do you want some? It's Chardonnay."

"Um. Sure. Yeah. Thanks. That'd be nice."

She stepped around me to pull a couple glasses from the cupboard, and I noticed that she smelled sweet. Vanilla something. Like cupcakes. "You probably need it after that trip, eh?"

I swallowed. "Oh yeah. You have *no* idea."

She handed me the glass, and I thanked her. "Come on through to the living room," she said, waving me forward. "We'll have a chat, and you can relax."

"Sure. Sounds nice. And thanks. I really appreciate it."

"Don't worry, Em. You live here now, so you're one of us. You can relax."

I live here now.

Maybe if I kept repeating it to myself, I'd start to believe it.

"I'm sorry, is it alright if I call you Em?" Avril said, as we entered the living room.

David was lounging on the couch, taking hits from a bong with his socked feet crossed on the pillow on the coffee table in front of him. The cloudiness of the glass told me the bong was well used.

"Oh. Actually, yeah. That's what my parents call me all the time, so I'm okay with it."

Gulp. Again.

I sunk into the thousand-year-old armchair that was angled to the couch, while Avril bounced into the spot beside David.

He offered the bong. "You want a hit?"

"No thanks," I said.

"What, you don't smoke?" he said, putting it on the coffee table.

"I'm not in the mood." I shrugged.

Avril's clap rung through the room. "Oh! You know what would make this better? Snacks."

"Oh, *God*, yes," David said.

"Whaddya fancy, Em?" Avril said, springing back to her feet.

"We have Cheetos, All-Dressed, Tostitos and salsa? Trail mix? You know, if you wanna be healthy."

Though my belly growled, I was much more worried about throwing up. "I'm good with the wine for now."

"Amazing. And you?" She pointed at David, then threw her arm at him. "Never mind. I know exactly what you want." She bounced off to the kitchen, leaving me alone with him.

I studied David again, shifting to avoid the spring that threatened to dig into my ass.

Who are you gonna be to me?

The arm holes of his tank top stretched almost to his hip, giving me a peek at his toned ribs and chest. The muscles on his arms were also prominent. His thighs were tight against his black jeans. There was a whole set of workout equipment in the corner of the room, and it was clear that he was the one who used it. He smiled, before he picked the bong back up, lit it, and took a deep hit. Though he looked fit, there were lines under his eyes. He was either tired or already stoned. "You must be right some happy to be here," he said, his voice smooth as he exhaled the smoke. Then I realized what was up with his accent—it was *East* Coast.

Shrugging, I gulped down some wine. It was already helping to relax my muscles. "I've been planning this move for months, but it's still weird. I've never been... well... this far from my family."

Something in David's lip pinched. Like he was biting it from the inside. "Everyone has to be a lone wolf at some point. Once you prove to yourself that you can make it on your own, you'll realize how powerful you really are."

Huh. That was much more profound than I'd expected, but I didn't believe it. Lone wolves tended to die, but a pack would always survive.

I said nothing.

David took another hit. "You're in school, right? Or you're gonna be."

My energy turned strangely solemn. "I start next month, but I'm worried, to be honest. Getting a master's is really challenging…"

What happens if I don't like it? What happens if I can't handle it? What happens if I moved all the way out here for nothing?

"I'm sure you en' got anything to worry about," David said, green eyes meeting mine again. We each seemed to be trying to make sense of the other. Tiptoeing around until we could find common ground. But I had a feeling—completely out-of-the-blue— that it wouldn't take us long. There was something about him that I couldn't place. He had a sort of familiarity that you don't often find in a stranger. Like a lover in a past life. And it comforted me right off the bat.

Avril came back and tossed a box of Oreos at David. He caught it with one hand and said, "You're a right saint, Av."

She grinned as she set a suggestive bowl of chips in front of me. "In case you change your mind, Em."

I downed the rest of my wine and debated asking for another. "Okay, I have to ask," I said to David. "What's your accent? It doesn't seem to match the Vancouverites I've met so far."

David chuckled. "I'm a Bluenoser."

"Uh, meaning?"

"He's from Nova Scotia," Avril said, plopping down beside him and throwing an arm around his shoulders. The way she touched his knee with the other hand made me wonder whether they'd ever slept together. "Dartmouth, to be exact."

"Ehyeah," David said.

I let myself laugh a little. "Ah, okay. Bluenoser," I repeated, tasting the word on my lips. "Huh. I never knew that's what they called Nova Scotians before."

David clicked his tongue as he turned his attention to the TV. "You learn something new every day."

Silence loomed, and I racked my exhausted brain for something else to say. "Dartmouth is what? Next to Halifax."

"Right across the harbour," David said.

"Huh," I said. "Thought so... Dartmouth to Vancouver." I mentally compared his move to mine. "That's far. I've never been there, but I can imagine that it's beautiful. What made you move here?"

Though David seemed a little high, his expression fell. His gaze flicked to me, then back to the screen. "My dad thought it was a good idea."

Avril flinched and gave me a look like I shouldn't have asked.

But underneath all the anxiety from the move, I was curious now. It tended to drive me, and curiosity was at the root of the big decisions I'd made in my life. It drove me to do my undergrad in applied ethics after suffering the "antibiotics incident." It drove me to question the meaning of my strange ability to see memory and scream some random's name. It drove me to consider doing my master's and move to here. It also drove me to get in fucking trouble. "How old were you?" I asked.

David frowned and didn't look away from the TV. "I dunno. Nine? Ten?" He didn't expand.

Alright, end of curiosity.

Had I already overstepped?

"How about you, Avril?" I asked, turning to her.

"Oh, me?" she said, coughing as she finished a hit from the bong. "Yeah, I've always lived in Ladner. I'm BC born."

"Oh, okay. And what do you do?"

"I work in senior care at a retirement home just down the street."

"Huh."

"Yeah, I mean, I like it," she said, picking at a loose thread on her jeans.

David wasn't helping with this conversation. He still hadn't looked away from the TV and was now acting like we weren't in the room with him.

"So, you're from Toronto then?" Avril asked.

"Born and raised," I said. "This is my first time living in another city, let alone another province." God, talking about Toronto was going to get old.

"Oh, I've always wanted to go there." She gave David a sharp nudge. "Right?"

He peeled his eyes off the TV and nodded absentmindedly.

"It looks like such an interesting city."

I shrugged. Toronto's familiarity versus Vancouver's shiny newness was less interesting to me. Or, at least, that's what I told myself.

Avril set her chin and looked at the TV. "Well, don't worry. We're going to have a lot of fun while you're here. We'll be your personal guides."

"For sure," David finally added.

"Cool," I said. "Thank you."

The three of us watched TV for a while. Presently on screen was a documentary that I'd never seen before. Something about the fitness industry and toxic influencers.

I sighed. My foot was bouncing up and down at the end of my crossed legs. I stopped it. "So, where's roommate number four?"

"Greg? Yeah, he's out," Avril said, with a wave. "He's meeting us at Sharkey's later, if you want to come."

"Where's that?"

"A short jog down the street." I was starting to learn that Ladner was a very small town. Everything seemed to be "a short jog down the street."

"Alright, sure," I said, fiddling with my empty wine glass. Now I'd regretted asking for it. It'd only amplified the fatigue from the flight. "Okay. Right. Uh. I think I'll grab a nap before then. I'm pretty tired."

"No worries," Avril said.

David kept quiet.

With a sort-of nod, I stood up, painted-on a smile, and made my way back to the kitchen where I put my empty glass in the sink. The small lobby of the house seemed oddly dark, the frosted glass only letting a fraction of light through, and it made me desolate. I was already missing the familiar smell of incense that greeted me when I climbed our staircase at home; the whine of an ambulance passing outside the door; our tabby cat, Sammie, perched on the top of the stairs, prematurely purring because he knew I was going to pick him up for a cuddle. Desperate to push the pining child from my head, I told myself that it was only the first day—the first couple *hours*, even—but it was hard. How do you cure homesickness?

Then I went back to my new room, casting a glance at the mountains again as I unzipped my hoodie and threw it on top of the drawers. I climbed into the bed, surrounded by the scent of someone else's laundry detergent. And I lay there with my head sinking into the pillow, squeezing silent tears from my eyes. I had no one else to blame but myself. I'd *wanted* this.

CHAPTER 5
CUPS

"What the hell do you mean by: you *saw* my memory?" Andy says, his breath turning to mist in the night air.

The two of us are standing at the edge. Up against the railing at a place called "The Devil's Punchbowl," which is a lookout over the city of Hamilton in Ontario. Below us, the city lights are sprawled. They twinkle in the night, helped by the fact that it's the middle of December. Most of the houses below are decked out in Christmas lights, and the colours shine, breaking through the raven-coloured landscape. It's the closest thing you can get to a mountain view in Ontario. In fact, the massive hill that we're perched upon *is* affectionately called "The Mountain" by the locals, but I can already hear the Vancouverites chuckling at us.

Andy is waiting for an answer, his hazel eyes turned dark. Behind us, there is a massive cross that stands on the edge of the cliff, visible from many parts of the Greater Toronto Area at night. The amber light illuminates the half of his face that is turned toward me, his brown hair windswept.

Normally, this is a very romantic place for us. It's only about an hour's drive from Toronto, and we come here to sit on the bench, watch the city lights, and make-out. We're still teenagers. Due to graduate high school in June. But tonight is different.

I turn away, looking out across Hamilton. In the distance, I can see Toronto's tiny skyline as the cold wind whips through my hair. It seems so far away... just out of reach...

"Em?" he demands, growing ever more impatient. "You were

about to explain to me what the *fuck* you are talking about?"
Fuck comes out harsh. Bitter. Sharp as a knife. Like he's talking to
someone he hates.

I sigh, breath clouding. This isn't how I imagined telling him
would go. "Andy... After the accident, it's like nothing's been the
same. I'm less like myself. And I-I've started noticing something
strange."

The look on his face says he doesn't believe me.

I'm not quite sure how to continue, but I give it a go. "I've started
to see things when I sleep."

He snorts. "Yeah. It's called dreaming. Duh."

"No," I say, firmly. "I'm not talking about dreaming. Obviously.
This is... I dunno... something *else*. The first time I noticed was
when I fell asleep with my mum on the couch." My eyes flash to
his. I've never explained this to anyone, not even my parents. Up
until now, it's been the only secret I've kept to myself. So, ignoring
his burning gaze, I press on. "Andy, I *saw* my parent's wedding day.
I saw it through my mum's eyes... It's like I've stopped dreaming
when I'm next to someone... My dreams have been replaced with...
memories."

For the second time, he looks like he doesn't believe me. "I'll tell
you what that accident did. It took my girlfriend and turned her into
a complete psycho." He pauses, ignores the pain that's sprung to my
face, and looks back toward the black horizon. "Em, it's been *two*
years since the accident. Stop blaming all your weird behaviour on
it. I mean, sure. You hit your head. But *Jesus*."

"Would you just listen?" I wrap my jacket tighter around myself.
The cold seems to be piercing through it. Into my bones and into
my very core. I want his touch to take it away, but tonight he's made
of ice himself.

"Sure," he says, not looking at me. "Alright. Humour me. What
memory of mine did you claim to see?" He makes air quotes around
the word "memory" like he's the one humouring *me*.

My spine chills like I'm about to explain a horror story. "You were at the EX with your sister. You were twelve? Thirteen? I dunno. It's hard to tell but you must have been young because she was still..." I trail off, hesitant to finish. The word that I mean to finish with balances on the tip of my tongue, but I'm too afraid to say it. *Healthy.*

He's now piercing me with a glare. I'm in dangerous territory, and we both know it.

I bite my lip, not able to meet his eye. Discouraged, I set my focus to the city in the distance again. I'm desperate for a distraction. So far away... "You were comforting her as the two of you sat on the Ferris wheel. She was afraid of heights, and she was trembling, but you didn't want her to miss the view. You sat her on your lap, and you held her. The Ferris wheel stopped at the top and you grabbed the frame, trying to prevent your seat from swinging and making her more scared. But then she wasn't afraid anymore. She was in awe of the view, and her eyes lit up." I smile to myself, thinking of his sister Steph before she got sick. She was always such a positive girl, with the power to light up a room with her giggle. "Steph grinned, pointing to the CN Tower like she'd never seen it before. You held her tighter. You were happy. I could feel the warmth that spread through you."

I look at him and he looks away. We're always moving in opposite directions, like two negative poles of a magnet.

He studies the horizon again, swallowing. It's been three years since Steph passed. She lost a long battle with leukemia, and the horrible disease broke her down over the years, slowly stealing away her bright spirit while he watched. He can't process the pain, and we barely talk about her, but that's the memory he's shown me. And, if anything, the fact that she's gone makes it slightly more believable. No one knows about it except for him.

"Andy," I say, wrapping my arms around him. "I'm not trying to hurt you, baby. I swear. I know it's a lot to take in, but I need you to believe me. Please. I need your support here. I've never told anyone before."

"When?" he demands.

I don't respond at first. My mind trips over the statement.

"When did you see it?"

"The night of our first time," I whisper. I'm talking about the night that happened over a year ago. The night that we made love. The night that he was so gentle, tender, and caring. The night that he held me as we slept, and I imagined that I would love him until the end of time. The way it used to be.

"Jesus," he says, shrugging me off. "I wanted that night to be special."

"It was! Andy, it was—"

"No, you don't get it, Em. That night was supposed to be about the two of us. But somehow, you've found a way to make it all about you. What sort of over-dramatic bullshit are you trying to pull on me now? You're looking for attention, as per usual, Em, and I'm sick of it. You want to go and hurt me, bringing up these painful things, just so we can focus on you? Is that what you want?" He shrugs as he steps away from me. "I'm sick of it."

Fuck you! I knew you wouldn't understand!

Suddenly, I want to scream at him. I want to grab him. Shake him to try to stir up some sense in him. But I don't do any of those things. I look out to the city lights and stay silent. I don't defend myself because what I'm asking him to believe sounds crazy. Let alone the fact that he's a master at breaking down my self-confidence.

Then he starts to walk away, turning into the cold and storming down the path. He wheels back for one final blow, jabbing a finger at me as his breath rises again. "You're cruel," he says, hazel eyes burning. He turns away.

And that's where he leaves me. Out in the cold. With my tears, the glowing cross, and the Christmas lights below. He leaves me, and the first crack splits through our relationship like it's made of glass.

"Emily?"

I pulled myself back into the present with heavy eyelids. The light in the room was different now. Darker, and golden, like the late afternoon, or evening. I woke up in a strange place that wasn't my room with a strange man with curly black hair looking down at me. His white smile was sparkling. He had a wolf tattoo on his arm. I didn't recognize him at first.

"Wakey, wakey, sleepyhead," he said.

"David?"

"Good morning." He chuckled. "Sorry to wake you, but you've been sleeping for, like, four hours and we're headin' out for dinner soon."

"What time is it?" I sat up and rubbed my eyes, ruining the minimal amount of makeup I had on. Half of it smudged onto my hand. I sighed.

"It's around 6:30."

"Oh."

"Yep. It's time to join Pacific time, princess."

I nodded, groggy. "Can you give me half an hour? I need to change and do some touching-up before we go."

"Well, you already look beautiful, but sure." He winked and stood up. My bed sprung back from the absence of his weight. "Meet us downstairs when you're ready."

I snuffed as I watched him walk down the hallway, black curls bouncing as he jogged down the stairs. I'd never met a man with such natural charm. It must have been a *Bluenoser* thing.

Stretching as I stood, I glanced out the window at the mountains in the distance. It was still light outside, but the clouds were already starting to reflect the evening sun, streaking brilliant colour across the sky. I changed quickly and threw on my favourite jacket. I let my hair down only to brush it out and tie it back in a bun again. My makeup didn't need as much touching up as I expected. Luckily, I hadn't looked as much of an idiot as I'd thought in front of David. I added a bit of eye shadow and refreshed my eyeliner. As I looked in the mirror, I gave myself a weak smile to lighten the energy, but my memory had made me miserable.

Andy.

Why was everything still about *Andy*? I'd escaped across the country, but it seemed I'd still dragged him along with me.

Shoving him from my thoughts, I left the room, finding Avril touching up her own makeup in the next one over. She'd done some winged eyeliner and was putting on some bright-red lipstick when I poked my head in. An overwhelming amount of perfume greeted me in the process. Her room was decked out in pink, and the walls were covered in framed pictures of cute and funny things that probably made her happy. First in my line of sight were the "hang-in-there" kitty, and a cartoon dinosaur with the word "Rawr" beside it.

"Emily! I take it you had a five-star snooze?"

"Yeah, it was nice."

Liar.

It would have been nice if I hadn't tortured myself with my own memory. "I certainly needed it."

"Good, I'm glad." She put the cap back on her lipstick and rubbed her lips together. "Are you ready? Greg's already at Sharkey's and he's *dying* to meet you."

Right. Roommate number four. Time to put my game face back on.

Or whatever game face I had.

"Ready when you are," I said.

"Amazing. David!"

David replied from downstairs with a muffled, "Yep?!"

"Get your coat! We're ready!" Avril grinned and grabbed my arm with one hand, while clicking the light off with the other. She led me down the stairs and to the foyer, tugging me like a little sister.

David met us there, pulling on a blue windbreaker that matched his tank top.

Avril was bobbing with excitement as she opened the closet. She took out a black leather jacket that instantly made me jealous and slipped on a pair of high-heeled boots. "This is going to be great! You're going to meet Greg, and we're all going to get along fantastically, and we'll turn into one big happy family. Just think! We're finally *full* again."

"The House-of-Wolves," David said, shoving his feet into his shoes. "Complete once more."

"Yes! I'm *so* excited!" Avril opened the front door, and the British Columbian air rushed in to greet us.

"House-of-Wolves?" I raised an eyebrow at David, wondering once again if he was aware of his spirit's animal form.

"That's right, princess," he said, touching my shoulder. "Welcome to the pack."

I watched him as he stepped outside, following close behind as I closed the door with a dull thud.

Wolf-spirited.

Apparently, I'd read the signs right. Had the Universe guided me to this house for a reason? Was it because I needed my new pack to survive here? Probably.

Avril and David led the way down the driveway, and I followed them, mildly surprised when we passed both cars and made our way across the small creek and to River Road. David cleared the creek in a single step, and I had no problem with the jump, but Avril needed to be lifted across by him, her high heels sinking into the soft soil and leaving her smiling in thanks.

Once we were all on the other side, we started walking toward town. The road was empty—a car passing by every couple of minutes—and the surrounding neighbourhood seemed quiet. In the distance was the faint sound of the river and the whir of a boat engine, but not much else. A little way down the road, we passed a yacht club and things changed. A lot of people seemed to be out on their boats; the locals not as bothered by the evening chill as I was. Was this normal for May?

We followed the river for a while, Avril chatting away as her high heels clicked on the pavement. I took the smile-and-nod approach, but I had a hard time concentrating on her. I was drawn by a mountain view that seemed to get better each time my eyes wandered toward them. It was either that, or David. He had his hands stuck in his pockets, his shoulders often shrugging toward his ears, his grin beaming as he turned to look back at me.

After what seemed like ages, we reached Sharkey's, which was a small restaurant on the dock at one of the local piers. Although seafood wasn't my favourite, I was grateful for the smell of fish and chips when we entered.

David and Avril immediately found roommate number four and greeted him from across the room. He was seated at a table near the window, grinning from over a pint of beer as he waved. He had a tawny coloured faux hawk, soft brown eyes, and a babyface. He stood as Avril ran up and hugged him, before clapping a hand in David's.

"This is Emily!" Avril said, enthusiastically framing me with fanned arms.

"Greg," he said, offering his hand. It was soft when I shook it. "Nice to meet you."

I had to resist the urge to pinch his cheek like a distant aunt straight out of Ontario. If the dictionary had a picture next to the definition of "cute," it could be his. "Nice to meet you too."

"Greggy here is the baby of the group," David said, nuzzling Greg's hair, before throwing an arm around his shoulders. "He's a measly twenty-three. 'Magine! He's the only one still in school, other than you."

"Just a pup, then," I said, with a smile.

Greg shrugged. "Yep, I'm the baby, I guess," he said, with a laugh.

And I legit stifled the *"Aww,"* that wanted to build in my throat. It was like I'd been united with the little brother that my parents never gave to me.

"Well, come on! Sit down, and let's get some more drinks," Greg said.

I grabbed the nearest chair, and screeched it horribly across the shabby, wooden floors. Everyone flinched, and the people at the bar tossed looks of annoyance over their shoulders. David stepped over to help as I tried to convince myself that my clumsiness was just fatigue. But, God, I felt like I didn't belong there.

We're on Vancouver time now. Pull yourself together.

The waitress made her way over and distracted the group from my awkwardness by taking our order for drinks. She rushed Avril and me, but smiled sweetly when she got to David like she was enjoying the fluid way he ordered a pint of *Granville Island* in that accent of his.

"Call me over if you need anything else," she cooed at him afterward.

Apparently, I wasn't the only one who could listen to him all day.

"So, Emily," Greg said, taking a sip of his pint. The head lingered on his top lip like a milk moustache. "How was your flight?"

My mood lifted a little. "Oh, yeah, it was actually... really good."

"That's great," he said, wiping his lip. "Is it a long one?"

"Not too bad. Just over five hours." I picked up the paper coaster that was on the table in front of me and started folding it into triangles, tighter and tighter. "Plus, I kind of connected with the woman I sat next to. She was incredibly kind."

"I love when that happens," Avril said.

The waitress returned with our drinks. She dropped David's pint first, and he gave her a grateful "Cheers," along with a sly grin.

"Isn't it great when you meet strangers that you just *click* with?" Avril was saying, as I gave the waitress a forced smile.

I nodded and immediately downed some wine. "Yeah, she

seemed nice. We even exchanged numbers. She wants to have coffee with me." I picked up the coaster again, twirling it between my fingers. "She convinced her grandson to give me a ride home so that I wouldn't have to take a taxi."

"And you were comfortable with that?" David asked. "Strangers in a strange city?"

I needed someone to rely on...

"Um, yeah? I mean, they apparently own a pharmaceutical company, so it's not like they were going to rob me or something."

David choked on his beer and looked at me like I'd told him I'd been abducted by aliens. It was a strange reaction, considering I hadn't said anything particularly shock-worthy.

"What?" I asked.

He didn't answer.

"Wait, Emily, did you just say that this guy *owns* a pharmaceutical company?" Greg cut in.

"Yeah, his name's Travis Roth," I said.

My new roommates flashed looks of austerity around the table. David put his head in his hand and sighed like he was getting a headache. The other two watched him like he'd just been diagnosed with something incurable, but not immediately life-threatening.

I threw confusion back at them. "A-Am I missing something? Do you know him?"

Silence. David took a deep breath and looked up. Avril pursed her lips. Greg opened his mouth like he had something to say, but then closed it again.

"He seemed nice to me," I added. "I mean, it was nice that he drove me home."

Finally, Greg spoke. "Yeah, I'm sure on the *surface* he was nice. But you don't want to get involved with the Roth family, Emily. Trust me."

I was very aware that I already was. I had Carol's number in my phone, and we had plans to meet for coffee next week. I mean, not *concrete* plans, but plans that I kind of felt obligated to. Especially since she'd been there for me from the minute I landed. Something that floated within the dreary energy told me not to mention that. "Um. Why?"

Greg spoke like it was obvious. "Because they're evil."

Evil?

I mean, sure, Barrett had seemed like a bit of an ass on the phone, and Travis had given off very conspicuous I-don't-actually-have-time-for-you-even-though-I'm-pretending-I-do CEO vibes. But evil? That made no sense. And if Barrett Roth really *was* my Barrett, then surely, he wouldn't be. I *knew* myself. I was the kind of person that decided to do a master's in Medical Ethics to fight that shit. My spirit would have never started spontaneously calling for someone who was immoral. Unless, of course, Barrett Roth *wasn't* my Barrett... And then the enigma of my life would be back to square one... Fuck.

"They're the spawn of the Devil," David grumbled from over his pint glass, pulling me from my thoughts.

"What? Did someone here get a bad batch of painkillers or something?" I couldn't help but try to lighten things.

Greg seemed unimpressed with my joke. "No. They're just horrible people is all. Greedy. Rich as fuck. They don't give a damn about anything except money, and they'll do anything to get it."

David's gaze landed on me and flared. "They're our enemies, Emily. Don't be fooled."

Enemies?

I was really confused. Who was I supposed to trust? The people that had first been there for me? Or my new roommates?

Curiosity elevated. "Um. Why?" I asked.

David's jaw tightened, but he didn't say anything.

"Oh, come on guys, they're not that bad," Avril cut in. Somehow, I wasn't surprised that she was the one playing Devil's advocate. From what I'd seen so far, it was natural for her to be objective.

"Okay, you can't just say that because one of your friends is screwing Barrett Roth," Greg said.

"Greggy," Avril rebounded, "I think she's been dating him for a year. I'm sure they're not just *screwing*."

"Oh, sorry," Greg said, with an adorable kind of sarcasm. "Screwing on the giant pile of cash he got from selling orphan's tears as some miracle treatment for cancer because he's like *super* evil. Does that sound more realistic?"

Now *that* seemed like the kind of investigation that I could sink my teeth into.

"Stop," David said sharply, tone asserting dominance although it was calm. "It's Emily's first night here and I'd rather not spend it talking about that sack of flaps. Okay?"

I wondered what the hell a "sack of flaps" was.

"Right," Greg said, eyebrows bridging. "Sorry, Dave. I didn't mean to—"

"It's alright, Greggy," David said. They gave each other weak smiles, and the conversation fizzled out. But my inquisitiveness wasn't satisfied.

"I still don't get it," I said. "This woman, Carol, she was so —"

"Emily, don't have a conniption fit," David cut in. "Jus' leave it, okay?"

I raised an eyebrow because I still had no idea what the *Bluenoser* was talking about.

He took a sip of his pint and smiled, his expression shifting like we'd already come to a mutual understanding. "You shouldn't call her back. End of conversation."

For the first time after my move, the faint, rebellious energy that ran through my blood rose. I got it from Mum, no doubt. And though it was weak, it was definitely there. But I didn't want to stir the pot. Not on my first day. Not when I was still so unsure about everything. Especially myself. So, I relaxed, took a sip of wine, and smiled back.

Alright, David. You've won. For now.

Something in me didn't believe him, anyway. The Universe had led me to Carol, and she'd seemed so genuine. How could a woman like that come from an evil family? And what about Travis? His driving me all the way to Delta had been such a selfless act of kindness; even with his moodiness. What was wrong with the House-of-Wolves?

As I sipped my wine, I couldn't shake the feeling that I'd end up seeing the Roths again. Nor did I *want* to shake it. How could two people that were so generous, so *welcoming*, and that went out of their way for a stranger, be so awful? There was something about it that didn't add up.

Discouraged by the negative air that wound around the table, I changed the topic and started to ask my roommates about themselves. I wanted to dig further into their lives.

David worked on the docks of Tsawwassen. He had a job at the port that kept him busy and paid, while being interesting enough. When I asked him if he ever wanted more, he shrugged. "I have enough to live." The way he tugged his lip and looked off across the bar told me he wasn't going to elaborate.

I left it and turned the question to Greg. He was studying plant and soil sciences at UBC. His focus was mostly agricultural, and he was interning at a commercial greenhouse before starting his third year at the beginning of the summer semester. He must have been trying to push through his degree, and I admired that. He came from a long line of ranchers from the Okanagan Valley—which, I understood, was one of the most beautiful areas in British Columbia—and his family owned a ranch outside of Kelowna. He was a self-proclaimed "cowboy," and I thought he fit that part well.

As Avril had mentioned earlier, she was a full-time caregiver, and she found her job fulfilling. Her family was also in Ladner, and they'd never had any desire to move anywhere else. She had two sisters—one younger, one older—and two mums that she loved very much.

I found myself grinning at the thought.

Two mums. What would that be like? I thought about "Mum-squared" and how much different I'd be if we didn't have Dad's down-to-Earth attitude to break up the crazy. I'd probably be doing Ayahuasca in the Amazon, determined to reach spiritual enlightenment.

In her spare time, Avril liked to keep up the gardens at the house, but she wasn't very good at it. I disagreed. Despite the dying succulents in the kitchen, the front yard looked good to me.

A basket of fish and chips later, I was done. It was almost midnight in Eastern time, and my mind was fried. I asked Avril if she wanted to walk home. She said yes, and we left the boys at Sharkey's.

Outside, the sun had set, and the moisture hung in the air, clinging to my jacket as I wrapped it tighter around myself. The river ran softly beside us as we walked, the docks drifting up and down with the wake. The North Shore Mountains loomed in the distance, bathed beautifully in the twilight. Quietness stretched between us, broken only by Avril's humming, the click of her high heels, and the distant drone of boats coming in for the night.

I shivered, and feeling obligated, sifted through my brain for small talk. I was tired and moody; therefore, not good at making it. So, I asked the first thing that came to mind, even though it was a little distasteful. "Are you and David, um, together?"

"Probably looks that way, huh?" She giggled. "But no, not really." She clipped one of her heels on the pavement and stumbled. I caught her arm, helping her straighten before she continued. "We've had our odd drunken nights, yes, but... It's not real." She crossed her arms over her chest and shrugged. "It's not for lack of trying on both our parts, either. It just doesn't work, and we've accepted it."

A shiver ran down my spine. I knew exactly how she felt. I'd tried so damn hard with Andy... "Sorry."

"Oh, no, no. It's fine. Don't worry about it. Like I said, it just doesn't work."

"Fair enough." I watched the taillights of a car disappear down the street, then sighed, unable to subdue the other burning question on my mind. "And, hey, what's with the Roth thing, anyway? What's David's issue with them?"

Avril hesitated, and her voice manifested in a series of "ohs" and "ums" until she settled on, "That's really not my story to tell, Emily. Sorry. I don't want to upset him."

"Oh. Okay..."

Because we wouldn't want to upset the alpha male, would we?

CHAPTER 6
MOUNTAINS BEYOND MOUNTAINS

"Hey Dad."

"Hey, honey. How are things so far? You settling in okay?"

"Yep." I was brushing out the tangled mess that was my hair, while watching myself in the mirror. "Things have been great so far."

"That's good. I'm glad you didn't have any trouble." There was a sadness in his voice. Like someone who's wishing you their best but is also mildly disappointed in your decision.

"Well... Dad... I..." ...was also painfully aware of the real reason I'd needed to call him.

"What is it, Em?" His tone switched to concern.

Frustrated with my hair, I tossed the brush onto the dresser. It hit my container of clips, and they fell off, scattering across the floor. I groaned. "I think I messed up in choosing this house."

"Really? Are you not getting along with your roommates?"

"No, it's not that," I said, snatching the clips one by one and dropping them back into the container. I went over to my bed and collapsed onto it. I hated this. I hated asking him for money. We were already stretched, and I didn't want my parents to pay for my mistake just because I sucked at being on my own. But I was at a loss of what to do other than beg my roommates. "UBC. It's far, is all... Dad, I need a car. And I don't have enough savings to buy one before the semester starts."

"Oh." His tone switched back to disappointment. "Well... honey..."

My guilt rose like tiny bug bites across my skin, and I started apologizing. I tried to keep the embarrassment out of my voice and instead worked to inject the subtlety of a little girl that needed her father. It always worked before, so it would work again. Especially with what the accident had put us through.

He sighed. "I can give you five thousand for now, but that's about all I can do. Is that enough?"

The guilt turned to hope, and I grinned in relief. Five thousand was *definitely* enough. I could work with five thousand. "Thanks, Dad. That's more than I could ever ask for."

"Alright, sweetheart. I'll transfer it to you when I get back to my office." There was the sound of him shifting, like he was trying to juggle his briefcase, the door to his lecture hall, and the phone. "Can you do me a favour, though?"

"Yeah. Shoot."

"When your mother calls, do your best to answer. She was so frazzled on Saturday that I thought she'd stuck her finger in an electric socket."

I swallowed.

"And I'm grateful you called her yesterday, but Saturday would have been better."

"I know. I'm sorry." I fiddled with the corner of my pillowcase. "But I was busy with my new roommates. And she can't expect a call every day. I'm trying to figure out my new life, here."

There was a thud, and I pictured him dropping his stuff on the podium. "That's fair. But try and remember that this is difficult for us too. We just want proof that you're safe."

My heart clenched. I didn't want to tell him how much I appreciated that. How much I missed them... "I'm safe, Dad. Okay? My new roommates have good energy. I can sense it."

"Alright. Good." He gulped a couple times—probably his coffee— and exhaled in what sounded like satisfaction. "Anyway, sweetpea.

My lecture's about to start, and I have to go. But before I do, can I offer you a word to the wise?"

"Anything, Dad."

"Next time, try to predict what you're getting yourself into, before you get into it."

A word to the wise. My dad was always good at disguising a novel behind a sentence.

We finished by telling each other how much we loved each other, and I hung up.

By the time I managed to haul myself downstairs for my first cup of coffee, it was after 12:00pm. It was Monday, which meant that my roommates would be at work, and I could take some alone time to get my bearings. The plan was simple: Open my laptop, sit at the kitchen table, and don't stop searching until I find a good deal on a car for under five grand. It'd be boring, yet productive, but I could deal with that. Especially after how busy yesterday had been.

Yesterday, after I woke up well rested and in a better mood, my roommates had given me a glorious, touristy introduction to Vancouver. We spent some time at Canada Place; we went to Gastown to watch the steam clock whistle on the hour; we forked over too much money to go up in the Lookout, where Greg pulled me from sign to sign, explaining each view with a wonder in his young eyes. It was a good time. A great bonding experience with the group. But as we wandered the streets, I couldn't help but notice that there were more homeless people than in Toronto. The perfectly manicured streets of downtown tried to mask it, but as soon as you moved beyond that, it was clear that the city had a housing problem. And one thing was blatantly obvious—the gap between the rich and the poor was as big as Capilano Canyon. It made me think about how grateful I was for my blessings, and I stopped sulking about my new life a little.

Back on that Monday, I made my way down the stairs with my slippers slapping lazily against them.

Ah... Alone time.

But as I glanced through the guardrail of the stairs and into the kitchen, I realized that I wasn't. David was sitting at the table; a spoon in one hand and his phone in the other. I stopped at the bottom of the stairs and watched him like a deer in headlights. He looked up from his phone, his thumb frozen mid-text, and gave me a smile through a mouth full of cereal.

I hadn't expected him to be there. I hadn't expected *anyone* to be there. I was in my pajama pants and a simple, brown spaghetti-strap shirt, *sans bra*. Which, I realized, was giving him a rather nice view, considering the kitchen was as brisk as the spring air flowing in from the window. He dropped his eyes back to his phone, pretending he hadn't noticed. And I tried not to think about how I'd wanted him to notice.

"Good morning," I said, walking over to the coffee maker, picking up the half-filled pot, and pouring it into an aged mug with a chip in the rim. It was forest green, with *Stanley Park* in faded gold.

"It's noon," David mumbled, with his thumb moving quickly over the screen.

I stirred some sugar in my coffee and then turned, taking a sip as I leaned against the sink. The afternoon sun was streaming in through the window, causing the dust in the air to drift like we were in some fairy-tale forest. It played off his black hair, the raven colour shining, making each curl seem like it was made of silk. I had to resist the urge to walk over and run one between my fingers.

"I wasn't expecting you to be home," I said, as the coffee warmed my throat. "It's Monday. I thought you'd be at work."

David set his phone on the table and lifted the cereal bowl to his mouth, draining the milk. "I took the day off," he said, in between slurps. "I figured we could spend some time together."

I figured we could spend some time together.

I repeated the phrase in my head, wondering what his angle was and what might be in the future for us. Was he just trying to be nice so that we could be friends, or did he see the potential for more?

Yesterday, he hadn't been particularly flirty, but from what I'd seen, he could be guarded. What did he see when he looked at me? He was obviously interested in me as a person, since he stayed home to spend time with me today. Was he looking for an alpha female, or another beta for the pack?

And why was I even thinking like that? It'd only been three months since my breakup with Andy. Was that really enough time to get over the man I thought I was going to marry? Was my new life making me crave a rebound? And did I even *want* David to be a rebound? He was my roommate. That was risky. And, if anything, he didn't *deserve* to be a rebound.

But what would be the harm in it, really? New life. New start. New *man?* What would be the harm in spending a little time with him and seeing where it went? What would it be like to gently suck on his bottom lip? To run my tongue across those perfectly white teeth? To pull my fingers through those silky curls?

Stop it! You're just looking for someone to cling to.

But what was the problem with that? I didn't have my parents, so I needed to create *some* sort of family unit. And David Mathis seemed like a good person to start with.

I spotted a pink cardigan that was slumped over the top of one of the chairs. It wasn't mine, but I put my coffee down, snatched it, and folded it around my shoulders. "You did, did you?" I finally said. My tone had dropped far more seductively than I wanted it to.

"Yep. I mean, you're going to be alone all week, so I figured that I'd give you some company for a day. In case there's anything you need to do." He raised an uncanny eyebrow. "Or want to do."

What an audacious, little bugger.

He was clearly a man that was used to leading the pack and getting his way.

Alright, David. I'll play.

I sat down beside him, smiling as I gripped my mug. "Okay. Sure. And I know we had a touristy day yesterday, but we never got to the Capilano Suspension Bridge. I really want to see it. Can you take me?"

He grinned back. "Now yer talkin' like a newbie."

Forty minutes and two cups of coffee later we were getting into David's rusted Mazda3. The sun was now shielded by the overcast sky, and it was drizzling, causing the low clouds to loom across the mountains in the distance. I pulled the hood of windbreaker down as I settled into the front seat. David shivered as he turned the ignition. He shook like a wolf—the misty rain flying off his jacket—before he reached over to crank up the heat. It wasn't lost on me that this was supposed to be *May* in Vancouver. The weather seemed sporadic and unpredictable. One hour it could be sunny and warm, and the next the sky could be dark and heavy; swinging the temperature with the chill of rain.

"It doesn't stop raining for most of the year, by the way," David said. "I have no idea why you want to live here."

I shrugged. "Wanderlust, I guess. Ontario is pretty boring. Besides, you also wanted to live here, Mr. Bluenoser, so you're one to talk."

He pinched his brow as he shifted the Mazda into drive. "I didn't, actually. I was forced to live here. It's different."

I looked out the window and wondered what that meant. The noisy fan was blasting nothing but cold air, so I closed the vent in front of me.

"I jus' try to make the best of it... Always have."

"That's completely fair," I said, appreciating the subtle vulnerability he was sharing. I turned and smiled. "Would you ever go back?"

Something crossed his face as he watched the road ahead.

Something that was hard to place. Something I was curious about, but knew he'd likely never tell me this early in our relationship. "Would if I could." I opened my mouth to ask a follow up question, but he shut me up by giving me an unexpected pat on the knee. "Anyway. Sorry. I don't wanna be a sook when you did all that work to move here. I guess it's not all bad."

I chuckled nervously. "Right. Thanks. Cheers for that."

David pulled out of the driveway, and I watched the misty mountains, as we drove down River Road toward Highway Ninety-Nine, heading north into Richmond. The drizzling rain refused to let up, and the wiper blades on the Mazda didn't get a break except for a brief period under the tunnel. The darkness there was only broken by the horrible orange lights that lined it. They made my eyes sore, but at least, I realized, things were becoming more familiar.

I passed the time by taking over David's aux cord, playing a couple of songs that brightened the miserable day and gave him clues about who I was. He humoured me, dancing in his seat with a swagger, while I subjected him to my horrible, muted singing. As we drove, I thought about how easy he was to be comfortable with, and when we were alone, I started to cherish our time together.

Good sign. New family. New start.

As long as I had my roommates, everything would be okay. As long as I had my roommates, I'd be safe. I was so relieved that they hadn't been a house of psychos and murderers. Or, at least, didn't *seem* like it yet.

We continued north toward Vancouver, chatting as the dark and foggy mountains continued to grow larger. The stress from the first few days of the move was starting to ease, and I found my playful side coming out a bit. As I focused on the sound of David's voice, I asked him to explain some of his Nova Scotian sayings to my ignorant, Ontarian ears. I learned that, to Nova Scotians, things weren't just good, but were "right some" good, and that "What are you saying?" was simply their way of asking, "How's it going?"; Which made so much more sense now that I remembered it was one of the first things he'd said to me. Speaking of my first night in Vancouver, to "salt the nail" meant drinking your pain away, and if someone had a "hole in their boat," they were a dumbass. It wasn't uncommon for a Nova Scotian to ask, "J'eat yet?" soon after you walked in the door, and "Get on your moose" was their way of telling you to hurry up and get there. I laughed a little more after each translation, and as David finished his lesson, I appreciated the little bit of his heritage that I got to see.

We got to Vancouver, finding our way to Georgia Street, and following it toward Stanley Park. It was around 2pm in the afternoon, so we hit a bit of traffic. The arrow lights that hung over the road told us that the two lanes to the Lions Gate Bridge were open, with only one open on the side that led back into the city. The coniferous trees of the park loomed over us, dark from the rain, suspending us into a west coast, forest world. I opened the window as wide as I could stand and took in the invigorating smell of the cedar as we got closer to the bridge. A couple of brave cyclists peddled through the rain on the bike path beside us, and from the corner of my eye, David smiled over at me. My face was probably full of wonder. A woman-child in her entirely new world.

Suddenly, the trees opened, and the green bridge appeared, towering and majestic before us, with two lions guarding the entrance on either side. It framed the snowcapped mountain peaks ahead, before exposing us to the magnificent views of Vancouver Harbour and the Burrard Inlet, as we made our way from downtown into West Vancouver. It was my first time going across the bridge, and I didn't want to waste a second of it, so I craned my neck in every direction and drank it all in. Even though it was a gloomy day, the views of West Van and North Van were beautiful. Grouse Mountain and Cypress Mountain sprawled on the other side of the bridge, each packed at the base with neighbourhoods.

"This is why," I finally said to David, as I focused on the incredible scenery. "This is why I wanted to come here."

"Fair enough," he said.

When we came out on the other side, we turned toward North

Vancouver and followed the city streets to The Capilano Suspension Bridge Park. It was a touristy nature attraction nestled at the base of Grouse Mountain. A must-see listed on all the Vancouver travel sites I'd surfed before coming out. From what I understood, it had a collection of boardwalk trails that wound through the trees, complete with a bridge that stretched over the roaring Capilano River. There was also some sort of walkway that clung to the cliffs.

"Not the best day for it," David said, pulling into a parking space and shifting the Mazda. "But you should take a walk around. Even though it's a complete tourist trap."

"Are you kidding?" I said, stepping out, putting my hood up, and closing the car door. "David, this is supposed to be iconic!"

"Yeah. Iconic for being tourist-trappy." He locked the car, laughed, and put an arm around me. "But it's fun to see how excited you are."

"Don't yuck my yum," I said, playfully pushing him. "I'm still new. I'm allowed to be excited, okay?"

"Right. I'll give you that one."

I trotted to his side, and we crossed the street toward the ticket booths, just as the rain stopped and the sky began to clear a bit. At the entrance, there was a billboard which housed maps of the park in different languages, and I snatched one in English, studying it with a grin. I was a little too into the stamp-game—clearly meant for kids—where you could stamp the map at locations throughout the park to prove you'd been there. The cool and rainy day had left it deserted, and I was happy that we were able to go through at my pace, which was like a fucking *snail*. I stopped at every sign, taking my time to read about the history of the area, and David was patient with me. He was a little more comfortable now that the rain had stopped, and he helped me find the first metal stamp, leaning on the handle with all his strength to make a strong imprint on the map after I'd slipped it between its jaws. I studied the totem poles as we walked past and snapped their many angles with my phone.

We followed the path until we got to the suspension bridge that the park was famous for, but the sight of it sent shivers down my spine. It was long—a lot longer than I expected—and was stretched high above the Capilano River, bouncing damply from the few people that had gone on.

David went down the steps like they were nothing, and I tried to swallow my fear as I followed him. At the beginning of the bridge, he turned back, shielding his green eyes from a sudden ray of sun that broke through the clouds. "Come on, Emily. What are you waiting for?"

I stepped on like a sloth. "I'm coming, just give me a sec." It was hard to adjust to the constant change in motion. Despite years of yoga, I had terrible balance, and Mum had affectionately called me, "The forever klutz of the Anderson family." Never to be repaired, no matter how much time I'd spent standing on a *Bosu* ball. I gripped the wet railing, the metal cold against my skin.

Meanwhile, David was fucking balancing in the middle like some kind of tightrope walker.

"David... I—I think I need you."

He grinned, walking back, and offering his arm. "You're too serious, Em," he said, as I dug my nails into his jacket. "You're never gonna move forward if you cling to the railing. Jus' let go and let your body balance."

"Easier said than done," I said, trying not to look down at the roaring river.

"And you're gonna have to trust me."

That's loaded, considering I only met you two days ago.

"Do you trust me?"

Despite the thought, I nodded sharply.

"Then let go."

"Okay," I huffed, letting go of the railing only to cling to him. My feet slid on the wood, but I caught myself for once.

"Now, one step at a time," he said, guiding me forward. "That's it. Let your body do the work."

I sighed. The bridge was shakier now that an impatient, middle-aged hiker couple had decided to blast past us. But David stayed with me, one step at a time, and after a while, I got used to the swaying movement a little. I relaxed enough to slip one hand into his, while the other gripped the top of his arm. The damp air threatened to pierce into the bones in my feet, but I put my awareness into the warmth from his touch to relieve it. Finally, we got to the other side.

I exhaled in relief. "Okay, I'm woman-enough to admit—that was a challenge."

"Probably not as bad as moving across the country, though, eh?" David chuckled. I found it hard to let him go. "You got this, Em. Jus' remember that, okay?"

There was a flutter in my stomach. It was the first time he'd used my nickname.

Is it too soon to move on?

I pushed the thought away.

On the other side, the park was incredible. Boardwalks allowed easy access to the trails, while protecting the natural fauna from the people. Nestled in the cedar trees were the planks of the tree-top trail, which served impressive views of the park and the Capilano River below. David and I climbed the stone steps up to it, with the coniferous forest sprawled around us. Ferns sprouted in a wild and crowded happiness from the forest floor. The trees in the park were bigger than any I'd ever seen, creating a thick canopy that shielded the ground below. The air here was pungent with freshness. And the energy there! Oh my God. It *definitely* wasn't Ontario...

The tree-top trails were awesome, and the smaller suspension bridges that sprung from tree-to-tree didn't freak me out nearly as much as the big one did. David kept being a *right* gentleman, and he waited for me in case I needed to cling on to him again. We made small talk about my family as we explored the treetops, and I grinned when I told him about my parents.

"What about siblings?" he asked, as we stepped onto a platform wrapped around the middle of a western redcedar.

"None." I leaned onto the railing to watch the river below. "I'm an only child. Well, unless you count our tabby cat, Sammie."

The breeze tossed his black curls as he took the place next to me. His arm rested against mine, and the hair on my arms stood on edge under my jacket. "You cat people are all the same. Crazy."

I nudged him, trying really fucking hard to ignore the prickling sensation. "So, what about you? Do you have siblings? And are they here?"

His expression tightened as he dropped his gaze to the river below. "Um. No. I guess, technically not. I almost had a little sister, but her birth went wrong."

My heart dropped, and I touched his forearm. "I'm really sorry. That's awful. It must have been so hard for you and your parents."

He swallowed, twitching his brows into a furrow. "Just my dad. My mum..." He trailed off, and I caught the meaning.

"I'm sorry," I repeated. Then I felt bad for asking.

He shrugged, but I caught the tension that hovered at the corner of his lip. "It's alright. It was a long time ago. Life's different now."

I shivered as I looked back out to the swollen river. The lush water rushed and bubbled up along the banks. "So... after she died, you and your dad came here?"

But now he was reserved. Careful. Showing those same signs that, even with his Bluenoser politeness, the topic was unwelcome. "Yeah. Pretty soon after. There wasn't much left for us there. We were estranged from my mum's family, and my dad isn't close with his, so we decided to move on. Or, really, Dad did."

"He must care about you a lot," I offered.

David flashed his eyebrows and ran his gaze upstream. "He did what he thought he had to."

"Are you still close?"

"Pretty much."

"That's good. I mean, I guess you two only have each other, right?"

He nodded.

"I'm glad he's still there for you."

Something on his face went sour. "More like the other way around." He peeled his grip from the damp wood and moved on.

"Oh..."

I hadn't thought about that. After an entire upbringing of support, it was hard for me to think of parents being any other way. *They* were supposed to be there for *you*. *They* were supposed to guide *you*. How could you survive the other way around?

"Well, if he ever comes to the house, I'd be open to meeting him."

I had no idea why I fucking said that.

David flinched. He paused and looked at me severely. "That won't happen."

Okay... This new tension was uncomfortable, so I pivoted toward the lighter side of things. In the cringey-est of cringe, I decided it was a good idea to flip my hair and say, "What, am I that unbearable already?"

Droplets from the trees rolled from David's curls as he turned and stepped onto the next bridge. "No. It's not you."

My chest tightened. "He doesn't come visit you?"

From ahead of me, his back rose and fell. He clenched and unclenched his right hand. I was beginning to believe I'd really overstepped and should really shut my dumb mouth.

"I'm sorry, David—"

But he'd turned back, and the look on his face cut my words like an axe. With one blink, he looked me over. Searching my face like he was trying to decide whether to trust me.

I shifted my expression friendlier and smiled. I even gave his shoulder an encouraging rub. Then, we spoke at the same time. "You don't have to—"

"'Cus he's in prison."

Those green eyes stayed glued to my face, but before I could respond, he moved on like he didn't want to hear it. As he circled the tree and went to the next lookout, I stood on the edge of the platform. Ringing like a gong. Pretending he hadn't dropped an emotional bombshell on me.

Oh, shit. I really shouldn't have pushed that.

My stomach dropped into my toes. He was the son of a prisoner. No wonder he didn't want to talk about it.

Up ahead, David had stopped on the next platform and was watching the park below. I moved beside him and tried to focus on an elderly couple walking on the trails with what was probably their grandkid. The little girl plucked a fir branch off the path, waving in the air like a big feather when she ran to them.

"Okay." Could I not think of anything else to say?!

He gave me a guarded glance. The kind that said, *Yep, you got me. You forced one of my secrets out.*

"David, I'm so sorry. I didn't mean to make you feel any kind of way."

"It's fine, Em."

But now my mouth decided to move a mile a minute. "It's just this is all so new and we're trying to get to know each other and I thought I was asking the right questions and —"

"Look. I get it. And I don't blame you, okay? But all you really need to know is..." He hesitated, and I stayed quiet, hoping that it would hold a safe space to speak. "Listen. Life isn't always easy. Sometimes you gotta jus' take it and... I dunno... *give 'er.*"

If there was ever a more Canadian way to explain life, I didn't know it.

I bit my lip and considered how different the world was for other people.

"At the end of the day, there's always gonna be challenges," he added. "And it's gonna be hard sometimes, but you gotta make do with what you've been given and not be a sook about it. That's jus' the way it is."

How could you be so insensitive, Em?

"Right," I said pointedly. "Compassion. One hundred percent, I should have checked that. God, it was really insensitive to push you about your dad."

How could I have assumed so falsely that his life was like mine? That everything was hunky dory from the minute he stepped off that plane? That he'd *want* to talk about his parents, and that they came with memories of sunshine and rainbows?

"Nooo." He pulled at the railing and groaned. "That wasn't what I was getting at. I didn't mean to make you feel shitty about it."

Acid crept into my throat. What would he think of me now that I'd assumed so wrong? Now that I'd fucked up so badly? I didn't want him to think that I saw him in a negative light because of his complicated past. Because, really, I didn't. He was beautiful, and calm, and kind, and someone who I saw as an essential future friend. I had to be more careful to squash the assumptions going forward. I had to be more careful with how I made him *feel*.

"Anyway," David said. "Don't worry about it. You didn't do anything wrong by asking. But all you need to know is that I've been on my own since I was sixteen, so I do what I can to survive. I don't deserve life to be like that, but I take what I can get. Avril and Greg are really the only ones I have here. My dad does what he can, but... Point is, I can only push myself so far."

A lone wolf that built his pack.

I thought back to his job on the docks. Was that why he didn't dream for more? Because he thought the world wouldn't give it to him, anyway?

David. What happened to you?

"If it makes any difference, I really appreciate you sharing all of this with me," I said. "Really. *All* of it. At the end of the day, I want to get to know you... I'm kinda alone here too... And I was hoping, I dunno, that maybe you could..." I shrugged "... help me with that. Help guide me through it? Since you've done it before?"

He smiled, and I hoped it was to restore the peace. "You're not alone, Em. And you don't have to be afraid. You're one of us now. The House-of-Wolves. All I want is for you to feel welcome. And I'll be there for you. I promise."

With the time we'd spent that afternoon, it was hard for me to remember that he was still a stranger. I touched his arm. Softly. Delicately. With appreciation. Trying to explain, wordlessly, how much that meant to me. It was incredibly comforting that I had someone here to depend on. "Thank you, David."

"No problem, princess." He jerked his head toward the path. "Come on. Let's forget all this shit and keep going. We still have that cliff walk to do."

"Right," I said, inhaling deeply. "Out with the bad energy, in with the good."

"Ehyeah," he said. "Totally."

We continued through the park, taking the next hour to work our way through, snapping a couple of selfies in between me trying to distract myself by reading the signs. While I learned all about temperate rain forests, corrosion, and our careless use of our planet's water supply, I urged my brain to stay present, but the man next to me now had my attention in a way he hadn't before. As I watched him, I couldn't help but wonder about his past; my theories as wide and roaring as the river below us. Why was his father in prison? And did it have something to do with why he hated the Roths?

My interest was peaked like the mountain that we stood on, and I started to worry that I wouldn't be able to let this go. There was more to this story—much more—and I really wanted to know. But how could I find out without being insensitive to David? And would curiosity kill the she-wolf?

CHAPTER 7
IT'S NEVER OVER

It's 3:30pm in a dusty therapist's office in mid-town Toronto. I'm sitting, uncomfortable, as I try to ignore the awkwardness of being watched by a middle-aged man over half-moon glasses. The window in the room is falling apart, and the white paint is chipped and peeling. Several strands of a spider's nest are weaved into the corner of its humidity-swollen wood. A shriveled housefly sits suspended in the middle, decaying like it's been there for weeks with no spider to claim it. Another fly lies on the ledge, buzzing around in helpless, tiny circles like it's on its last legs of life. I can visibly see the dust drifting in the air. I'm choking on it even though we've only been here for twenty minutes.

Beside me, Mum shifts, taking my hand like she knows I need comfort. She's sitting up too straight, and her beautiful, blonde hair is falling down the length of her back in waves. It stops just short of the belt of her faded capris, and from her ears, her favourite dream-catcher earrings are dangling. They swing in silver circles with three feathers hanging from the bottom. She clears her throat, causing the old man to give a start.

I follow up with an annoyed look, flourished with teenaged angst. I'd been hesitant to see a therapist in the first place, but he's made this *so* much worse. And he's met the quality level of someone we haven't had to pay for. But that's the reality of the Anderson-family life in my teens. It's a constant struggle for money as my dad works his ass off and my mum fights to establish herself in a city with a cruel reputation. Half of my paycheques from my part-time job at the coffee shop are going to our utilities.

A low hum comes from the back of the therapist's throat. "Yes, well. Ummm." Nothing useful. "Can you kindly explain yourself again, Emily?"

I sigh like it's a lot of work. Because it kind of is. "I don't know how or why. But ever since my accident, I've been seeing other people's memories while I sleep."

He sniffs like I'm ridiculous. "Right…" That doesn't help either. "And what happened with this accident then, eh?"

I roll my eyes and open my mouth to answer, but Mum takes a sharp breath and cuts me off. "She damaged part of her parietal lobe and suffered a coma for two days." I realize that she's absentmindedly twisting the emerald ring on my finger. Drawing the hope from it that, from now on, I'll be safe.

"Parietal lobe, eh?" he says, scribbling on his notepad. "Mrs. Anderson, could I speak to you alone for a moment?"

"Absolutely not," Mum says. "Anything that you can say to me, you can say to Emily too."

He grumbles. "Yes, well, right…" Clearing his throat, he looks over his glasses, leaning forward like he's about to tell a small child some really bad news. "Emily, it seems that you may be suffering from some sort of mild post-traumatic stress disorder, or PTSD for short. But there's nothing to worry about. It's a common ailment, and I will prescribe you something that will sort it all out." He leans back in his chair, seeming satisfied with his half-assed diagnosis.

"But… No… That's not it…" I stammer. "It's real…" I'm not sure what else to say. Trying to explain it to other people is like pulling teeth.

"I'm afraid that what you are describing is physically and biologically impossible. It may *seem* real in your mind, because of the PTSD, but it is, in fact, not." He holds his hands out in a shrug and repeats, "It's impossible."

"It's *not* impossible," Mum jumps in, quick to defend me. "Sir, she has described details about my wedding day, from *my* perspective, that no one else could know. Things she couldn't have known unless I told her. And I didn't."

He sighs and grabs his prescription pad from the small drawer in the top of the roundtable beside him. The faded lamp on top wiggles in protest. "I'm afraid that sometimes children will take fascination with their parents in times of trauma," he says, as he scribbles down the description of whatever-drug-he-thinks-is-going-to-fix-me in blotchy ink. "Protective figures. They get very attached to the people that make them safe. Perhaps there are ways that the information was gained that you haven't thought of, eh?" He tears the paper off the pad, and it separates with a loud *riiiiip!* He offers it to Mum. She takes it even though her jaw is dropped. "Take two a day, with food."

Mum sits back on the couch, looking as defeated as I am. She falls silent, and I hope she can figure out what to say next, because I fucking can't.

The therapist furrows his bushy brow like he's thought of something else. Will it be helpful? Probably fucking not. "Miss Anderson, I believe the PTSD has caused Emily to seek additional attention, as it often does, and this jargon about memory seeing is a fragment of that, that's all. A cry for attention. Like I said, it is *not possible.* Are you quite sure that Emily is getting enough love and affection from you and your husband at home? You may want to assess that a little deeper."

Mum wrinkles her nose and crumples the prescription into a ball. "Fuck you." It bounces off the therapist's nose, and he looks really offended by it. "We're done here."

I shoot Mum a look at her uncharacteristic behaviour, but she ignores it and grabs my hand. She yanks me off the couch and toward the door without another word. Then she drags me out onto the sidewalk, her steps pounding on the concrete as we make our way toward the nearest streetcar stop. Outside, the air is muggy with the odd heat of mid-May, and it causes the smell of nearby market stands to become overwhelming. It stinks like fish and various seafood mixed with rice noodles.

The drone of the crowds drowns my thoughts. Mum's not paying attention either (big city selective hearing) and she's still storming our way through the crowd, visibly upset. That's the thing; she doesn't get upset often, and most of the time it is expertly controlled. But when that all goes south, it goes there *quickly*.

"Mum, slow down," I plead, pulling back my hand.

She lets go but continues forward. "Useless man!" she says, as we get to the streetcar stop. "Who does he think he is? Huh? I mean, he pretty much accused you of lying, and me of being a bad mother. How is that supposed to help us here?" She makes her way into the TTC booth and plops herself down on the bench with a huff. Her earrings swing wildly from her earlobes, as she winds herself into a knot of frustration.

I sit quietly, like a ghost. All this *bad energy* is my fault, and I'm too young to be able to process that.

A woman passes the front of the booth, swaying, and reeking of cheap liquor. "Y'all got a cigarette?"

Mum ignores her, and I shake my head.

She goes away, and I sigh, turning back to my mother. The air in the TTC booth is stuffy, and it smells like someone pissed in the corner because they probably have. "You believe me, don't you, Mum?" I ask, nudging a greying cigarette butt with my foot. I wonder if the woman would be desperate enough to pick it up. I've seen people smoke them straight off the street before. Which makes me really sad.

Mum loosens her arms and turns to me. "Of course, I do, honey."

Despite the words, there's a hint of hesitancy, and it makes my guts churn. I'm a freak, and there's no getting away from it now. I'm a freak, and I'm broken, and no one knows what to do with me. Including the woman who's never failed to guide me before.

I melt into the bench and rest my back against the warm glass. My throat tightens, and I hide the sudden hopelessness vibe that I've fallen into. I close my eyes. Try to ignore my noisy city. But the smell in this part of town makes me hungry.

From the next seat over, Mum exhales like she's trying to rid herself of the negative experience, and I raise my head to watch her. Exhale the bad, inhale the good. It's one of her constant mantras. Finally, she unwraps her arms and looks at the busy street. Her eyes glaze over. My weird problem is also hers, and I can tell that's what she's thinking about.

"Em," she says, her tone much softer now. "I don't know what the answer is to this, but..."

"What, Mum?"

"Well, this is gonna sound a bit crazy. But what if we *found* this person that belongs to the name you've been screaming? What if we found *Barrett*? What if your subconscious is giving us a clue on where to go next? What if they can provide some sort of indication in the answer to all of this? I'm thinking they're the key to something big in your future."

I scoff and throw too much attention into the street. "That's insane, Mum. There's no way that this person exists. It's just a name, and I'm fucking crazy. That's all."

"Em..." Her voice is stern. "This ability is a gift from the Universe. Therefore, it must have meaning. You're not crazy, honey."

"And you thought *therapy* was going to help us with that?"

She pauses, pursing her lips. "I don't know what I thought. I was only doing what the doctor suggested."

The defeat in her voice makes me apologetic. She's only doing what she can to help, and I'm being a bitch. "Sorry, Mum."

"It's alright, Em. I'm aware of how frustrating this is for you."

"*Frustrating* doesn't describe the half of it."

"Meditation," she says, suddenly. "We have to do more targeted meditation. And you have to try to dig deep."

"I don't want to dig deep."

"It's the only way we're going to find meaning."

I cross my arms. "Yeah, well, I don't want to *find meaning*. I want it to go away so that my boyfriend doesn't question why I'm shouting some other person's name."

A few heartbeats pass where she doesn't say anything.

My irritation deepens. I shrug heavily. "And anyway. Even if this theoretical name belongs to an actual *person*, we live in a city of three million people. And that's Toronto alone — not even the GTA. How exactly do you propose I find him?"

She clicks her tongue. "Oh, honey, that's the easy part," she says, giving me a smile that doesn't make sense in all this. "All you have to do is follow your heart. Believe me. Follow your heart, and you will find them."

CHAPTER 8
LOOKING FOR A STRANGER

It was Thursday night, and I was sitting in my room, on my laptop, staring at *Google*. The first time I'd done this, I'd only had a single name—*Barrett*—but now I added the other. My fingers moved lethargically when I typed in *R.O.T.H.* and it took me a long time to hit Enter after. Did I really think this was him? And even if it was, what would I do with that? How could I even *fathom* the idea of finding this mystery person, and what would it mean for my future if I did? What signs would I need to follow? What would it add something to the meaning of my move? But fate seemed to be guiding me, and I couldn't ignore that. It was what drove me to shoulder my courage. Finally press Enter.

Up popped a plethora of links and information on him. The smaller font under his name declared *Chief Financial Officer and Senior Vice-President of Roth Pharmaceuticals.* Below that was a collage of three different pictures, and links to some website that sourced his stock trading history and net worth, his *LinkedIn* profile, and his leadership page on the company's website. I stared at the main photo—him dressed to the nines in front of a muted background—blinking as I searched his face.

He was the spitting image of the man that I'd seen in Carol's memory. His father. What was it? Josh? Jacob? I couldn't remember. Anyway, he looked *exactly* like him. He had the same dark eyes and dark red hair, which was shorter on the sides and medium length at the top, swept back in a fiery wave. But those black eyes were also *gorgeous*, and in the warmth of the studio light, they reminded me of melted, dark chocolate. He had a gorgeous smile, complete with perfectly straight teeth that were probably paid for.

The reaction that shimmered through my body was hard to place. It was like someone had slipped some arsenic inside the chicken parm I'd had for dinner.

How can this be him? This billionaire pretty-boy...

We were from completely different worlds, and I couldn't even imagine the number that I'd see if I clicked on that link to his net worth. This man ran a multi-billion-dollar pharmaceutical company; that likely made money from breaking the ethics code in one way or another. I was about to dedicate more of my education to uncovering injustices like that and holding such companies accountable for fixing them. I mean, yeah, pharma companies were a necessity. They provided life-saving—and life-*changing*—treatments to billions across the globe. And yes, I'd been one of those after my accident and yes, I was grateful for it. But they also tended to have wildly high profit margins and products that were priced on the side of obscene. I wondered what number I'd find if I searched for Travis, as the CEO, and clicked on the link for his net worth.

Ugh. It made me shiver. After suffering the antibiotics incident, I had a hard time letting things like this go. At least the smaller pharma company that was responsible for that had paid for it in the end...

This makes no fucking sense.

I scanned the other two photos of Barrett like they held the meaning *Where's Waldo* style. The second was another studio photo where he looked slightly younger, and in the third he was standing at a podium at some sort of conference, one hand spread in front of him like he was gesturing his presentation. In all three he was suited flawlessly and stuck in a posture of confidence. I was very aware that I was lying in bed, wearing an old pair of Roots sweatpants and a lovingly stained hoodie.

Scrolling down the page, I read the blurb that the search engine had pulled from the company's website. It again mentioned his title, before continuing with, *Roth Pharmaceuticals, is a company that is proud to be North America's largest, and inherently Canadian. We are driven by our commitment to bold, purposeful values, including becoming a world leader in research and innovation, and becoming the most sustainable pharmaceutical company on the planet.*

I raised an eyebrow.

Huh. Interesting.

Drifting to the other side of the page, I noticed that there was a link to an article titled, *The Two Brothers at the Top of the Pharmaceutical Industry: Barrett and Travis Roth Continue to Flourish Despite the Death of their Father.*

And the word "death" hit me like a brick.

My phone instantly shocked me out of it when it pinged with a text. It was Carol. Which was an uncanny coincidence given what I was reading.

Hello, Emily! she said. *I hope your week is going well. I've made reservations at the Teahouse in Stanley Park for four o'clock tomorrow. I wonder if you'd be free to join me?*

Oh yeah. I'd forgotten that I was supposed to meet her for coffee this week. I picked up my phone, but my fingers hovered over the screen.

Then David's suggestion from my first night ran through my mind. "You shouldn't call her back," he'd said. "End of conversation."

But how could I *not* meet her? The Universe was giving me very clear signs toward the mystery man that I'd been calling for over a decade of my life. I couldn't ignore them. They'd only come back stronger if I did.

I thought about it for a moment, and then texted, *Hey Carol! That'd be lovely. I'll see you then.*

Hey, even if this didn't go anywhere, I didn't owe David any explanation on why I was meeting her. Especially when he wouldn't tell me *why* he hated the Roths.

Somewhere downstairs, the front door opened and closed. Sighing through my nose, I turned my attention back to the screen. I started to type *Father of Barrett Roth* into the search bar, but David came up the stairs, and I closed the browser like I'd been watching porn.

He threw his backpack into his room and then wound around the banister toward mine. "Hey, princess." My spirit warmed at the new nickname he'd given me. "What're you at?"

"Not much," I said, smiling innocently as he collapsed on the bed beside me. "I was just about to start a movie. Do you wanna watch it with me?"

"What one?" he grumbled, rolling into a pillow.

"Forest Gump?"

"Ugh."

"What? It's a classic. Don't tell me you don't like it."

He groaned. "But it's so *boring*."

I put a hand to my chest in fake offense. "It's a cinematic masterpiece!"

"Still boring."

"Whatever. We're watching it anyway," I said, giving him a playful nudge. "How was your day?"

He shrugged. "Had to train a newbie at work. That's always painful. The gym kicked my ass. And I had an appointment that kicked it some more after."

"Yeah, I was wondering why you were home so late." Now that I thought about it, he didn't look so good. There was a blueness to his skin that I'd never seen before. "Are you feeling okay?"

"Jus' tired," he said. "And I wanna eat, but I don't wanna cook."

"There's leftover chicken parm," I suggested. "I can heat it up for you, if you want."

"You're an angel, Em," he said.

My spirit warmed a little more.

"Did I hear you were watching Forest Gump?" Avril said, coming out of her room with a grin on her face.

"No—" David said.

"Yeah," I cut in. "Care to join us?"

"Oh, heck yes!" Avril trotted over, jumped on the bed, and wiggled up on my other side.

"That makes two," I said, nudging David again.

He sighed.

"Three!" Greg added, coming out to join the watch party. Shortly after, he crawled up beside Avril, and I tried to balance the laptop on my knees so that everyone could see.

"If we're gonna watch this thing, we're watching it downstairs," David griped. "That way I can lay down and pass out from how boring it is."

"I'll get the popcorn!" Greg said, springing up and thundering down the stairs. "Meet me there!"

As we pulled ourselves from my bed to flock to the living room, I realized my heart had swelled in a way that it hadn't since I'd left home. I was starting to bond with my new family, and that was the best sign of all.

On Friday evening, the wooden gate to the gardens of The Teahouse groaned like it was unhappy to be opened. The small restaurant was quaint but dripping with expense at every turn. It was west facing, just at the edge of Stanley Park, and had stunning views of the Burrard Inlet, Bowen Island, and the Sunshine Coast beyond. The recent warmth had allowed the daffodils and lilacs to bloom, and they wrapped the patio in brilliant colours. It was here that I found Carol waiting for me, waving with a broad grin as I came in. The sun caught the sparkle of her diamond bracelet and blinded me, but

I blinked though it and grinned back. I hugged her after she got up from the table. Her head was draped in a massive purple sunhat, and she was wearing a muted plaid shirt that was a stark contrast to her fancy bracelet.

I pulled back my chair, sank into its cushions, and asked her how she'd been. The gingham-green tablecloth brushed my knees and tickled me as I tucked into the table.

Carol answered honestly and told me she'd been lonely because her daughter was vacationing in Spain with Travis's wife, Jalpa, leaving their Estate emptier.

Hard life, I thought bitterly.

"I can't complain, though," she said, sipping her cappuccino. "It *has* given me a little extra time with Travis. Which has been nice."

Ignoring the discontent within, I put on a polite smile.

Rich people problems.

"Spain, eh?" I said instead.

"Yeah, she's got this thing for the Spanish coast." She flicked her sparkling wrist. "She prefers to drag Jal along for some reason. It doesn't bother me, really."

She went quiet, and I leashed the burning questions that wanted to burst from my throat from the moment I'd sat across from her. I cleared it and jerked my chin instead. "That's a beautiful bracelet. It looks new."

And fucking expensive.

"Thank you, Emily. It is." She held it against her wrist so that I could study it, but she was barking up the wrong tree. "It was a welcome home present from Barrett. Isn't it stunning?"

I suppressed a flinch at his name and tried not to think of the weight of my student loans. "He has good taste."

She laughed, the sound as lovely as a songbird. "Yes, he knows his grandmother well. That's for sure." With her cappuccino suspended in one hand, she flagged down the waiter. "We must get you a coffee."

He appeared out of nowhere, and I ordered a latté made with almond milk. He scribbled down my order and smiled before making his way inside.

Then Carol and I made dreaded small talk about my upcoming school and the sporadic weather, and then fell into a comfortable silence as we both enjoyed the view. The early-evening sun was sparkling from the sea—rivaling her bougie bracelet—and the mountains beyond were layered in shades of blue, each one lighter than the one before. It was breathtaking, and I couldn't believe these were my views now.

The waiter came back with my latté, pulling me from my thoughts. I took a sip immediately after, and the sweetness flowed down my throat like waves of happiness. Carol smiled and told me that she enjoyed my company. Considering we hadn't spent much time together, I was touched, and I thanked her.

"But there's someone who would enjoy it more," she added. Then she turned and dug through her purse before returning with an envelope, which she handed to me. On the front, my name was elegantly scrawled.

"What's this?" I asked.

She grinned, her expression brightening. "It's my attempt at helping you fit in, my dear. Open it."

With my curiosity peaked, I slipped my thumb under the seal and pulled the invitation from the envelope. It was black, and the words that danced across the card in a fancy red font told me that I and a guest were cordially invited to the eighth annual "Roth Pharma Banquet"; a night in celebration of the success of the company. It was in two weeks.

"I know it seems strange," Carol said. "But after all the droning on the boys do about the company, it's actually a very fun night. I thought you might like to come so you can meet Barrett."

I swallowed as I caressed the smooth card.

An invitation to meet *Barrett.*

"I mean, you said his name on the plane," Carol said. "Perhaps that was fate guiding you to a new friend."

I blinked, shocked to hear this from her. I wasn't sure if she had any spiritual beliefs or was just using the "pop-culture" reference to fate, but she was bang on the money. The Universe couldn't be any clearer with the signs. Was it just hammering it into my thick skull because I'd missed so many over the years? Or was it because I'd ignored the path to figuring out what this name meant to me for so long? Was this realignment?

"I'm sorry, Emily. Did I overstep?" Carol asked. It was the look on my face. I was sure it was sending the wrong message.

"No! No." My voice barked out much louder than I'd meant. "I'm just... grateful, is all. Gratefully surprised." I smiled. "I've never met anyone that's been so eager to help me build a new life before. Thank you so much, Carol."

Of course, I *had* to accept this. If I didn't, it would keep coming back in different ways. I was sure of it. The time was now whether I wanted to face it or not. But I was also painfully aware of something else— If I was even going to *consider* accepting, David couldn't know...

She smiled back. "Well, I thought it would help you feel more at home. And I'm aware that Barrett can be... well... *Barrett*. But I really think that you two would get on!"

I had no idea what she meant by "Barrett being Barrett," but I believed the last part. Was he some sort of key to my future in Vancouver?

"Yeah. Thanks. I'll think about it."

"Fantastic," she said, beaming at me. "For what it's worth, it's also a great networking opportunity for you. After all, you're going into Medical Ethics, right? Wouldn't it be of benefit to get some exposure to pharma?"

I hadn't actually thought of that. All the work I'd done in the years between gaining my undergrad in ethics and applying for my masters was in Public Service. It'd given me great experience, but no beneficial exposure to the medical industry. This could also be a chance to learn.

"That's a great suggestion." I tapped the invitation against my fingers, before I put it back in its envelope and slipped it into my purse. "Thanks very much."

An image of the House-of-Wolves shaking their heads with their arms crossed flashed into my mind. I was about to disobey my alpha's orders in the worst way, but did I care?

Well, yeah.

I felt bad for not listening to David. But how could I help it when curiosity and fate were in the way?

Carol flapped her hand toward my purse, her bracelet blinding me again. "There's an RSVP link on the card. Don't forget. Also, it's formal, so make sure you wear a beautiful dress, honey."

My brain punched me with the number in my draining savings account. "Right."

"Your guest, too."

"Right," I said again.

Really, the only person that I could contemplate taking to this thing was Avril. She was the only member of the House that was *okay* with the idea of being around the Roths. And hadn't she mentioned that her friend was dating Barrett? Perhaps she wouldn't be opposed to sitting through it with me.

The vibe at our table had risen a little, so we finished our drinks and ordered some wine and dinner — which Carol offered to pay for. Because of the number in my bank account, I didn't refuse.

After every sip of *Sauvignon Blanc*, I got braver and more comfortable. So, shortly after our plates had been cleared, I decided that it was time for me to get to some of those burning questions. I *had* to learn more about the Roths.

"Carol, can I ask you something?" I said, after I'd finished a good quarter of my second glass.

"Sure, sweetheart. Anything."

"Well, it's about Travis." My nose tingled from the gulp of wine. "I'm wondering how he became CEO of Roth Pharma. I mean, he seems so young."

She put her wine down and thought for a moment. "He had little choice. His father, John, was taken from us, and it forced him into the unjust position of being the man of the house, as well as a CEO, at barely twenty-four."

Something tightened in my chest. The thought of losing a father was unbearable, and I felt horrible for them. "I'm so sorry. Was it illness? Cancer, or something?"

Her posture stiffened, and she looked at me for a long time. "No, Emily. He was murdered."

My ears rang, and my jaw dropped. "*Murdered?*"

"Yes," she said, way too matter-of-factly. "A man killed him."

A flurry of questions buzzed around my brain, but I couldn't catch one, so I sunk back into my chair instead. "Whoa. That's so heavy. I'm so sorry. Like, so, so sorry, Carol."

She tried on a smile, but then dropped it when it didn't fit. "It's alright. It happened twelve years ago, so it's gotten a little easier over time. Marginally. Bit by bit."

I leaned forward on the table, trying to show sympathy. This was a sensitive subject, and I had to be compassionate. "The man who..." the options of my next word reeled through my head, and I grabbed the least offending "...*attacked* him. Do you know why? Did you ever get that justice?"

Carol's face went two shades lighter, and she started to study me in the same way David had when he was questioning whether to trust me. Searching every inch of my skin for evidence. Calculating what she should say. Like I'd done with him, I threw in a well-intentioned smile and hoped it would be enough.

She fiddled with her napkin, rolling the fabric at the corner tight between her manicured fingers. "My opinion," she said slowly, "is that the man was not of sound mind. During the trial, he changed his plea in the middle of the courtroom. The police told us that there was a debt of some kind. A debt that he owed John."

"A monetary debt?"

She nodded, her expression stern.

"Oh."

How fucking horrible would it be to have your father killed over money? To me, it seemed insane. Such an unbelievable waste of life...

I thought of Dad and my skin froze. Nausea hit me right after, and I was sure it wasn't the wine.

"Are you alright?" Carol asked.

"Yeah, I'm just... horrified. I mean, it's horrible. I feel so bad for you and your family."

She bit her lip and looked away. "It's something we're familiar with."

Now the lull was uncomfortable. Desperate to soothe it, I reached inside and caught one of those flurrying questions, trying to frame it with as little awkwardness as possible. "Carol? What was John like?"

She tapped her fingers on the table; the napkin still rolled tight between her thumb and index. "Well, he was... He was... You've caught me a little off guard. Sorry." She flushed before nodding surely. "He was a wonderful man and a great father. And good son-in-law, at that." Then she picked up her wine and downed it, setting the glass on the table with the daintiness of a butterfly landing. "But he was also a businessman. Immersed in his work all the time. Not unlike the boys are now. Which worries me a little, to be honest... John had his ways of... well... *dealing* with things. He was stubborn when it came to that, you know. But he was a good man."

I took note of how she punctuated "good man." Like it was two words. Good. Man.

Carol's gaze then drifted out into the garden, touching the flowers as she grazed it over them. "Both of his boys miss him dearly. He was taken from us much too soon."

"Yeah. I believe it."

Carol's eyes started to glisten, and she shook her head as she looked out to the sea. "Emily, can we stop this discussion, please? The case is closed, and it wasn't John's fault. He was taken unfairly."

I reached across the table and took her hand. The way the tablecloth was moving told me her foot was bouncing under it. "I'm really sorry, Carol. I didn't mean to upset you. And I can't imagine how hard the past twelve years have been for your family."

She nodded and dabbed the corners of her eyes with the napkin. "Yes, well. They have been difficult, honey. Difficult in ways that you simply could not fathom..." She trailed off, and I saw the pain flash across her face before she squashed it. "Let's move on, okay? Talk about something happy. Oh, I have an idea! How about we order some cheesecake?"

Not wanting to upset her more, I dropped the whole John thing and agreed.

The sun was sinking over the Burrard Inlet by the time we'd finished dessert, gracing the sky and sea with the start of a beautiful sunset. I shivered with the chill that it brought, and even though the waiter had lit some of the heat lamps, it was starting to get cold. So, we decided that it was time to leave. As we made our way into the parking lot, Carol hugged me and told me that she'd see me at the banquet in two weeks.

Something guilty churned on the inside, but I covered it and told her that I was looking forward to it.

As I waited for my Uber, I watched her drive away in a bright white Tesla, disappointed that the Roth family was still a mystery.

At least I've left with an envelope that holds the possibility of clarity, I thought. *I just have to woman-up and be brave enough to use it.*

Yeah, right. How was that gonna happen when I'd feel so guilty for keeping it from David? And what I'd heard about the Roths so far had made my blood run cold. How much deeper did this whole murder thing go...? And how did I fit into all of this...?

CHAPTER 9
SHOULD I STAY OR SHOULD I GO?

On the weekend after I'd met Carol, David took me to a dealership so that I could find my car. At first, I was lost—the salesman pressuring me to finance for a bigger budget—but David had scoped out the lot and found a Toyota Yaris that fit within my means. It was forest green and had over 200,000 kilometers, but it ran okay and was enough for me. I was so freaking relieved. It was another step toward building my life in BC, and David had been there for me. That was at least *something*, right?

On Friday, two weeks later, I'd picked it up and driven it home, so I decided to celebrate. I invited the House out to Sharkey's to have dinner on the patio, and we took the opportunity to overindulge with a few drinks. By the time we were watching the sun set over the Fraser River—empty fish and chips baskets piled high—everyone was tipsy. It was almost a month since my move out west, and I was getting closer to my roommates while also building trust in their support system. We were developing the foundations of blossoming friendships, and my love and affection for them was starting to flow naturally. They made me feel like part of the pack, and that helped reassure me that it was safe to let everything settle. At least, a little bit.

Long after the sun had set over the mountains, we stumbled down River Road, with David and Greggy belting out some song that I'd never heard. I grinned and linked arms with Avril as we walked, savoring her warmth and the soft melody of her giggle. We were acting like besties, and this eased the anxiety I'd had about sharing my secret invitation to the Roth Banquet with her.

And though I'd led Carol to think that I was *definitely* coming, it took me a full week to decide whether to go. If I went, and I met Barrett, and I came upon some life-changing revelation, would I even be ready for that? Could I handle it on top of how much my life had already changed with the move to Vancouver? I mean, my roommates had been a great support, but I'd only *just* started to get settled. Was I ready to stir the pot by going after the signs the Universe was giving me?

Besides, there was David and the way he'd reacted to the Roths on my first day here. What did that all mean? And why did he hate them? Sure, I'd learned firsthand that pharma companies could be wrought with masked immorality, but did that really make them evil? What had happened to make David feel strongly enough to transfer his beliefs to the other members of the House? It had to be something big, right? What if I went to this thing and got slapped with the cold hard lesson that the Roths *were* evil? Would the Source want me to do something about it? Was it somehow tied in with my Medical Ethics master's?

Ugh. It was all so overwhelming! How was I supposed to figure this all out when there were so many question marks?

Well, I'd never find the truth if I didn't take that leap.

Should I stay or should I go?

I'd asked myself that question before my move, and it had all turned out okay. Basically. Well, *shaky*, but okay. And if I could survive that, then I could survive a night with the Roths, and the potential lessons that came with it. Right? So, I decided I was going. For sure. I was *definitely* going.

I went online, and I RSVP'd, and that was that.

Then, a week before the banquet, I managed to ask Avril if she'd join me. I really didn't want to walk into a room of strangers in a strange land without one of my new family members by my side.

"I dunno, Em," she'd said, with her expression strained. "It sounds a bit... not up my alley."

"Yeah, but it could be if you gave it a chance?" I pointed out. "Come on. We can count it as a girls' night, or something."

"Hmmm. Maybe. But I'll really have to think about it."

"That's fine. We've still got a week, so take your time."

"And why do you want to go so bad? I'm surprised you even met with this Carol woman after what David said."

I paused, contemplating what angle I wanted to show. "I'm going into Medical Ethics, so a night to rendezvous with a pharma giant would be huge for me. I just wanna learn. You know, get my foot in the door. It's a great networking opportunity and could help my future career."

"Hmmm. I guess that makes sense."

"Plus, didn't you say that your friend is dating Barrett Roth? Wouldn't this be a chance to see her?"

This time, it was her that paused. "Yeah. I mean, I do see them sometimes. But *don't* tell David!"

"You keep my secret, I'll keep yours."

"Promise?"

"Pinky swear." I offered my finger for her to hook, and she smirked as she took it.

"Okay. I'll come. But we keep it on the downlow."

I breathed a sigh of relief. Convincing her had been more painless than I'd thought. She must have valued her friendship with Barrett Roth's girlfriend, which gave me hope that, one day, she'd value mine in the same way. "Thanks. I really appreciate it."

That weekend, we'd snuck out of the house and went shopping for dresses in downtown Ladner. Avril settled on a short, strapless, light-pink one, while I went for a more conservative, long, one-shouldered, royal blue. When we got home, it was easy for us to sneak them upstairs because David and Greg were in the living room getting stoned.

Back on the Friday after we'd had dinner at Sharkey's, I stormed up the stairs with my feet heavy from white wine and changed into my pajamas. I'd just finished pulling a tank top over my belly when David knocked on my door with a drunken rhythm.

"Em. Hurry up. I need to show you this."

"Okay, okay." I giggled as I stumbled and opened it. He was grinning on the other side. He'd changed into a dark blue t-shirt that had a cartoon Thunderbird on the front. It had its wings flexed up like a bodybuilder, and the letters UBC were printed in gold underneath.

"Whaddya think? Greggy got it for me."

"With love, from my heart to yours!" Greg called from inside his room.

"Right some," David slurred. He turned around and walked back so he could pull Greg into his doorway, giving him a hug, a kiss, and a noogie on his faux hawk. "And I love you, bu'y."

"I love you, too, ya big softy," Greg said, patting David on the chest before he freed himself from his best friend's grip.

I laughed and leaned against my doorframe, one hand bracing on the wood. "I gotta admit, it's pretty badass."

David stumbled back over to me, a waft of beer following his tropical smelling cologne. "I knew you'd like it," he said, pushing past me and into my room. He collapsed on my bed with a satisfied sigh and pulled a joint from his pocket, popping it into his mouth and preparing to light it.

"No, no, no." I bounced on my knees as I landed beside him, pulling it away. "Not in my room, Mr. Wolf!"

We started to wrestle, and I teased him before I returned it. Even through his bloodshot eyes, his grin was adorable. "Shit. Sorry. I forgot we en' in mine."

Ignoring the sudden drunken urge to grab his shirt collar and make-out Hollywood romance style, I dropped from where I'd been propped over him and settled on my back. The waves of my hair draped over his shoulder, creating a contrast of blonde against the skin of his arm. "We can go smoke it outside if you want. It's a nice night."

His chuckle was heavy from intoxication, and he threw his left arm behind his curls. "Nah. I'm comfy here."

I couldn't ignore the prickling from where my arm was touching his, or the soft and subtle way in which his fingers were caressing the edge of my hand. It was the area between my thumb and index finger, and as I tried to wrangle my body's response, I wondered whether that was an erogenous zone, or whether I was just drunk.

"What're your plans for tomorrow?" His sexy Eastern burr worked against my wrangling.

I shrugged, studying the constellation of water damage on the popcorn ceiling above us. "Not much during the day. Except that I should do schoolwork. Avril and I have plans tomorrow night."

He turned his head and smirked. "Where was my invite?"

My heart sped up. The way that it does when I'm about to tell a lie. "We're having girl time. You'd hate it."

His head turned back but shifted even closer to me. "Girl time."

I swallowed and nodded way too quickly. "Yep." I hated lying to him, but I wasn't up for the negative energy explosion if I'd mentioned where we were *actually* going. "Why? What are your plans?"

This time, it was him that shrugged. "I may go see my dad. Seeing as you're busy, anyway."

"Okay. Makes sense."

He rested his head against mine and continued the delicate touch with his fingers. I realized that I felt a lot closer to him but was also confused on what to do next. He started humming the same tune he'd been singing outside, and I listened to the deepness of his voice, trying to tell myself that I didn't want him. We were roommates—that was it. Platonic roommates that were starting to become good friends, and I couldn't let the wine fuck that up for me. I *wouldn't*

THE VEIL OF OPPRESSION

let the wine fuck that up for me. He had a history with Avril. It was *wrong* to want him. I gave myself all sorts of excuses. And that all worked. That is until he turned and hovered over me...

His tone started dripping with seduction instead of drunkenness. "Em. I've really enjoyed the time we've spent together so far."

"Yeah?" I raised my lips closer to his.

"And I'm really glad you're a member of the House now."

"Yeah?"

"Do you—?" He paused and pinched his eyebrows, bloodshot eyes glazing as he reached under his supporting arm. "The heck's stabbing me?"

The colour drained from my face when I realized it could only be one thing. The corner of the invitation. The very one that I'd held and studied—wondering what this all fucking meant—before folding and stupidly tucking it beneath my bedsheets the night before.

Shhhiiiitttt!!

His face turned mischievous, and the way that he grinned as he pulled it out told me that he was ripe to tease. I snatched at it to stop him from catching the words. "What is that?" he asked. But I was out of luck. He'd grabbed it back to confirm what he'd seen. "What is this? Where'd you get this?"

I hesitated. "David... Just let me explain—"

"Emily. Where *the fuck* did you get this?" He sat up and wobbled it between his thumb and index finger; the sound pulsing with my guilt.

I sighed and sat up too, pulling my knees to my chest. "Do you remember the woman that I met on the plane? Carol?"

He nodded, bloodshot gaze unblinking as it pierced mine.

"Well, we met up for coffee the other day. And she gave it to me." I shrugged. "It's really nothing. Just a banquet. I thought it might be a good opportunity to meet a few people and network..."

His voice escaped in a growl low enough to rival the animal tattooed on his biceps. "I told you not to call her."

I dropped my knees, and the comforter parted under my feet like a fabric version of the red sea. "And I don't understand why. What's the harm in me meeting her?"

He swung his legs over the side of the bed and stood. "The harm is that I told you about the Roths! They're the Devil's spawn, and I don't want you getting involved with them!"

"David. Come on." I turned up my palms. "She's a nice woman. You're getting the wrong idea here."

"I don't care," he said. He started to pace as he jabbed the corner of the invitation at me. "You can't go to this thing, Em. I thought you understood about the Roths. The fact that you even *considered* this is so deceiving."

"David, please. It's not like that. I'm not accepting to hurt you. And also—by the way—how can you tell me not to go when you won't even tell me *why* it hurts you?" I reached out for the invitation, but he yanked it out of my range. If I weren't under the influence, I probably would have pulled something.

"Girl time? Really, Emily? And you were going to take *Avril* to this thing?" His tone was filling with rage. Bad energy explosion detonated. "So you're fucking *lying* to me now?"

Frustration flooded through me, and I smacked my bed. "I only said that because I knew this is how you'd react!"

He gripped his curls and mimed ripping them out. "Why can't you jus' understand that anyone that gets involved with them lives to regret it?"

"Why, David? You can't just say things like that and not explain yourself!"

"Because I'm tryin' to protect you!"

"From what?" I knee-hopped toward him, teetering on the edge of the mattress. "I have *nothing* to go on here! You won't give me any rhyme or reason to this whole Roth thing, but you want me to choose your side? How's that fair? I'm not even aware why there *are* sides!"

The argument came to a silent standoff. He watched me, calculating his next response with his green gaze burning. Then he looked away and drew a deliberate breath before he responded with control. "After all the bonding we did over the past month, is it too much to ask for you to trust me?"

"It is when you don't trust me back." I bit my lip and continued quieter. "If you trusted me, you'd let me make my own calls. Not order me around like some beta wolf."

His response was to shake his head, wrinkle his nose, and drop his voice above a whisper. "You have no idea what you're dealing with." He turned toward my door and stormed out. I watched him stop at Avril's. The sound of Greg and her laughing came to a dead stop. "You were gonna go to this?" David held the invitation like a playing card of blame. "You were going to celebrate their sins with them? Sipping wine and champagne? That's fucked up, Av."

"David, my friend's going to be there. And I wanted to support Emily with her networking. I swear, that's—"

"Oh, *jog on*." David whipped the invitation at her with an angry flick of the wrist. He pulled the joint from his pocket and hammered down the stairs.

Avril came out of her room with the invitation trembling in her hand. She met my eyes, and though we didn't say anything to each other, we shared the same shocked expression from across the hall.

CHAPTER 10
GHOSTS AGAIN

It was a tad embarrassing to pull my cheap Toyota Yaris up to the sprawling black gates of the Roth Estate the next evening. The massive property was nestled on Cypress Mountain in West Vancouver and was at a high enough elevation to serve gorgeous views of the neighbourhood below and the city in the distance. In fact, it seemed to be the highest of all the estates on Cypress. Nothing was above them but the rolling peaks of the mountain.

Avril and I dropped our jaws as we passed through the elaborate wrought iron gate and made our way up a lengthy drive that was framed with coniferous trees on either side. The Estate came within view below a darkening navy sky, and it only grew bigger as we drove toward it. It was an extensive French-style château, made of white stone with a dark roof draped over its multiple wings. It had an abundance of uplighting—making it look like a clone of Versailles, or something—and the lengthy stone driveway ended in a wide circle that hugged the front. A marble fountain stood boastfully in the middle, competing for attention against the Estate. Its water was loud and overbearing, even from the car.

The length of the driveway was lined with cars ten *thousand* times more expensive than my own, and we could see the crowd of people gathered in the ballroom through its gigantic arched windows.

A shiver spread through me as we pulled next to the fountain, and a couple of valets strode to either side of the Yaris. My energy turned uneasy. I had a strange sense that I didn't belong here.

"Good evening, Miss," the valet said, as he opened my door and offered me a hand.

I stepped into the cool spring air and thought about how stupid it was to be helped out of a four-cylinder Toyota like it was a Lambo, but I shrugged it off. Tonight, I knew I was going to have to play the part and ignore my relative poorness. Only if to follow the signs. Ugh.

"Could I kindly see your invitation?" the valet said.

"Oh. Yeah." I fumbled through my clutch and found the folded card, sticking it out to him.

He looked at it, then my car, and handed it back. "On behalf of the Roth family, I welcome you to their Estate. May I please have your keys?"

I shifted my clutch to the other hand and gave him the worn fob of my ancient hatchback, urging my face not to flush in embarrassment. After all, when my forest-green symbol of middle-class-ness was out of sight, I could be anyone. No one would know that Avril and I were imposters in this crowd. We wore the right heels to mask it—even if they were found at a second-hand shop and had their labels rubbed off.

The valet thanked me, and Avril beamed from across the rusted roof of my car. "So fancy," she said, as I moved around the hood to join her.

After David's blow-up the night before, it took me over an hour to convince Avril to come; and she very nearly hadn't. I mean, it had been hard—much harder than the first time—but at least she was helping me face this crowd of rich people. And now that she'd owned the decision, she seemed to be in the right spirit, so I appreciated that. Though David was furious with us—and we'd both have some reconciliation to do after the banquet—at least we could embrace tonight, learn some shit, and possibly meet the next person that would change my life.

I studied the modern castle with my fingers tapping on my

clutch. "It *is* impressive," I admitted. "Do you think they had to blast away part of the mountain to get this much land?"

Avril shrugged. "No idea."

"Ladies, please follow me to enter." The other valet turned our attention, and we shot a look at each other before we followed, heels clicking across the flawless square-fitted stones of the driveway.

Though the multi-car garage was past the left-side wing, they'd built a rotating platform that sat under the windows to the ballroom. Presently perching there, in glimmering *rosso magma* (or translated for normal people—*red*), was a Ferrari. Its mere presence was demanding attention, even without the slow rotation.

I snuffed at it. Like most rich people, the Roths were no strangers to showing off, and they clearly weren't afraid to be assholes about it.

Up three levels of broad steps was the main entrance. The oversized double doors were made of frosted glass, lined with black wrought iron that swam through them in elegant filigree patterns. Together, they formed an arch, which matched the rest of the Estate in its château-style grandeur.

It was at the entrance, that an usher with a clipboard stood. His bowtie was squeezed so tightly to his neck, that it looked like it was trying to choke him. "Good evening, ladies. Can I have your names please?"

I cleared my throat and tried not to look at it. "Emily Anderson. This is my guest, Avril Warner. I RSVPed a week ago."

"Anderson..." He scrolled his pen down the list and then marked it with a sharp point. "Nice and easy. Right near the top." The doorknob filled his entire palm when he turned it. "Please make your way to the right from the foyer and into the ballroom. Service staff will be there to greet you if you need. Have a pleasant evening."

The foyer presented itself in a grand reveal of shimmering light. A crystal chandelier that hung above the staircase. There were two hallways that led to areas at the back of the Estate, and I remembered from Carol's memory that the kitchen was there, with the gardens beyond. The staircase rose to the second floor in polished white marble, each edge of the twenty-five to thirty steps rounded to perfection like they'd been carved by hand. A ruby red carpet ran down the middle, flowing on each stair like a bloody waterfall, until it reached the tiles and disappeared in a sharp edge at the bottom of the first step. The handrails were the same wrought iron that wound through the front door, and they framed the staircase on either side. The gap between the top and bottom swirled in filigree patterns of black and gold. I studied their design as we stepped onto the alternating diamond-shaped tiles that lined the first floor.

"How much do you think this place is?" I whispered, leaning over to Avril.

She smirked, twisting her pinky at the corner of her mouth like a villain. "A hundred, billion dollars."

We giggled and I hooked my arm with hers as we pushed forward. The echo of our heels was immense through the space, and it was barely covered by the roar of voices from the people already in the banquet.

We walked through another set of French doors and into the ballroom. A real, honest-to-God *ballroom*. The ceilings must have been at least twenty feet high, and there were floor-to-ceiling windows. On one side, there was a balcony that showcased the Estate's sprawling view from its perch on the mountain. The room itself looked like it was made for dancing, but today, cushioned chairs were lined up in rows leading up to a stage. On the screen behind the stage, the name "ROTH" was projected in red capital letters, with an animated fade slowly running from left to right, giving it a shimmering effect.

Avril and I were greeted at the door by a waiter, who offered us a glass of champagne. We both took one without hesitation, nodding like we highly approved. My eyes skimmed the top of the crowd for a friendly face, but I didn't see any at first. Which wasn't helped by the fact that there were only two possibilities for friendly faces, and people were clustered.

Then I caught Travis entertaining a larger group. He was wearing a black suit with a dark purple tie that matched the strapless dress of the Black woman beside him, who was just as drop-dead gorgeous as him.

Must be his wife.

Her ebony skin was smooth and flawless, and her thick black hair was tied in an elegant updo, accented with a diamond hairpiece that sparkled when it caught the light of the ballroom's chandelier. They were focused on a man in the group who had bright blonde hair and intense blue eyes, who also had a modelesque brunette next to him. I watched as Travis's wife grinned up at him, her ivory teeth sparkling in a stark contrast to her skin.

As I stood there, toes aching from being pinched in used designer heels, imposter syndrome started to sneak up on me. These weren't my people, so what was I doing playing the part of rich-girl networker while David sat upset at home? Having authentically played the part of my person from the get-go?

This is so stupid. Why did we come?

"What's wrong, Em?" Avril asked. She'd caught a face that I didn't realize I was wearing.

I shrugged and took a sip of the champagne, which was smooth and tolerable. I'd never been a big fan, but I realized that it was probably because I'd only had the poor-girl's version. "It's David," I admitted.

Now I couldn't get him off my mind. He hadn't talked to me all day and was giving me the silent treatment mixed with avoidance. I hated being in this negative energy with him, and I hoped that Avril wouldn't pay more of a price for supporting me. I had a long road ahead, but I had to get through *this* night first.

I shook it off.

Okay. Let's re-frame. If anything, maybe I'll get a chance to talk to Barrett...

"Don't worry," Avril added. "It'll be okay. Give him time."

The champagne bubbles were a happy contrast to the dread. "I know. But I hate fighting with him. Especially over something so ridiculous."

She put a gentle hand on my arm. "To him, it's not though. Believe me. He has a bad history with the Roths, and he really cares about you. This isn't easy for him."

I bit my lip and nodded, honesty sneaking out. "I just don't understand all this. The Roths have been nice to me so far. What could be so bad about them?"

She tilted her head like she was calculating what to say. "I think you'll find that their true nature is masked."

"What do you mean by that?"

She raised an eyebrow but didn't answer, choosing instead to swallow more champagne. I wondered how she was going to make up with David herself.

I glanced back at Travis and caught his eye, relieved to see him flash me a brief smile. He excused himself and his wife from the other group. They glided across the floor toward us, and I straightened my shoulders into better posture.

"How about we try not to think about it?" Avril said, before they arrived. "Let's ignore how weird this is and have a good time. Okay?"

"You're right," was all I could say. I clinked my champagne glass off hers. "Cheers."

"Cheers," she agreed.

Suddenly the Roths were there, and I fought to pull my thoughts away from David.

What did they do to make him hate them so much?

"Emily," Travis said, his honey-smooth voice bursting through my thoughts. "I'm so glad you could make it. It's great to see you."

"Nice to see you too, Travis. Thank you so much for having us."

"My pleasure." He flashed his perfect grin and placed a gentle hand behind his woman. "This is my wife, Jalpa."

Jalpa smiled and extended her hand. "Hello, there. Jalpa Roth. But you're free to call me Jal."

"Nice to meet you," I said, shaking her hand.

"This is Emily Anderson," Travis said to her. "She's a guest of Grandma's."

Jal's voice was as warm as a cozy blanket on a cold winter's night. "Well, any guest of Carol's is a guest of ours."

I smiled and turned to Avril. "This is my friend, Avril Warner."

Avril shook Travis's hand, and then Jalpa's. "It's so nice to meet you, Travis, Jal," she said, beaming at them.

"The pleasure is ours," Travis said.

Avril giggled nervously and jerked her chin toward the CEO. "I'm also a friend of Rebecca's."

Travis raised his chestnut eyebrows. "Barrett's Rebecca?"

Avril nodded. "Yep. I've met him quite a few times, actually."

"Very well," he said, smirking as he tipped his champagne glass toward her. "Then you don't need any warnings about my little brother ahead of time."

Avril gave a singsong laugh in return. "Oh. *No.*"

"You may need to warn Emily, though." Travis added.

Jalpa nudged him. "Oh, stop."

Then his attention got caught by someone else across the room, and I realized that we weren't going to get much more of their time. Travis Roth was in demand that evening, for obvious reasons. "Welcome again, ladies," he said. "Please, make yourselves at home. I'm sorry, but I'm being beckoned again. Would you please excuse us?" He gave us a final smile and moved away with Jal in tow. She waved at us as they left.

I raised an eyebrow at Avril, before we dropped our empty

champagne glasses onto the tray of a passing waiter, thanking them. "Warn me about what?" I asked. "What did he mean by that?"

Avril chuckled. "Well, Barrett is... Well... you'll see."

Barrett's what?? Why does everyone keep saying shit like that?

She clasped her hands, drew her lips into a tight smile, and tapped her toe on the hardwood. "Damn. Jal's a lucky woman, isn't she?"

Mildly annoyed at her ambiguous answer, I rolled my eyes. "I bet a lot of the women don't come to this thing just to listen to their business strategies, or whatever."

Avril looked across the room at Travis and ran her gaze up the length of him. "Or, if they do, they at least enjoy the benefit. I'd heard he was a smoke-show. But in person... damn."

I twisted and watched him shake hands with two other men in the group, his welcoming grin never failing. I nudged Avril's arm and urged her on. "Come on. Let's get another drink and find Carol. Oh, and if you see Barrett, let me know."

We wound our way through the crowd, snatching another glass of champagne from a nearby waiter before we got distracted by the world's best hors d'oeuvres collection. As the staff fluttered around the room, I tried not to think about the possibility of them being paid for by big pharma immorality. My sightline never gave up its search for Barrett, but I imagined, like Travis, that he was buried in the crowd somewhere, hosting. I swallowed my last bite of spinach puff. Impatience snuck out of my nose in a sigh.

Then I saw Carol near the stage, standing with a group of women around her age. She was dressed in a gorgeous white gown, which was beaded with small pearls across the waistline. There was a tall woman beside her—another middle-aged real-housewives type—who had her chestnut hair wound in a tight up-do and had a grey gown tight to her frame. I watched her for a moment, and she watched me back like she could feel my gaze.

That must be Carol's daughter, Ava.

It was obvious, because those eyes—which were presently giving off an icy tinge—matched the pale brown of Carol and Travis. I could also see Travis in her, and I realized then that he looked like his mum, not his dad. It was another interesting polarization between the Roth brothers; Barrett a clone of their father, and Travis getting his looks from their mother.

Carol followed Ava's attention and started beaming when she saw me, her arm waving in a big fan above her head. Ava looked like she was embarrassed by it. Carol then touched Ava's arm and motioned toward us before they excused themselves and made their way over. I caught the muted annoyance that played across Ava Roth's expression before she quickly masked it.

"Emily!" Carol said, holding out her arms to me as she neared. "You look gorgeous, honey. I'm so glad you came." She pulled me into a snug hug, her diamond-clad fingers digging into my arms. I hugged her back, trying not to spill my glass of champagne down her dress. "It's so good to see you."

"Of course," I said, with a little laugh. "I wouldn't miss it." I turned to Avril and introduced her.

"Nice to meet you," Carol said. She pulled Avril into a similar hug, and Avril looked at me like she'd been shocked by static. I grinned, not surprised by Carol's warmth in the least. "Welcome to our home, you two."

Avril cleared her throat as they separated. "Thank you so much for having us, Carol. This property. Wow. It's incredible!"

"It will do, don't you think?" Carol motioned around the ballroom with the champagne lapping at the sides of her glass. "Yes, yes, well. John, you know. He had this place designed and built after they started trying for a second son." She sipped her drink and smacked her lips. "We were living in Point Grey before, in a modest five-bedroom. Much too small, eh, Ava?"

Oh, yeah. Only five bedrooms? Who could possibly live in that?

"Anyway," Carol said. "I was just happy that my gracious son-in-law welcomed me into their home after the passing of my dear, late husband."

I watched Ava swallow like she was desperate to clear the pesky emotion from her throat.

"Of course, it was another five years until the Estate was complete and Barrett was actually *born*. Stubborn boy that he is. Travis was eight by then, and we didn't *want* them to be that far apart in age, but you can't rush these things, you know." She wagged her diamond-studded finger at us. "It's been—gosh—nearly thirty years since we moved in." She turned to Ava. "Oh my God. Is *that* how old Barrett is now?"

"Just shy of a year, mother." Ava's tone matched the iciness of her gaze.

"Yes, yes, of course. And Travis will be nearing *forty* soon." Carol put her hand to her chest. "My, my. I've made myself feel my age. Never get old, girls. Never." We chuckled, and Carol sighed contently.

"So," I said, failing to hide my intrigue, "are you saying that John had the Estate built because of Barrett?"

Carol grinned. "Well, yes. But don't tell Travis that." She double tapped a finger against the side of her nose. "Ironically, it now belongs to him alone. And all in all, it's provided a great home for us over that time."

I looked around the room in question. I could feel energy from years of practicing with Mum, and the walls here were giving off a subtle hint that this was a lie. A little one. But still a lie.

"It wasn't long after," Carol said, diverting me from them, "that John built himself a new Tower in which to work out of. I'm sure you've seen it. It's the pinnacle of Vancouver's downtown skyline. You know, big glass building with 'Roth' on it? It was there that he hid from us most of the time." She laughed and turned to her daughter, who fixed her with a cold stare.

The widow of Johnathan Roth didn't seem to find this funny at all.

Carol jumped like she'd been prodded. "Oh! I'm sorry, darling. I haven't even introduced you! This is, of course, my beautiful daughter, Ava."

Ava's handshake was as devoid of warmth as the rest of her. It manifested in a brief squeeze that left my finger joints aching. She was careful not to act rude, and she welcomed us as her mother had, but it seemed much less genuine. We spoke briefly about who I was and where I came from—same story that'd been on repeat since my move—but unlike everyone else, Ava didn't pretend to care. When she asked me what neighbourhood I grew up in, I wanted to answer with one of Toronto's best, like "Forest Hill" or "Lawrence Park," just to get *some* reaction out of her. Instead, I was honest and told her I was from Davenport. It wasn't a bad part of town, but it was certainly middle class.

Her eyes glazed like she could see straight into my bank account.

I reminded myself after that there weren't a lot of people on Earth as rich as the Roths. They were at the top. There was no point in trying to impress them.

As Ava scanned the room for someone else to talk to, I studied her, and my blood ran cold again. Her husband had been murdered. What must that be like for her?

Then, Travis and his team began to move to the stage, signaling the start of the presentation. Carol pulled us toward the cushioned chairs, and we followed the wave of the crowd, before settling together along the edge of the middle aisle.

Carol stood there for a moment; head on a swivel as she clicked her tongue. "Ah, *Barrett,*" she hissed. "I wanted you to meet him, Emily, but I'm afraid it will have to wait. That boy runs on his own timeline." Apparently, I wasn't the only one who'd noticed he wasn't around.

CHAPTER 11
BLINDING

Carol settled into the seat beside me, with Ava to her right. Avril was sitting on my left. I watched as Jalpa stood beside the stairs to the stage, giving Travis a quick kiss before he made his way up. She greeted the other members of the team that were presenting as they followed behind.

"Every year, the boys pour their hearts out into this event," Carol said, focused on her oldest grandson as he mingled with his team on stage. "It's the one time they gather their team, celebrate the successes of the past year, and calibrate on the direction going forward. Travis started it eight years ago and he's been hosting it here every year since."

I glanced around the room as the crowd settled in their seats. The only people left standing were the service staff, ushers, and Jal at the edge of the stage. No Barrett. Nowhere in sight. "They certainly get a good turnout for it. That's for sure."

Then, the entry of two people from the foyer drew my eye, and I finally saw him. For the first time in a decade, I finally fucking *saw* him.

And my heart stopped.

And the air hung suspended.

And time slowed to a grinding halt.

And goosebumps spread across my skin.

My first time seeing Barrett Roth in person stunned me like I'd been smacked over the head with a brick. Suddenly, I couldn't breathe.

He, on the other hand, made his entry into the ballroom like the epitome of overbearing, masculine confidence. Dressed to the nines in a flawless suit, he had a supermodel woman clinging to his left arm.

She was dressed in a red gown that matched his tie, her long red hair draped over her shoulder, and her sparkling grin cast its presence around the room. She had dark brown eyes, similar to his, and their hair would have also been the same if he'd been wearing his natural copper-red, but he wasn't.

Instead, his hair was brown. A couple of shades lighter than his brother's. It was still short at the sides, but longer at the top, like the picture I'd seen online. And it still swept over his head in the wave that peaked at the front.

I legit *gulped* when I thought about how attractive it looked on him.

In a show of affection—or maybe, just a show—he spun the woman around like they were ballroom dancing, and the crowd clapped and whistled for them. They beamed at each other, and he gave her a quick kiss before they separated. Her gaze was glittering, and fixed on him, as she moved to take her seat.

On his way to the stage, Barrett snatched an hors d'oeuvre from the plate of the nearest waiter, munching and swallowing before he met Jal, who gave him a wry look. They hugged, and he gave her a kiss on the cheek. After parting, she straightened his collar, tightened his tie, and brushed his shoulders, laughing at something that he'd mumbled into her ear in the process. Then he gave her hand a squeeze, and she watched him with a hint of fondness as jogged up the stairs to join the rest of the team on stage.

The applause got louder as he greeted people one by one, before ending with Travis, who dipped his chin as his lips formed the word "brother." Barrett grinned, and they pulled each other into a strong embrace before separating with a kiss on the cheek. Then Travis held his shoulders—Barrett's hand lingering on his brother's back—and they shared a few words privately, each ending with a nod of acknowledgement. Finally, Travis let him go, and made his way toward the podium.

As he fell in line behind his brother, the youngest Roth's attention swept the crowd. Someone shouted "Yeah, boss!" and Barrett smirked like he really fucking liked it. Someone else followed up with a wolf-whistle, and the room roared in laughter.

Now Barrett looked like he was fighting a grin. He fixed his eyes on the culprit, ticked a finger between himself and Travis, and mouthed, "For me? Or him?"

"Him!" someone shouted.

Barrett nodded, tilted his head, and mouthed "Fair enough." He finished by putting his finger to his lips and tapping his ear before he pointed to Travis again. The crowd finally lulled, and he settled into a gratified smile.

My eyes were burning, and I realized that it was because I couldn't fucking take them *off* him. I wasn't sure how long it had been since I last blinked.

Suddenly, like he could sense my stare in the same way Ava had earlier, Barrett's black gaze moved straight to mine. Jolted by an invisible, electric connection, I suppressed a jump and froze in response. He held me for a moment—the energy charging between us like a building-sized battery—and it was definitely... something. But then he smirked and broke it, turning his attention back to Travis. And as I fought the shockwaves pulsing across my skin, he clasped his left hand over his right wrist and raised his chin like a prized stallion.

Who are you supposed to be to me?

With a few quick blinks, I yanked myself back. I refused to be star-struck by this billionaire pretty-boy. Universe fated or not.

"Welcome, Everyone," Travis began, smiling over the crowd. "On behalf of Barrett and myself, I'd like to thank you all for coming tonight. As you are all aware, this event is of great importance to us. It gives us the chance to celebrate collaboratively as a company and align our values and beliefs going forward. Not only that, but it serves as an opportunity for us to open our very home to those we hold dear and allows everyone else to be spoiled for the night." He smiled as a wave of chuckling drifted over the crowd. "There's no shortage of champagne, or hors d'oeuvres, so please, enjoy yourselves and I promise I won't drone on this year. I can't speak for my brother, though."

"I never drone," Barrett said, releasing his perfect grin.

Again, people laughed.

The two brothers smiled at each other, before Travis continued. "I want to start with a brief overview of the incredible successes of this year," he said, as the slides on the screen changed to match. "Starting with our greatest accomplishment. Five years ago, shortly after my brother joined me at the head of our company, I stood in front of you in this very room and announced our aggressive sustainability plan. Your murmurs of surprise and excitement swiftly followed. It was the very first commitment that I assigned Barrett responsible for, and he immediately took it to heart, grateful for the challenge—as all of you have been."

Beside him, Barrett raised an eyebrow and nodded.

Travis paused and looked over the crowd. "In the months following, our competition wasn't hesitant to announce their incredulity and skepticism. The name *Roth* was deemed one of optimistic insanity, and they waved us off like lunatics. My younger brother and I became accustomed to hearing all about how crazy and foolish we were to dedicate our company to achieving such a dream. They told us we hadn't a clue what we were doing. They told us that we were introducing a liability to the business. They told us that it was *impossible.* They were hungry and eager to watch us fail."

He paused again, and the air hung like everyone was holding their breath. "And, well—as you all know—at Roth Pharmaceuticals, we thrive on the impossible."

Excited murmuring started to bubble.

"Those that doubted us were envious of our mission, and our failure would only serve to prove that it could not be done," Travis said. "So, we simply *didn't* fail. And today—five years later—I am ecstatic to announce the success of your hard work. We are now, officially, *the* most sustainable pharmaceutical company in North America, and are now the first carbon zero pharma company in the world!"

The crowd went wild, and the senior leadership team on stage celebrated by shaking hands and giving each other pats on the back. Avril and I clapped along with them.

Huh, was all I could think.

I'd never heard of a pharma company that'd taken on something like that and done it. Quite the accomplishment.

But what could it be hiding?

As Travis continued, he announced that, next, they would be become the most sustainable in the world, and he gave special thanks to the team's Chief Sustainability Officer, and his brother: the Chief Financial Officer and Senior VP.

Barrett beamed as Travis stepped down to shake their hands, before Travis began congratulating the blonde woman beside him. He kept smiling at her as he stepped back to the podium.

Next, he spent fifteen to twenty minutes going through the directional blueprint of the company, each goal referred to as a "pillar of their foundation." They ranged from continuing aggressive goals in sustainability, advancing in pharmaceutical technology, providing the safest products on the market, investing in their people, and financial security.

All boring corporate stuff that made a lot of sense.

And though I found myself fading in and out of listening, I admired the incredible public speaker that Travis was. His words were clear and confident like he'd had years of practice, and his verbiage was never broken by an "um" or "ah."

I wished I could be like that. It would come in very handy with the teaching assistant role that I'd be starting at UBC next week.

By the time that Travis wrapped up, I'd gained a significant amount of respect for him. The amount of time and devotion that he poured into the company as the CEO was evident through his speech, and it was obvious that he was invested in the company's future. Not only that, but he was *excited* about it, which breathed a life of energy into the team as they moved to a brighter future together. He seemed to be sharp and deliberate, which was reflected in the culture of those that worked for him.

I began to consider—just for a sec—that maybe I'd been wrong about big pharma all along. After all, the company that made the antibiotics that poisoned me after my accident wasn't Roth Pharmaceuticals. They were a smaller competitor, desperate enough to push noncompliant products out the door to make a quick buck. I was so fucking happy they'd went bankrupt after that scandal... But also, furious enough to pursue an entire career dedicated to ethics.

But then, why would David think they're evil?

I shoved the thought away because I didn't know for now, and inquisitiveness would have to wait. The ad hoc investigation would need to be continued. More evidence was needed...

On stage, Travis finished and handed the podium over to his brother, causing my attention to snap back like an elastic. I studied Barrett as he shook Travis's hand and took the clip-on mic from him. The crowd clapped for their CEO. Travis stood in his brother's previous position and nodded in thanks.

Barrett smoothed the papers on the podium and flashed his perfect grin as he waited for the crowd to quiet.

The sound of my pounding heart only got louder when they did.

"Wow," he said, shaking his head. "Wow, wow, wow. I must be honest; I am *practically* at a loss for words." He stepped down from the podium, choosing to walk the stage instead. "Don't say anything about that," he said, as an aside to someone sitting on the other row. The audience chuckled, and his black eyes scanned us.

I wasn't sure whether to hope for them to land back on me or pray to avoid it.

"I am *astounded*. I am *inspired*. I am *invigorated*. I am just so bloody-fucking-*proud*." The crowd laughed again. "I know," he said, as he continued to stroll the stage. "Do you see what comes out of my mouth when I'm at a loss? Do you see what you've done to your CFO with your incredible work? I am so humbled by all of you, and I am confident that—and *Travis* is confident that—we have the right people in this room to take us toward our brilliant and exciting future."

He shook his head. "Do not get me wrong with that. It is not as if it needed to be proved. But now it remains unequivocal. Irrefutable. Indubitable. And all the other fucking words for *undeniable* that you can think of. Because you have made it so. And since I am at a loss, I will simply say this. Thank you." He stopped at the edge of the stage, and the microphone boomed as he put a hand to his heart. "We have so much to celebrate, and so much to look forward to. And there isn't an alternative team on this *Earth* that I'd want to move forward with."

There was a brief bout of clapping before it lulled.

"Now I," Barrett continued, "am quite aware of—and I *relish* by the way—the loving nickname that I've been gifted with over the years. Quite appropriately. Quite suitably. *The Bad-Roth*. Isn't that right?"

There was muted laughter, flourished with nervousness.

"I am notably happy with it, and believe me, I am aware of how it is deserved." He raised his chin and kept walking. "My brother being the angel counterpart, of course."

Travis shook his head like his little brother was a rascal.

"The ying to my yang," Barrett said, grinning back at him after he passed. "Good cop, bad cop: Good-Roth, Bad-Roth. I see the play there. You are all quite clever. And don't doubt my sincerity when I say that I enjoy playing the bad guy. I do. I really... Really... Do.

But it serves a pragmatic purpose, you see. So, in contrast, I will conclude with this." He stopped beside the podium and faced the audience. "I—*we*—appreciate and celebrate each and every one of you for your unwavering hard work and dedication of service. And from the bottom of my ice-cold heart, thank you. Thank you all."

The audience cheered and clapped, and I found myself unconsciously joining in. He had me under a spell that I couldn't seem to break...

"Now," Barrett said, jumping back up to the podium and moving the slides forward, "I wouldn't be much of a CFO if I didn't torture you with a quick breakdown of the numbers. So, let's get on with it, shall we?"

A high-level overview of the company's financials popped up, and I finally tuned out a little. He explained them and went into detail about expansion after. Even though I wasn't paying attention to what he was saying, I couldn't peel my eyes away. He was just as smooth as his brother at public speaking, with quite a bit more humour thrown in—like he knew he could get away with it.

If I could've used one word to describe Barrett Roth, it'd range somewhere between "overconfident" and full-blown "cocky"; while Travis seemed to be more on the humble side. Both were fascinating to watch, if anything else, but I was also really confused.

How was I supposed to feel about the man standing on the stage in front of me? The co-owner of an evil company that really seemed like it wasn't. The man people had named The Bad-Roth, but that thanked them wholeheartedly for their unwavering dedication. The man that—probably—belonged to the name I'd been calling for over a decade without ever knowing why. Even standing there, he was a mystery outside of being a corporate bigwig. An enigma. Who the hell was he, really? And why did it matter to me?

Barrett finished up, and the presentation was passed to the next member of Roth Pharma's senior leadership team. I trailed his every move as he settled himself in line beside Travis, their mirrored poses giving away their family resemblance.

The resounding theme throughout the whole presentation was one of positivity and growth, and I had to admit, after it was finished, I'd gained respect for their business. They seemed to be doing an incredible job, and their values *seemed to be* sound. So, their reputation with the House-of-Wolves grew into a bigger question mark, and it made me dizzy.

I really don't wanna fucking think about it right now.

They concluded with an awards ceremony—Barrett and Travis each winning one of their own—and when it was over, the whole thing turned more casual. People dispersed back into groups to mingle, and Carol was so popular that Avril and I had to let her go.

We parted from the crowd to grab a couple more drinks and another plate of hors d'oeuvres to help settle our grumbling stomachs. I was in mid chew of a prosciutto-wrapped-fig when a shrill voice hit us from the edge of the crowd.

"Av?"

Avril turned, choking down her tuna tartare. "Oh my God. Beck!"

And striding toward us in her silky, red dress was Barrett's supermodel girlfriend. She pushed between us with outstretched arms and a waft of obnoxious rose petal perfume. "It is so good to see you. I didn't know you were coming!"

Avril stepped aside, munching as she brought me back into the circle. "I'm actually Emily's guest. She was the one invited."

Barrett's girlfriend turned, red lashes flashing as she gave me a once-over. Her grin hid any cracks she saw in my middle-class flaws. "Rebecca Morgan," she said, extending a hand of manicured, red nails. Each was filed to a sharp point. And, man, her grip was harsh. I barely had time to say my name before she giggled and cut me off with, "Or rather, the *future* Rebecca Roth."

Avril's jaw dropped in between her next bite of pimento croquettes. "Oh my God, he's proposed?"

Rebecca's plump lips fell, bunching cherry-red at the corners.

"Well... not yet." She glanced across the crowd, to where Barrett was flashing his perfect grin around a group of admiring employees. "But we're getting there. Believe me, he will. We must get started on our beautiful babies."

I almost spat up my champagne.

Hell will freeze over before a man like that *proposes to anyone.*

Rebecca's gaze pierced me, and she gave me another once-over. "Something funny, Emily?"

"Oh... No..." I waved my hand and faked some coughing. "A piece. Popcorn shrimp. Caught in my throat. Sorry."

It was a bad lie. The Roths weren't even serving popcorn shrimp. It probably wasn't expensive enough.

Rebecca narrowed her black eyes, but Avril saved my ass. "Good things come to those who wait, right?" she said.

Rebecca glanced back across the room. "That's right," she muttered.

I swallowed some liquid courage and cleared my throat. "So. Uh. How did you two meet?"

"Oh," Avril said, latching onto the change in topic. "We were in the same ballet class when we were little, and it just sort of blossomed from there."

"Oh, that's so nice," I said, in a tone way faker than I'd meant.

"Yeah, I can't even count how many painful recitals we've been through together," Rebecca said. "Right, Av?"

Av?

"We sure got used to wearing a lot of makeup," Avril said.

Some things never change, I thought, giving Rebecca a once-over back.

Then I nodded, but my interest was pushing a breaking point.

From over Rebecca's shoulder, I saw Barrett excusing himself from the group and weaving his way through the crowd. He was headed for the balcony. Alone. Very much alone.

Now or never.

Seizing opportunity like someone had stabbed it into me with a needle, I passed my ceramic plate to Avril. "You two catch up. I've gotta introduce myself to someone."

The doors that opened onto the balcony allowed the spring air to flow freely, and I took a deep breath as I stepped through, hoping the scent of cedar and sea would make my feet go forward. My heart was hammering under my ribcage, and my stomach jittered like a cage of rowdy finches. I'd never been so nervous to meet someone in my life.

But the view was captivating from the moment I went outside, and it hooked me long before Barrett did. This was the east side of the Estate, and it was perched on the edge of a cliff, giving sprawling scenery of the land below. From here, you could see the rest of West Van below them, with a clear view of Stanley Park, Downtown, and everything beyond. All the way to Washington. I was sure that, on a clear day, you'd even be able to see Mt. Baker, standing proud in its ever-snow-capped peaks, from well beyond south of our border.

The sun had set, leaving streaks of red and orange below a draping, navy blanket of stars. The Lions Gate Bridge stretched in its twinkling, white lights, connecting this land with that of the south. I recognized the dark trees of the park, winding in a wild peninsula, between the bridge and the downtown core. Tonight, the five white sails of Canada Place were lit up with a dark red, and the Lookout tower sparkled with intensity as the sunlight began to fade. Vancouver Harbour's black sea shimmered with their reflections.

Barrett watched it all with his back turned to me, lighting up a cigarette, before he leaned his elbows on the stone railing. I watched him exhale the smoke in a deep sigh, and his shoulders relaxed under the support of the stone. It was like he'd shrugged off a heavy jacket that he'd grown tired of slugging around. He flicked the ash from the end of the cigarette causing it to flare in the growing darkness, and drew another puff, before he looked back to the view. And my rowdy finches choked on a cloud of guilt. He was clearly trying to get some alone time, and I was about to interrupt that.

For a moment I thought about turning around, but an invisible force pushed me forward like a heavy palm in the middle of my back. The click of my heels told him that I was there, and as he turned to look at me, I caught the glint of annoyance in his black eyes before they shifted warmer. He pushed himself from the railing and regained his private-school-perfect posture, rising above me before I climbed three steps to his level. We stood in silence, and I became captivated by his eyes. The warmth of the city lights below had molded them into that colour of melted dark chocolate again.

I struggled to make words. It took a vehement, mental shove. "I—I'm sorry, Barrett... I—I didn't mean to disturb you..." These were the first words I ever said to him, and I immediately wanted to grab them back and start over.

"Yes, well. I suppose it's my duty to be in demand as host," he said, his irritation singed by cigarette smoke. "Please. Join me." He motioned to the spot beside him on the railing. I automatically drifted to it. His tone made me swallow. Heavily.

Get a grip, Em. You were meant to meet him.

"I wanted to take this opportunity to introduce myself," I managed, placing one hand flat on the stone while motioning into my chest with the other. "I'm Emily Anderson. I'm a guest of Carol's."

We shook hands and then he surprised me by bowing and giving the back of my right a soft kiss. "It's a pleasure to meet you, Emily." My hand tingled like a limb that'd been sat on for too long, and I was speechless. I must have worn it on my face, because then he smirked. "Forgive me if I've offended you. My brother and I were raised with a bit of old-school chivalry." He turned and flicked away more cigarette ash. Harder this time.

I blinked. "No, no. Not at all. I've just never had a man do that for me. It's actually quite... nice."

He turned his head and smiled again, but I saw the way he was studying my face. Ebony eyes making micro-movements on my skin. Calculating who I was and what he was going to do with me. He turned back and took another drag. "I'm pleased you think so," he exhaled.

I cleared my throat and leaned on the railing. Mirroring his previous stance with the stone brisk under my bare elbows. "The sustainability goals that you've met," I said, not sure what else to talk about, "they're very impressive. Congratulations on that."

"Thank you. I share your sentiment. The Earth is worthy of preservation, and we, as industry leaders, must do our part."

Which surprises me. Aren't you supposed to be the bad guys?

We watched a returning boat make its way through the harbour, its wake rolling from the bow. "It's beautiful, isn't it?" he added.

The gentle wind played with a loose strand of my hair. "Without a doubt."

He nodded and cleared his throat. "My father gave me many pieces of advice, but there's one that sticks with me in this context. 'Never buy a property without a view.' And he never failed to deliver on this."

His father. The man that was murdered.

My stomach pinched into an uncomfortable knot. "It makes sense that he'd tell you that, considering this is the one he built for you."

His black eyes hit me with a chill, though he was careful to keep his expression neutral and his tone calm. "He did, did he? And how would you know?"

I straightened my spine, not wanting to aggravate the nerve that I'd obviously hit. "Oh, well... Carol mentioned it earlier when she was telling me about the Estate."

He took another drag of his shrinking cigarette. Though he didn't say anything, I saw the way he ground his jaw after he'd exhaled.

A tense quietness fell, and I tapped my fingers on the stone as I racked my brain for what else to say to him.

Who are you supposed to be to me?

Barrett drew his last drag and killed the cigarette on the stone, placing the butt into a glass ashtray that sat to his right. "So, what's your story, Emily?"

"M—My story?" I hadn't thought he'd want to know anything about me.

"Yes. You know, who are you? Where are you from? That sort of thing."

I am the awkward daughter of two of the most loving people on the planet, who smacked her head during an accident, causing her to dauntingly scream your very name after waking out of seeing other people's memories...

"Oh..." A giggle jammed up in my throat. "There's not much to know, to be honest."

He raised a copper eyebrow. "Humour me. I'm attempting to be polite."

Something in my gut simmered, but I shrugged and told him my over-used story about my move while he tried not to look bored. Then I told him about meeting his grandmother on the plane.

"Ah, yes," he said. "Her frivolous and strange preference for public flights. Apparently, I'm not the only one who craves an occasional taste of normalcy."

I had no idea what he meant by that. And even if I had, I couldn't relate to it. We'd grown up in vastly different worlds, and I never had the *choice* to experience life in the lower-middle-class. I was sure there was no way he could handle it if he were forced into it. He'd probably never done a load of laundry or touched a broom in his life. Resentment shot through my veins.

Over-privileged asshole.

But—I quickly reminded myself—*I'd* also never felt the crushing weight of running a multi-billion-dollar company on my shoulders. And I knew which life I'd choose out of the two. Mine. Without a doubt, mine.

Clearing my throat, I tried to steer our conversation toward the positive. "Travis actually gave me a ride home after we landed too."

"How very generous of him," he said, flatly. "He wears the Good-Roth badge well, don't you think? And this was what? A month ago, you said?"

"Yeah, I've only been in Vancouver for that long."

He smirked in a way that sent shivers down my spine. "Well, kid. I'm afraid you haven't seen anything yet."

I watched him for a moment, confused about the whole thing. I'd thought that meeting him would trigger some grand revelation. But so far, all it had resulted in was the differences between us being highlighted, and him being a bit of a jerk. Maybe this wasn't my Barrett after all...

Who are you? I thought, studying the faint freckles that ran across his nose.

Then his attention got pulled over my shoulder, and voices told me that other people had now joined us. I turned, finding the blue-eyed, blonde-haired man that I'd seen talking to Travis and Jal earlier making his way toward us with the brunette woman.

"Well, look who's decided to grace us with his presence," Barrett said, a contrasting grin spreading across his face. He moved away from me and down the steps.

The blonde man returned his grin with a matching set of perfect teeth. "I knew I'd find you out here, you braw slotter beast." His accent confused me. It verged on Scottish in a way that wasn't full Scottish.

Barrett put an arm around his shoulders. "I assume that's my grandmother's greeting kiss you're wearing?" He was right. The blonde man had a distinct smudge of lipstick on his left cheekbone.

"Aye. Like a badge of honour."

Barrett ruffled his hair. "As you should."

"Ah, get off, you numptie," the blonde man said, playfully pushing him away.

I stepped down to join them, but Barrett looked at me like a pain in the ass that he'd just been reminded he had. "Ah, yes. I suppose I should introduce you to our guest, here. Shane Thomas, Emily Anderson. Shane, Emily is a guest that Grandma invited for... well... I don't believe you mentioned that, Emily. What was your interest?"

"Networking," I said, trying not to let my face ice over. "I'm studying Medical Ethics. She thought it'd be good for me."

Though I'm starting to question why.

"Ah," Barrett said. "Right. How practical she is." He motioned to Shane. "And Emily, this is my lifelong best friend—and thorn in my side—Shane Thomas."

Shane raised an eyebrow. "Smooth, Roth. Always the gentleman, aren't you?" He shifted his expression warm and stepped forward to shake my hand. His eyes were as aquamarine as the Caribbean Sea. "Pleased to meet you, Emily." Now his accent had become more Canadian. I wondered what his heritage was.

"Nice to meet you, Shane," I said.

Barrett motioned to the brunette beside Shane. "And this exquisite woman is his girlfriend, Melissa Mitchell."

Melissa and I shook hands, and she shot him an arch expression. "Flattery won't work on me, Mr. Roth. I can see straight through that silver tongue, remember?" She smiled at me. "Nice to meet you, Emily."

Barrett smirked and slapped his best friend's back. "Which is precisely why you were attracted to a loyal man instead of a handsome one."

Shane shook his head, his breath escaping in a muted chuckle. "Oh, feck off, Bear. At least I'm not parading around on stage every year, trying to play *Bad-Roth* while simultaneously hoping all the lassies in the audience cream their pants for me."

"Shane!" Melissa smacked him on the chest.

I looked between them and wondered what Shane had meant by, "*trying* to play the Bad-Roth."

"Bonnie presentations, though," Shane said, smirking at Barrett.

"Yes, well. We all have agendas, don't we?" Barrett said.

"Believe it or not, he's a massive softy behind all this," Shane said to me, throwing a thumb at his best friend.

Barrett stepped back and cocked his head. "Do we *really* want to go there? How about I reveal the fact that Mr. Thomas, here, can't get through the ending of *Homeward Bound* without crying like a—"

"Alright!" Shane said, nudging Barrett in the ribs. "Point taken. We're both giant softies on the inside. I admit it. Happy?"

Barrett grinned and put his arm back around Shane's shoulders. "There's a reason that we fell in love."

Shane pushed him off again, before he sighed and pinched the bridge of his nose. "And, trust me, I question that decision. Every. Single. Day."

The four of us shared some polite laughter before we fell into an awkward silence, and I sensed that this was a good time to excuse myself from their little group. I was starting to feel like I was overstaying my welcome, and that I was holding them back from having the conversation that they really wanted. That, or I was starting to fade from a few glasses of champagne, a heap of hors d'oeuvres, and too much time in a haunted Estate that was so foreign to me.

Either way, I was tired and massively disappointed by the lack of direction that the banquet had given me. I was even too exhausted to think about "networking" with anyone else who had the potential to help my future career. After Barrett, I was so done.

This can't *be him. Can it?*

The chatter of the group turned to murmurs in my head as I

watched Barrett and thought about the man that he was presenting himself as. Or the man that he *was*. I hadn't spent enough time with him to tell which was which. But I couldn't help but be taken aback by the things that Shane had said about him. Who was he underneath it all?

I don't know what I'd expected to find when I met the stranger whose name I'd been shouting, but it wasn't him. I'd been waiting for over a decade to find out, yet here he was. The cocky, silver-tongued, billionaire pretty-boy. Take him or leave him, Em.

I looked up to the stars and turned my palms up.

What the hell am I supposed to do with this?

As the others started to fall deeper into conversation, I cleared my throat and told them that it had been nice to meet them. The three of them said goodbye and continued their chatter seamlessly when I clicked away. In the doorway, I turned and shot a longing glimpse at Barrett. The imprint of his kiss was still sizzling on the back of my hand.

Who are you, Barrett Roth? And why was your father murdered?

Inside, Avril was still talking with Rebecca, but she looked as ready to go as I was. Chuckling on the inside about how awesome a person she is, I walked up and "reminded" her that we had another commitment back at the house. Rebecca rolled her eyes and didn't hide it, but she let us go, mentioning to Avril that it would be good for them to catch up again soon. We used the same excuse about our "commitment" to say goodbye to Carol, and I thanked her for inviting us.

"Did you get a chance to talk to Barrett?" she asked before we could walk away.

I faked a smile and nodded. "Yep."

"Good! Stay in touch with him, honey," she said. "It'll help you."

I really doubt that...

Five minutes later, I was handing the valet a pathetic five-dollar tip and starting my car. As I started to wind my whining Yaris around the fountain, I thought about David again.

You said you were trying to protect me from the Roths; but protect me from what? The fact that one of them is a dedicated businessman, married to his job just as much as he is his beautiful wife? Or the fact that the other is a presumptuous prick who I'm surprised is even tied down with a girlfriend?

The more I learned about the Roths on the surface, the less it all made sense.

In my scratched rearview, I watched the Estate shrink away, questioning what all this meant. But it stood strong and silent, in all its glory and brilliance, effortlessly masking the lies that I was sure it held.

CHAPTER 12
ENJOY THE SILENCE

It's a dreary fall day in Toronto, and my high school friend, Mia, and I are walking down Eglinton Avenue, heading toward a lunch date with a few of our friends. We're only sixteen and facing the beginning of grade ten, blissfully unaware of any real-life challenges as we wrestle with the pettiness of our high-school drama. Although our lunch hour is short, our school is close to the shops on Eglinton, and isn't too far from Yonge Street, so it's easy for us to escape into some retail therapy. But I never buy anything. Buying brand-name junk and showing it off is Mia's job. I'm too strapped by paying some of my family's utility bills and scrounging what I can for university tuition.

The temperatures are dropping, and I study the contrast of the fall leaves against the overcast sky. A couple of the shops have brilliant autumn displays in the windows, and I smile as we pass one where pumpkins, leaves, and gourds surround a small hay bale. On top sits a stuffed scarecrow, who lists lazily to one side with his stitched mouth wide.

Ahead, there's a lineup for a pop-up Halloween store, and my smile turns into a grin when I think about the upcoming Halloween party that I've purposely not mentioned to my parents. (Someone's already secured a keg, and that's not something I want them to know.) Not only is it my first Halloween party in high school, but it's the first party that Andy and I will be attending together. I've been surfing the internet for couple's costumes for over a month.

Mia sighs dreamily as she hooks her elbow with mine. "I love fall. It's so beautiful. The way that the colours come out." She nudges me. "Very romantic, don't you think?"

"Well, I wouldn't call it romantic," I say. "But yeah. It's my favourite time of year."

She flashes her raven eyebrows. "A great time to finally mention to your parents that you've got a *boyfriend*?"

I break into a nervous chuckle. "We've only been dating for a month, Mi. And I can already picture the look that's going to be on Dad's face."

"Oh, come on," she says, pulling my arm as the heel of her boot crunches a leaf below her. "Your dad is great! He'll understand."

I raise an eyebrow as I turn to study what's in the next window. "He'll understand, but I don't expect him to be happy about it."

"He will be. Once he sees how *awesome* Andy is." I watch her reflection in the window as we stop, pretending to browse the rack of shoes on the other side. "Speaking of that, how have things been going?"

The colour flushes to my face, and I look at the sidewalk. I'm still new to the idea of young love, and it flusters me. "Honestly? Really good." I shrug. "We had fun at the movies the other night. He even bought me a packet of cherry candies because I mentioned they were my favourite."

She tugs my arm, and we continue down the street. "That's so sweet!"

"He *is* sweet," I say. "Really sweet, actually. I like him, Mi."

She leans into me, and I catch a whiff of her cherry blossom perfume. "Did you make-out with him?" Because these are the kinds of things that *truly matter* to us in high school.

I beg my face not to blush more. "I might've."

"Atta girl!" she says, nudging me. "I want to see more of *this* Emily!"

"So do I." I giggle before coming back to Earth. "But in all seriousness, Mi, he just makes me comfortable."

"Like you can be yourself around him?"

The fall breeze tosses my blonde waves. "Yeah, I guess so."

She nudges me again. "That's a good sign!"

"I guess so," I repeat.

Down Eglinton, the cars come to a crawl. The traffic has stalled because someone's blocking the right lane by trying to do the most horrible parallel park job I've ever seen. The horns blare in a symphony of annoyance, but the driver doesn't care.

"What about you and Chad?"

She waves her hand like it's nothing. "Oh, I'm dumping Chad. He's an idiot. I'll have another boyfriend in time for the Halloween party."

"You think so, eh?" In all honesty, I have no doubt about it. She's a social butterfly. It's not unrealistic for her to do these things.

She raises her chin. "Positive."

God, I wish I had her confidence. "Well, happy hunting."

She shoots me a wry smirk. "You know I'm good at it. It won't be hard." She jerks my arm and points across the street. "Oh, look! There's your knight-in-shining-armour now."

I follow her gaze and see Andy on the other side. When he realizes we've spotted him, he shoots us a grin and waves. Sixteen-year-old Andy has not yet transformed into the cold and bitter man that he becomes later.

I grin and wave back. As I watch my handsome boyfriend, I'm struck with a sense of pride and happiness. It's probably just the "honeymoon" phase, but I don't care. He's hot, and sweet, and I feel like I could fall head-over-heels and not even notice. We stay locked on each other from across the street, and he smiles like he's feeling something similar. The hazel of his eyes makes them warm and beautiful. The hues of brown catch in the light of the overcast sky.

This odd moment in the middle of Eglinton is when I realize that I might love him, and it feels good. Really good. Our blooming relationship is still unstrained by the challenges that it'll face later.

From down the street, someone's blaring "For Those About to Rock" by AC/DC from their car window. Raised by my dad's classic rock obsession, I could probably belt the lyrics off by heart, but I'm not paying much attention. My focus is still on him—my knight-in-shining-armor—as he looks for a break in the traffic so that he can join us. Spotting the ideal moment to j-walk is a skill that is essential to growing up in Toronto, and he's no exception to this.

Suddenly, a speeding Acura appears, and we find out who's blasting the song. It's peeling down Eglinton, doing much more than the speed limit, and I panic when I realize that Andy's about to make a break for it. The car's coming much faster than he realizes, but there's no time for him to turn back.

"Andy! No!" My scream pierces the air, joined by the horrible sound of screeching tires.

The driver of the Acura pumps the brakes and swerves onto the sidewalk to avoid the stalled traffic, but they end up slamming into the building behind us and ricocheting back. The impact isn't enough to stop the speeding vehicle, and Mia and I stand there like helpless rabbits caught in its headlights. Somewhere, a boy is screaming, and I have no time to realize that this is the returned panic of my boyfriend. Without thinking, I try to shove Mia out of the way, but it's too late. We meet the cold hood of the Acura and are tossed in two different directions like a couple of rag dolls.

Everything goes black.

The pavement is cold beneath me as I come to. My vision is blurred, and I can see distorted shapes through a red lens. Hot liquid stings my left eye. I'm confused. Disoriented. Pain pulses in shockwaves and drowns me with a sensory overload so strong that I can't tell what's fucked up and what's not. The voices echo through my ears before they merge with a ringing that only gets louder and louder. It smells like burnt rubber, smoke, and spilled gasoline. I try to talk, then to scream, but I can't. My voice manifests in a bubbling groan.

The shape of what I think is a person drops to my side, and I blink to get the blood to clear from my eye, but it doesn't. "Oh my God, Em. Don't move. Please, don't move!" It's my boyfriend's voice, dripping in controlled dread.

"Andy..."

He lifts my head and places something soft beneath it. My vision comes in and out of focus, and when it returns, his shape is less blurred than before. "I'm right here. It's okay." The top of my head burns as he holds it. "Everything's gonna be okay. You're gonna be alright."

I release a couple of pain-ridden huffs before my voice squeaks in anguish. The tears are working to clear some of my vision, and it's enough that I can see the intense anxiety playing on his face. His hazel eyes are glimmering in response to my broken state. Sirens in the distance give me little relief, but I beg them to get me out of this horror when they get here. Dizziness takes my consciousness, before it lets up and gives it back. "Where's Mi...?"

Andy glances somewhere behind him. "People are helping her, Em. Don't worry."

I turn my head to follow his gaze. Between the legs of strangers shooting around in chaos, I see her blurred shape lying on the ground. I blink, pleading for the red lens to clear, and for a fraction of a second, it does. Her body comes into focus, bleeding and mangled. She's unconscious and not moving. Grief rises from my core and starts to battle the pain. I use what little breath I have to start screaming, before I'm drowned out by the taste of my own blood. And the world goes away again.

The room fades into view with a blinding white, and my eyelids are heavy. One by one, the things around me become recognizable—bed, curtains, window, grey-speckled vinyl tiles—and I realize that I'm in the hospital. My chin wants to sag into my chest, and my limbs are as heavy as lead, but I fight to stay conscious. I blink a few more times and start to feel the plastic tubes stuck up my nose. From somewhere beside me, something is beeping, and my first thought is that I want it to stop and let me sleep.

A warm hand touches my forehead, and I turn toward, brain lagging. It takes several seconds for me to recognize my own mum. I catch the floral smell of her shampoo as her wavy blonde hair drifts next to me, and I see the shimmer of tears in her blue eyes. Though she smiles, the strain in her face works against her.

It takes me a moment to find my voice, but when I do, it comes out in croaks, like a frog. "Mum?"

She brushes a strand of my hair behind my ear, but it falls back because the tubes are wrapped there. "Hi, Em."

I groan and try to pull myself up, but I can't put weight on my left wrist. It's wrapped in a thick cast, and it thumps to the bed beside me when my muscles refuse to lift it.

"Easy, easy!" Mum fixes the cast and places a hand in the middle of my back. She uses the button on the bed to shift it into a seated position.

I cradle my cast in my lap and release a slow breath, trying to reconcile with the pain coming from every movement. "What happened?" I search my memory, but nothing comes back.

"Honey, you're in the hospital," Mum says, stroking my forehead. "Do you understand that?"

I smack my lips, which are dry and desperate for water. "Yes."

Mum nods, and her touch starts to soothe what little it can. "Do you remember anything?"

My brain is filled with a fog so thick, that it could be rolling out of the trees of Stanley Park on a rainy day in Vancouver. I shake my head. I don't have the energy to go through it.

Again, Mum nods. "You and Mia were hit by a car on Eglinton. You have a broken wrist, a couple of fractured ribs, and a bad concussion." Her voice hitches and she wipes her face. "Em, you've been in a coma for two days."

A coma...? What...?

I blink and run my unbroken hand over the left side of my head, which is bandaged and sore. My hair's been reduced to peach fuzz there. They must have shaved it.

Mum takes my hand away from the area. "You have no idea how amazing it is to see your eyes open again," she whispers.

My jaw droops and my mind glazes in confusion, but I pull myself out just enough to give her a weak smile.

Across the room, I can see Andy curled up in one of the hospital chairs, with his neck stuck at an uncomfortable angle. Affection numbs some of the pain. I'm grateful for him.

Mum follows my gaze. "He's been here almost as much as your father and me. He's been really worried about you, sweetheart."

"He's good like that, Mum."

Too bad it wasn't for long, grownup me adds over the memory.

She squeezes my hand. Between my fingers, there's something solid that wasn't there before. "I really like him, sweetpea. I wish you'd told us you had a boyfriend. That's such exciting news."

On a normal day, I'd be ecstatic, but right now I don't care whether she likes him or not.

What am I gonna do? How can I be alive with all this pain?

Wrestling my weak and stiff muscles, I pull my hand from hers to check what's bothering my fingers. The three emeralds of the ring glimmer from the fluorescent lights, and they're harsh on my eyes. I twist my hand to study them, and I'm really confused. I've only seen this silver ring outside the protection of Mum's jewelry box a handful of times. It's a family heirloom that's believed to have protective energy, but I've never seen anyone in my family ever wear it before. It's meant to be kept safe in a jewelry box. It's not meant to be worn.

Mum's tears drop onto the bed sheets below. "I was so scared, Em... I thought we were going to lose you... I had to put it on. I was hoping it would save you."

I try to blink away my grogginess. The left is harder to blink than the right, and I feel pressure there. I must have a black eye on that side. "Thanks, Mum."

"Just promise me you'll never take it off," she says. "From this day forward, you'll never take it off."

"I promise." I squeeze her hand and relax into the bed. Then I begin to search through my broken memory, but the pieces are starting to come back out of order. Like a puzzle that's been strewn across the floor. "Where's Mia?"

"She's alright," Mum says. "She suffered a broken hip and ankle, but they got her into surgery, and she's been recovering for the past couple days. She has a bit of a bump on the head too, but nothing like what you have. She was discharged a couple hours ago."

I sigh in relief. "Was anyone else hurt?"

"The driver. He crashed into a storefront behind you and was killed upon impact. The police suspect he was impaired, but nothing's been confirmed."

Anger rises, and as soon as it starts, I want it to go away. I shouldn't be feeling glad that someone was killed. I shouldn't be feeling vindicated. It's not right, even if he's paid the ultimate price for what he's done to us.

"Honey, I'm just thankful that you two are okay."

I nod, but the sheets are bunched tightly in my right hand. From between my fingers, the emerald ring pushes back, returning me to the present.

"It's going to be alright," Mum says. "You're awake now, and everything is going to be alright. You're strong, Em, and we're going to get through this. We just have to concentrate on getting you better." She pushes the strand of hair behind my ear again. "And don't be surprised if your father and I never let you leave home again."

I can tell that she's expecting a laugh, but my voice escapes in a whisper of self-pity. "It's not fair."

She strokes my cheeks. "I know, sweetheart. But you and Mia are alive, and that's all that matters."

I take a deep breath and plead with my tears to stop, if only for her sake. This has already been enough for her without watching me suffer the "why me?" mentality.

I sink into the hospital bed, wipe my face with my good hand, and try to focus on what's on TV across the room. The pillow has shifted down my back. Mum adjusts it, and I catch the concern in her face. That's not all. She hasn't told me all of it. "What's wrong, Mum?"

She swallows as she sits down, blinking rapidly. "Em... I need to ask you something else. While it's still just the two of us."

Somehow, I smile through the pain. "Anything."

A few heartbeats pass before she speaks. "Honey... Who's Barrett...?"

CHAPTER 13
TEARS IN HEAVEN

"Oh my God! Someone please help him!"

Back in Ladner, I sat up in my bed, my breath heaving, and my face broken out in a cold sweat. I grabbed the pillow next to me, threw it across the room with a scream, and tucked my knees to my chest. I couldn't feel the ancient scar under my fingertips, but I knew it was there. It'd been ages since I'd dreamt of the accident, but time hadn't made the memory any less painful. I put my arms across my knees and rested my head on them. Then I thought about how badly I wanted to go home.

Who's Barrett? Mum's question echoed in my mind.

Andy's voice joined in, punctuating his disapproval over the several years after. *What the fuck, Em? You're screaming another man's name when you wake up! What's* wrong *with you?*

My loved ones were tired of hearing me scream the sentence after waking up. I could tell. It was always a variation of "Oh my God! Barrett! No! Someone please help him!" and I didn't blame them for being sick of it. Especially when we had no idea who the hell I was screaming for.

Who's Barrett?

I gripped my thick hair and pulled. After meeting the man who belonged to the name, I still had no idea.

"Em?" There was a knock on the door that could have only been Greg. It was Friday morning. Avril and David would be at work.

"Yeah," I said, inhaling as I raised my head. "Come in, Greggy."

"I heard you scream," he said, appearing from behind the door. "Everything alright?"

"Yeah. No. I mean. I had a nightmare, is all."

"You look really flustered. D'you want me to get you some water?"

"No. I mean. Thanks. I'm fine."

Greg looked skeptical as he sat on the edge of the bed beside me. "You sure?"

I threw up my arms before resting them back on my knees. "No. Actually. I'm not." Sighing, I dropped my chin on my arms. "I think I fucked up, Greggy."

"Really?" He raised a compassionate eyebrow. "How?"

"The whole Roth Banquet thing. I shouldn't have gone. And I shouldn't have dragged Avril. It wasn't worth it."

I'd taken a chance on the Banquet and learned *zip*. Now David was pissed, and I'd pissed him off for *nothing*. I hadn't even taken the chance to fucking network like I said I would!

"Hmmm," Greg said. "To be honest, it was a questionable choice."

"I know. But I wish someone would have told me *why* it was questionable before I went." I eyed Greg expectantly. "I still don't understand why he hates the Roths. All they do is show off their money, while—in stark contrast—going into great detail about how their company is saving the world."

Greg shrugged. "It's a long story. And it's not mine to tell."

"Ugh!"

"I'm sorry, Em. But it's true. I mean, I may be David's best friend, but I can't speak for him."

Sucking the air through my nose, I twisted my hair into an ad hoc bun and let it fall out again. "I get it."

"Sorry, Em."

"It's fine." I paused, returning my chin back to my arms. "Do you think he'll forgive me? David, I mean?"

Greg chuckled. "Yeah. Of course, Em. It's *David*. I mean, he's been through the wringer in his life, but he's a chill guy underneath it all."

Hmmm.

Despite what Greg was saying, it was hard for me to picture. The House-of-Wolves had been like living in a cold-war zone all week. David and I had barely spoken, and we seemed to be moving in opposite directions. When he was home, I had to stay late at the library to prep for school. When I was home, he found excuses to go out. On Thursday morning, I'd planned on making him a nice breakfast and some strong coffee before he left for work, but by the time I gathered the energy to drag myself out of bed, I'd found that he'd already left to go to the gym. I'd been living there for almost a month, and I knew David wasn't an early riser. He was more of a get-up-half-an-hour-before-work-and-rush kind of guy. He always went to the gym *after* work.

"Talk to him," Greg suggested. "Explain your side. You were trying to make headway on your future career, and you didn't mean any harm. He'll get it... Eventually."

"You make it sound so easy."

"That's because it is, Em. At the end of the day, David's very level-headed. I mean, look at Avril. She's made up with him already."

He was right. Even though she'd been my accomplice on the night, Avril was no longer in David's crosshairs. It was just me.

"And a case of *Grandville Island* never hurt," Greg added, giving my knee a pat before he got up. "Doesn't matter the beer. He likes them all."

I huffed.

There was nothing going on that day, and I wasn't sure what else to do but take Greg's advice. So, I got in my Yaris and braved the drive downtown to the Grandville Island brewery. If I was going to go with my tail tucked between my legs to David, I was going to go with an olive branch of his favourite beer.

By the time I pulled in the driveway, the sun was lowering over the river and the mountains, promising a sky later peppered with stars. I hauled the beer out of the trunk of the Yaris, my eyes grazing over David's Mazda as I struggled to slam my rusted hatchback shut. His windows were covered in a thin fog from the cooling night, which told me that he'd been home for a while. I mentally crossed my fingers that he'd be lounging in the living room, surrounded by weed smoke. Whatever helped me here was a bonus.

I was greeted by the warmth of my new home when I pushed through the chestnut door. I slipped my shoes off, making my way into the kitchen with the twelve-pack at my hip. Greg and Avril were sitting at the table, playing a game of what looked like blackjack. I wobbled past and heaved the beer onto the counter. There was a thud of rattling.

"Hey, Em," Greggy said, breaking his concentration to greet me.

"Hey." I ripped through the cardboard and started unpacking the bottles to load them in the fridge.

"That's a lot of beer," Avril said, dealing a card that made Greg groan in loss. "Do you mind sharing?"

"Technically, they're for David. But for you, anything." I popped the top off a couple of bottles and set them on the table. They were chilled at the brewery and my trunk had kept them cool.

"You're that nervous to talk to him, eh?" Avril said, giving me a sympathetic look.

I sighed. "No. Well... yeah... A little."

"It'll be okay, Em," she said, taking a swig of beer. "David's very level-headed."

"So I've heard," I said. "Speaking of, do you know where he is?"

The two of them shrugged.

"Must be in his room," Avril said. "No one's in the living room"

I twisted the caps from the two bottles I'd set aside, tilting my head. "Okay."

"You got this, Em," Avril said.

"Wish me luck." I pushed off the counter and walked toward the stairs, hoping she was right.

At the top, David's door was propped open, and his room was dark—except for the dull glow coming from his TV. It cast ominous shadows across the hallway. I nudged the door open with my shoulder, expecting him to be sitting up and glaring at me, but he wasn't. He was tucked under his comforter, black curls falling across a face that was resting in sleep.

With the beer bottles hanging stiff in each hand, I paused and watched him, debating whether to turn around or push forward. If I turned around, I'd be letting him snooze, which was not only much kinder, but would probably leave him in a better mood later. But later would likely be tomorrow, and I'd have to live another day in *silent-treatment* land. If I pressed on, I'd be waking him, and would risk having to wrestle with his grogginess along with his annoyance. But at least I'd get this settled tonight. Maybe. Potentially.

Biting my lip, I decided to let him sleep. He was obviously tired, and I didn't want to be inconsiderate.

I tucked my tail between my legs, went back to my room, and started to surf the ol' Instagram.

Almost an hour later, I heard him groan deeply. Like he didn't want to be conscious but knew that he should be. Bolting up, I grabbed the beer bottles from my nightstand. I'd almost forgotten about them, so they'd gone warm. There were puddles on the wood. Shit. Uh. Better than nothing?

The ancient carpet muffled the sound of my footsteps as I walked over and peeped out into the hallway. David was definitely awake and rubbing his forehead. I studied him as the light from the TV fell across his face and curls. Even in the ever-changing glow of what was on screen, he looked... hollow.

"David?" I called softly.

He drew a breath through his nose. When he turned to look at me, he looked like a wolf that'd been woken by being jabbed with a stick. "Em?" His voice was rough and groan-y.

I smiled and crept tentatively into his room. "Hey there, sleepyhead. Sorry. Didn't want to wake you. But don't worry, I come in peace." I stuck a beer bottle out and offered it.

He sat up with a yawn. The comforter fell into his lap and exposed his bare chest. He took the beer with a muffled, "Thank you."

"Sorry it's warm..."

He shrugged. "Meh. It's beer."

"Heh," I said. Was he in an okay mood or not? Sometimes, with that Bluenoser politeness, it was hard to tell. "Do you mind if I sit?" I asked, motioning to the bed.

"Yeah, no, go ahead."

"Um. Okay. Thanks." I lowered myself like a mother robin on her eggs. Then I looked at David's chest and had the strangest craving to run my tongue across the delicate black curls. Blinking, I pushed my lust into the submission-zone and put way too much attention on the TV. Lust wasn't going to help me here.

David sighed and leaned back on his headrest. "I needed to get up, anyway. How long have I been asleep?"

"I dunno. I only got home a few minutes ago. Were you lying down after work?"

He took a swig. "Must've been."

I drew from my bottle of liquid courage too, but it wasn't enough to help me. "So, why the nap? Did you have a long day?"

He shrugged again.

I started to think I'd made the wrong decision. I should have come to him when he wasn't still fighting unconsciousness.

Pushing myself to speak, I folded my legs and turned toward him with my beer balanced in my lap. "Listen, David. I'm sorry about the whole Roth Banquet thing. I—I wanna tell you that I didn't go to annoy you, or anything."

His gaze was sharp when it flashed over.

"I—I just thought... ya know... that it'd be good for my future career. But you were right. It wasn't worth it. And it didn't really work out anyway..."

He didn't say anything.

"I can't stand being in this tense energy with you," I admitted softly. "This week has been really hard, and it's partly because I haven't seen you. I feel like you've been avoiding me."

He picked at the corner of the label on the bottle. "I don't wanna talk about it."

"Yeah, but, we should," I said. "I don't want this to go on, David. I need you. I mean, you're the closest friend I have here, and I don't want to fight with you anymore. Especially over some *pretentious* billionaires that I'm not even sure why you hate."

"It's complicated, okay? And I understand that you're curious, but it's none of your business, and it jus'... sucks. Talking about them. Thinking about them. It sucks for me. I don't wanna do it."

"Okay. I get that."

"And it hurts when you don't trust me."

I put a hand on his knee. "It's not that I don't trust you, David. But we've only known each other for a month, and we've just *started* to build a foundation. Unconditional trust takes time, and in order to build it, you kinda have to trust me back..." I waited for him to say something, but he didn't. "Look. All I ask is for the freedom to make my own decisions. About people. About facts. That kind of stuff. Trust me, if there's something bad about the Roths, then I'll sense it in time. I'm pretty good at that. I get it from my wannabe-hippie mum."

He shot me a half-smile, and my nerves jolted with a hint of progress. "Not hard to believe."

I giggled and bumped him with my shoulder. He bumped back,

and we got into a bit of a playful tussle, which was an even better sign.

"Listen," I continued after, "at the end of the day, I'm never trying to hurt you. I'm just trying to piece together my new life here... Determine where everything fits... Where *I* fit. What my future looks like... It's all such a mystery."

"You don't have to have it all figured out," he said, drawing a swig of beer. "You're super smart. It'll come with time."

"I know," I said, picking at my own label. "But it's hard, and I need you in my corner. And Avril. And Greg..." I trailed off, wondering how much vulnerability I should show. "To be completely honest, this whole move thing is still terrifying, and I need my new family so that I can feel safe. I need there to be peace."

He took my hand, his warmth soothing and kind. "It's gonna be okay." There was a moment where we were silent, and he wound his fingers slowly in and out of mine. Our bodies were still communicating—connecting—and his touch was telling me, again, that he'd be there for me. And it was so fucking nice. "I don't wanna break down that foundation of trust. Believe me. I like you, Em. It's been nice spending time with you. And I'm glad you're part of the pack." His face fell. "But I have a bad history, and there are things that you don't need to know."

"Okay," I said.

I wasn't sure how much further I'd get than that, so for now, I'd take it. I mean, I *wanted* to know him. I wanted it so bad. But maybe I'd have to be okay with learning it slowly. Maybe I'd have to be brave enough to offer that piece of unconditional trust first.

"Look, I know I fucked up. So, I appreciate you looking out for me," I said. "And I'm never going to disregard your advice, but at the end of the day I need to be able to make my own calls. I didn't go to that banquet to hurt you or to make you uncomfortable. I went to learn, and that was it. Please believe me."

"I do, Em. But I'm scared too." He shook his head, curls bouncing in response. "'Cus I can see it coming."

My tone was soft and encouraging. "You can see what coming?"

He hesitated. "You get involved with the Roths and they turn you against me."

"David," I said, taking his hand in both of mine. "You don't have to be worried about that. No one is *ever* going to turn me against you. I'm always going to be on your side. House-of-Wolves, right?"

He searched my face, green eyes brimming with severity. "You sure about that?"

Why would he say that? A few seconds ago, we'd talked about our desire to build trust. What could the Roths ever do that could turn me against him? I didn't even *like* them, for christssake.

"Positive," I said. But his face was still stoic, so I gave his knee a few pats to snap him out of it. "Now, can we move past this and have a warm beer while we watch some TV?"

He blinked heavily, but to my relief, nodded. "I'd like nothing more. C'mere." He lifted the duvet so that I could get under, and I hesitated, wondering if it would flare my lust at the wrong time.

"Oh. Yep. Thanks." Too late. My body seemed to have made the decision on its own. I shimmed closer to him and lay my head on his shoulder. I was very aware of the heat radiating from the fabric of his pajama pants.

What would be the harm in becoming more than friends?

I shoved the thought away. We'd just made up. And I wanted to bask in our friendship without complicating things.

We watched TV as I enjoyed the simplicity of his closeness and inhaled the sea breeze flowing from his window. I knew that my decision about the Roth Banquet had left a bitter taste in his mouth, but at least he'd forgiven me. I'd be okay with leaving it at that.

Then I got an idea.

"Hey," I said, after a few minutes. "Why don't we go out tomorrow?"

"Out?" he echoed.

"Yeah. Let's go downtown to a bar. You know. Have a few shots. Get a little tipsy. Do some bad dancing."

"*You* want to go out?"

"Yeah. All of us. It's my last Saturday of freedom before school starts, and I want to take advantage of it." I giggled, spreading my hands in an arch with the beer bottle pinched between my thumb and forefinger. "The House-of-Wolves: Out on the town."

He laughed. "Alright. The nerdy master's student wants to go out. Why not?"

"There you go," I said, before I mocked his accent with a playful drone. "Why not?"

He nudged me, almost making me spill my beer all over his bed, and I laughed with authentic joy. Then I put my head back on his shoulder. It was a relief to be playful with him after all we'd been through. I was grateful to have my David back, so for now, I couldn't be happier.

David's a kid, and he's wandering the streets of Dartmouth sometime in the evening. The warm breeze tosses his much shorter curls and ruffles through his light green t-shirt as he wanders what looks like a downtown market. I can feel that there's a smile broken out on his face. He walks up to a woman at the fruit stand and asks her for a basket of strawberries. The woman smiles and calls him "me love" as she hands them back. He thanks her.

As the sun grows lower in the sky, he heads back down the street with *home* in mind. Ahead is a group of boys his age who call out to him when he gets closer.

"Yo, David!" one of them says. "Where're you at? Come play soccer."

"I can't," he says. "I gotta go straight down the line home. My mum's havin' my baby sister today."

"Wow! Good luck!"

David gives them a wave before pushing forward, and I realize how determined he is. He winds his way through multiple back alleys—most of them filled with a mix of garbage and stray cats—ignoring the stares of the sketchy people he passes along the way.

Over the haze of memory, I worry about him.

But he gets to the wooden door that backs onto the alley safely, and steps into a concrete house that is painted bright blue. The kitchen is tiny and has an Eastern, nautical touch.

From a room at the back of the house, a woman cries out, and the voices that follow seemed strained. David freezes and swallows. The sounds are making his skin crawl. He steps forward and tries to peer around the doorway to the other room, but at the same time, a man steps through from the other side, jumping at the sight of him.

"David!" The man's complexion seems pale, and there's sweat beading on his forehead.

Not knowing what else to do, David lifts the strawberries like an offering. "I got 'em, Dad."

His dad pushes past him, stepping over to the sink. He grabs a steel bowl and fills it with water.

"Is everything goin' okay?" David asks tentatively.

His father searches through the kitchen until he finds a clean set of towels, nearly yanking the drawer from its track when he pulls it out. "She had you at home with only a midwife. Your mother's strong, bu'y. Everything's fine."

"Okay. Well, can I—?"

"Go on out to the park, now," his dad says, waving David away. "Or keep walking about. This en' a place for you right now. You'll be in the way." He goes back into the other room with the bowl and towels.

David shivers. There's something bad about those voices, and his dad's mood doesn't sit right with him.

Shrugging it off, he makes his way back out the wooden door, and walks around the house to the road on the other side. He follows it for a bit, picking up a branch and running it over the concrete as he tries to ignore the pit in his stomach.

He comes upon a woman tending her front garden. A tree towers over her yard that has apples growing on its branches. She calls him over, and he grins, jogging up to the concrete wall around her lot.

She smiles. "David. Good evening, ducky. What're you sayin'?"

"My baby sister's gonna be born tonight, Mrs. Forde," David says, raising his chin.

"Holy mackerel!" she says. "It seems like your mother's been pregnant for a dog's age. Finally!"

"I know," David says. "I'm so fussy today. I can't wait."

"I bet." She pulls two apples from the tree. "Here. Have these. They're ripe, juicy, and aren't riddled with pesticides! Jus' a little treat for you on this happy day."

David hesitates at the gift, but the rumble in his stomach pushes him to take the fruit. He's hungry, and I wonder why he didn't take some of the strawberries from home for himself. "Thank you, Mrs. Forde!"

"You're welcome, David." She puts her hands to her hips and studies him with an affectionate smile. "Tell me how your mother makes out tomorrow. I'd like to come see the little one as soon as she's well."

"I will. I promise." They nod at each other, and he gives her a final wave before he continues down the street.

Slipping one of the apples into his pocket, he takes a small bite out of the other, exposing the sweet inside. As he chews, content rises from his core, and he savours the flavour. Then he meets the trail that leads to the local park. It's small, but there's enough room for him to soak up the sun in the grass, and the flower beds lining the trail soothe his spirit with their colour.

And, God, he's so cute.

He goes to the middle of the park and sits down in the grass with a huff, munching on the apple as he looks up into the trees. The thought of joining the other boys to play soccer runs through his mind, but he can't seem to get his anxiety to settle, and he's more comfortable with the idea of being alone right now. Besides, he tells me, he could be called back home at any minute. He could be needed, and he could help. He wouldn't be in the way.

A tinge of resentment for his father breaks into his thoughts—*Why don't he let me help?*—but he pushes it away. He respects his father, and he'll keep to that.

Instead, he steers his thoughts toward his baby sister and how lovely it'll be to have her around. His dad works a lot, David tells me, and his mum is always busy helping him. It'll be nice to have some company. To have someone to take care of and protect as they grow up. It'll help him learn to be a man, and he can't wait to love his little sister with his whole heart.

I'm super touched by his thoughts.

Having finished the first apple and tossing the core aside, David takes the second out of his pocket, which attracts a skinny seagull. He squawks as he approaches, and David narrows his eyes. Usually, he'd chase the pest off, but today the birth of his sister has put him in such a good mood that he decides to relax, peel a piece off the fruit, and toss it into the grass. The bird jumps but doesn't hesitate to scoop it up before looking for more. David sighs and tosses him another piece before devouring the rest himself. The seagull swallows the fruit and turns his begging look back.

David scrapes his hands together and shows him that they're empty. "No more."

The gull tilts his head in question, but knowing that the benefit is over, flies off to look for someone else to mooch from.

David chuckles before he lies back in the grass, tucking his arms behind his head and studying the colourful clouds above. The gentle breeze sways the trees, and it's hypnotizing, so it's not long until he's drowsy. Relaxing into the earth, he closes his eyes, warmth spreading through him when he thinks about holding his baby sister in a few hours.

By the time he wakes, the sun has set, and the sky is dark. He can hear the surrounding city, but he can't see it, so he bolts upright, pulling himself to his feet. It's dangerous to be in the park at night because druggies hang out there. And if they don't take you, then some stranger very well could. He's been warned of stories like that. It's high time he got out of there.

He follows the path back to the road, and then the faint streetlights home. As he passes Mrs. Forde's house, he finds it quiet. She's either gone to bed or not home. He looks at her tree and contemplates stealing another apple, but then thinks better of it. His belly rumbles to push the idea, but he pushes back. It's very wrong to steal, and it wouldn't be right to do it to a neighbour. With a longing sigh, he moves on.

He winds his way back through the alleys, and the closer he gets, the more horrified he feels. There are ambulances casting red and blue lights on the buildings surrounding his home now, and there's screaming coming from inside. He approaches it from the back garden this time, flinching at the appalling sounds. Unsure of whether he should go in, he stops at the decaying gate, and watches the house. The door at the back is open, but no one's visible, and he can't see into the bedroom well enough to tell what's happening. The only thing he can see from the window is a chair, and all he can do is watch and wait, because he knows that it's best not to go in. He'd just be in the way, like his father said.

Suddenly, his mother gives a piercing howl that stretches into the night, followed by the blubbering of hopeless crying, and a lot of shouting from the people in the room. The sound shakes him to the core, and he's frozen, gripping the gate as his unblinking gaze locks on the bedroom window. His mother screams again, and it drowns out the screaming of everyone else. Then, everyone's shouting over each other, and he's not sure whose voice to focus on. There's a mix of his father saying, "Hold on!" and a stranger's voice relaying, "We gotta get her to the hospital! It's the only way to save the baby!" over and over until it's drilled into his head. The symphony of shouting comes to a horrific climax before the night is plunged into silence. It's like someone's simply clicked off a radio.

David's rapid breath and pounding heart take over, whooshing between his ears as he waits. Every second is more painful than the last, and he prays that this will all be over soon. The absence of a baby crying tells him that it won't be over in the way that he wants it to be, though.

Suddenly, his father comes into view of the window and confirms this. David watches him collapse into the chair like his body is made of stone, and dread washes over him. His dad drops his head into his hands and breaks down in uncontrollable sobbing, and as his back heaves, his cries become almost as piercing to David as his mother's were moments before. David isn't sure whether to run to him or throw up. The nausea that's hitting him is swiftly pushing toward the latter.

Someone dressed in uniform comes into view and places a heavy hand on his father's shoulder. "Sorry," they say. Like it's all they can manage.

David starts hyperventilating. He wants to go to his father and jump into his arms so their grief can be shared, but the dismay is starting to consume him like a colony of termites through a plank of wood. He's way too young to know how to process any of this, and it paralyzes him. Chokes him. Makes him feel like he's drowning in his own sweat. Only one thought comes to mind, and it's drenched in his fear for the future.

What're we gonna do now?

CHAPTER 14
TURN UP THE LOVE

I could taste the bile at the back of my throat. When I woke up, I didn't scream, but I was still in David's bed. And my clothes from yesterday. Beside me, he was asleep, shoulders rising and falling with each breath. I watched the sun play off his raven curls, too choked up to be disappointed that he'd let me fall asleep during the movie and hadn't tried anything romantic. I reached over and brushed his brow with my thumb.

That night must have been so horrible for him...

He stirred at my touch and fought his eyelids. When his green eyes unglazed and settled on me, at first, he smiled, but then his expression darkened. "Em, you okay?" I hadn't realized I'd been crying until he brushed a tear from my cheek.

I was so devastated for him. When we were at Capilano, I'd described him as a lone wolf who'd built his pack, but I hadn't realized how painfully accurate that was. His father had been all he had when he came to Vancouver, and now that man was in prison. David had been on his own since he was sixteen, so it was no wonder he built a new pack with the House-of-Wolves. The concept was so terrifying to me. How'd he possibly survive that?

"No," I finally admitted.

"C'mere." He opened his arms, and I shuffled into them. I settled against his chest and inhaled his skin. It smelled like it was infused with coconuts. Or shea butter. Or coconutty shea butter. "You're trembling. What's got you so shook up?"

THE VEIL OF OPPRESSION

THE VEIL OF OPPRESSION

"I was thinking about family... What happens when they're gone..."

"Oh, Em." He held me tighter. "But your parents en' gone. They're jus' far away."

I meant yours...

I latched onto his misinterpreted direction to cover for my ability's emotional backlash. At least I didn't have to throw out the excuse of a nightmare, for once. "It's so strange... School's about to start, and what if I fuck it up? What if I don't like it? What if I can't make it on my own? What if this whole move was for nothing?" Oh, shit. In covering my ability, I'd started listing off true fears.

"Even if you don't like it, the move won't be for nothing," David said. "It'll teach you something, anyway. Plus, it brought you to us. And you'll always have *us*." It felt like he'd kissed me on the top of the head, but it was too soft for me to be sure.

I nuzzled into the soft curls on his chest. "I'm so grateful I have you," I admitted, in a whisper. "You're an incredible man, David Mathis."

He chuckled softly. "I dunno about that. I'm a survivor, that's all." He squeezed me. "But I'm grateful to have you too, Em. You're a beautiful woman with a heart of gold. Questionable decisions sometimes, but a heart of gold."

I managed a small laugh. "I'm so sorry about the banquet."

"I know. And after sleeping on it, I realized that you were right last night. If you wanna hang around the Roths to further your career, I can't stop you. And I can't really be mad at it. It's not fair." He paused. "Plus, it'll only lead you to learn the truth about them in time. I have to trust you on that."

I blinked. I totally wasn't expecting that. Avril and Greg were right. He *was* level-headed.

"Heck, maybe you can even make them pay with all the badass Medical Ethics knowledge you're gonna gain."

My voice was soppy, but the question came out clear. "Make them pay for what?"

"For all manner of sins," he said.

"But what *specific* sins—"

"Let's not worry about that for now, okay? All you need to know is that I've tried to stand against them before, and I've failed." He swallowed.

"Wha? Stand against them for what—?"

"Look. At the end of the day, my point is, that I jus' want our House to stay strong. And for that, I gotta be confident enough to let you be free. Investigate what you wanna investigate. Prove to yourself that you're strong and you gonna make one hell of a Medical Ethics person one day."

I laughed at his description of my future. "Professor," I corrected him.

"Huh?"

"Medical Ethics *Professor*. That's what I want to be. A professor. Just like my dad."

"There you go," he said. "And you're gonna do it, Em. It's only when you try that you're gonna learn how powerful you really are."

I cuddled him deeper. He had no idea how much better he was making all this. "But what about you?" I asked, as my curiosity turned. "Did you ever think about changing careers? I mean, you seem to be really into fitness and not so much into, well, working down at the docks. What's stopping you from making a change?"

He was quiet for a minute before he said, "I know I could become a personal trainer if I wanted, but I'm happy with what I got, and I don't exactly have the energy to change it. For now, I'm secure and safe. I gotta good family with my roommates. It hasn't always been like that in the past... There's no need to stir that up. That dream isn't worth my time right now."

But you never wanted to make it come true?

I decided not to push it. We were having a moment of connection, and I didn't want to fuck that up by making him feel like I disapproved of his life choices. "Okay."

There was a hum from his throat. "Enough with the heavy. We saltin' the nail tonight, or what?"

I pulled away to raise an eyebrow at him. "Salting the nail?"

"You know. Drinking it all off. Getting plastered. Getting paralyzed." He grinned.

"Um, *hell yeah* we are."

"Then I'd better make a good breakfast for everyone."

By the time the four of us were stumbling down Cordova Street—on route toward the upscale club that I'd found through a quick Google search—I was feeling alive. Even with the misty rain that was falling. My tender moment with David had soothed a lot of my anxiety, so now I was loose enough to let myself have some fun. I hooked one arm in Avril's, and the two of us walked in sync, sprawled across the street like a couple of teenagers. Conveniently, the boys ended up behind us, and I was tipsy enough from our pre-drinking at home to be showy about the nice view we were giving them as we strutted through the moody Vancouver weather.

Although the club was dark and hazy—the walls illuminated with purple uplighting—it was warm and packed with people. All the circular booths around the dance floor were taken, so Avril set out on a mission, targeting one that was only half-taken by a group of guys. With a flirty smile and a gentle toss of her blonde hair, she began to persuade them to let us use the other half. I assisted, shrugging off the jacket that I'd borrowed from her to expose the smoke-show of a top that I was wearing. Men have the uncanny ability to choose when to be simple and easy, so I wasn't surprised when they turned into a group of bobbleheads, shifting over to make room for us.

Avril shrieked, "Thank you!" as she settled into the booth. She immediately got offers for drinks that she politely refused.

Then, our own boys were there to get them for us.

"What are you having, Em?" David asked, as I finished taking off the jacket, tossing it into the booth beside Avril. I liked the way that his gaze brushed my collarbone and shoulders.

"White wine, thanks."

He nodded and took Avril's order before starting toward the bar with Greggy.

I snatched his hand. "David?"

"Yeah?" he said, turning back. His green eyes and raven curls were soft in the low light of the club, and *fuck* was he sexy.

I smiled to cover my lust. "Really. Thank you." I was relieved to have things back to normal, and I wanted to drive home how appreciative I was of his understanding.

He flashed me his beautiful grin. "Of course, princess." He squeezed my hand, before he continued toward the bar with the pup-of-the-House.

I held my smile as I watched him disappear into the crowd, then slid into the booth with Avril. She was locked in a shouted conversation with the guys that we'd just conned, and I found myself hesitant to join. Although they were the typical, decent-looking type that seemed to wander the streets of Vancouver in abundance, I had no interest in flirting with them. My thoughts were solely on the Nova Scotian that'd just walked off to the bar.

I'm single. Might as well enjoy it.

Plus, he'd been so kind this morning. And warm. And lovely. And cuddling him had felt so fucking *right*. Maybe I was ready to get over Andy. Maybe there wasn't a harm in becoming more than friends.

I wondered whether this was me talking, or the alcohol.

Avril was being polite, but she was showing the same signs of disinterest in these guys as I was. So, when one of them raised his chin toward David and asked, "Is that your boyfriend?" I lied and said yes. Avril nudged me under the table, so I threw in, "The one with the brown hair is hers."

Several of their faces dropped.

"The one that looks like a teenager?" someone asked.

I grinned and put a hand on Avril's shoulder. "Oh yeah. Bit of a cougar, this one."

"She's only joking," Avril said, brushing off my hand and trying to redeem herself. "He's actually twenty-six. He just has a baby face." Poor Greggy; the pup-of-the-House. She'd had to add three years to his age to make the *concept* of dating him imaginable.

Under the music, the group of guys started muttering to each other, but they didn't say anything else to us. In fact, after that, they lost interest completely, which was what we'd wanted, anyway. Avril and I exchanged furtive glances and silently praised each other for our combined success as we waited for the guys to return with our drinks.

Soon, they did; the two of them bringing beer bottles, wine glasses, and a tray of shots that Greg was balancing on the palm of his hand like a waitress. I slid out of the booth to help dish out the drinks as David set my glass on the table.

"Thanks, babe," I said, keeping up my act while hoping he'd write it off as me being tipsy.

He shot me a half smile but didn't say anything about it.

Then the song morphed into *Turn Up the Love* by Far East Movement, and it made me want to dance like a mad woman. "I love this one!" I slurred, downing a healthy gulp of wine before turning back to David.

He was still standing at the edge of the booth, but now he wasn't looking at me. He was laser-focused on someone across the dance floor, with his shoulders stiffened and his right hand clenched. At first, I was confused, but as I followed his sightline, I understood why.

Barrett Roth was in the middle of the dance floor, absorbed in a make-out session worthy of a soft-core porno with his supermodel girlfriend. Though the song was upbeat, they listed from side-to-side, his arms wrapped around her shoulders. A glass of what looked like scotch was hanging from his hand.

David's jaw tensed, and I realized that I'd completely forgotten whose "territory" we were in. How the hell had I managed to find the *one* club upscale enough to host pretentious billionaires?

Nausea burned my stomach as I watched Rebecca take her mouth off her boyfriend and turn, her smile seductive as she ground her ass into his groin. Pleased, he held her hips with one hand while brushing aside her hair with the other, nipping at her neck. She turned back and started kissing him again. He crossed his arms to rest over the top of her shoulders again, his grip lazy on the top of the scotch.

Then, like he could sense that we were looking at him, Barrett raised his dark gaze to meet David's. They watched each other as Barrett kissed his girlfriend before he pulled his lips away and raised his chin to give David his full attention. Even though they were a dance floor apart, the stare down burned with tension and sent shivers down my spine. Barrett rested his chin on Rebecca's head as she cuddled into his chest, eyes unblinking and fixed on David's as his mouth curled into a cocky smirk. In a movement that seemed glazed with vindictiveness, he raised his glass from behind Rebecca's back and gave David a nod.

David looked like he was trying not to chew his lips off.

"Come on, David," I said, laying a gentle hand on his shoulder to turn him away. "Ignore him. Please?" I snatched a shot off the tray and shoved it into his hands. "Here, have this."

He took it without looking at me, gaze still locked on Barrett's.

I snatched another and nudged him, finally breaking their stare-down. "Come on. House-of-Wolves, remember?" I raised my shot. "House-of-Wolves."

Snapping out of it a little, David grinned and raised his in return. "House-of-Wolves."

We tossed them back in tandem, and then he slammed his glass on the table, threw his head back, and broke into a loud howl. Avril and Greg followed his lead, and I laughed as I joined in, releasing the negativity into the haze of the club. The proud declaration of our pack's presence turned most of the heads that were on the dance floor, and I didn't doubt that people were writing us off as a bunch of drunk idiots. But I didn't care. I found my howl empowering, and I let my spiritual-freak flag fly.

As I brought my head back down, I looked across the dance floor, and found Barrett still smirking at us. I held his black glare before I tossed back another shot, shaking it off as I grabbed my wine glass. "Come on. Let's dance!"

Taking David's hand, we watched the Bad-Roth together, before I pulled his attention to the other side of the club. When she left the booth, Avril gave Barrett a smile and a wave, but the pup-of-the-House wasn't so generous. Greggy gave him both middle fingers.

As we moved to an area of the club where Mr. Roth wouldn't be in sight, the beat dropped, and shockwaves of bass trembled in our bones. We broke into some energetic, booze-fueled moves, and I threw my head back in a laugh at Greg's hoedown style, before joining Avril in some fluid motions. My focus was still on David. I grinned as I watched him release the tense moment from earlier by getting lost in the music. Which was the whole point of what I was trying to get us to do by suggesting we go out.

The song merged with one that I didn't recognize, but I was so immersed in the music that I didn't notice a stranger's arms until they were wrapped around me. His lips grazed my neck with disgusting moisture, and I tried to push him away, but he held me in place. This made me shriek and struggle more, and then David noticed. The rage from his earlier encounter with Barrett surfaced through the burning green of his eyes, and he lunged forward to pull the strange man off me.

I stepped behind him.

The two men were then at each other's throats, exuding testosterone as they screamed at each other over the pumping bass line. The other members of the House stepped in to separate them, but I was so emotional that I couldn't help. I stood back from the crowd, my breath rapid and my heart pounding. Being held in place while a strange man groped me was not something that I'd liked, and I secretly hoped that David would teach him a lesson.

Face stiffened in anger, David turned away from the fight and sheltered me. He took several deep breaths and his expression started to soften as he held me, but I could feel the tension through the muscles of his arms and chest.

"You alright?" he asked.

"Yeah, yeah, fine," I said, melting into his arms.

"Ripe asshole," he growled. "What the fuck did he think he was playin' at?"

"It's okay, David," I soothed him. "I'm alright. Just a bit shook up is all. But I'm thankful you were there for me."

He held me tighter. "Some men will never fuckin' learn."

We danced for a few minutes, gradually settling in each other's arms, and I thought again about how grateful I was to have him on my side. He'd really shown up for me since my move; from welcoming me, to taking me to Capilano, to helping me buy a car, to moments like we had this morning. He made me feel safe and supported. Like I had someone here that I could depend on no matter what. He made everything seem like it was going to be okay...

I melted deeper into his arms, as intoxicated by his touch as I was from the wine. The trauma from a few minutes before had already been healed, and instead I thought about Rebecca and Barrett. How much I longed to have a moment of what they were having. A man's lips on mine. And if I was going to have said moment, there was no one I'd rather have it with than the man who was holding me.

Would he reciprocate if I revealed how badly I wanted to kiss him?

Tipsy Emily made the move before I could think about it. I shifted to wrap my arms around David's neck, running a hand through his curls and raising my lips close to his. He dropped his chin to bring them closer, and my insides vibrated. I braced for the elation, but he turned his head at the last second, expression dripping with dilemma. Then he distracted me from his change of heart by asking if I wanted another drink.

I dropped my arms, stinging in embarrassment. Nodding, I took off before he could see the look on my face. As I battled my wine-soaked emotions and a room filled with strangers, I refused to cast a glance in the direction that Barrett was in. I didn't want to put salt in the wound by watching him revel in what I'd wanted.

David was following, and as we joined the massive crowd around the bar, he seemed to be trying to gauge the severity of what he'd done. I looked away, biting my lip hard to distract myself from the stinging at the back of my eyes. My body language was fucking *betraying* me, and I couldn't veil it.

David stepped behind me and wrapped his arms around my shoulders in apology, once again surrounding me with warmth. I sighed as I rubbed my cheek on his biceps, grasping the crook of his elbow with a longing hand. He gave me one of those ghost kisses on the top of my blonde waves.

Fuck. What am I supposed to do with this?

The bartender then called on David, and he stepped forward, separating us.

As soon as the second glass of wine hit my hand, I gulped it down and asked for another while he had the bartender's attention. He shot me a questioning look, but seemed eager to make it up to me, so he ordered the second glass as I tried my best to compose myself.

After that, the night turned fuzzy. I remember deliberately not dancing with David for the rest of the night, and my mood picking back up when I got too drunk to care. Sometime around 2:00am, I think I leaned on Greggy as we left the club, but the rest of the night turned into a massive blur.

And I walked out of that place with some memories that I wanted to forget, but the one thing I *couldn't* was the stare-down between

David and Barrett. The hold of Barrett's obsidian gaze. The way he sarcastically nodded. The furtiveness of his sardonic smirk…

David Mathis. What happened to you?

CHAPTER 15
THUNDERSTRUCK

My month of freedom ended quickly, and before I knew it, I was pulling my Yaris into the parking structure on my first day at UBC. The morning was busy. I had three lectures and a meeting with the professor who would potentially support my master's—Dr. Tsuyuki. He was kind, quiet, and incredibly sharp (which was a bit intimidating) but I was confident that he'd help push me through this. Whatever got me through my master's alive was a benefit, and I had to be ready for the stress.

We spent a good hour in his brisk office inside the Biological Engineering building, chatting, and discussing the overview of the program. He was flawless when he spoke, and he smelled as fresh as his office. Some sort of mix between pine and clean laundry. I explained my background at the University of Toronto and the work that I'd done in Public Service since graduating from my bachelor's. He was happy with the experience that I had, and by the end of the meeting, I was relieved when he stated that he was excited to work with me. I grinned and told him likewise.

"Have you considered what your thesis is going to be about?" he then asked.

"Um, I was thinking of something along the lines of analyzing why patients would refuse life-saving medical treatment," I said. "I think that sort of thing would be really interesting."

"Hmmm. Interesting, yes. But that's more of an undergraduate-level topic."

"Okay... Well, what about medical care for prisoners with long-term sentences." I swallowed, thinking about David's father.

"Ah! A fascinating subject," Dr. Tsuyuki said. "But it's been heavily researched in the past. How can you challenge yourself to look outside the prominent topics?"

Then my mind felt like a deflated balloon. I rubbed my forehead. Medical Ethics was such a broad field, and there were so many topics to choose from. How was I going to think outside the box while researching something worthwhile to me?

"You don't have to decide today, Emily," Dr. Tsuyuki said. "Take your time to really consider your options."

But I'd started thinking about the fraudulent antibiotics that put me back in the hospital after my accident. "Pharmaceutical companies," I threw out. "Quality vs. profit. That kind of thing."

Dr. Tsuyuki raised an eyebrow. "You may be on to something there. Quality vs. profit has also been overdone, but how about thinking more along the lines of moral product development?"

I opened my laptop and typed out some frantic notes. "Moral... product... development..."

"And, you know, Vancouver is the home of one of the biggest pharmaceutical companies in the world. You may be able to leverage that to your advantage."

I stopped typing and looked up. "Roth Pharmaceuticals," I said.

"Roth Pharmaceuticals," he echoed, dipping his chin with a smile.

Huh. I wasn't sure how I was going to leverage that for my thesis, but at least I'd made some connections there. Perhaps the Roth Banquet hadn't been such a waste after all.

"Let's schedule our next meeting in two weeks' time," Dr. Tsuyuki said. "By then, I want you to have a more solid idea of your thesis topic."

Great. Wonderful. Now I'm not stressed at all.

After the meeting with Dr. Tsuyuki, my brain felt heavy. My circuits were shot for the day, and I knew this because I turned the wrong way outside of his office, walking the maze of hallways for a good two minutes before I realized I was, in fact, going the wrong way. Then I had to rush back past his office, hoping that he wouldn't see me and think I was "the hopeless Torontonian," lost on her first day.

The last lecture wasn't for an hour afterward, so I wandered around the campus, stopping in at the bookstore that was *filled* with images of Thunderbirds to showcase the school's mascot. I picked myself up a UBC hoodie to play my part as the classic newbie. As I pulled it over my head, I savored its coziness and ignored the subtle chemical smell, before heading to the library for some quiet time.

For the first forty minutes or so, I cleaned up my scattered notes from my previous lectures before I started a new file called *Meetings with Dr. Tsuyuki*, typing out my initial thoughts and feelings. I glazed over the jumbled words on the screen, and I tapped my two front teeth in thought. Thesis-based master's *with* courses. I was in for a tough year, that was for sure.

It'll be worth it, right?

Well... maybe. After all, times were tough for graduate students. Having a master's wasn't always a benefit over having an undergrad. But if I wanted to teach this kind of thing, I'd have to suffer through the education that it took to get there.

After I'd finished organizing my notes, I sat back, stretching my arms and folding them behind my head. I closed my eyes to give them a break from the computer screen, then I leaned forward and propped my chin on my hand. A group of undergrad girls were sitting around a table across the room, and their obnoxious giggling told me that they weren't having as busy a first day as I was. My head pounded to remind me that it needed a coffee.

Turning back to my laptop, my attention snagged on one particular note—*Roth Pharmaceuticals*. I started thinking about the Roth Banquet, and the accomplishments that the Roth brothers had presented.

How can I leverage what I've learned so I can use it to my advantage?

And what could they be hiding behind all those monumental accomplishments? Also, how was this all linked? Roth Pharma and my thesis-slash-purpose in BC? The House-of-Wolves vs. The Roths? Barrett and me? It was all jumbled up like a broken mosaic, and I had no idea how the Universe wanted me to piece it all together.

But one thing was for sure—Dr. Tsuyuki hadn't mentioned the pharma giant by accident. He'd been guided to tell me that, whether he'd been aware of it or not. More likely not. Few people believed in the things that my family did, and he was an ethical scientist. They were much more difficult to convince when it came to the hocus-pocus, spiritual stuff. But I was sure. Again, the signs were there, and I just had to follow them.

Where do I start?

Pulling up Google, I typed in *Roth Pharmaceuticals*, which spat out a long list of website links pertaining to the company. I clicked on their home page, which—not surprisingly—pulled up an elegant website worthy of a multi-billion-dollar pharma giant. Flashing across the homepage were the company's commitment for quality, pharmaceutical safety, and sustainability.

But I wasn't interested in any of that. I clicked on the "About Us" tab, which served up a novel about the company's history:

Founded in 1971, Roth Pharmaceuticals is the largest pharmaceutical company in North America. We started with a small facility of 1000 employees in Richmond, British Columbia under the leadership of Nicholas Philip Roth. The company quickly expanded after Johnathan Philip Roth joined his father at the head of the company in 1985, and the company now employs over 150,000 people in Manufacturing, Research and Development, Distribution, and more. Presently run under the leadership of brothers Travis Benjamin Roth and Barrett Nicholas Roth, Roth Pharmaceuticals owns multiple manufacturing facilities across the country. Including the original facility in Richmond, BC, we have additional facilities in Surrey, BC, Victoria, BC, Edmonton, AB, Toronto, ON, Montréal, QC, and Halifax, NS. We also have two Research and Development facilities in Vancouver and Halifax. We currently produce over 2000 brands of specialized pharmaceuticals, and are rapidly expanding into other health-related industries including medical supplies—

Okay. Whatever. Blah, blah, blah. What else?

Below the introduction were some photos of their original processing facility, a faded one from the eighties of Nicholas Roth and Johnathan Roth, and a current one of Travis and Barrett; dressed-to-the-nines, as they beamed at their professional photographer's camera. Below the picture were links to a few historical articles from published works with titles like: *How Nicholas and Johnathan Roth Made the Most Impressive, Powerhouse, Father-Son Team in the Industry,* and the one I'd seen before—*The Two Brothers at the Top of the Pharmaceutical Industry: Barrett and Travis Roth Continue to Flourish Despite the Death of their Father.*

The last one struck me like a tuning fork.

John was murdered...

I hadn't thought much about that since the Roth Banquet, but now I was intrigued. Carol had said that John was killed over money, but, to me, that seemed like such a surface-level explanation. A mask of a lie, perhaps...

I pressed the back button and typed in *Johnathan Roth.* Up came a photo of John in a suit and tie complete with a short biography, multiple links to the company, as well as news pages covering his death twelve years ago. I clicked on the first one, and the webpage appeared, complete with the video covering the story. Desperate not to miss a word, I plugged in my headphones, turned up the volume, and pressed play.

A manicured news anchor appeared, sitting behind the desk with a somber look on his face. A photo of John hovered on the screen behind him. "Horror on the streets of Downtown Vancouver today as a man open fired in front of a coffee shop on the corner of Georgia and Howe, killing another man and leaving him dead on the scene. We now go to Dana Saunders with the story. Dana."

The shot changed to Dana, dressed in a charcoal skirt suit, standing in front of a coffee shop which was sectioned off with police tape.

"That's right, Calvin," she said, an Irish tinge to her accent. "It all started here outside the beloved *Café du Diable*, where it is reported that a man allegedly *shot and killed* another man in broad daylight this afternoon, in front of a sixteen-year-old boy and many onlookers. The victim is forty-eight-year-old Johnathan Roth, President and CEO of the city's revered Roth Pharmaceuticals, who was pronounced dead at the scene. Police have informed us that he succumbed to multiple bullet wounds before paramedics arrived. The suspect is forty-five-year-old Joseph Mathis—"

I jumped like I'd been struck by lightning and slammed the pause button.

Joseph Mathis.

My ears started ringing.

Mathis... As in *David* Mathis? *My* David?

That would make him not only the son of a criminal, but the son of a murderer...

Shivering it off a little, I pressed play again.

"It was reported that his behaviour was irate and that he was infuriated before the incident occurred," Dana finished.

The screen jumped to a witness of the shooting. "I had no idea what was going on. It all happened so fast. He was screaming and then suddenly, he shot him! It was so loud that I thought fireworks were going off in the street!"

Back to Dana: "The identity of the sixteen-year-old boy has not been released; however, it's been reported that Mathis also threatened him before police arrived on the scene and detained him. So far, no relationship between Roth and Mathis has been identified, and police are urging anyone that witnessed the shooting or has any additional information to come forward—"

I paused the video and put my hands on my forehead. I was having trouble reconciling what I knew about David's father and what this newscast was telling me. It didn't sit right with me, but there were way too many coincidences to ignore the inevitable fact. This was the link between them. This was why David's father was in prison. He'd *murdered* Johnathan Roth in the middle of the street.

But why?

Below the newscast video there was a link to another one called: *Travis Roth breaks his silence after the conclusion of the Mathis Trial.* I clicked on it with a finger as fast as a Ferrari.

Up popped the video of a twenty-something Travis, standing in front of a sea of microphones with a teenage Barrett by his side. There was anguish on his face, and everyone hushed as he started to speak. He put a gentle arm around his little brother's shoulders. "Although nothing can bring our father back, or end the pain of the loss, I believe that justice was served here today." He gave a pained smile. "We are deeply touched by the outpouring of love and support that we have received over the past few weeks. Nevertheless, our family would greatly appreciate the privacy to grieve in peace during this difficult time. Thank you, Everyone."

A roar of press broke out, "Travis! Travis! Barrett! Barrett!"

But someone grabbed my shoulders, and I gave a massive start.

"Hey, Em," Greg said, shooting me an adorable grin as he leaned into view. "Whatcha watching?"

"Nothing." I slapped my laptop shut. "Just—uh—trying to kill some time before my next lecture."

"Good." He sat beside me, pulling a couple sandwiches from his backpack. He handed me one along with a coffee. "I brought you some lunch."

Though I had leftovers in my backpack, the sandwich was a welcome break. "Um. Thanks, Greg... I mean—you're so kind. Thank you. I really needed it."

He shrugged as he took a sip of his own coffee. "Yeah, well, you had a really packed day today, so I figured it's the least I could do." He raised his chin, motioning to my sweater. "I see you're already decked out in the swag."

"It's my first day. I need to look the part." I sat tall, but sweat was beading on my forehead.

"Sweet." He shot me another charming smile, and although I was a little annoyed with him for interrupting my snooping, it was impossible to be mad at him. It was like trying to be mad at a puppy. "How was this morning?"

I sighed as I unwrapped the sandwich. It was ham and cheese. Not my favourite, but I bit into it gratefully, anyway. "Busy," I said, as I chewed. "Looks like my Mondays, Wednesdays, and Fridays are going to be packed for the next, you know, *forever*."

He laughed. "Well, you're the one that insisted that your Tuesdays and Thursdays be kept free."

I pointed at him with the bitten corner of my sandwich. "That's because I'm eventually going to have to get a job."

It was true. I'd saved up enough to live on short-term, but it wasn't enough to be comfortable in the long run. I'd need some extra financial security eventually, but I'd cross that bridge when I came to it.

"You could always go work with David," Greg joked.

"Yeah, I dunno enough about operating a crane." I sighed again. "I'll find something. But I want to concentrate on getting this semester started first."

He slurped his coffee and smacked his lips. "I hear that."

"'Ow was your morning?" I wolfed down my sandwich like I'd been starving.

He shrugged. "Not bad. I've got a few interesting courses this semester, so I'm happy about that. I'm a bit sick of doing all the generic prerequisites."

"I know, Greggy, but it gets better." I wiped some mayo from the corner of my mouth. "After the first couple years—when you start to study what you really want—it becomes rewarding. Trust me."

"I believe you." He glanced at his watch. "Oh, shit. Sorry, Em. I've gotta go." He shot up and gave me a brief squeeze before taking off in a flurry. "I'll see you at home."

"Thanks for lunch!" I called after him.

"No worries!" he called back.

My heart pulsed as I watched him dart off.

The next ten minutes I sat there suspended in my thoughts as I finished my coffee. I was still fixated on the Roth-Mathis incident, and though I'd closed all my browser windows without looking into it further, I couldn't help but wonder: *Why would Joseph Mathis murder Johnathan Roth in the middle of downtown Vancouver?*

In doing so, he'd landed himself in prison for the rest of his life, leaving David to fend for himself at only sixteen. It seemed reckless and made no fucking sense.

God, he must have been desperate...

I huffed as I packed up my things for my next lecture.

One thing was for sure: David wasn't going to tell me anything about this. If I were going to solve the mystery of Joseph's decision, I would need to do so on my own, but I wasn't sure where else to look.

I pushed it out of mind as I slugged my backpack over my shoulder. This wasn't worth my time for now. I had a master's degree to pursue, so I had to turn the war ships toward Roth Pharma.

After the day was done, I drove south on Highway Ninety-Nine back toward Ladner, rolling down my window and enjoying the warm spring air. On the radio "A Horse with No Name" by America, was playing, which was one of my dad's favourites. I grinned as I pictured my parents dancing to it in Mum's original studio when I was little, Dad enthusiastic with his toneless singing. I'd joined them, holding their hands with each of mine, and I jumped up and down with all my strength, because that was what I'd considered dancing when I was that age.

Then a pit grew heavy in my stomach, and I thought about David. I had a new family now, but how much did I *really* know about them?

CHAPTER 16
RED RIGHT HAND

I caught sight of David's Mazda when I pulled into the House-of-Wolves, and my throat clenched. After what I'd learned at the library, how would I be able to look at him the same way? I wouldn't, I told myself, but that didn't mean I was going to treat him any differently. It wasn't David's fault that any of this happened. He didn't make his father into a murderer.

Pulling my feet over the threshold of the House-of-Wolves, I leaned into the chestnut door, engulfed by the warmer temperature on the inside. Someone had cranked up the heat, but it was June, so I had no idea why. Kicking my shoes off, I locked the door and walked over to the kitchen, dropping my laptop on the table as I ran a hand through my hair. The muffled sound of the TV in the next room told me that my alpha male was likely in there, so I shrugged off my coat and left it on the back of the chair before I went to meet him.

David was working out in the living room with a grey hoodie pulled up over his curls.

I tilted my head. "You know, most people don't consider a hoodie to be optimal workout gear, Mr. Mathis."

David smiled, but it was obvious by the lines in his expression that he wasn't okay. "Yeah, well. I'm a little colder than normal today."

"I'm surprised you're even working out at home. That you're even working out *at all*. Are you feeling okay?"

He shrugged before lifting a weight onto his shoulder. "Gotta keep up with them gains."

"Um, not when you're looking like that, you don't." I stepped forward, and he paused, studying me as I lowered his hood. Though there was sweat on his brow, he quivered, and his skin was verging on white. There were circles under his eyes, and breath seemed a little wheezier than working out would cause. "Did you even go in to work today?"

He lowered the weight and sighed. "No," he admitted. "I feel like shit."

"It certainly looks like it." I stroked his curls and found them drenched in sweat. "You look like you might have the flu, actually."

He shrugged again. "I'll live."

I placed the back of my hand to his forehead and found him warmer to the touch than he'd normally be. But it was hard to tell because he'd been working out, and the house was so fucking hot. "I've got some ginger in the fridge," I said. "I'll make you a tea that might help. And for the love of the Source, sit down. You don't need to make things worse by forcing yourself to exercise sick. You know this, Mr. Mathis."

He groaned and set the weight aside. "Alright, alright. You've got me."

Back in the kitchen, I pulled out the ginger root, stripped off the skin, and grated it into a metal tea strainer. I boiled the kettle and then pulled the honey out of the cupboard, coating the bottom of a large mug, before I placed the strainer over the mouth. The savory smell of the ginger hit me as I poured the hot water over it, and I breathed deep, letting my concoction steep.

Releasing a bit of exhaustion, I leaned against the countertop, as the steam rose from the mug behind me and tickled the back of my arm. I shifted away from it, and pulled out my phone, finding a missed text from Mum.

Happy first day at school, sweetheart! Facetime tonight?

I sighed and thought about this. Though I was trying to prove my independence, I hadn't talked to my mum in over a week, so I knew that I should probably agree. *10pm your time ok?*

As I waited for her reply, I put my phone down and lifted the tea strainer, stirring David's tea.

The counter vibrated: *Sounds good!*

Topping the mug with some cold water, I lifted it to my lips to test it, and was pleased to find it a perfect blend of spicy and sweet. I had no idea if it would make David better or not, but it was what Mum did when I was sick, and it always seemed to work.

I went back into the living room, serving it to him with a smile and urging him to drink. He sat on the couch with a lot of added groaning, and cupped it with both hands, before he sat forward, resting his elbows on his knees. He hung his head. I rubbed his back, the hoodie bunching from under my fingers. Even through it, his skin was radiating like a furnace.

Hmmm. He was clearly worse than I'd thought. Maybe the tea wouldn't be enough? I wondered whether I should drive him to the clinic.

He drew the strength to sit back up and sip the tea, shivering at the first taste. In the grip of his hands, the mug looked tiny. "You're too good to me, Em."

I shifted closer and widened the circles that I was rubbing on his back. "You're worthy of it," I told him. Then, I frowned. "You seem really bad. If you're still like this tomorrow, I'll drive you to the doctor."

"En' no point," he grumped, as he sipped.

"David, if you have the flu, you're gonna need treatment."

"I jus' need sleep, Em," he said, placing the mug on the table. "Will you switch places with me?"

"Uh. Sure."

We did so with some awkward shuffling. He grabbed one of our pillows and set it in my lap so that he could lay his head there. I was oddly happy that he wanted to. I pulled the blanket from the back of the couch and covered him with it, then continued stroking his curls.

After a deep breath, he fell silent. His muscles began to relax beneath the trembling, and I tried to distract myself from my wandering thoughts by watching the documentary that was playing on the TV. It was about supplements this time.

"David?" My voice then hovered above a whisper.

His voice was muffled by the pillow. "Yeah?"

"When we were talking about your dad the other week, I don't think you told me his name."

"You really care?"

Though he couldn't see me, I nodded. Then swallowed. "Just curious."

He melted into the couch. "Same as my middle name. It's Joseph."

Right. Of course it is. Murderer confirmed.

I stayed quiet and, luckily, he was too sick to press me for why I was asking. Struck with the revelation, I told myself that I'd only asked to be sure. I kept playing with his hair, and after a short time he fell asleep. I ran my index finger across his left hand, studying every crease and mole that stood out against his pale skin.

My David. How can you be the son of a killer?

Curling my fingers around his, I shifted forward, letting my head sink into the back of the couch. The fatigue of the day spread over me, and I let myself drift with my hand in his, knowing full-well there was a chance I was going to see something that I didn't want to see.

David is a child again—ten or eleven—and he's jogging down the hallway of a two-bedroom apartment with grimy, grey walls. He runs to the back bedroom, where there isn't much more than a bed, a nightstand, and a horrible view of the building next to them. It's so close that you can see what the neighbours are watching in the apartment across. He grabs a beach bag from the bed and runs across the hall to the tiny bathroom, snatching some towels from the rack inside, before heading back down the hall to the kitchen. The kitchen is sectioned off in a corner of the apartment that has laminate flooring. The kind they threw into every kitchen in the sixties and seventies.

There, Joseph is standing at a circular wooden table that's like the one we have at the House-of-Wolves, leaning over a map of Vancouver. David joins him, propping himself up on a chair as he studies the map with his father.

"So, where d'you fancy for a swim, bu'y?" Joseph points to the West End. "First Beach, Second Beach, or Third Beach?"

"Hmmm," David says, leaning on the table. "Some guy at school told me that First Beach is the best. I think we should go there. And they don't call it First Beach, anyway. It's English Bay Beach."

There's a glint of pride in Joseph's eye when he looks at his son. "Alright," he says. "If we don't like it, we'll try the others. We have enough time."

David nods, but all this talk of beaches reminds him of home, and his stomach feels sour. "Dad? Are we gonna stay here forever?"

Joseph's face teeters on the edge of apology, and he seems like he's holding back. "Yes, me love. This is our home now. We'll have a better life here, and now we're Vancouverites."

I feel David pout. "What if I don't wanna be a Vancouverite? What if I wanna go home?"

Joseph lays a gentle hand on his shoulder. "David. This is the choice I made to give us a better future. There's nothing left for us in Dartmouth. I know it's hard, because everything's different here, but *this* is home. And I know you don't understand, but one day, you will. We're doing what's best for you."

David questions this at first, but he trusts his father, so he doesn't push it. "Okay."

"Good," Joseph says, standing up straight. "You got that lifejacket I bought you?"

"I don't need that. I swam the sea everyday back home."

"The sea here en' the same sea in the harbour at home," Joseph says. "It can be right mean and rough. Go get the lifejacket."

"Dad..." David groans, but Joseph points down the hall, so he pulls himself from the chair. He trudges back to his room, and wrenches open the door to the closet, where he's stashed the lifejacket. He snatches it from its place.

A knock on the front door draws his attention. It's overbearing. Tapped by someone adamant not to be ignored. David hears Joseph open it with muffled surprise, before the deep voice of a stranger responds. Gripping the lifejacket in his hand, he sneaks back down the hall and peers around the corner. The sting of adrenaline mixed with curiosity tells me that this child version of David is not used to having visitors. Fear pops up and he shrinks back into the cover of the hallway, because his father has invited in a man with copper hair, black eyes, and perfect teeth.

Oh my God... Johnathan Roth, I think over the memory.

"Thank you, Joseph," John is saying as he steps inside. The wrinkle of disgust that shimmers across his face when he looks around the drab apartment is concealed immediately after. He's dressed in a black suit with white pinstripes, complete with golden cufflinks set with rubies. He looks very out of place. "How are you settling in? Are you getting along alright?"

"Yes, Mr. Roth," Joseph says. "Thank you." He twists his hands together, making his skin scrape. "Can I get you something, sir?"

"No, thank you," John says. "I will not be staying long. I merely wished to check on you. See how you're doing." He catches David peering around the corner and smiles. "Ah, David, isn't it? Come here, lad. Let me get a look at you."

At first, David's paralyzed, but the glint in John's obsidian gaze tells him that this man is not a good one to disobey. He swallows and pushes himself forward, clutching the lifejacket as he grapples with the instinct to turn and run the other way.

John flashes his perfect grin as he kneels and puts a heavy hand on David's shoulder. He smells pristine; like he's never been dirty in his life. "There's a good boy. How are you? Do you like it here so far?"

David's eyes flash to his father for guidance—*Should I tell the truth? Or lie?* Joseph encourages him toward the latter with a subtle nod. Looking back at John, he pulls forth some courage. "Yes, sir. It's very nice. We're happy here."

John smiles. "I am pleased to hear it. What's that you have there?"

"M—My lifejacket." David holds it up. "We're gonna go to the beach today."

"You are?" John morphs his voice into a humouring kind of wispy, and Joseph flinches from the whip of his black glare as it snaps to him, then back to David. He grins again. "Excellent. We're not short on good beaches, so enjoy yourselves." To David's relief, he removes his hand and stands.

Joseph's mouth falls open like he's not sure what to say, and David moves over to him, taking his hand.

John studies father and son, and I can't tell whether the smile that he gives them is genuine. But I can take a good guess that it's not. "Well, I won't keep you," he says. "Nevertheless, is there anything you need, Joseph?"

"Sir?"

Frustration flashes across John's face. "Is there anything you *need* from me?"

"No, Mr. Roth. We're right some fine with what you've provided already."

"Are you quite sure?"

Joseph nods.

"Hmmm." John clasps his hands and raises his chin. The rubies of his cufflinks sparkle like they're mocking the Mathis family. "I've been informed that you are having trouble making your appointments. It is also my understanding that you've missed the last three in a row. Is this true?"

Joseph hesitates. "I'm sorry, sir. I had a mix-up with the dates."

John nods, but the twitch of his eyebrow reveals that he thinks this is a lie. "I see. Well, I hope the expectations outlined in your contract are clear. Do you need me to review it with you?"

"No, sir. I'm very sorry. It won't happen again."

"I should hope not," John says. His black eyes settle back on David, who shifts like someone's holding a flame to his skin. "Some things are too precious to risk for a mere mix up of dates." Then he fixes a glare on Joseph and holds him. The tension is so thick that it could be sliced with a knife. "I'm happy to see you're settling in alright," he says, releasing them and turning to take the door handle. "Give me a call if you need anything clarified."

Joseph steps over to widen the door. "Thank you, Mr. Roth," he breathes.

John flourishes his exit with a scowl. "Have a good time at the beach." Finally, he's gone; footsteps made by expensive soles receding down the hallway.

Despair floods David system as he watches his father close the door. Though Joseph's eyes are wide, they fix on nothing. He looks like he's gone into shock.

CHAPTER 17
I SAT BY THE OCEAN

On the Friday following my first week at school, I decided to take a drive to Stanley Park to have some quiet time to myself. Winding my Toyota around the roundabout at the entrance, I followed the road to the collection of totem poles in search of some peace and tranquility.

It was early June, and the weather had been fantastic so far. The temperatures were perfect, and we seemed to have an abundance of sunny days, which I understood was normal for Vancouver at that time of year. That Friday wasn't any different, and a gentle breeze blew, causing me to be comfortable in the thin sweater that I was wearing. I parked my car and wandered the gravel path over to the totem poles, fascinated while they towered over me in brilliance and colour. Walking from pole to pole, I stopped at each sign and read about their history and meaning, before my thoughts started to wander back to my old life...

It's March in Toronto, and Andy walks through the front door to my house with a small snow drift trailing him. He closes it and shivers, looking at me with the same coldness that blows outside. Breaking our eye-contact, he clasps his hands together and blows his breath into them, before rubbing them on the thick arms of his peacoat. As

I watch him, my first thought is that my boyfriend doesn't look like himself anymore. He's become frigid, stiff, and cruel—just like the Ontarian winters we were raised in—and I'm desperate for the end.

Since the accident, nothing's been the same. He's slipped down a slope of gradual resentment, and I know it's because I've been subconsciously calling another person's name. I have no control over it, but I've told him about it, so now he can hold it against me. I'm used to him taking out his frustration in subtle, little jabs that sting like a spider bite. Not enough to be painful at first, but sure to bug me later.

It's been ten years, and my ears ring when I think about this. About how many days it's been. About how much time we've wasted, just because it's easier to cling to someone familiar than to break up with them. Our relationship is not only toxic, but it's stagnant. Putrid. A festering structure held up by rotted wood that should have been bulldozed long ago. And I can't take it anymore. If I never break up with him, I'll never leave. And if I never leave, then I'll be stuck. Decaying in place, like our relationship. Wasting my life in the comfort zone.

I look at the fireplace and shiver too. Then I wait for the sarcastic greeting that he's sure to shoot me at any minute. I'm nervous because we're about to have a conversation that he's not going to like.

He slips off his shallow boots and tromps across our worn hardwood floor, standing next to the couch that I'm sitting on. I notice that he hasn't bothered to remove his coat. It's a sure sign that he's not going to be here for long. "Em?"

I look away, as our tabby-cat, Sammie, darts into the room, hopping up on the arm of the couch and begging him for attention. Andy runs his hand along Sammie's back, before picking him up and setting him on his lap as he sinks into the couch beside me.

"Alright," he says, with a tone softer than I expected. "What incredibly difficult conversation are we about to have now?"

I sigh, trying to ignore the anxiety that seems to swell whenever he's next to me. I can't even remember the last time I kissed him and meant it. "Andy. I called you because I've decided on something that you're probably not going to be happy about."

He snorts. "Shocker."

"I figured it would be better to talk about it in person." I hate how submissive and quiet my voice is. I wish that I could stand up to him with strength.

"Alright. What is it then?"

I mentally prepare for the backlash, as Sammie steps across us and onto my lap. His paws pinch into my thighs, but I'm grateful for his support even if he's oblivious that he's giving it. "I received an offer letter from the UBC." I gently wind Sammie's tail through my fingers. I need all the comfort that I can get right now.

Andy furrows his brow. "Okay..."

"Andy." I swallow. "I'm going to accept it. I want to go. I think it's the best decision for me right now."

He laughs, but it's bitter. Sammie decides that he's had enough and jumps to the floor with a quiet *thud*. "Wait, let me get this straight. You think moving to *BC* to do your *master's,* where you're an *entire country away from everyone you love*, is the right decision for you right now?"

I study the flames and nod.

"Em, you can't even make breakfast without your parents' advice. How the hell are you going to live on the other side of the country? And even with the *abundance* of universities in Ontario where you could do your master's—including all of those in the city we *live* in—you chose the *University of British Columbia*? What the fuck are you thinking?"

"Andy..."

"What do your parents think about this?"

I shrug. "They're both supportive. They know it's what I want."

"Really." He casts a glance over my shoulder and toward Mum, who's unsuccessfully eavesdropping from the doorway to the kitchen. "You're okay with this?" he says, raising a brown eyebrow. "Lil? You're okay with this?"

Mum rubs the citrine crystal on her necklace between her fingers. "Andy, I know it seems difficult, but you need to be a little understanding—"

"*I* need to be understanding?" he snaps, motioning to me with a flat palm. "My girlfriend is literally abandoning me, and *I* need to be understanding?"

"Andy—"

"Mum, *please*." My blue eyes plead with hers. "Can you give us some space?"

She bridges her brow, before she backs up and leaves.

When I pull my gaze—fucking kicking and screaming—back to his, I find him glaring like he thinks this is crazy. Which, I suppose, to him, it is. He's never been further than a couple hours from Toronto in his life.

"We've been together for ten years," he says. "How could you make a decision like that without talking to me?"

"Because it's my life, Andy. I deserve to decide for myself—"

"Okay, so what? My opinion means nothing anymore?"

I hesitate, because he's kind of hit the nail on the head, and I'm not sure how to say that without being cruel. His opinion means nothing because I *don't want to be with him anymore*. I don't *want* the same old stagnant life anymore. I don't *want* the comfort zone. I want *purpose*.

"You don't care, do you?"

"Stop putting words in my mouth. It's not like—"

"This is fucking painful. You're going to be so far away, and you didn't even consider how that would make me feel, did you? I'm hurt, Em. Like an arrow to the heart. This fucking *sucks*." He puts his head in his hands, and I try to ignore the gaslighting. Problem is, it's working a little. He knows how to push all my buttons, and he's making me feel more guilty with every punch.

When he raises his head again, there's a flare in his hazel eyes that isn't from our fireplace. "But it's not just about that, is it?"

I swallow and try to absorb some warmth from said fireplace. This cold is too much for me. I can't take it.

The grinding at the back of Andy's teeth is so strong that I can hear it. "You have a hidden agenda, don't you? This whole BC thing is just a way to cover it. You know exactly what you're doing, Emily. You *knew* this would end us."

When I speak, my voice is weak. "I think it's for the best." I force myself to look him dead in the eyes and tell the truth. "I don't love you anymore, Andy. It's been a long time coming."

He snuffs. "Okay. Sure. *It's been a long time coming.* Would have been nice if you could have let *me* know." He jerks his shoulders. "So, what? Is that it? You make me come all the way over here through the cold so that you can tell me you don't love me anymore and you're disappearing across the country?"

I nod again. The guilt-meter's rising.

"This could have been a phone call, Em. You can be such a little bitch." He barks out a laugh and gets off the couch, making his way to the door, where he starts to jam his feet back into his boots. "Well, then I'm happy to inform you that your wish is granted, Miss Anderson. It's fucking *over.*"

Tears start to stream down my face, hot against my skin. "I'm sorry, Andy. I never wanted it to end this way."

He steps toward me with his boots leaving puddles of melted snow on our hardwood. "You're a fucking liar. You were just waiting for an excuse, weren't you?"

I watch his blurred shape in silence.

He growls as he turns away. "Fine. Go to Vancouver then, Em. See if I give a fuck. Go to Vancouver, then." He yanks the door open, causing a rush of air to push inside, flourished with another group of snowflakes. "I hope all your dreams come true out there."

Then, the door slams, and he's gone. Just like that. My boyfriend of over ten years is gone.

Free from him, I burst into tears, and Mum rushes forward to take me in her arms. Though it's a bit of a relief, I bury my face in her chest, and she strokes my hair, not phased when her fingertips brush the deep scar that she knows I have there. Patient and compassionate, she lets me take the time I need to release my heavy emotions. And there, in her arms, I shed the last tears that I'll ever shed for Andrew Moore.

As I continued to wander the totem poles in Stanley Park, I drew some inspiration from my new world to help ease the pain of the day-dreamt memory. The sea breeze tossed the thick waves of my hair as I followed the gravel path to the SeaWall, where the city skyline stood in its magnificence. Andy's voice echoed through my mind: *Go to Vancouver then, Em. Go to Vancouver, then.*

The evening sun played on the windows of the downtown core and made the harbour shimmer like millions of diamonds. The Lookout and the white sails of Canada Place stood proud among the condos and offices of Coal Harbour, like they were encouraging me wordlessly. I crossed my arms over my chest.

Well, Andy. That's exactly what I did. And I still believe there's a bigger reason that I'm here.

There was something about Vancouver that couldn't compare to home. Something that made me come alive every time I watched the mountains or the skyline. Something that made me believe that I had a bigger role in life than being stuck in my comfort zone. Something that told me I belonged.

I thought about my new family here and how supportive they'd been, before thinking of David specifically. He was feeling better now, but on Tuesday he'd pulled himself out of bed, still sick, and forced himself to go to work. He'd dismissed my suggestion of going to the doctor and shrugged it off, stating that he was fine. I was worried because he clearly wasn't. He was barely able to function that morning, but he claimed that he couldn't miss another day of work. Something about needing the money. I'd stood in front of the door with my hands on my hips, but he'd given me a gentle smile and a quick half-hug before he left me with my worries.

And I was also confused about the most recent memory I'd seen. It was clear that Johnathan Roth had some sort of hold on the Mathis family, but what the hold was, I didn't know. What would make the CEO of a pharma giant come to someone's apartment and intimidate them? And what did he mean when he confronted Joseph about missing the "appointments"? What appointments?

Carol had said that John was murdered for a monetary debt, but what was Joseph doing to pay that debt? What did he get sick of? What was big enough to make him pull the trigger?

What did he do to you, David? What did he do to make your father risk everything to take his life?

I wished I could ask him outright, but there was no chance in hell that he'd ever answer it, and even less chance of me wanting to be that disrespectful. But this whole murder thing had my gears grinding, and I didn't think that my curiosity would be able to let this go. There was something that Roth Pharmaceuticals was doing that was fishy here. Fishier than the smell of the sea that was presently wafting toward me.

David Mathis, what happened to you?

I didn't know, but I really wanted to find out. If anything, it would only bring me closer to him, and maybe it would help me fulfill my purpose here. The Universe would give me the signs. I knew it would. I just had to be patient. But one thing was already clear— There was a hidden history between Joseph Mathis and Johnathan Roth, and it was a history so damaging that it left ripples of hatred between their sons.

Two mothers pushing strollers pulled me out of my head. They broke their conversation about getting their kids to sleep through the night to say hi to me, and I said it back as they passed. Then I glanced beyond them as they followed the SeaWall further north. And there on the hill—like a human validation for my intuition— Barrett Roth lounged shirtless in the grass.

I blinked a couple times. Nope, I wasn't dreaming. Here he was again, and now I'd have to decide what to do about it. I watched him for a minute while I mulled it over. He was lying on his back with his arms folded behind his head, the red hair on his underarms and chest betraying the faux brown of his wave. He was wearing a pair of jogging shorts and running shoes, with a coin-sized heart monitor strapped around his right biceps. Now that he was shirtless, I saw that he had two tattoos. One that was sprawled across his left shoulder, and the other was on his right forearm below his elbow. I was too far away to tell what they were. Though he had good muscle tone, and certainly wasn't a small or skinny man, I could see the faint outline of his ribs framing the top of his abs.

Where did you come from, Barrett? Why here? Why now?

My first idea was to turn and run back to my Yaris before he spotted me, but my instinct held me firm in place. Instead, I felt it shift and push me *toward* him, and I fought against it, afraid of the strange electric feeling that held me the first time I met him. He made me feel like I couldn't find my footing. He made me stumble from the lightning bolts of his black gaze.

Then I remembered what had happened last weekend. How he and David had locked in that resentful stare-down, with Greg giving him a *double-whammy* afterwards. What was I supposed to say about that? Was I supposed to apologize, or play it cool in the face of the enemy?

Drawing a determined breath, I let my feet push me forward

before my brain could churn it around any further. If I was going to find out what happened to David, how Barrett and I were fated, and how all this shit was linked, I'd have to be brave. It couldn't hurt to play both sides a little.

I moved toward Barrett with my soles sinking in the grass, reminded of something that Mum had once said: *Coincidence is a disguise of fate.* Hopefully that would be enough to get me to open my mouth and make words come out.

When I was close enough to get a good look at him, I saw that his eyes were closed, and he was basking in the sun like a cat on a windowsill. The tattoo that draped over his left shoulder turned out to be a realistic, black-and-grey tiger; its front half clawing onto his chest with its mouth open in a defensive snarl. The back half disappeared behind his shoulder and was hidden in the grass.

Tiger spirited, I thought. *Oh no.*

I'd never met a person whose spirit had the animal form of a tiger (that I was aware of). But I bet if I flipped through Mum's massive book on the subject, I'd find words like cunning, cocky, stubborn, self-centered, overconfident, a tendency to be assholes. All accurate of what I'd seen from Barrett Roth so far.

Explains a lot.

The tattoo on his forearm, I now noticed, was a silver crown with incredible detail. Its base spanned the width of his arm, and it was jeweled with sapphires; each point rising in the form of a *fleur-de-lis*. In the center, a diamond-shaped sapphire held a punctuating *fleur-de-lis* at its top, with two others tilting from either side of the sapphire to form the front of the crown. I thought it was beautiful. Then realized how damn close I was to be able to think it was beautiful.

The grass sprouted from under my white sneakers as I froze, and my heart lurched like it was trying to power my voice. "Barrett?" I hadn't meant for it to come out like a question, but it was a *start.*

He opened his eyes and propped himself on his elbows, raising a copper eyebrow. Tilting his head, he sat up, resting his arms across his knees. "Hello."

"Hey!" I summoned all my keep-it-cool-ness as I lowered myself next to him. "Fancy meeting you here."

Oh God, Em. Play it cool, *not* corny...

He smirked, listing a finger toward me. "Emily, right?"

"That's right." I crossed my legs and begged my heart to slow down.

He looked out to the city. "I've astonished myself. I'm horrible with names. Especially in the absence of my assistant whispering them into my ear." His raven gaze moved to mine, and the hairs on my arms started to rise. "It must have stuck with me."

We fell into an awkward silence, and I racked my brain for what to say to him that wasn't a direct question about why his father was murdered. "What are you doing out here?" I asked, instead.

"Running," he said, simply. "It is my refuge."

I choked down the beginning of a hiccup. "You come all the way out here to run?"

"I live here, Emily. This is my *backyard*, so to speak."

Right. Carol *had* mentioned that he'd escaped downtown after moving out of the Roth Estate.

"Oh, really? Where?"

He pinched his right eye closed and pointed to a high rise across the harbour that was next to the Convention Center. "There."

"Coal Harbour," I said. "Cool." Because only a man with money to burn would own a condo in Coal Harbour. An area so expensive that only the elite rich can afford to live there. "Must be nice." I couldn't keep the sarcasm out of my tone.

He chuckled and ignored it. "Very much so."

I bit my lip as I continued to study the skyline, still highly aware that his attention was on me. It was like being caught in his grip—a tiger's grip—and part of me could feel his father's energy coming through him.

Hesitant, I glanced over and shot him a smile. "Uh, listen. I wanted to tell you that I'm sorry for the way that my roommates acted the other night. We were, um, drinking, and it was kind of rude of them."

He pinched his brow in and out of a furrow. "I'm sorry?"

I wasn't surprised that he didn't remember what I was talking about. He was probably too busy being the CFO of his family's company to deal with such mediocre things. Such *kid's stuff*.

"Um. The other night when we saw you at Limelight." The confusion stayed on his face, so I added, "You know. When they, uh, gave you the finger and... *other* gestures."

To my relief, he grinned. "Kid, if I had a dollar for every time someone gave me the finger, I'd be a richer man than I am now. Don't worry about it." He shifted in the grass. "And anyway, I don't recall what you're talking about. I was a bit fucked up myself."

"Oh. Okay. Fair enough. Sorted." Swallowing, I plunged my hand into the grass and began to pull it out, strand by strand, as I questioned how much I should share with him. I was very aware that this was unfamiliar (enemy?) territory, and it felt like walking on eggshells. I crushed bits of grass between my fingertips. They left my skin green and waxy in revenge. "I thought I should apologize, anyway." I shrugged. "I know that you and David don't have the best relationship..." I trailed off, unsure of how else to say it.

"David..." He drew out the name.

"Mathis," I said.

"Mathis," he echoed. "That's right. You were with him. I remember now. And who is David Mathis to you?"

"My roommate." I tried to keep my tone factual and calm because I wasn't sure how he'd respond. "We live together down in Ladner."

He smirked and held me for a moment before he said, "Do you not realize that you're fraternizing with the enemy?"

I sighed to show him that I didn't find this as funny as he did. "That's not the way I see it, Barrett. I don't want to get caught up with what happened between you two. At least, not without having enough information to make my own judgement of either side."

This, oddly enough, was what seemed to trigger him. His expression shifted cold, and his gaze dropped even colder. God, he looked like his dad. "What is it that you think you know, Emily?"

I straightened my spine like he'd pushed my back up against a wall. "Nothing, Barrett. He hasn't really explained anything, to be honest. All I know is that he doesn't like you. And, I mean, I don't *know* you. So I don't want to use that as judgement."

I was hoping that my vulnerability would get him to slip up and reveal something useful to me. Or, at the very least, get him to start *thinking* about trusting me.

But he snuffed and looked back to the view. "I don't fault him for that. I'm not an easy man to like, and I'm conscious of it." His expression fell as he skimmed the city. "I am the son of Johnathan Roth. What is there to like?"

"What does that have to do with anything?"

At first, he didn't answer. He blinked as the breeze tussled the top of his faux brown hair. Then, with his voice in a murmur, he said, "Everything."

Without thinking, I laid a gentle hand on the toned muscle of his biceps, finding his skin warm beneath. He tensed at my touch, but the turning of his head was mild. Like he was curious why I'd do such a thing. "I'm very sorry about what happened to your dad," I said.

His Adam's apple dipped in his throat as he swallowed, but I caught the tensing of his jaw and the flare through his obsidian as he tried to mask it. "That's very kind. Thank you, Emily."

I dropped my hand, not wanting to hold the heaviness that told me I'd overstepped. Our time together was coming to a quick and natural end, and I had a feeling that soon he'd be literally running away from me. But I couldn't let him go without bridging the connection. I *had* to make sure that I saw him again. My intuition was sure of it.

I inhaled bravery before I spoke. "Hey—uh—Barrett? I know—I

mean—I *think...*" With a sigh, I pulled my phone from my pocket and opened it, offering it to him. "I think you should put your number in there."

His face shifted into a smile so slow that it was almost mocking. "You're asking me for my number?"

"Yeah. You know—uh—Carol. She thought it'd be good for us to be friends. And I, uh, need friends here. You know. Because I'm new?"

He drew his lips into a tight O and nodded. "Utilizing my grandmother as leverage for my number. I don't think I've encountered that one before, Emily."

I huffed out a genuine chuckle. "It's all I've got." I craned my neck as I watched him navigate to my contacts. "Oh, and—between you and me—David's opinion of you isn't going to affect mine."

One copper eyebrow flashed as he tapped the keyboard with his thumbs. "Duly noted."

"And I'm going to decide whether I like you or not, on my own terms."

He grinned. "Guess I'd better not fuck it up then."

I laughed, enjoying the contrasting warmth from his smile when he looked over at me.

Then his attention locked on my face again. "Let me make an enquiry of you, Emily. If I may."

"Alright." I said, picking at the grass, and trying not to playfully question the preppy language that he seemed to use. "*Enquire* away."

He shifted his focus back onto the phone as he finished entering his number. "Tell me what you think of my brother."

"Travis? Well—I mean—he was a little standoffish when he drove me home, but I think it's just because he was busy. After the Roth Banquet, I realized he's actually really kind, generous, and respectful." I chuckled. "Easy on the eyes, to be completely honest." I shrugged, releasing some of the broken grass to drift away on the breeze. "I mean, so far, I think I like him."

"Right," he said, as he handed me my phone. "Well, I'm not my brother, kiddo. Try to remember that before you think about texting me to *rendezvous* as friends."

I wasn't sure what he meant by that, but I swiftly pulled myself up, slipped my phone into my back pocket, and brushed the dirt from my butt. The success of getting his number was telling me that it was the best time to leave. "Right. *The Bad-Roth*, isn't it?"

"So they say."

Braver now, I shot him a playful smirk of my own. "Hmmm. I think I'll be the judge of that."

He smirked back, and I gave him a small wave before I walked away, making a bee line toward the parking lot by the totem poles. There was something about having his number in my phone that rejuvenated a bit of that power that Andy had taken from me over the years. I reveled in it as I skipped across the bike lane ahead of some motivated cyclists.

As I stepped down to the pavement of the parking lot beside my Yaris, I let myself bask in a small bit of the confidence that had been returned after being robbed by my ex-boyfriend.

Or maybe it was just the aftereffects of an encounter with Barrett Roth— A man with such an abundance of his own that he could have given me some along with his number.

CHAPTER 18
I HOPE YOU DANCE

The next morning, David Mathis knocked on my door and asked if he could come in. I ran my fingers through my disaster-of-a-hairdo and brushed it to one side to try to make it look *some sort* of good. "Yeah. Come in, David."

My door swung open, and he appeared, carrying his warm grin and a fresh cup of coffee. I inhaled as he moved to my side and sat down by my feet. "Morning."

Returning his grin, I tried not to think about how I had his enemy's number in my phone. "Morning, sunshine. I hope that's for me."

He went to take a sip. "Nah." Then, after catching the fall in my face, he clicked his tongue and offered it. "Of course, it's for you, Em. You're too serious. Relax."

"Hey, I don't joke around when it comes to coffee." The heat of the mug was welcome in my fingers, and the first sip was as delicious as it was needed. "You're an angel, David Mathis. Thank you."

"My pleasure." His smile was as warm as the green in his eyes, and I got lost for a moment as I watched him. He was so hot that I could've slipped my feet under his thigh to get the chill out of my toes. "You got plans today?"

I slurped my caffeine fix. "Not really." Then I nudged him with my foot. "I figured I'd hang with you."

"Okay. Right on." He picked at a piece of fuzz on my comforter and dropped his gaze. "But I, um, was gonna go see my dad. And this is gonna be weird and stuff. But I thought… I dunno. Maybe you could come with me? I mean, maybe meeting him will help you understand a bit about why I feel the way I do about the Roths. I know I haven't told you much, and you wanna know, but it's… a lot."

I set the coffee on my nightstand and shifted forward to take his hand. "I imagine it is, David. And I can't tell you how much I appreciate how vulnerable that offer is for you."

His grip tightened around mine. "It's jus'… after we talked about trust, I realized how much I wanted to build that with you. And yeah, it's only been a month, but I wanna share a bit of my world with you. To be honest, I've never got this close with someone so fast, but you've been so kind and caring, and I love hanging out with you. *You've* been the angel, Em. And I know you wanna know me. I want that too. I mean, within certain bounds… And I wanna know you." He tossed a hand through his curls. "Fuck, I'm really not being smooth here."

"It's okay." Giggling, I kissed his hand before I could think about it. "I'm touched. I really am. And I want to see the real you, so you don't have to be afraid to show him."

He smiled, and for a moment, looked at my lips.

I thought about the club and how hurt I'd been that he didn't want to kiss me, but sober Emily had already let that go. We were still determining what was right for us. Still learning about each other as we did the awkward dance between friends and *maybe something more*. He'd had a right to be hesitant, and there was no harm in taking it slow. But I very much wondered if he was going to kiss me then…

"The Roths are kinda the reason he's in there," he said, pivoting back to his dad with all the tender smoothness of a second hand on a clock.

I hesitated. If he was going to be vulnerable, then so was I. "Yeah, I know. I kind of… looked it up online?" Then I braced for a reaction, but it never came.

Instead, he shrugged. "I figured you would at some point. You've been looking at Roth Pharma for school, and a quick Google search about them would have easily revealed it."

"I'm sorry," I said. "I should have told you that I looked it up..."

He shrugged again. "I've been a dick about it in the past. I don't blame you."

We fell silent for a minute. Sitting there. His hand in mine. I thought about the energy that was flowing from my heart chakra to his, and how fucking incredible that was. Then about how much I was turning into my mum.

"So, do you wanna come?"

I jolted. "Y–Yeah. Of course! I'd love to come. What time?" His vulnerability in asking me to meet his dad was so deep and I was honoured that he'd asked.

"Whenever you decide to get dressed and—well—shower." He leaned forward and nudged my shoulder. "*Hint, hint.*"

"Oh, shut up, ya Bluenoser."

"Heh," he said, breaking out a covert grin.

I made a face, and we broke into a playful tussle. Every time he tickled me, I felt like I'd was having a near-death experience and catching a glimpse of heaven. The spots he hit always seemed to feel good without also feeling annoying. Some sort of David-magic.

He ended up on top of me, and the pull from his lips like a gravitational field. I couldn't seem to keep mine out of orbit. I propped myself on my elbows, mouth moving forward, destination: David, when—

I just felt honoured to have been invited to meet a murderer, my thoughts rudely interrupted.

I paused.

It sounded strange—I know. But maybe my introduction to Joseph would give me another piece to the puzzle of Johnathan Roth's murder. And it could only bring David and I closer... Which I wanted... Which I really, really wanted.

Seeing the look on my face, David smiled, pulled himself up, and gave my leg a pat. "Come get me when you're ready."

A tad disappointed, I turned, grabbed my coffee, and drained it. "Just give me two shakes. I won't be long."

Outside, a gentle rain was falling. I let it refresh my skin when I walked over to David's Mazda, tilting my face to the sky, and letting it pepper me. He unlocked his car, and I slid onto the worn fabric of his passenger seat. He started the whining engine, cranked the temperature dial to hot, and turned up the fans. It wasn't cold, but it was cool enough to not sit right with him. I'd learnt that he liked the heat.

We set off, and I took over his aux cord to throw on our trip's soundtrack, asking him where the prison was.

"Mission," he said. "It's about an hour away."

The rain had moistened the roads, but it didn't slow us down. Within minutes, we were out of downtown Ladner and heading toward the highway. I spotted a Tim Hortons along the way and—dying for a Timmie's fix and a bit of breakfast—I asked him if we could go through the drive-through. Like the good friend that he was growing into, he agreed.

We ordered some coffee, breakfast sandwiches, and donuts, then, fueled up for the drive, we set off on route to the highway.

I ate my sandwich like I was feeding my inner she-wolf, and then popped his halfway from its bag so that he could eat it one-handed after he merged onto the flowing highway. After he was finished, I offered his donut to him in the same way, which was easy because he'd ordered a chocolate glazed. I, however, had been adventurous and had chosen a powdered, raspberry-filled one. I struggled as I held the bag below my mouth to catch the sliding sugar. David shared his glances between me and the road and chuckled while he watched me munch on it.

"I'm aware this looks ridiculous," I told him. "But it's *so* worth it." When I was finished, I wiped my powdered fingers on a napkin, and stuffed it back in the bag. "See? Didn't even get any in your car, either."

"That's because you left it all on your face." He reached over and wiped the corner of my mouth with his thumb, licking it off.

Gulp.

My groin ached, and I opened my coffee to distract myself. "Hey. We should have picked up a donut for your dad." I paused. "Does he even like donuts?"

David smiled. "Apple fritters are his favourite, but they won't let us take it in, anyway. They don't let you bring anything that isn't sealed."

"Right. Makes sense." I licked the stray dough from my teeth. "Do you ever bring anything for him?"

He flashed his eyebrows as he scanned the highway ahead of us. "Almost every time I see him. He'd be pissed if I didn't."

"I bet he looks forward to it."

David nodded, throwing a glimpse over his shoulder before merging into the middle lane. "Yep."

I watched the couple in the car next to us mime an argument. "I mean, it must be hard for him. Being locked up in prison." David's jaw tensed, and it reminded me of how sensitive this topic was for him. I cleared my throat and switched to a more positive tone. "So, what are we bringing him today, then?"

He hovered his hand over the heat from his vent. "Jus' a couple of his favourite magazines and a big packet of chocolate-covered almonds." He paused. "And you."

Wiggling my fingers around my coffee cup, I tried to control the fuzziness flowing through my veins. "I have to be honest; I'm really touched that you asked. I know how important your dad is to you."

"It jus' *feels* right," he admitted.

And yep. Said fuzziness definitely wasn't coming from the coffee or the air vent.

I took small sips and relaxed, thinking of David's memories as I watched the fog loom over the mountains to the north. From what I'd seen, Joseph had been a loving, caring father, who'd taken the chance to move to Vancouver for a better life for his son. What he'd done seemed uncharacteristic, and therefore must have been triggered by something *John* had done. What were these "appointments" that he was bugging Joseph about? And what did Joseph mean when he said that they were alright with what John had already given them?

"David?"

"Yeah, Em?"

I hesitated with how to frame my question, before settling on a gentle curiosity. I didn't want to hurt him. "How did you do it?" I tried. "I mean, after your dad went away, you had no one. You were alone, and you were so young. How'd you survive?"

I watched him graze his teeth over his bottom lip as he calculated what else he was going to share. "Honestly, I was shocked, but I had no choice but to pull myself out. I was sixteen, so I was old enough to start work. People at school helped me find a job. I struggled with a foster family until I was nineteen and then left them. Then I jus'... learned to take care of myself." He grabbed his coffee and downed some.

I ran my eyes along the length of the swollen Fraser River in the north. "Where did you live after foster care?"

He swallowed the coffee. "I got another apartment in the Downtown East Side."

"Yeah, but you were only nineteen. Even if you were working, how could you afford an entire apartment on your own?"

He paused, drumming his fingers on the steering wheel. "I had help."

"From, like, a roommate or something?"

A flare of green told me I was pushing it. "Okay. Now you're asking questions that you don't need to know the answers to again."

"I'm sorry, David. I don't mean to cross the boundaries of what you're willing to share. I really don't." I dropped my voice just above a whisper and spoke before I realized that I said it out loud. "I just wanna understand why your dad did what he did."

He visually winced. "I don't want you to know that."

Triggered. Joseph must have been triggered by something.

"John must have done—"

"Emily, stop!"

His demand plunged us into silence, and I dropped my gaze to the car floor in regret. I didn't mean to twist the knife that was lodged in his heart. I really didn't. "I'm sorry..."

The wrinkle of his nose was a sharp contrast to the cheery pop song that was streaming from my iPhone. He took that time to compose himself, but the Mazda lurched as his foot fell heavier on the gas.

We passed a few other cars through the spray from the rain, and then he merged back into the middle lane, quieter now. "Listen. At the end of the day, I really like you, and I'm happy when you're around. And I know I said that I wanna show you part of my world, but not so you can pry, okay? It doesn't matter. Things are how they are." He shoulder-checked to pass a slow Ford. "There's a sayin' in my family that goes: If you en' at the christening, you shouldn't be at the wedding. You understand what I mean?"

"Yeah. I think I got that one."

"I wanna focus on the present and the future. Not the past."

The thought of my accident popped into my head, and I realized I wanted the same thing.

"Right?"

Though my curiosity was far from quenched, I smiled. "Right."

"Okay."

I exhaled and took another sip of my coffee before I turned the emotional tables and nudged him. "For the record, I'm happy when I'm around you too."

He smiled back, but I could tell he was still uncomfortable, so I dropped the subject of his past completely. I scrolled through my phone and found a Bob Marley song, hoping that it would ease some of his tension. And I was vindicated when it made him grin.

Soon, we were leaving the highway, and we crossed over the roaring Fraser River, passing a sign that said, *Welcome to Mission!* I watched a train go over the parallel railway bridge, its engine darkened and slick from the rain. I tried to track the streets we were following, but it was hard because the route wasn't straight forward.

David navigated it like he'd been doing it for years.

We left the town from the north, and began to climb the base of a mountain, before coming to a winding drive that was marked with black signs that said things like "Correctional Institution." A sense of gloom loomed over me when we came to the first gate.

We stopped for a brief exchange, before being waved through by the security guards. Inside, multiple facilities were sprawled across the plateau of the mountain, with a driveway leading off to each one. This prison system was so extensive that it housed minimum, medium, and maximum-security buildings, and I swallowed as we turned down the path to the maximum.

Then we came to a second gate, where the wall was topped with towers of armed guards and double sets of barbed wire. David and I were both asked to provide ID, but the guards were familiar with the man beside me and his rusted, grey Mazda. They let us through without any issue, and it gave me a good indication of what I'd face if I ever came back alone. Then I wondered why I'd ever come back alone.

David weaved into a spot in the parking lot that was marked "Visitor Reception," humming as he shifted the car into park.

"What?" I said.

He asked me if I'd worn a bra, and I started to blush. Of course, I had. Why wouldn't I? He cursed under his breath and tried to hide a smirk when he told me I'd have to take the underwire out.

"*Excuse me?*"

"Uh. Yeah. Sorry. It's a thing." The way he was getting flustered was painfully cute.

"And why, exactly, were you thinking about my bra?"

"Um. Well. You know. Mental inventory, and stuff."

"Uh huh."

"I'm sorry Em," he said, stifling a chuckle. "I should have told you to wear one of those sports ones. I don't usually have to think about this kind of thing."

"Yeah, well, I can't take the underwire out," I said. "It's not that kind of bra!"

"Well... then... uh..." He adjusted something on the dash that very much didn't need adjusting right then. "You're jus' gonna have to take it off, I guess."

"Here? You're telling me that I need to take it off *here*?"

"Either that or they make you take it off in there. It'll set off the metal detector."

I paused. "You're being serious, aren't you?"

"'Fraid so, princess."

I sighed and pulled off my jacket.

Fuck, I'm about to look like such a dumbass in front of him!

Luckily, I'd chosen to wear a fitted, black sweater with a t-shirt neckline, and my bra was convertible, meaning that it could be undone at the straps. Eyeing David, I shifted forward and reached up under my sweater. He stared out the windshield and looked like he was trying not to laugh.

After a minute of struggle, I pinched my face. "*God.* Alright. You're gonna have to help me. I can't get the shoulder straps."

He let his smirk fly, but kept his eyes averted as he slipped his hand up my back to release the straps. My hunger flared at his touch, and I didn't think my face had ever been so hot when I pulled the bra from under my sweater and wrapped it in my windbreaker. Afterwards, I shifted myself and adjusted my bun.

"You look great," David said.

I gave him a playful smack. "Oh, shush. I just hope, for your sake, it's not freezing in there."

He grinned. "I hope, for my sake, that it is." Dodging my second smack with a laugh, he popped open the car door and stepped out into the rain, grabbing the bag for his dad from the trunk.

I pulled my jacket around my shoulders and followed him, shivering as the spring drizzle sprinkled my neck and face.

Inside the visitor's entrance, there was a vestibule with a second set of doors which were locked until they buzzed us through. On the other side of that, a woman with a short, blonde bob sat behind a sheet of plexiglass. She smiled at David as we came through.

He flashed one back as he stepped up to the counter. "Hey Margret. Long time, no see! What are you sayin'?"

She shrugged and nodded. "I've been doing alright. Thanks for asking, David. I only got back a couple weeks ago."

"Glad to see you're feeling better."

"Thank you." She turned her friendliness toward me. "And who's this?"

David put an arm around my shoulders, his hand enveloping my right with all of its warmth. His touch immediately reminded me of my bra-less boobs. "My girlfriend, Emily."

I shot him a look, and he returned it with one that said, *Play along.*

"Ah. Lucky girl, then! Hi, Emily." She tapped the dip in the counter that ran under the plexiglass. "Can I just get both of your IDs?"

David nodded, and I crossed my fingers that my Ontarian license would fly as I slipped in under the plexiglass with his British Columbian. I hadn't yet made the effort to get it updated. That was next month's problem.

Margret raised an eyebrow and looked at me as she held the blue Trillium-stamped card, but she dropped it back without saying anything. "I'll add her to your father's list of approved visitors, then." She clacked away on her keyboard, before slipping David a small key. "Right. You're all set. You know the drill, Mr. Mathis."

"Like clockwork," he said. Then he began to walk me through the process of signing the visitor's log and locking up our things. They made us leave everything but the key, and I was even asked to slip off my ring.

"D—Do I really have to?" I asked Margret. "I—It's really valuable."

"Afraid so," she said. "I don't make the rules. And don't worry. It'll be safe in the locker."

I watched the glimmering emeralds with apprehension as the door to the locker closed.

Margret waved us through to a hallway that led to the metal detectors.

"Your *girlfriend*?" I said to David under my breath, as we walked under the blinding florescent lights.

"They're pretty strict, so it makes it easier if you're related in some way. Less hassle, ya know? It was the only way I saw around it."

"I see." I elbowed him. "You could've at least bought me dinner first."

He grinned. "Alright. I owe you that."

And hey, I couldn't really be mad, considering I'd pulled the reverse on him at the club last week.

Guards were waiting for us at the metal detector, which had an x-ray like what you'd find at airport security. David placed the key and bag with his father's gifts in the bin, and then removed his shoes before they waved him through without issue. I followed suit, but the machine blared when I stepped through, and the guard pulled me to the side to scan me with a handheld one. It beeped as he ran it over my wrist, and I pushed up my sleeve, rotating my arm to show him it was bare.

"I have pins from an old accident," I said.

He nodded, and then searched my shoes, before clearing me to proceed with David.

"You broke your wrist?" David asked, as we followed the hallway toward another set of doors.

"Yeah. When I was a teenager." Images of my accident flared, and I shoved them away. Afterward, I didn't elaborate.

We were let through the first set of doors, and then came to a second, which led into the visiting areas of the prison. To the right were booths with receivers for non-contact visits, and to the left was an open room for contact. A kind guard told David that Joseph had been behaving himself, so they were still going to give us a contact visit, even though this was the first time he'd brought a guest. David grinned as he thanked him, and we were told to go to the left and wait inside. Joseph would be along shortly.

The area for contact visits looked like a high school cafeteria. There were two sets of doors on either side—one for the visitor, and one for the prisoner—with guards stationed at each one. Inside, the room was filled with the quiet murmur of other prisoners receiving visits from their loved ones.

The plastered seat chilled the back of my thighs when we sat at a table diagonal from a couple, of which the man was incarcerated. He was dressed in a red jumpsuit, his hair hung in straggles from his head, and he had face tattoos. I shivered when he looked at me. The woman he was with turned and glared suspiciously. Her matted hair didn't form any kind of shape.

I swallowed and pulled my sleeves down, before looking away.

"You okay, Em?" David's warmth was welcome as he put his arm around my shoulders.

Though I was tapping the table, I broke out an assuring tone. "I'm fine. Just a new world, is all."

His green eyes softened with understanding. "There's no need to be fussy. My dad's not a monster. He's only being punished because he slayed one. You'll see."

Easy for you to say. I think nervousness is reasonable when meeting a murderer.

Despite the thought, I put a hand on his knee. "I believe you, David."

He looked at me like no one had ever told him that before. Then squeezed me. "Thanks for coming."

We exchanged smiles, and I fought the urge to kiss him in the middle of a damn prison.

Suddenly, the door at the other end of the room clicked, and my heart leapt as Joseph Mathis stepped through in chains. The guard escorting him started to unlock the cuffs around his wrists and ankles, and as I watched, I realized that the man across the room was different to the one I'd seen in his son's memories. His features were now worn and dull, and the wrinkles on his skin were prominent from the stress of prison life. He had multiple scars on his face that looked like they were once deep cuts—the most notable being the one which was drawn across his right cheek. It ran all the way from the corner of his mouth to his ear. The black curls which once matched David's were gone, and his head was shaved down to the scalp. He was dressed in a red sweatshirt and pants, with the number that now identified him marked on his chest. He rubbed his wrists, and I thought about a wolf that had been snatched from the wild, beaten into submission, and forced to spend the rest of his life in a cage.

Joseph blinked lethargically. He spent a moment soothing his bruised skin, and I wondered how long he'd spent in handcuffs to get them. Then, his sunken eyes flared with what looked like hope. He'd seen David, who'd left our table to go to him. Joseph shot an apprehensive look at the guard, before he used what little energy he had to jog forward and catch his son. The two met in a tight embrace emanating with love, and Joseph kissed David on the cheek, his fingers braced in the back of David's curls. The other prisoner watched them and let a little bit of endearment play on his lips.

When they pulled apart, Joseph held David at arm's length, and they exchanged a few words in private. As David spoke out of earshot, he looked back at me, and I thought about how I'd never seen him happier. Joseph held his shoulders as they walked over, and I stood to meet them.

"Dad," David said, as we came together. "This is Emily."

Though Joseph's smile was fatigued, it was welcoming. "Hello, me love."

God, he sounded like... well... a *dad*. An average, every day Canadian dad, forced to live an unprecedented life.

He clasped my hand in both of his, and I recognized the same warmth that came from his son. Then I remembered that those hands had once held the gun that ended the life of Johnathan Roth. "So, *this* is Emily." He shot a furtive glance at David, who cleared his throat as he sat beside me.

"Nice to meet you, Mr. Mathis," I managed.

His dull grin widened as we separated and sat. "Please. Call me Joseph. And thank you for coming to see me. David never brings anybody, so it's a nice change." David's expression fell, and Joseph offered his upturned palm on the table. "Give me your hand, bu'y." He gifted his son with a compassionate squeeze and smiled. "What I mean to say is, he's never really been comfortable, considering what I am."

I picked at my thumbnail. "To be honest, I was a bit surprised when he asked me. But he's been an amazing friend since I moved, and we've become close."

"For sure," David agreed.

"He's always been a good boy," Joseph said, "so I'm not surprised.

But I'm sorry to tell you there's not much to be excited about. I'm nothing but an old dog, locked in a cage for the rest of his life."

"Not for the rest of his life," David said, shooting his father an admonishing look. "Not forever."

Joseph squeezed his hand again but said nothing. His weary gaze turned back to me. "Anyway, it's nice of you to come. I don't get to see beautiful things very much anymore."

"Thank you, Joseph." But I was staring at the hand that held David's. The hand that I was sure had trembled before it gained the strength to pull the trigger. Three times.

David shifted like he could read my thoughts. "So, Dad. What are you at?"

Joseph frowned and then shrugged. "Last week we got in some new blood. A young man. They say he murdered his wife and child." He turned and shared a captious exchange with the other prisoner, whose face turned as cold as ice. "Proper bastard," Joseph spat when he turned back. "Anyhow, everyone's having a conniption fit because it takes a special kind of evil to destroy his own blood." He paused. "Those young boys, they're all forming groups again. Getting upset. Things have been tense. I'm an old man staying out of the way. You spend enough time in hell, you see every devil, and you know which to fight. Anyway, that's only what he's been convicted of. There are two sides to every story."

"Every dog's got his day," David said.

"That's right, son," Joseph said. "It en' the first time I've encountered such evil."

My intrigue lit up like a torch. "What do you mean by that, Joseph? When have you—?"

David cleared his throat in disapproval.

Joseph's jaw tensed, before he blinked like he'd forgotten I was there. "Emily. I'm sorry. I'm talkin' as if it's only me and my boy. There's no need to talk about such things. Let's talk about somethin' else." He jerked his chin at David's gift bag. "What'd you bring me today, bu'y?"

214

David pulled out the chocolate-covered almonds and a couple of magazines. A copy of *Men's Health*, and something about boats. "Thought you'd like these, Dad."

Joseph's expression brightened as he took the almonds. "Ah, I've gotta be careful with these. Those boys inside will swap stuff for them, for sure." With a scarred hand, he sprawled the magazines on the table, before picking up the boat one and sifting through it. "My son knows me. Thank you, David." He landed on something and laid it flat between us. "Hey. Look, bu'y. It's an old dayboat, like the first one I had for fishin'. You remember?"

David grinned. "Yeah, Dad. That's why I thought you'd like it."

"Did you do a lot of fishing back East?" I asked.

"Oh yeah, I've spent my fair time on the sea, Emily. That used to be my job before..." Joseph trailed off; energy saddening with every second. "Anyway. It doesn't matter. I'm being a sook." Father and son exchanged solemn glances, and I wondered what made them leave the East when they both seemed to miss it so much.

Hoping to raise the vibe, I asked a question that I'd thought about, but had never gotten around to asking David. "Um, what does *being a sook* mean, by the way?" I motioned to myself. "Sorry. Ontarian. We don't use that."

Joseph smacked a hand on the table and looked up with a playful tinge. "Seriously? Does this boy not speak Nova Scotian anymore?" His gaze flashed between us. "Well, get on yer moose, Dave. You need to teach this beautiful girl!"

"Oh, trust me, Joseph, he speaks plenty of Nova Scotian. I'm just slow to learn." I laughed.

"Good," he said, flipping back through the magazine. "Even though we come from away, I never meant you to be so westernized that you forget, David. Holy mackerel."

"Uh... What's a mackerel?" I asked.

Father and son broke out into joyous laughter, and I was so touched that I had no time to be embarrassed about it.

Joseph held his stomach before he settled an appreciative eye on me. "Ah, Emily, me love. It's been a long time since I've laughed like that. Thank you."

I was proud that I'd given him some happiness in such a dark place. "Glad to be of service."

Who could imagine that my shortcomings in Eastern slang would come in useful?

David reached under the table and squeezed my hand gratefully. Part of me wished that he'd never let go.

"Well," Joseph said, beaming as he shut the magazine and rested his arms on the table. "If he hasn't taught you already, then by God, we'll teach you together."

We spent the next half-hour in a lighthearted discussion of Nova Scotian slang. For an Ontarian, the accent was tough for me to imitate, but my practice made Joseph laugh more, which in turn lowered my guard with him. Beneath his roughened exterior, I could see the softness on the inside, and this made it harder for me to understand what had turned him into a killer. Sitting at the prison with him was like sharing a round of drinks at the kitchen table of a friend, and soon it became difficult for me to see him for what the numbers across his chest said he was.

Still, the burning questions danced at the tip of my tongue: *Why did you...? How could you...?* But the mixture of pride and happiness on David's face kept them away.

By the time the guards called Joseph to be returned to his chains, the other prisoner and the person visiting him were gone, and two hours had flown by. Hugging Joseph felt oddly natural to me now, and as we said goodbye, he whispered to me to come back to visit him and take care of his son in the meantime. I stepped aside and let David and him have their final moment together. Then Joseph kissed David forehead and left us, waving from the prisoner's door as he was put back into the cuffs.

David and I did the reverse of what we'd done to enter, and

as we left, I had a brooding sense that Joseph had been hinting at something when he said, "There are two sides to every story." Of course, this was the case with the murder of Johnathan Roth, but how much would I really learn about the polarized sides? I wanted to get to know David deeper, but I had to be careful with how much the murder intrigued me. I didn't want to disrespect him or break the trust that we were building by crossing boundaries. Our relationship was like a crystal swan. One wrong move, and the whole thing would be cracked. And I didn't want that.

When we walked back to the Mazda, the sky was clearing in tandem with our moods. David pulled me into a prolonged hug in front of his dented hood, and I savored it as he murmured "Thank you," into my ear. But I didn't need him to thank me. As we held each other, his energy was telling me much more than his words ever could.

CHAPTER 19
I FOUGHT THE LAW

In the next memory I see, the sterile, white room fades into view like the beginning of a bad film, and David shifts to keep the cold platform beneath him from stiffening his back. The sheets are scratchy against his skin, and they reek of medical-grade bleach, which irritates his nose.

Where is this? I think. *A surgery room? A hospital? A clinic?*

It could be any of them. The medical equipment that surrounds the walls and the mounted lights above give me no clues on how to separate them.

Where are we, David?

A nurse—at least, I *assume* she's a nurse because she's wearing smocks and a lab coat—looks down on him. Her face is as stern as stone. "Mr. Mathis? Are you ready?"

He sighs, half in annoyance, half in impatience. "Let's jus' get this over with."

Her pink lipstick bunches into a sympathetic pucker. "I'm sorry. I'm sure this isn't your favourite."

I feel the flare of disgust, and something tells me he's sneering. "Get on with it."

She moves to his right, and he watches her walk over to an IV pump that's running into his arm. The end of the line disappears into his skin under a haphazard strip of medical tape, stuck crookedly across the inside of his elbow. I can see the edge of his wolf portrait. His voice sounds so similar to how it is now, that this could have been last week. He's not younger in this memory. This one's more recent.

The nurse flicks a thick needle, and he looks away. "I'm going to administer the injection now, Mr. Mathis. It may be cold but remember that this is normal. Cold is good."

Bullshit, he thinks.

"Tell us how you feel."

He looks in the direction of the other voice and sees two people in lab coats tapping away on iPad screens. They're too far away for me to read their clip-on badges.

There's a sting at the IV entry site, and David hisses. "You said this would be cold. It's not cold. It's hot."

Both people look up from their iPads. "What do you mean it feels hot?" one says.

A burning pain begins to branch off from the IV site, and it spreads down his arm, through his shoulder, and up into his neck. It's like his veins are being filled with fire, and panic smothers him as it scorches across his chest. "Stop! Stop! It hurts!" He yanks the line from his arm, splattering blood and liquid across the sheets.

"Mr. Mathis!" The blonde nurse jumps forward to pin him, but agony is already doing it for her.

David starts to writhe, and he clenches the sheets as the medication paralyzes him in suffering. "Stop! Please! Help me! Please!" The fire rips through him, and he releases a blood-curdling scream; no longer able to beg. It's like someone's strapped him to an electric chair, eager to watch him flail to death.

"What's happening?!" The man and woman have joined the nurse to pin him down.

"I—I don't know! We've never had this reaction before!"

Sultry tears dampen David's cheeks in between his screams, and the words that he can get to leave his lips are desperate cries. "Help me... please... please help me... make it stop..." His voice is reduced to a bubbling croak, and his jaw locks open in a silent scream.

"Do something!" the woman says to the blond nurse. "We're getting muscle seizure!"

David's now drowning in caustic veins and muscle spasms, so he has no choice but to submit, trembling as he struggles to breathe. Though I can only sense a resonance of the pain, I feel the horror and panic that he's suspended in as he wishes for death.

Anything... he thinks. *Anything. Please, jus' make it stop...*

And if I was there, I'd do anything, just to save him. But this is a memory, and it's already happened. So, I'm helpless. Stuck with the experience of his torture, as I beg my ability to pull me out—

"Emily," Dr. Tsuyuki said. "Your thesis?"

I blinked myself from a memory of a memory. It was the Monday two weeks after I'd started at UBC, and we were sitting in his office, having our follow up meeting. I was supposed to be telling him what I'd nailed down for my thesis, but the thought of it reminded me of David's memory from the night before.

After getting stoned on Sunday afternoon, we'd moved up to my bed and fallen into a nap together. Then I'd shot upright—slapping a hand across my mouth after calling for Barrett—shocked by a memory more vivid than any I'd seen before. Luckily, David hadn't been woken by my screaming, so I didn't have to worry that he'd ask why I was belting out his enemy's name. Instead, his eyelids were shifting in the hold of a dream, and the way that he smiled in his sleep told me that it was a peaceful one.

I'd lowered myself beside him, more confused than ever, inquisition in overdrive.

Was he chronically sick and receiving treatment? And did that have something to do with those "appointments" that John Roth was badgering Joseph about? Did Roth Pharma give David treatment, and Joseph was paying for that somehow?

Now that I thought about it, David did seem to be sick often. Was that why he was so adamant on not going to the doctor the last time? Was that memory a bad reaction he had to his treatment because it was fraudulent like the antibiotics I'd been given after my accident? And if he *did* have a chronic illness that needed treatment, how bad was it? Oh my God, what if it was terminal? What if he didn't want to tell me because it was terminal?!

Hot tears had streamed down my face unannounced, and I'd reached over, stroking the curls of his trimmed beard. We were only starting to build on our foundation of trust, so I couldn't expect him to tell me everything. But whatever that memory was about—whatever he was hiding from me—it was big with a capital B.

"Your thesis?" Dr. Tsuyuki prompted again.

I rubbed my brow. "Yeah. Sorry. I'm a little air-headed today." I paused and took a deep breath. "I've decided I want to analyze the quality assurance strategies of pharma companies around the globe when products are non-compliant. You know, what happens when things go wrong? And what risk matrices to they use to determine if the product should still go out the door?"

"Ah, interesting," he said. "It will make for some challenging data analysis, but I like the idea."

"Okay. Cool. Me too."

Dr. Tsuyuki smiled. "Emily. You still don't look sure."

Okay, so I wasn't *one hundred percent* sure. But I was running out of time if I wanted to start my research, and I was supposed to have an answer for him today. So far, this was the only solid idea that I had. And, if anything, at least I'd be a bit vindicated if I dove into the potential root cause of what had happened to me during the antibiotics incident. I knew that I wasn't *supposed* to have a personal stake in my thesis research—internal bias and all that—but at the end of the day, wouldn't that help drive me?

"I'm sure," I said, throwing in a nod to punctuate it.

"Okay." Dr. Tsuyuki sat back and clasped his hands together. "I'd suggest you start by reaching out to some good pharma contacts, because—oh boy—you're going to need them for this one. Keep me in the loop about what support you need. I have some close contacts at Roth Pharmaceuticals, if you need them."

"Yeah. That sounds good. I have my own contacts too. But it couldn't hurt."

I mean, sure. I had Barrett Roth's phone number, but how did I expect that to help? Was I supposed to just text him up and say, *Hey, can you tell me all the ways your company creates immorality in the world?* Not likely.

"And I think you should consider extending your master's to thesis based. Two years instead of one. This is going to need a lot of research."

Two years??

How could I even *consider* being away from my parents for that long?

"I—I can do that?"

"If it's what you want." He spread his hands. "Just a suggestion."

I swallowed. Maybe I *was* fucking up by choosing this topic... "I'll think about it," I said.

"Great. I'm glad we got that fleshed out today. And how are you doing with your TA work so far?"

"Bit of a challenge," I admitted. "But I think I'm starting to work out the kinks."

In all honesty, I was awkward at teaching, and it was taking me longer than expected to settle in. But the undergrad students were bright, and they asked questions that made my brain do overtime. It was a welcome challenge if I wanted to be a professor like my dad. Sometimes I wondered how he did it.

"Fantastic," Dr. Tsuyuki said. "Keep up the good work. Now, do you have any questions for me before we wrap up?"

"Um. No? I mean, I think those will come in as I start my research."

He laughed. "I don't doubt it."

I started to gather my stuff, giving myself a mental reminder about which way to turn out of his office so I didn't look like an idiot this time. "Thanks, Dr. Tsuyuki."

"Have a good day, Emily."

CHAPTER 20
A MATTER OF TRUST

The following week, Avril got an invite from Rebecca Morgan to join a camping trip in Squamish, which—inevitably—meant that Barrett Roth would be there. She'd immediately gone to David to check if he had a problem with it.

"Whatever," he'd said. "I can't stop you from catching up with your friend."

It wasn't necessarily a *no*, but it wasn't a *yes* either. So, she took it at face value. "Em, do you want to come?"

I'd sat silent, watching David from across the living room as I curled further into our ancient armchair. After the connection we'd shared from visiting Joseph *et cetera*, I was hesitant to do anything to upset him. But the thought of my thesis was pulsing at the back of my mind, and I needed the excuse to see Barrett again. Plus, the Roth-Mathis history had grown as interesting to me as ever, and maybe more time behind enemy lines would help me understand what had happened. If a big pharma company was causing an injustice somehow, I wanted to know.

"Are you sure you'd be okay with it?" I asked David.

He shrugged as he stood up. "Trust," was all he said as he walked out.

I shot an uncertain look at Avril, then got up to follow David to his room.

"Don't shut me out," I said, as he threw himself on his bed with a huff. "If this really bothers you, I won't go."

David propped himself up on his elbows. "You've been worried about your thesis lately," he said. "And if spending time around he-who-must-not-be-named helps your future career, Em, then I en' going to stop you."

"Yeah, but I don't want to risk driving a wedge between us."

"You won't. We talked about building trust. This is me giving you the chance to do that."

I paused. "Are you sure?"

He pulled his lips to one side, and for a minute, I thought he'd changed his mind. "Go. Seriously. Avril's gonna need someone to watch out for her, too."

"Okay..."

"But jus' be careful around him." He sat up and took my hand. "Promise me that. Don't believe a word he says, because it's all lies. He's bad to the core, no matter what he shows on the surface."

I nodded, winding my fingers between his. From what I'd seen of Barrett Roth so far, I had an inkling that *some of that* was true. "Thank you."

"For what?" David asked.

My gaze hovered on his lips. I really wanted to kiss him, but I held myself back. "Giving me the chance to be trusted."

David smiled and said, "You deserve it."

When Friday came, I was running to my car with my laptop bag swinging at my side, when I realized that I'd be very late for the pickup time. Avril and I were supposed to carpool with Rebecca, and though I cringed at the thought of listening to them chat between bad pop songs—*Don't you just love this one, Av?*—I couldn't argue with efficiency. But my last lecture had run long, and my students had pinned me with a lot of solid questions, so I wasn't going to make it.

"Shit." I hissed, unlocking my car, and balancing my phone while I dialled Avril's number. When she picked up, I explained, but she said they'd already left because she'd called me multiple times with no answer. I sighed and asked her to send me the address.

"Actually, Em. I heard that Barrett's heading up later if you want to carpool with him. Might as well save the gas, right?"

"*Av!*" I heard in the background.

"Barrett?" My heart rate sped up.

"Y—Yeah." Avril sounded like she instantly regretted telling me. "You okay with that?" Her voice went muffled, but I could hear her apologizing to Rebecca. She was probably annoyed about the idea of me riding with her "future fiancé," but it was too late now. I'd already been given the offer. And Avril was right. It made more sense than me driving up on my own.

I paused and thought about whether Barrett would be annoyed that someone had volunteered his precious time. Then I pushed myself out of it. If I wanted to move forward, I'd have to be brave. "Yeah, good idea. He knows where he's going, right?"

She chuckled. "Well, I should hope so. We're going to the Roth's private campground. He's only been going there since he was, you know, *born*."

"Right." I hadn't been told that. "Makes sense. Alright. I'll give him a call."

"Okay, have fun. See you tonight!"

I stared at the black screen long after she'd hung up. Barrett's number had been in my phone since we met in Stanley Park, but I'd never reached out to him. There was something that held me back every time I'd thought about it—Mum would call it a "metal block" —and he scared me a little. My stomach fluttered as I scrolled through my contacts. I didn't *want* to call him, but maybe I could reframe this "pickle" into an opportunity. Maybe asking for a ride from Barrett Roth would be a good thing? Maybe?

Then again, probably not.

Pushing past the fear, I clicked on his name and raised my chin, putting my phone to my ear.

I shouldn't be this anxious all the time.

I had a wannabe-hippie mother. Shouldn't my blood run with incense and weed smoke by now?

"Barrett Roth." His voice jolted me like a volt.

"Oh. Uh. Hi, Barrett. It's, uh, Emily."

Silence.

I swallowed. "Emily Anderson."

"*Emily*. Right." He didn't mask the confusion. "How are you?"

Adjusting my rearview for no reason, I watched the foot traffic up on the lane behind me. "Good. Um. Just finished my last lecture of the day."

There was a sound of shuffling, which was followed by muted strain. "Right." He sighed. "Well. How can I help you?" He was *probably* a man with limited time, and he *probably* wanted to make it clear.

I bit my lip. Oh God. I shouldn't have called. I should have just taken the hit and driven up myself. "Um. W–Well... I kinda missed my ride with Rebecca to the campground. She mentioned you were leaving later, so I thought I'd ask if I can come... you know... with you?"

"Huh." I imagined him putting a hand on his hip. "She failed to mention we'd have an extra guest, but no matter. There's plenty of space." He paused and I pictured him checking his fucking Rolex. "Of course, I'm happy to accommodate. Can you be here in an hour?"

I hesitated when I remembered he was downtown. "I dunno. I need to pop back to Ladner first, and I'm at the university. Can you give me two?"

To my relief, he chuckled. "Alright. I'll make an exception, just this once. Of course, I could always send you a car if that would help."

Send me a car. Typical rich guy.

"Um, no. I don't think I need that. But thanks. Do you mind texting me your address?"

"I can do that. Listen, when you pull up, park on the curb out front. I'll have my doorman, James, valet your car. Tell him you're there to see me, and he'll guide you."

"Okay. Will do."

"Take care, Emily. And see you soon."

He hung up, and I pulled my phone from my ear, finding it warmer than normal. The little hairs on my cheek were trying to cling to it like the sound of his voice had sent static through it. My nerves tingled, and I shook it off before I tossed it in the passenger seat and shifted my car into drive. Somewhere along the way, my phone pinged with his text, but I cranked up my music and rolled down my window to let the sea air refresh me.

Who is Barrett Roth? And why does he always make me feel that way?

I tried asking the Universe, but They left me on "Read."

The drive home ate up my first hour—made worse by the Friday traffic under the Massey Tunnel—and by the time I backed into the driveway at the House, I was pushing it. Leaving my purse, I snatched my laptop bag and bolted inside, thundering up the stairs to my room before I started to throw together a bag. I packed light: just the essentials to survive the wilderness of the west, along with some much-needed product to keep my hair under control. And by the time I was done, I was starting to regret turning down that car. After all, what was the harm in knowing a man as rich as Barrett Roth and taking advantage of the perks?

I shivered, not wanting to think about the potential answers.

Back outside, I was fighting to close my rusted hatch like I always did, when David pulled his Mazda into the driveway. I grinned as he walked over, but all he gave me was a weary smile as he put his palm flat on the hatch and used his trainer-like muscles to close it. He was looking rough and was wearing those dark circles under his eyes again.

"Where're you to?"

My face fell at the roughness of his voice. "Camping, remember?"

"Right." His lunch pail hung limp at his side.

I smiled and gave his chest a pat. "It's only two days, and I promise I'll be careful. And how about we do something fun when we get back? Just the House-of-Wolves?"

He shrugged. "How about jus' you and me?"

My internal butterflies began to dance. "Or yeah. You and me."

Then he pinched the bridge of his nose and closed his eyes, bracing a palm against the Yaris. I stepped forward to cup his face. His skin was cold. Very un-David-like.

"Are you okay?"

"Fine. Yep. Fine."

"You don't look fine."

"I'm tired, Em. I'm gonna go eat and go to bed."

"Are you sure you don't want me to stay?"

He rubbed his brow. "It en' about me. I'm a big boy. Now go before I change my mind."

I caught a glimpse of his watch, which reminded me that I had taken up a chunk of the hour that I needed to get downtown. "Hey, why are you home so late? You should have been done by 3:30."

He grumbled: "I had an appointment."

Dread pierced my gut. "What kind of appointment?"

"I need to get inside. Get on your moose and head 'er." *Get on your moose* was a term for going somewhere fast and *head 'er* meant to start going there. I'd learned that from our time with Joseph.

I stepped forward, letting his tropical cologne engulf me. "You sure you're okay? I'm worried about you."

"Yep. It's nothing."

When I wrapped my arms around him, I heard a soft wheeze in his chest. "I need a hug for the road."

He rested his chin on my head. "Don't turn your back on them mountain roads. They're a right bitch."

I chuckled as I held him. "Yeah, yeah. Be careful and shit. I know."

"Jus' saying. Ontario is flat, so you en' used to that."

"Ontario is very hilly," I corrected him, as we pulled apart. "And I'll be fine."

Plus, I'm letting the British Columbian drive.

We looked at each other, wrapped in a strange energy of longing.

"I have to go," I finally said.

He nodded and walked away. "Have a good time. We'll be talking." Nova Scotian for *see you soon.*

I stood by my car door, watching him as he trudged into the house. Every time he looked like that, I'd get anxious. Especially after seeing his horrific memory. And I was starting to take notice of how often he was sick. Adding mental notes to my ad hoc investigation. And I earnestly wanted to help him, but since he wasn't an open book, I chose to take this route. Plus, he was right. He was a big boy, and he didn't need me to take care of him.

Right?

David Mathis, what's happening to you?

The streets of Coal Harbour were as pristine as you'd expect any wealthy neighbourhood to be. Bright, unmarked sidewalks; A plethora of over-the-top water features; Flora and hedges perfectly trimmed and tamed; Stunning, mountain views. Barrett's building was on Cordova, and it rose thirty floors in glass trimmed with a light grey, granite siding. I gaped up at it as I fought my trunk for my bag and imagined the outrageous cost of the condos inside. This was not a place that everyday people lived. It was a place for the wealthiest one percent, and they wanted everyone else to know it.

The sprawling silver address marked over the double doors told me that I had the right building, so I went into the vestibule and studied the LED screen. I was about to start pressing buttons, but the door buzzed and opened, and an older man waved from the front desk. I stepped into the lobby and was hit by the fresh smell of hospital-grade air filtering. The ceilings inside were easily twenty feet, and they were punctuated by an eclectic light feature that was probably crafted by some Italian designer with a cigarette hanging from his mouth.

"Miss Emily, I believe." The man stood and met me beside the desk. He had kind eyes.

"Are you James?" I asked.

He spread his hands in welcome. "That would be me. I believe Mr. Roth is expecting you. Is that your car on the street?"

I nodded and glanced back. My Toyota stuck out like a sore thumb.

"Well, then. If I may just have your keys, I'll park it for you."

I shifted my bag and handed them to him, finding his skin soft as our fingers brushed. "Feel free to take it for a joy ride, if you want."

"Thank you. That may be the best offer I've had all day." His chuckle was as endearing as a loving grandparent. He motioned around the corner to the three silver elevators. "Please make your way up to see Mr. Roth. And don't worry about a thing. I won't wreck your car on my joy ride."

I smiled. "I can tell that you can be trusted." We went our separate ways, but as I approached the elevators, I realized I was missing something. "Oh! James?"

He stopped and looked back.

"Uh. What floor is he on?"

He chuckled again, warming my heart. "Press the button for the penthouse. He'll buzz you up."

"The penthouse. Of course." I was glad I'd whispered it to myself because James didn't deserve my sarcastic tone. He was too nice, and probably got enough lip from the pompous *elite* that lived here already.

Barrett Roth—you are ridiculous.

The thought was confirmed when I reached the top and stepped into a large lobby that led to the double doors that were presently open into his penthouse. To the right was a floor-to-ceiling window that faced east, giving a sprawling view of the city below, including the Lookout. To the left, a massive portrait with a golden frame took up the entire wall. It was a silly photo of Barrett and Shane—professionally taken. Barrett had his arm around his best friend and was kissing him on the cheek. Shane had one bright-blue eye closed in a wink, his right hand forming the rock and roll "devil-horns." I snuffed out a laugh as I stepped across the marble tiles to study it. Then jumped at the sharp sound of a clap.

"Well, look who made it." Barrett Roth walked from his open doors, dressed in a white polo shirt, a dark pair of jeans, and a flawless set of white sneakers.

I smiled, trying to ignore the jolt that he always seemed to give me. "Yeah, sorry I'm late. Traffic was a little worse than I thought." I cleared my throat. I'd never been a good liar. "I was just admiring your picture here."

He grinned as he put his hands on his hips and looked up to the portrait. "Shane Alistair Thomas. I love that motherfucker more than anything."

I raised an eyebrow. So far, it'd been rare for him to use a word so... *improper.* "You two have quite the bromance, huh?"

He turned his grin into a smile as he ran his eyes over the image. "It's more than a bromance, Emily. I'd call it a loving friendship that has lasted—and will last—a lifetime. I would die for him, and I'm not concerned about what anyone thinks of that." And I must have worn my surprise on my face because his obsidian gaze shifted. "What?"

I managed to shrug. "That's just kind of lovely and honourable," I explained. "Aren't you supposed to be the bad guy?"

I'd said it as a joke, but it was a serious question.

"Stay tuned, kiddo." Then, Barrett motioned inside. "Would you like a tour? I figure it would probably dock my chivalry points if I didn't offer one."

I glanced inside. It looked super fancy. "Um, aren't we late?"

"Time is dictated by me, Miss Anderson. I am not dictated by it." It seemed like this was a very *Barrett Roth* thing for him to say.

"Um. Okay then. What the heck."

When else was I going to get the chance to see a multi-million-dollar penthouse in Coal Harbour?

"Let me take that for you." He stepped forward, and I caught his musky-sweet scent as I slid my bag from my shoulder and handed it to him. It was intoxicating. Like David's, but in a way that I was much less comfortable with. "We'll be departing momentarily, so I will leave it here for now." His lean runner's muscles moved under the polo shirt as he shifted my bag and set it aside on the marble, and I had to snap myself out of staring. He welcomed me inside with a hand across my shoulders that made my skin tingle.

The entry to the main floor of his condo housed another lobby and had more of those twenty-foot ceilings. On the left side there was a powder room, gym, home office, and a spare bedroom. At the back, there was a giant sliding door that led out onto a patio with a pool, hot tub, an outdoor kitchen, and sprawling views of the harbour and mountains on the North Shore. Beside the sliding door was the kitchen, which was decked out in marble countertops and high-end, stainless-steel appliances that a billionaire CFO like Barrett would never need to use. On the right side was a breakfast nook that was nestled in a circular set of floor-to-ceiling windows that showcased a view of downtown. Then, there was a dining room and bar, and a living room that was big enough to fit the House-of-Wolves inside.

The staircase curved above the breakfast nook, and the second floor was exclusive to the master bedroom. Up there, he had a California-king bed that wore immaculately clean, ruby-red sheets. On the wall opposite the stairs, there was a sliding door that led out onto another patio, and he had a master bath, a walk-in closet that housed so many clothes and accessories that it was hard to believe it belonged to a man, and a laundry room.

After we'd finished the tour, I was drawn to the second-floor patio, so I stepped out to watch the city below. People were going about their evening lives on the street, unaware of how we towered above them. Joggers trotted by. Dog walkers went through their usual start and stop motions at each tree. A businesswomen clicked by on her polished heels with her cellphone to her ear. All were blissfully ignorant of our existence at the top, and it was strange to be looming over the rest of the world like we owned it. It was all very—hardwood floors, and glass railings, and gold faucets, and black marble tiles, and "look how much money I have."

I tried really hard not to be impressed, then felt stupid when I did. I wasn't supposed to idolize wealth. I was supposed to idolize the things that truly mattered. Like human connection.

Barrett stepped out beside me. I watched as he raised his chin to the wind and let it brush through his faux-brown hair.

"This is incredible, Barrett," I found myself saying. "Truly an amazing penthouse."

He shot me a smirk. "Thank you, Emily."

My eyes glazed over the distant mountains in the east. Mt. Baker—all the way down in Washington—was just visible enough to see its forever-snow-capped peaks. "I can't believe you actually *live* here... You realize that most people could only dream of this place, right?"

He nodded without looking at me. "I'm a lucky man, Emily. I always have been."

I rested my chin on my palm as I braced my elbow on the railing. "You're a very *rich* man, there's no doubt about that."

Once again, my mouth had spoken before I'd given it permission, and I looked over to find that there was a fall in his expression. It was so subtle that I wouldn't have recognized it if I weren't so in tune with the emotions of other people.

Mum had always told me to be aware of the unspoken pain and struggles of others, and to be gentle with it. What we see at the surface isn't necessarily reflective of how things are below. And it was clear to me from that look on his face that something was missing. Something was fundamentally wrong, but I had no right to judge that. After all, his father *had* been murdered in cold blood in front of a coffee shop when he was only sixteen. Who was I to judge what world he really lived in?

I wanted to put a hand on his shoulder, but something held me back. "I'm sorry, Barrett. That was insensitive of me."

There was a slight narrowing of those ebony eyes before he turned away. "Don't be. It's the truth." He paused at the doorway and looked back. "Now, are you finished gawking at where I live? Can we take our leave?"

I countered his sudden venom with a playful tone. "Sure. Let's *take our leave* then."

It only took him a moment to lock up—*Who's really going to break in up here? Spiderman?*—and by the time he grabbed his bags and cooler and joined them with mine in the elevator lobby, James was waiting for us. He greeted us with his grandpa smile and mentioned that he'd come up to take the bags down. Barrett thanked him but refused to let him move the cooler. Instead, he shifted it onto the trolley himself, his toned muscles tensing under his shirt again.

James clicked his tongue. "Come now, Mr. Roth. There's no need to fuss over this old man. I'm stronger than I look."

Barrett smiled as he adjusted the cooler. "I'm well aware, James, but I don't need you injured." He stood straight and put his hands on his hips. "There's no need to show off because there's a beautiful woman around."

My skin prickled weirdly.

James looked at me. "*Show off*, Mr. Roth says. I've no need to show off, Miss Emily. There's a young man in here yet!"

Barrett chuckled. "That's the spirit." He tested the resistance of the loaded trolley. "Are you quite sure you're going to be alright with this?"

James waved his concern away. "Don't fuss, Mr. Roth. Now. What is it that Mr. Thomas always says?"

Barrett grinned. "*Dinna fash.*"

"Ah, yes. *Dinna fash.* What a lovely inherited accent he has, eh?"

Barrett smiled as he glanced up at the portrait of him and Shane. "I'm not going to tell him that. It'll go straight to his head." We shared a laugh, and then he brought out his wallet. "I appreciate the assistance today, James." He offered him a hundred-dollar bill, and I blinked at it. I didn't even know they existed.

Again, James waved it away. "No, no, Mr. Roth. You are always so kind to me, and I appreciate that in return. There's no need."

"Then take it to buy the missus something special. You're aware of my opinion on abundance. It's not useful if it's never shared."

James tenderly accepted the bill. "Alright. Thank you, Mr. Roth."

Barrett lay a hand on his shoulder as the elevator dinged, and I wondered if James felt the same static that I did when Barrett touched him. "Tell her also that I thank her for the casserole. It was delicious and much appreciated. Better than anything my chef whips up."

James laughed, then grunted as he pulled the trolley into the elevator. "I'm not going to tell her that. It will go straight to *her* head. Especially considering your chef is the best in the city."

Barrett helped push the trolley from the other side. "Oh, no, you must. See, having it go to her head equals a happy wife for you, and the potential of more casseroles for me. So, it's symbiotic."

"Always thinking strategically, aren't you?" James said.

Barrett raised an eyebrow. "Is there any other way to think?"

I found myself smiling at him before I snapped out of it a little.

Wait a minute. Aren't you supposed to be the bad guy?

We took the elevator down to his private garage, and I stood stunned as I stepped out. There were six spots, all filled with cars whose collective worth would be in the millions. The red Ferrari that we'd seen showing itself off on the platform at the Roth Estate stood glimmering at the back left, with a generic, black Mercedes next to it, and a silver Porsche next to that. On the back right was a gold Lamborghini, next to a blue, convertible Maserati, and then—the most incredible of the bunch—a Chevy Chevelle from the seventies, which was a deep ebony with two white stripes creating a bright contrast up its hood.

"Wow..." I gravitated over to the Chevelle and ran a hand across its polished hood. It was so well preserved that it looked like it had travelled through time.

"Ah." Barrett joined me, the glint in his obsidian eyes matching the car. "I was going to let you choose which one we'd take, but it seems you've already chosen."

I grinned as my hand bridged a loving connection with the roof of the muscle car. "This one. Definitely this one."

CHAPTER 21
CAT PEOPLE

As we made our way toward the north on Georgia Street, the sky was sprawled in a bright blue, with fluffy clouds drifting throughout. The city was alive, and I smiled as I inhaled the sea breeze from the Chevelle's open window. The patios of the cafés and bars were packed with people enjoying an evening drink, and the streets and SeaWall of Stanley Park were crowded with those craving a walk without rain.

The roar of the Chevelle echoed from the buildings around us, enhanced by Barrett's overzealous revving every time he shifted down. It was clear that he genuinely enjoyed driving it, and his happiness lightened the mood. "Oh, baby," he breathed, as he ran his hand across the steering wheel, the Chev rumbling beneath us. "Sometimes you need to be careful with this one."

"I don't doubt it."

Oh my God. Why'd I just say that so sexily?

Playfulness flashed through Barrett's eyes, and he held me there before looking back to the road.

I dropped my gaze and ran a hand across the leather seats. They were as soft and creamy as butter. Both sets—front and back—were continuous like they often were in classic cars, so I was sharing the front with him. The steering wheel was a big circle of black leather, and the simple dials on the dash included a cassette-tape radio, with an old cigarette lighter perched below.

"This car emanates love," I said, as we wound our way toward Stanley Park.

Honestly, it wasn't something that I expected he'd own, but I was beginning to see that there was much more to him than the enemy of David Mathis. And, though he tried to hide it, I saw the look of appreciation when he glanced back over at me. The ebony had softened in a way I hadn't seen before.

"I'm not surprised you can feel that," he said.

The sun flashed through the massive trees, bathing us in and out of light. "Where did you get it?" I asked.

He smiled as he watched the road ahead. "My father bought her as a project car for me when I was fifteen, and she was a complete wreck when she came to me. The engine wouldn't start, and the paint was a dull and faded grey. Nearly *everything* was broken. I couldn't fathom what the hell I was going to do, but then Kirk..." he paused and swallowed "...my friend, saved my ass and agreed to help me. It took us nearly two years to get her into the state she deserved. What you're looking at now is a product of the dedication of two teenagers who... Well... anyway... The point is, she wouldn't be what she is today without him."

I shuffled a little closer. "Tell me more about Kirk."

Hesitating, he shifted gears ahead of the slower traffic approaching the Lions Gate bridge. "Well, I assume you can tell by the Chev that he's a car genius. He was the only one of my friends that didn't pursue a post-secondary education, but that doesn't matter now, because he owns a successful repair and restoration shop over in Burnaby. The Chev was the first car he restored, and now the majority that his team work on are rare luxury vehicles." He bit the inside of his lip, and his muscles flexed as he shifted again. "I'm incredibly proud of him."

I smiled as I turned and wiggled my fingers through the passing wind. "Sounds like you have a lot to be proud of."

He nodded but didn't answer in words. A strange expression shimmered across his copper-red brows. "He'll be there tonight. You'll have the chance to meet him."

"Looking forward to it," I said.

Our conversation ended with a bit of tension, and I turned away from him to rest my arms across the base of the window, dropping my chin to meet them. I closed my eyes and sunk into the refreshing scent of cedar and pine from Stanley Park. When I opened them, the concrete lion that guarded the right base of the bridge swung by, and the park ended, opening the view up to the east. In between the cable supports for the bridge, the harbour was shimmering, and it wound between the city and the mountains before disappearing as it curved to the north. I watched the fading layers of land in the distance, thinking of Mission, then of Joseph, and then of how strange it was to be sitting beside the man whose father he'd killed; almost like we were friends. I sat up and looked at Barrett, who quickly looked forward like he hadn't been watching me.

Where did you come from, Barrett? Why here? Why now?

With a deep sigh, he reached for a pack of cigarettes that was sitting in a slot below the radio, pulling one out between his teeth. "Do you mind?"

I shook my head. Cigarette smoke didn't bother me. It reminded me of the streets of Toronto. "No, go ahead."

He took the smoke between the fingers of his left hand, then clicked the lighter on the dash with his right.

I fiddled with the emeralds of my ring and encouraged my body to relax as we bumped over the north side of the bridge.

He took the exit that followed the signs for Highway Ninety-Nine, west toward Whistler. We stewed in awkwardness, and I realized there was something about him that made me nervous, so I was determined to fight it tooth and nail. I was an upbeat, friendly and— for the most part—a happy-go-lucky woman. I wasn't about to let my energy be dulled by the presence of any man.

But I also couldn't deny that this one was different. This one was the one whose name I'd been involuntarily shouting for a good chunk of my life, without ever knowing why. Of whose existence I'd doubted and waved off like it was nothing, even when my mum was sure that it meant something. This man was likely to change my life if I let him...

After he'd lit the cigarette, it was clear from his long draw that he felt the tension too. So, I steered the conversation toward the one person that would bring the high vibes back. "Is Shane Scottish or Canadian?"

He exhaled, flicking ash out the open window. "He's a mix of both. His father is a full Scot, while his mother is Canadian."

"Right. Makes sense. His accent confused me when we met."

Barrett turned the Chev through the streets of West Van, on route to the highway. "Some words he always says as a Canadian. Others, always a Scot. He also speaks a Scots language, so sometimes he'll throw that in the mix, just to make it all the more confounding." We climbed a steep road, then turned to merge onto the highway. "I cannot call myself a master of language, and to make matters worse, Kirk is half-French." His expression fell. "Between the fluency of their alternate languages, I sometimes get lost."

"Huh," I said, surprised he was admitting something like that to me. "Obviously, I know about French, but I never knew there was a *Scottish* language."

"There is more than one," Barrett pointed out. "The version of Scots that Shane's family speaks hails from their native Aberdeen."

I ran a finger along the fuzzy rubber seal of the Chev's window. "Ah. Okay. And what about his parents?"

"His father, Michael Thomas—affectionately known to me as *Uncle Mike*—is the CEO of one of the major energy producers in BC, and his mother sits on their Board." He exhaled, and the Chev growled as he shoulder-checked and merged us with the moving traffic. The smell of burning gas followed us pungently, and the whistle of the wind made it harder to hear. He raised his voice in response. "Their business is astoundingly different to ours, with astoundingly different challenges. Shane is more junior in his company than Travis or me, but, then again, he has the luxury of having his father still alive to learn from. We are not so lucky."

Sorrow shot straight through my stomach like it did every time I was reminded of his father's murder.

We fell silent again, and I thought about John. Just over a week ago, I'd sat across from the man who'd taken his life, chatting like we were old friends. I'd even hugged him goodbye. What would Barrett think if he knew that about me? Would he consider that a betrayal, even if we hardly knew each other? I'm sure that he wouldn't hesitate to kick me to the curb, or that I wouldn't be sitting in his timeless car at all.

Guilt clouded the thought.

Barrett's gentle tone made it worse as he changed the topic. "Are you homesick, Emily?"

I sighed, studying the scattered barges on the sea to the left. They were far below us as the highway rose higher on the side of Cypress Mountain. "Honestly, yeah. But it's not Toronto I miss so much." I shivered at the thought of Andy. "It's my parents. I don't think I'd miss Ontario so much if they were here with me. There's something about Vancouver that seems right. Something that feels like home. Or... I mean... that *will* be home. Someday... Maybe."

He nodded as he slid the built-in ash tray from the dash and killed the smoke. "I can understand that feeling."

The properties of West Van rose in layers to our right. Each was probably more expensive than the last. "Have you always lived in Vancouver?" I asked.

"Yes," he said, drumming his fingers on the open window. He shifted the Chev into a higher gear, which quieted its sexy drone, and made it easier for us to hear each other. "The Roths have lived in Vancouver for many generations now. This is our city, and it will be forever."

Something about that last sentence seemed ominous.

He reached over and made me suppress a jump by touching my

shoulder. "Don't despair," he said. "It won't be long until you fall in love."

I raised an eyebrow. Though I didn't doubt it, I questioned whether it would be with Vancouver alone.

The Sea to Sky Highway ran along the edge of the coastal mountains and led north toward the ski town of Whistler. It served breath-taking views of the Howe Sound as the ocean snaked between the snowcapped peaks of the Sunshine Coast and those that towered over the highway to the right. The trees grew wild, balancing from cliffs that mixed in colour from grey, to burnt sienna, to red, like they were woodland acrobats destined to thrive. Layers of mountains framed the view in every direction, fading from a forest green to a light blue, as they sat above water that glimmered like a million tiny diamonds. The beauty was jaw-dropping, and it felt like we were driving through a scene straight from a fantasy film.

I gawked as I took out my phone and snapped pictures and videos with no filter needed. As I captured it all, I could feel those obsidian eyes on me again. But when I met them this time, Barrett was smiling. My excitement seemed touching to him, and again the Bad-Roth showed me without words that he probably had a heart.

We made small talk as he twisted the Chevelle over the mountain highway, and by the time we neared the end of the drive to Squamish, he was starting to feel more like a friend than an enemy. After the remaining tension between us dissipated, I realized just how damn *easy* it was to talk to him. Which was something I never thought would happen with a billionaire.

I learned that he'd inherited the Roth Campground—where we were headed—after his father died, and that Travis got a property in Whistler. The Roth Estate was inherited by the two of them, but Barrett had sold his share to his brother to buy the penthouse in

Coal Harbour. I wondered, as the widow, where his mother's share fit into all of this.

Then, he told me about how him and Shane were avid snowboarders—not surprising for men raised in mountains—and that they'd often stay at the property in Whistler on the weekends in the winter.

When we weren't talking, he was happy singing and dancing to whatever song came through on the classic rock station. David Bowie's "Let's Dance" turned out to be one of his favourites. "Go Your Own Way," by Fleetwood Mac was a close second.

I sat there hiding my smile and pretending that I didn't find it a little attractive.

About an hour down the road, the town of Squamish came into view, surrounded in all directions by towering peaks. It sat nestled on the shore of the aquamarine Howe Fjord, and a colossal cliff face rose on the land east of the town. As we wound down the road toward it, Barrett explained that this was the *Stawamus Chief*. The Squamish Nation of this area considered it of spiritual significance, he told me, and it was a great challenge for hiking and mountain climbing. The massive peaks of Garibaldi Provincial Park loomed in dazzling white and grey in the north, he told me, and the peaks of Mount Tantalus and the Serratus Mountain stood to the west.

All-in-all, my first impression of Squamish was that it was a lovely little town with an awesome natural setting.

Before we could drive through it, though, Barrett turned right, and then took us through some elevated residential areas until we came to a gravel road that led into the backcountry. We followed that for a few minutes, twisting and turning along a path that looked like it was built for logging. The gravel pinged from the bottom of the Chevelle as we rose further into the mountains. He steered it through the more challenging bits with care and experience, and after gripping the windowsill until my knuckles turned white, I was very thankful that he'd driven. I couldn't imagine doing it in my Yaris.

Finally, we reached a large black gate that disappeared into the woods on either size. The trees were clear cut in the surrounding area, but it still looked out of place in the middle of the forest. Barrett entered a code on the keypad, and the gate slid to the side, closing itself behind us once the Chev had passed.

We drove down the paved driveway for a little, before a white house came into view above a bright blue lake. Though I was sure that the Roths would consider this a modest "cottage," to the rest of the world it was a five-bedroom mansion with all the amenities of a standard home. It was two levels and had a wooden deck that wrapped around the second floor.

The driveway sloped down to the lake, branched off to a boat-launch, and then rose back up toward the house. But we wouldn't be following it today. Though the house was open to anyone that preferred to stay there and not outdoors, Barrett said, for this visit, we'd be camping.

He turned off the paved driveway and onto a dirt road that led to the outdoor area away from the house. There, the Roths had built five campsites set in a semi-circle, and the largest at the top had a full outdoor kitchen in addition to its firepit. A washroom building sat off the path that branched from it.

Four, gigantic, *glamping-style* tents were already pitched at the largest site, and it was here that I saw Avril's Honda Fit tucked in the parking area, next to a red Jaguar SUV, and a blue Toyota Tacoma pickup. Barrett revved the Chev—likely to draw attention—before pulling next to the other vehicles and bringing the rumbling muscle car to a rest.

Shane was already coming over when we stepped out. *"Enfin!"* he said, throwing up his arms. *"La Belle Chevelle!"* He pivoted toward the campsite and added, "Impressed, aren't you Kirk?" before turning back and saying, "What's the matter, Bear? Can't help yourself from showing off in front of a bonnie lass?"

Barrett threw an arm around his best friend and tussled with him, before planting a kiss on his forehead. "That's rich, coming from the man with the atrocious solid-gold Lambo that he doesn't have space for. When, oh when, are you going to free me from having to store that monstrosity?"

"Ah, get off, ya great numpty." Shane pulled himself away and pointed at him. "And Dinna do that. Dinna hate on the Lamb. Because the answer is that you will *never* be free, Barrett Roth. *Never.* As long as you love me, you'll be forever in my debt."

Barrett shook his head. "Then I am willingly enslaved, brither. You don't have to ask twice." He dropped to his knee to catch a huge dog who'd trotted up to him.

I wondered whether *brither* was some sort of nickname.

Shane turned his grin toward me and offered a hug. "Hello, Emily. Nice to see you again."

I stepped into a new masculine scent and squeezed him. "Nice to see you again, Shane. And who's this?" I motioned to the dog, whose curled tail wagged as Barrett ruffled his fur.

"This is Dixon," Barrett said, grinning up at me with his chin nested in Dixon's fluff. "Shane's Malamute."

Shane grunted as he started to unload the bags from the Chevelle. "I give you fair warning—he's a lady killer."

I giggled as I dropped beside Barrett and got a face full of Dixon-kisses. "I can see why."

But then Barrett's energy turned apprehensive as he locked on someone across the campsite. I followed his gaze toward a muscular man with honey blonde hair who was sitting in one of the Muskoka chairs around the fire. A beer bottle resting on the arm of the chair was sitting in one of his massive hands. Barrett sighed through his nose before he smoothed Dixon's fur and kissed him on the head. "Come on," he said to me. "I'll introduce you to Kirk."

We moved across the campsite, and Rebecca trotted up to throw her arms around Barrett's neck and pull his mouth to hers. I was surprised when a little jealousy floated to the surface from my core.

"I'll tend to you momentarily, babe," he said, ignoring her pout as they pulled apart. "Let me greet everyone first."

Rebecca "*Humph-ed*" away, and I tossed a wave toward Avril and Shane's girlfriend, Melissa, before Barrett and I went over to Kirk, who stood to meet us. He was a quite few inches shorter than Barrett—who was the tallest of the three men—and had a strong jawline that matched his chiseled mechanic's build. His dark blue eyes brewed like the start of a thundercloud, and they fixed unblinking on Barrett as the two men met. Barrett swallowed, and Kirk held him there, saying nothing as the muscles of his jaw tensed. His expression was stern, and he stood stubborn in silence.

Finally, Barrett spoke breathlessly. "Hey, Ki."

Kirk pulled his lips into a tight line. He dropped his gaze and blinked a couple of times, with his focus moving to different spots along the forest floor like he was suffering in some internal complex. He looked back at Barrett before grabbing him and pulling him into a tight hug. I watched Barrett's polo shirt bunch under Kirk's grip, and Barrett wrapped his arms around the top of Kirk's shoulders, dropping his mouth to rest on the right. He sniffed and squeezed his eyes shut.

And, oh boy. I felt like I *really* shouldn't have been there. Like I should have just turned, walked away, and given them some space. But I was frozen. Whatever this reunion was between them, it was emotional, and full of unspoken history. The energy kinda trapped me like a snare.

David's voice echoed in my head: *If you en' at the christening, you shouldn't be at the wedding.*

When the men finally separated, Kirk's tone was gravelly. "Roth."

A line appeared between Barrett's brows. "It's good to see you."

Again, Kirk blinked before dropping his eyes to the dirt.

Sensing the strain like a damp fog, I shifted my weight and dragged my foot across the ground.

Kirk then looked at me. Though his expression was solemn, he raised a curious eyebrow.

Barrett cleared his throat like he wanted to divert the attention away from himself, for once. "This is Emily Anderson," he told Kirk. "She's a friend of Avril's. And, well, I hope a new friend of mine."

Kirk drew his pained expression into a half-smile and offered his right hand. His grip was gentle, and completely unexpected from those roughed-up mechanic's hands. "*Enchanté*, Emily."

"Uh. Yeah," I said. "Likewise."

Now that he'd moved, I caught sight of the crown tattoo that was on his left forearm. It had the same placement and a similar size to Barrett's sapphire-studded *fleur-de-lis*; although Kirk's was on the opposite arm, and was gold, gothic, and studded with rubies.

"Emily," Barrett said. "This is Kirk Richards. He's my"—he hesitated—"*other* best friend."

Kirk's eyes snapped to him like he'd been stung.

Barrett dropped his in response.

Woah. I never thought he'd be so submissive with someone.

It was a stark contrast to what I'd seen of Barrett Roth so far.

I tapped my foot, tortured by the tension as I searched for something to say. "So..." I threw a thumb back at the Chevelle. "Barrett said that you re-built that whole car with him back when you were teenagers."

Kirk slowly looked to the Chev, where Shane was busy offloading things from the trunk. They caught each other's eye, and Shane shook his head. With one blink, Kirk shot a look at Barrett that dripped with accusation. Barrett refused to look back. "A long time ago," he finally said.

"Well, it's gorgeous." I cleared my throat. "You two really did an incredible job. It looks like it's travelled through time, and it was so fun to ride in."

Again, he gave me his half-smile. "Thank you." Apparently, Kirk Richards was a man of few words. He seemed reserved and quiet, yet sure of himself. A far-cry from the outspoken cockiness of Barrett, or the bubbly playfulness of Shane. It made me curious about why they were friends, and I was looking forward to learning more about him.

"Emily." Barrett's private-school-perfect tone drew me from my thoughts. "Kirk and I require a moment to speak. Please excuse us." He smiled. "It looks as though the girls have broken into the wine. Perhaps you'd like to join them?"

I clasped my hands and stretched my arms in an awkward movement that I hadn't meant to do. "Sure. I'll just—uh—go over there with them, then."

Barrett nodded. "Thank you." Hovering a guiding hand in the middle of Kirk's back, he turned them toward a path that led from the campsite, and they escaped into the forest together. I watched Kirk drift further from Barrett as they walked.

Huh. Strange.

Turning the other way, I sat at the fire beside Avril, my back melting into the Muskoka chair as I released the tension and tried to relax. She handed me a very full glass of wine, which I accepted with thanks.

"Figured you'd need it," she said. "How was the drive up?"

Rebecca watched me like she was looking for the slightest sign that any flirting had happened.

I shrugged. "Good. The scenery was amazing. Not much to report." As I drew my first sip, I couldn't help but focus on the path that the two men had disappeared down. Then I looked at Rebecca, who looked back like she couldn't decide whether to like me or hate me. "Maybe it's not my place to ask, but what happened between those two?"

The three women swiveled their heads, each waiting for the others to speak. Then, raising her chin like "the obligated partner," Rebecca said, "Well. They've been friends for a long time, and they're close, but they haven't spoken or seen each other for a year."

The alcohol tingled at the back of my throat. "Really? Why?"

What would cause two friends that were so close to not speak for an entire year?

"Well—"

"Leave it, Rebecca!" Shane's order came sharp from where he'd settled at the outdoor kitchen, weirdly starting to prep for dinner.

Wait. Billionaires *cook?*

Rebecca slapped the back of her hand against her knee. "Shane, I'm just answering a question—"

"That you have no right answer, so just *fecking* leave it." He wheeled around, pointing the spatula at her. Rebecca glared, but he ignored it and turned to me. "And, Emily, lass. I'm not trying to be rude, but it's best if you don't pry. It really isnae any of your business."

"I'm sorry, Shane. I didn't mean to stir anything up."

He narrowed his bright blue eyes. "Yeah, well, if you want to ken, ask Barrett when you're not a stranger to him, but be prepared for him to politely tell you to feck off."

Uh. Ouch?

The spatula vibrated as he pointed it at Rebecca again. "She has no *clue* of the true depths of our history, and therefore, has no right to answer you. Also, *she* will tell you all the awful things about him well before any of the amazing things."

Rebecca's response was sharp, like the lashing of a snake. "Fuck you, Shane!"

He shrugged dramatically. "You ken what, Rebecca? Feck you right back." Then he mumbled something that sounded like, "*Gypit Hoor,*" along with some other Scots words that were probably rude.

She sneered.

Whoa. This is intense.

"Okay, okay. That's enough. We all just need to calm down." Melissa stepped in with a voice of peace and reason. She pulled herself up from her chair and moved over to her partner, rubbing his back and neck as she tried to soothe him.

I took a big gulp of wine and swallowed it along with my guilt, before I spoke to Avril under my breath. "Struck a nerve."

She frowned and said, "You seem to be good at it."

The group fell silent, and to distract myself, I pulled out my phone and texted David to ask him if he was feeling any better.

A moment later, it buzzed with his response, and I smiled as I read it in his voice: *Two hours in and you're already texting me. 'Magine that! LOL I told you it'd be better to stay here.*

I snuffed. *No, it's nice. I was just worried about you is all.*

If it's that bad, it's not too late to come home.

Two days, I reminded him, smirking at my phone. But I couldn't help but wish that I was there with him instead, lounging on the couch and watching a fitness documentary he'd very likely be way too into.

When I pulled myself from our virtual check-in, Avril and Rebecca had started a separate conversation, and Melissa was helping Shane to prep some burgers and sausages. With a whine and a huff, Dixon settled himself at my feet, and I pulled them from my sneakers so that I could run my toes through his fluff.

Soon, the flames from the fire began to hypnotize. The length of the day was making me tired, which wasn't helped by the heaping glass of wine on an empty stomach, or the warmth of the dog under my feet. My eyelids began to fall heavy, and I think I fell into a quick snooze somewhere between watching Shane and Melissa break into an ad hoc slow dance and hearing him whisper "I love you" to her.

I smiled and thought about how I longed to hear the same thing. And from a partner who'd mean it this time...

A while later, I woke up when Barrett and Kirk came back from the woods. They weren't all the way to bright, but their energy seemed a little better now. I watched Barrett lay a hand on Kirk's shoulder before they separated. He then moved to give Rebecca a kiss, while

Kirk settled in his previous place across the fire. Dixon looked up at Kirk and then stood, leaving my feet cold as he trotted over to greet him. Kirk smiled as he stroked Dixon's ears, but I saw the sadness that lingered in his stormy eyes.

Stretching out his back like an oversized cat, Barrett started whistling to the song that now surrounded the campsite—someone must have started it while I was snoozing—and he made his way over to the kitchen with Shane. There, he started some playful banter with his best friend, praising him for dinner and telling him all about how he was, "the most astounding motherfucker on the planet." But, despite the loving interaction with Melissa, Shane was still in a sour mood from earlier, so he responded with bitterness. Barrett furrowed his brow and asked him if everything was okay.

Shane shrugged it off with *more* bitterness. "You fecking do this," he said, shoving the spatula in Barrett's hands. "You're much better than me."

"Shay," Barrett said, stopping him before he could storm off. "What's happened? Are you sure you're alright?"

"Yes, brither. *Dinna fash*."

Barrett gave him a pat on the shoulder, "Grab a drink and go sit down."

With a reluctant sigh, the half-Scot took a beer from the mini fridge, angling it on the stone of the counter so that he could pop the top off with a smack from the heel of his hand. He took a swig while he leaned there, crossing his arms as he watched Barrett's every move. There was a glint of concern on his face that told me that he wanted to speak with his best friend privately, but Barrett didn't notice until he looked at him again.

He smiled reassuringly. "Go sit down, Shay," he repeated. "I'm fine. Really."

Nodding, Shane left him, and took the chair beside Kirk.

Then—to my pleasant surprise—Barrett started to play host. He grabbed the wine bottles, topping up the women's glasses as he waited for the burgers to be cooked. Once we were served, he grabbed another beer for Kirk, along with one for himself, and grinned as he clinked bottles with his two best friends. "Cheers, boys," he said.

The three of them took synchronized swigs, and Barrett moved back to the barbeque to flip the burgers, his shoulders moving in a natural rhythm with the music. I watched the muscles move under his polo shirt and thought about how different he was around his friends. How different he was from the perception of what David had painted him to be.

The House-of-Wolves—well, David and Greg, at least—were adamant in their beliefs that the Roth men were some kind of "devil's spawn," but I didn't really see that with Travis *or* Barrett. They'd both shown me snapshots of men who were loving, caring, and protective of their family and friends—but that also could've been a deceptive, big-pharma strategy.

Anyway, I was starting to wonder if Avril had been right when she'd played Devil's advocate with the rest of the House. This story was complex, and it clearly needed a more in-depth analysis than I'd thought.

I listened to Barrett singing, before he hummed, mid-swig of beer. "Oh! I almost forgot." He jogged over to the cooler and pulled out a bag of peanut-butter cookies, tossing it across the campsite to Shane, who caught it with a loud, crinkling sound. "From Grandma with love."

Shane gasped like a kid on Christmas Day and ripped it open. "Fecking *love* that woman!" He broke a cookie in two, and devoured a half, shoving the other unexpectedly into Kirk's mouth. The two chomped away—Kirk looking like he was trying not to choke—and groaned. "Ahhh... Feck... Yes... Oh my God... Bear..." He went over to Barrett and served him a full cookie in the same manner that he had with Kirk.

Barrett had no choice but to chew and mumble, because his hands were occupied with the grill. "Fucking exceptional."

"Right?!" Shane said.

Barrett chuckled as he turned and leaned on the countertop, snapping off the end of the cookie that couldn't fit in his mouth. "You know, sometimes I make the deplorable mistake of forgetting that my grandmother is a genius. And this is a welcome reminder."

I grinned and thought of Carol gleefully baking cookies for her grandson's camping trip.

"Oh," Shane mumbled, with his mouth still full. "It's undeniable. I mean, that's better than *sex*. Don't you think that's better than *sex*?"

Barrett smirked. "Really depends on the person you're with." He looked carefully over at Kirk, who was just as careful to look away.

Then Rebecca stood up and stormed off into the tent like he'd insulted her. Which was super weird. What did she have to be insulted about?

There was a strange glint of amusement in Barrett's obsidian as he watched her, and he didn't follow.

Uh oh. Trouble in paradise?

Avril sighed and stood up. "I'll go," she said to no one in particular, following Rebecca and disappearing into the tent.

"Aren't you forgetting the ladies, Thomas?" Barrett said, washing down the cookie with another swig of beer.

Already on his second helping by the time he'd collapsed back into his chair, Shane grinned at Melissa and tossed her the bag.

Barrett shook his head. "Always the gentleman."

"What, brither?" Shane shrugged. "The lass can catch, can't she?"

Melissa broke off a piece of cookie, grinning as she threw it back. "Asshole."

He snatched it mid-air and gobbled it, spreading his arms in a playful shrug. "Give me all you got, baby."

That was when Kirk laughed for the first time that night. "Get a room, *vous deux*."

"No, I think you should stay for the show." Shane nudged him jokingly.

Melissa sighed in a defeated kind of acceptance before handing me the bag. "Here, Emily. Have one."

"Thanks." I chose one and blissfully bit into it, but my eyes wandered from the tent to the unfazed man at the grill.

The plot with these Cat People seemed to be thickening with each passing second, and something told me that it was going to be a longer weekend than I'd originally thought.

CHAPTER 22
WANDERLUST

The next morning, I came back into the world with the glow of the sun on the tent, the happy symphony of the birds, and the smell of fresh coffee. I groaned as I sat up and stretched out my shoulder, which was stiff from the elevated air mattress. Avril was still deep in sleep beside me, and I smiled as I watched her, grateful that I'd gained such an awesome family member.

Energized and ready to start the day, I tossed the sleeping bag from my lap and met the chilled air. I changed, slipped on my shoes, and let myself out into the misty mountain atmosphere, which clung to my skin as I stepped outside. I shivered and wrapped my windbreaker tighter to my small frame but inhaled the cedar and pine. It was rejuvenating, and I took several deep breaths as I made my way over to the kitchen, where the coffee was already steaming from a metal kettle. I poured some into one of the clean mugs left on the counter, and mixed in a bit of sugar, before I stood sipping it with the steam tickling my nostrils. Then I wondered where everyone else was. The soft sounds of snoring from Melissa and Shane's tent—along with a matching sound from Kirk's—told me they were still asleep. But Rebecca and Barrett's tent seemed quiet. Maybe the unhappy couple was up?

I shrugged it off and sipped as I leaned against the counter. It was probably the best damn coffee I ever had. The morning essence was made even more amazing by the solitude, so for now, I'd enjoy the simple act of *being*.

I let my thoughts wander, and the first place they drifted to was David Mathis and how he was feeling now. Smacking the hot coffee between my lips, I pulled my phone from my pocket. *7:30am.* Not too early to call—though he might be a little cranky if I happened to wake him up. I'd have to play the "I was worried about you" card, but at least it wasn't a lie. I *was* worried about him. *And* the plethora of things he seemed to suffer from.

After a few rings he picked up with his voice rougher than yesterday. "Morning, Em."

I swallowed the coffee in my mouth. "Oh, shit. Did I wake you up?"

His muted chuckle was a welcome sound. "Yeah, you did. But I wanna hear your voice first thing, so it's okay."

I threw in my gambit. "I was just worried about you, is all. How are you doing?"

"Fine. Jus' tired is all." He was downplaying things again. He didn't *sound* fine at all.

A white and grey bird landed further down the counter and studied me with a curious eye. I'd never seen one like it before, so I quickly snapped a pic in the space between our conversation. "I've been thinking about you," I admitted to David, before my brain could stop me.

I could hear the grin in his voice. "Miss me already?"

"Something like that... I wish you were here is all..." It was a weird thing to wish, considering whose property we were on. "I wish things were different..."

He sniffed, sounding even sicker. "Things are how they are, Em."

Even though he couldn't see me, I nodded. I had the distinct feeling that we were hinting at the same thing without ever saying the words. What would it be like if his father had never murdered Barrett's?

"For the record, I miss you too," he said.

Warmth spread through me, and I grinned like a crushing

schoolgirl as I hugged my jacket. "So, what are your plans on this beautiful Saturday?"

"Probably jus' going to work out, then order Chinese food and get stoned with Greggy." He moaned out a stretch.

I chuckled. "That sounds counterintuitive."

"Nah, see, I'm sick. So, if I'm gonna work out, I'm allowed to feast on deliciously greasy noodles."

"Except that you shouldn't be working out sick!" I added.

"Gotta get them gains somehow, princess."

I sighed. "I should've stayed home."

"It's all good, Em. Big boy, remember?"

"Yeah..."

The clunking sound of wood-meeting-the-ground drew my attention toward the beach, and I looked over to see Barrett alone down there. Rebecca wasn't with him. Now was my chance to get more one-on-one time with him.

"Um, David? I've gotta go. We can catch up tomorrow when we get back. Try to get some rest and feel better for me."

"Alright, princess."

"Okay, go back to sleep."

"Yep. Bye."

I was smiling when I hung up, but the sounds from the beach snapped me out of it. I drained my coffee before I turned to follow the signs. The truth was, I really did miss David, but I had a whole weekend ahead to learn a new set of information. So, I followed the path down toward the beach, and there I met our host, prepping a canoe and paddles for a trip out on the water. Dixon was with him, looking particularly cute in a doggie-lifejacket that matched the one that Barrett was wearing.

Mr. Roth was bright-eyed, and bushy tailed; moving with speed I'd never seen before, as he tossed the paddles into the canoe. Damn.

That coffee must have been stronger than I'd thought. "Good morning, Miss Anderson!"

"Good morning, Mr. Roth." Dixon ran over to me, and I kneeled to receive my morning kisses.

"Did you get the chance to enjoy some coffee?"

I giggled as I pushed the overenthusiastic malamute from my face. "I did. And I also saw the most beautiful bird up there. Have you seen this before?" I stood and pulled up the picture on my phone; hit with his musky-sweet cologne as we came together.

"Ah," he said, tapping on the screen. "*That* is a Whiskey Jack. I feed them when I'm here. They were probably expectant of that. Were the seeds gone?"

"Yeah. Didn't notice any."

He grinned. "Quintessential."

Who the fuck uses a word like quintessential*?*

Trying not to laugh, I shoved my hands into my jean shorts, still gripping my phone in the right. Was there an end to the things that I didn't know about him? "You're up early," I pointed out.

"I couldn't sleep any longer. There is no measure of the ways this property can be enjoyed, and I prefer not to take that for granted."

I nodded toward the canoe. "Where're you headed?"

"I'm glad you asked, Miss Anderson." He turned away and disappeared into the boat house, returning with a third life jacket. "I was about to take Dixon on a romantic tour, but now that you're awake, I'd like you to come with us. There's something spectacular that I'd like to show you."

My fingers brushed his as I took the lifejacket, and excitement shot through me like a shock. "Sounds like fun."

"I'm pleased you think so."

As I pulled the lifejacket over my windbreaker, he squatted to lift Dixon, whose legs hung limp as he carried him to the canoe. Then, Barrett offered me his hand, and I gripped it tightly as I stepped in, cursing my shitty balance when it wobbled beneath me. I took the spot at the very front, and he launched the boat into the water, hopping in from the shore as we began to glide across the misty lake.

"Are you going to be comfortable at the very front? Would it not be sensible to move back one seat?"

"Pfft. Yeah." I waved him off. "I always go to the front. Trust me." In truth, I'd never been in a canoe, but I didn't want to look like a silly city-girl in front of him. All I knew for sure was that you sat down and paddled.

The playfulness of his laugh told me that he'd seen straight through me. "Alright, then."

I took a paddle and plunged it through the chilly water. "For a man that lives in a penthouse in downtown Vancouver, I never thought you'd be so in tune with nature."

"Nature is all we have, Miss Anderson. And I enjoy connecting with it more than most other things in life." His paddle dipped in from behind me. "As I said yesterday, I am a lucky man. Made even more so as the current proprietor of this land." Again, his answer was a surprise.

We glided further into the lake, the sound dropping to only Barrett's paddle and the roar of what sounded like a hidden waterfall ahead. After my brief start, I set my paddle across my lap to concentrate on the amazing scenery. The glistening water ran down the sharp edge of my paddle, before it fell in tiny droplets to rejoin the water below. Across the lake, the sun shone on a surface that seemed to be made of glass, dampened from the morning fog that still hovered over the water. The only break in the clear aquamarine came from the gentle wake of the canoe, and the ripples from Barrett's paddle as he pushed us along. That *incredible* smell of forest wafted through the humid air, and again, I gratefully filled my lungs.

"This place is absolute heaven, Barrett," I said, in love with the morning. "I could live here. Easily, I think. Just wander the woods all day."

When I looked back, his eyes were that dark chocolate colour that they seemed to go when he was tranquil. "This has always been a peaceful place for me."

I smiled when I turned back. "I can see why."

The clouds parted and let more of the sun through, bathing us in golden light. I lifted my chin toward it, closing my eyes and slipping into a state of bliss as I absorbed its energy. It activated me much more than any coffee could, and when I opened them again, I'd turned playful. I re-joined the effort, and my paddle splashed as it skimmed the top of the water. Wearing a wry grin, I twisted started throwing some back at Barrett.

Freezing globs of lake water sprayed me in return, and I gasped. "Barrett!"

I could hear the grin through his voice. "You brought your phone, didn't you?"

"Maybe?" I shivered.

"Foolish, but to be expected of an amateur. There's a waterproof pocket on the chest of the lifejacket. Slip it in there, and it will be protected." I did what he said, and when I was finished, he added, "Good. Now I don't have to be remorseful for doing this."

A frigid wave washed over me, and I cried out in shock, Dixon joining with a whine. The menacing laugh that Barrett broke out after told me that he was enjoying it. "Alright, alright! You win! I surrender!"

"That's a dangerous admission, kid."

"Fuck, that's cold!"

"It's glacial fed. Did you expect any different?"

Twisting, I stuck out my tongue and got his perfect grin in return.

"Perhaps don't start fights that you can't win, Miss Anderson."

I hid my smirk when I turned back and decided to punish him by refusing to paddle again. Not that I was much good, *anyway*.

Then, a cramp in my knee reminded me of how uncomfortable I

was. The bow of the canoe came to a point right at my shins, forcing my feet to be awkwardly tucked under the seat, and I realized that this tiny spot at the front was probably just a brace of some kind. The front seat was *behind* me, and Barrett had been fucking with me the whole time.

Hmmm, could be a problem.

"Um, Barrett?"

"Yes, Emily?"

"I'm sitting on the bow brace, aren't I?"

"It took you that long to figure that out?"

"Uh, yeah? How long were you going to let me think it was a seat?"

"Well, we're balanced, and you looked so cute, basking in your ignorance. I simply could not help it."

I huffed out a laugh. He was unbelievable. "Whatever. But you were right. I'm uncomfortable. I need to move back."

His tone dripped with uncertainty. "What? Here?"

"Uh, yeah?"

The following sigh told me that he didn't have faith in my balance. "Alright. What I'd like you to do is swivel, pull your legs over the side, and then move—*slowly*—to the front seat."

"Right."

"And I cannot stress the word *slowly* enough," he said. "This canoe is a little top heavy and is notorious for tipping."

"Oh. Great. Way to tell me that now, *Mr. Roth.*"

"Would you like help?"

"I'm good. I can do this." Truth was, I was reassuring myself as much as him.

The swiveling and pulling my legs over part happened with no problem, but as I stood, the canoe wobbled in warning. I fought to rebalance it before I stepped one foot toward the other seat. Then, (over)confident that I could do the same with the second, I looked up to tease Barrett. "See? Easy-peasy."

But Murphy's Law immediately put me in my place, and in the distraction of looking up at him, I caught my other foot on the edge of the seat, slamming into the side of the canoe. I heard Barrett cry, "Shit! Em!" as he braced to rebalance it, but it was too late. My fall had caused too much momentum, and the moody canoe tossed all three of us into the water.

The frigid lake hit my chest like a pile of bricks, and I gasped as the lifejacket pulled my head above the water. Barrett drew a similar inhale from somewhere beside me, but Dixon was doggie paddling happily, tongue hanging from a wide, doggy grin.

When I'd caught my breath, I started to sputter. "Oh my G-G-God! I am *s-so* sorry."

Barrett swam over to Dixon and reached for the handle of his lifejacket. "Emily, go to the other side. I need you to counterbalance while I lift him in. Dixon, come *here!*" But the Alaskan malamute was done, and he swam away toward the shore. With a shuddering sigh, Barrett recognized a wasted effort and let him go.

"I'm s-so sorry, Barrett!"

"It's alright! It's alright. You didn't capsize it. That makes it easier. But we have to re-enter together from opposite sides."

I did as he said and swam to the other side, quivering as I waited for his signal. Then, we acted as counterweights to each other, and with a strained heave, I pulled myself up as he climbed over the opposite side. He had the added disadvantage that I was much lighter than him, so it was a bit more of a struggle, but he made it.

We were both speechless and panting while we recovered from the effort. I sat on the *actual* front seat and rested my arms across my knees, dropping my head as I begged for the sun to warm me. He collapsed toward the stern, the seat behind him bracing the top of his back as he threw an arm over his eyes.

"Oh my God. I'm such a klutz." I gripped my hair and realized that my old scar was raised from the cold. "I can't believe I just did that..."

But Barrett started laughing, which was a very welcome sound.

"I literally *just* warned you." His laughing got louder, and I let it dissolve some of the embarrassment.

Releasing my tension with a heavy exhale, I decided to join him, and our duet of laughter echoed across the lake. And by the time we let it calm, I felt a little closer to him. What'd been the harm in going for an ad hoc swim on a summer morning, anyway?

He grinned as he pulled himself upright, smoothing his faux-brown hair back into its signature wave. "Ahhh. That was fun, blondie."

I chuckled, grateful for his reaction. "I'm so sorry."

"Think nothing of it. This was not the first time that's happened, and it won't be the last. And—nevertheless—we were going to get wet on this trip, anyway."

I wrung out my ponytail before twisting it up into a bun with the hair-tie I'd kept around my wrist. "What do you mean?"

"You'll see. It's all part of the fun, kiddo." He shot me a wink, shimmied off some water, picked up his paddle, and pushed us further onto the lake.

Who are you, Barrett Roth?

I took a beat to unclip my lifejacket and pull off my soppy windbreaker. It stuck to my skin like clingwrap, and I had to peel it away from each arm before I draped it over the brace in front of me. The humidity of the air drew goosebumps over my body, but it was better than sitting in a soaked coat.

"I hope you're comfortable now, Miss Anderson." Barrett's lively tone drifted from behind me.

I vibrated again, but pointedly said, "Yes, I am."

"Thank fuck. Pick up a paddle, will you? I'm going to need your help for this."

I turned to stick my tongue out at him, but I clipped my lifejacket back on and did what I was told.

We glided toward the east side of the lake, where a cliff face rose, coming to its highest point around a rounded corner. The lake had an offshoot there, which was hidden if you were standing at the campground's beach. It was a private and intimate area, sheltered by the curve of towering granite. The sound of roaring water got louder as we went around the corner, and I discovered that this was where the waterfall was. It fell from the peak of the cliff, crashing to the lake below in a thunder of mist. The force began to push us backward, and we had to paddle to keep ourselves in place.

The mist sprinkled my face as I looked up. "Wow..." I was starting to realize how incredibly lucky we were to experience this nature.

"Ava falls," Barrett said, over the roar of the water. "My father named it after my mother when we took possession of this land."

"That's very romantic!" I called back to him. "I'm glad you showed me, Barrett. Thanks!"

"Oh, but we're not done. This isn't what I wanted to show you."

I raised an eyebrow, the mist covering the right side of my face as I turned to him. "Huh?"

"We must go *under* it."

"*Under* it? What, there's something on the other side?"

"Yes. Something very special."

It took me a moment to figure out whether he was fucking with me again or not. "How're we gonna do that?"

"With a lot of hard work, but I assure you, it's worth it." He set his paddle at a right angle to the water and ran a strong stroke that jerked us forward. The flow immediately pushed back. "Like that. See?"

I copied him, trying for myself.

"Good. Now, I have done this myself many times, in a kayak or on the seadoos, but with the canoe it requires both of us. Paddle straight through the falling water, and whichever way you want the boat to turn, you paddle on the opposite side. Got it?"

I swallowed but jerked my head in a nod. "Right. Got it."

"Brace yourself. It's going to be frigid."

"I'm ready. Just don't stop."

"You don't have to say it twice, kid."

There was a surge of power from the back of the boat as he began to push against the current. I did what he'd said and paddled like mad, fighting to keep the boat centered toward the middle of the waterfall as we started to push through. The icy water took my breath as it slammed onto the top of my head and knocked out my bun, but I kept going. Once I was through, I blinked the glacial water from my eyes and kept focused on the path ahead as the current changed, now helping to propel the back of the boat. I heard Barrett whoop and sputter from behind me, as he cleared the water from his face. The sound of his voice echoed down the cave ahead of us before it faded.

I wiped my face with both palms—thankful that I didn't have any makeup on—before I righted my bun. "Holy shit."

He laughed and the boat wobbled as he crouched forward, opening the storage compartment that sat under the yoke. "You okay, Em?"

Hearing him use my nickname made my stomach flip. I exhaled, shaking the water from my skin. "I think so." Again, the echo pulsed down the cave ahead. "How far back does this go?"

He clicked on an electric lantern, causing the earth around us to sparkle in a brilliant concave. "It takes about a minute or two to paddle to the back at a leisurely pace." He handed me the lantern, before he pulled a second from the compartment. "Place that on the seat ahead of you. We will need it to guide us."

With a flat palm, I wiped the water from the front seat and then set the lantern down as he did the same at the back. The balanced light reflected off the minerals of the cave like a semi-circle of stars, strewn in various patterns across a velvety night sky. The current from the waterfall was causing us to drift into the mountain, but our speed increased as Barrett dipped his paddle back in the water and gently pushed us forward. I was too awestruck to help.

I grazed my fingertips along the stone as we passed, finding it cool to the touch. "What kind of rock is this?"

"Mostly granite and sedimentary rock such as sandstone and shale."

I twisted, failing to hide how impressed I was with his answer. Apparently, Mr. CFO knew more than just finance facts. "This is granite?"

He smiled. "Yes. This area is composed of a great deal of it."

"Wow..." The rush of my breath boomed around us. "This is incredible, Barrett. How did you even find it?"

His warm chuckle pulsed down the cave. "I can't take the credit. It was Kirk who found it." He took care to steer us around a few of the stalagmites coming from the bottom of the cave, and I brushed my fingers against the various stalactites that passed. "One day, long ago, when Kirk, Shane, and I were merely a threesome of pubescent teenagers, we pulled our seadoos up to the waterfall. Mr. Richards was adamant to show off his strength—of which he's always had an abundance—so he plunged his arm through the falls and held it against the weight of the water as he reached for the cliff face on the other side. Lo-and-behold, to our surprise, his hand met empty air, and that's when he discovered that there was a cave here."

I watched the rock twinkle above me. "Well done, Kirk. There's something to be said for boyish overconfidence."

He chuckled again. "Quite. We, as men, are built to prove ourselves. Time and time again."

We neared another stalagmite, and I pushed off its surface to help guide us around it.

"My father was thrilled with the discovery," he added. "Especially when we found out that the walls of this cave held something priceless."

With perfect timing, we came to the end, and the lantern light revealed what he was talking about. I gasped. There, on the walls, was a broad collection of native pictographs, preserved perfectly in their lines of red. Carved petroglyphs were peppered among them, and my jaw dropped as I shifted forward to get a closer look. A metal handle had been drilled into the wall just above the water's surface, and it was here that Barrett anchored the boat with a piece of rope that he pulled from the center compartment. His intoxicating smell surrounded me as he stepped across the yoke to kneel beside me.

I gawked as I studied the collection. "Wow..." My voice had dropped into a whisper. "I'm speechless, Barrett..."

"I'm not surprised. So far, they haven't failed to take anyone's breath away." He reached out and traced a petroglyph with his index finger.

"They're quite rare, aren't they? Pictographs and petroglyphs?"

"Only if you're not sure where to look for them," he said. "BC is full of them. We have many First Nations, and the native influence remains quite abundant—and massively pivotal—here. As it should. This is their land, no matter what colonist lies we tell ourselves. I'm sure you've noticed that already."

I nodded slowly, thinking about the signs and totem poles at Capilano. "How do you know so much about this, Bear?" I asked, turning toward him. "The details of the land and its history?"

He paused, and his lip folded like he'd bit it from the inside. "The Earth is the love-of-my-life..." He brushed his fingers across the rock. "Well, *one* of the loves-of-my-life, anyway. I have a passion for geographical sciences... Environmental sciences..."

I blinked. This was very much *not* the person that strutted up on stage at the Roth Banquet. He was showing me another side of himself—the *authentic* side—and it was *this* Barrett that I wanted to get to know. "Then, sorry, I don't mean to sound insensitive, blame the curiosity, but why are you running numbers at the family business?"

He winced like I'd struck something inside before covering it by furrowing his brow. I worried that I'd overstepped again. "The duty and honour of my birthright will always take precedence over passion, Emily. The very same as it will for my brother. Travis—as capable and competent as he is—cannot run our company alone. I am bound by obligation, as is he... As we will always be."

My heart ached a little. It had never occurred to me that the life that he was living may not be the one that he wanted. I couldn't imagine what it was like to be chained to your family business, whether that made you rich as fuck or not. "I'm sorry. I didn't mean to make you feel any sort of way."

"It's quite alright. I can see your genuine kindness." He smiled. "You haven't offended me."

Something tingled. Deep in my gut, where I couldn't ignore it. I turned my attention back to the wall, but it didn't help much. "So, tell me what they mean, Bear." I figured if he'd started using my nickname, then it would be okay for me to start using his.

"Well, it's a lot of interpretation," he said, running his hand along the images. "When we discovered them, my father sought out a Squamish Elder to help us understand their meaning. He explained that pictographs were often painted on rock to depict visions or dreams of the natives. Sometimes they depict reality as well." He pointed to a line with rays coming out of it; "This one is thought to depict a fir branch, which they were surrounded by." A straight line with dots around it; "This is meant to symbolize offerings made by the younger people of the tribe." What looked like an animal, an oval shape with four legs, a tail, and horns; "This is a cow." Lastly, he pointed to a circle that was surrounded by a bigger circle, with two lines coming out of the sides, top, and bottom; "This is thought to be a symbol for happiness."

"Incredible. And what's the red paint?"

"Typically, it was made from red ochre, which are iron oxides mixed with clay."

"And they somehow managed to get all the way down here to paint them?"

"Well," he said. "The cave would have been pre-existing, as these caves are carved by underground rivers that flow toward the lake. So, there's really only two ways that they could have done so. The lake and the river above freeze in the winter, which turns the falls into a light trickle that runs down the cliff face. That would have allowed them to walk in on foot. Or, alternatively, they did exactly as we just did, and they sailed in via canoe."

My eyes panned the illustrations. "So, what First Nation did they belong to then?"

"Squamish," he said. "This is the unceded territory of the Squamish First Nation, so there is no doubt about it."

I was so incredibly *grateful* to experience such an amazing part of the history of the land and its First Nations. "I'm speechless," I repeated.

Then he took my right hand with his left, which made tingling climb up my nerves. "Here. Check this out." Folding my fingers to match the shape of his, he guided my index over a petroglyph. "Do you feel that? That's an arrow."

I held my breath, paralyzed by his touch as my fingertip grazed the carving before us. The fine hairs across my body stood like they were energized by the electric connection made by our touch, rising like blades of grass to the sun. I turned my head and found his black eyes sparkling and beautiful in the dull light. And I had no clue how many moments of tension passed. Just that we were locked in them. It was the most romantic setting I'd ever been in with someone, and I fought the urge to lean forward and place my lips on his as we watched each other. He dropped his gaze to focus on my mouth like he was fighting the same, before drawing a sharp inhale, dropping my hand, and sitting back on the yoke to distance us. My skin craved his touch as soon as he broke it.

Oh shit... I thought, pulling myself from the spell as thoughts of David immediately rose to the surface. *This complicates things...*

Turning back to the pictographs, I did a mental 180 to distract myself, and I thought of Johnathan Roth. What sort of expectation did he have for his sons? I could feel his youngest watching me now, but this time I didn't mind the attention of his gaze so much. Maybe I even *welcomed* it now...

After a while, I spoke. "Barrett?"

"Yes, Emily?" he answered, softly.

"Do you miss your dad?"

He glanced back to the pictographs. "Every day."

"It must be really hard living without him."

"It's gotten easier over time, but it's never been the same." He paused as he dropped his eyes. "Sometimes I feel lost, like I don't know what I'm doing, and I wish he was here to simply... *tell* me. And I'm aware that Travis sometimes feels the same, though he never says it. Running a company that is worth billions in a billion-dollar industry is never easy when you haven't had much guidance."

I smiled at him. "For the record, I think you two are doing an incredible job. Judging from the banquet, you're steering the company in the right direction and doing some great work. I mean, you may have money, but it's not like you don't work hard for it."

And this was coming out of *my* mouth? In what world did I ever think I'd be praising the co-owner of a big pharma company? I was literally studying something that existed to keep them in line.

But Barrett Roth had shown me that there was more under the surface. He'd given me a little peek at who he was, and I wanted to see more. I wanted to know the *real* him. Pick him up. Study him from all angles. Heck, maybe even be *friends* at some point. After all, it could only help my future career. Right?

Then Joseph's words found a contrasting place in my mind—*There are two sides to every story*—and I wondered what plotline in *this* story was murder worthy.

Barrett was now failing to hide his own bewilderment, before he shifted his expression softer. "That's kind of you, Emily. Thank you. I'll remember it when I'm in need of encouragement."

"It's true though," I said, quietly. "Call me a spiritual observer of the truth."

We smiled at each other, and that strange romantic tension grew between us again. It was like I could spend hours in that cave. Bathed in the warm light of the lantern. Getting lost those eyes of his. Absolutely and irrevocably lost... There was something about them that had me hooked... A moth that had drifted all the way across the country to meet its flame.

You say you're the Bad-Roth, but you're only hiding behind him.

Who are you gonna be to me?

Barrett broke the mood by standing and untying the canoe. "Come on. Let's get back. I have breakfast to make."

CHAPTER 23
ALL THAT I'VE GOT

After dinner, Kirk went to the back of one of the campsites to chop wood and, seeing the opportunity for some alone time with him, I offered to help. After spending that morning with Barrett, I was excited to get a chance to talk to someone who'd been friends with him for so long. And maybe Kirk would give me a little nugget that would help me tie all this messy history together. Maybe he'd be able to tell me a little bit more about John and give me an indication of the motive for his murder.

Plus, you know, Kirk was handsome and single—as far as I knew—so anything that distracted me from how I'd started feeling for Barrett was an advantage.

With few words to start, we formed an efficient team where he split the wood, and I loaded it into a wheelbarrow. But the quietness let those pesky thoughts about his best friend to rise. I started thinking about Barrett's hand and how I'd glanced at it while we walked back to the campground from the lake, stopping myself from reaching out and taking it. I'd be in the wrong with a move like that, for sure. *More* than in the wrong, actually—I'd be aiming way left of the proverbial field. He was in a relationship already, and even if he weren't, we weren't compatible.

Were we?

I mean, we were from two separate worlds, and my attraction to David made so much more *sense*.

But between the moments that Barrett and I had spent in canoe and the Chevelle, I couldn't ignore how deep the bonding experience had been with him. It was effortless. Easy. *Right.* In these past two days I'd felt like I'd connected faster with him than *anyone,* and it *was* his name that I'd been shouting for years. Was this it? Was this really *my* Barrett? The person that I was fated to? And if so, what should I do with my feelings? What should I do with my conflicting attraction to David? What should I do about the Roth-Mathis feud, and the possible root cause being big pharma oppression?

Ahhh! It was so fucking overwhelming!

I decided to turn my attention to Kirk so I didn't have to think about it.

In between sips of bourbon, he seemed to enjoy slamming the axe onto the chopping block, the wood splitting in sharp cracks beneath it. Watching the bulging muscles of his shoulders and back, I thought about how easy he made it look. When I told him that he was good at it, he smiled and offered me the axe to try. I watched the shimmer of the blade like an assault weapon. I could already see it bouncing across the campsite and wreaking havoc after slipping from my hand. But Kirk was quietly encouraging, and after some convincing, I agreed.

"I'm not gonna be any good anyway," I said, taking the handle and adjusting my posture.

"That's okay," he said. "Doesn't mean you can't try."

I proved myself right when I missed the wood completely on the first swing. With his massive arms crossed, Kirk told me to try again. On the second attempt, I used all my strength and somehow managed to contact the wood, but it refused to split, giving me only a stubborn crack.

"Here," he said, stepping forward to help. "It's much easier if you hold it like this."

My tone teetered. "It's harder than it looks, Kirk."

"I know." I could smell the bourbon above his woodsy cologne and the imprinted scent of campfire. "But you just need practice."

His warm hands encompassed mine as he shifted them on the handle of the axe. "There. Try now."

The new position was much more comfortable, and I gave it everything. I focused my glare on the wood, splitting the cracked piece with ease.

"There you go. *Bon travail.*" Kirk picked the pieces and tossed them in the wheelbarrow before setting the next one. "Now. Again."

This time, I impressed myself when I split it on the first try, and I dropped the axe to my side, putting my other hand on my hip. "That's surprisingly satisfying." I couldn't lie—having a successful split did make me feel a bit like Wonder Woman.

"Yeah," he said. "Especially when you've got something to be angry about." He shot a subtle glance at Barrett in the other campsite.

The grin on my face faded as I followed his gaze. Rebecca's arms were wrapped around Barrett's neck, and he was holding her hips as they swayed in another of their soft-core make-out sessions.

A gentle mountain breeze chilled me. "Here." I offered Kirk the axe. "I think that's enough chopping for me."

He took it with a nod, knuckles turning white with the sudden tightness of his grip. He set the next piece and split it with the loudness of a thunderclap, making me jump.

"So," I said, trying to diffuse the strained energy. "On the drive up, Barrett said you were French."

"*Oui.*" Kirk snuffed quietly and broke out his half-smile. "A quarter—the way I see it. My *maman* comes from a small town north of Québec city, and my *grand-père* is also French-Canadian. My *grand-mère* is actual French-from-France, though."

"Um, but wouldn't that make your mum entirely French?"

He shrugged. "I don't think of French-Canadian as French; just Canadian. If you wanna get technical, she is, and I'm half-French. But I prefer to think of myself as a quarter pure-French."

"You sound so Canadian, though," I said, chucking a piece of wood in the wheelbarrow. "I mean, you don't seem to have an accent unless you're speaking French."

"*Merci*," he said, taking a break to sip his bourbon. "I've worked hard on it, so it's good to know."

"But then, how'd you get so good at French?"

"My family speaks it exclusively at home. My *maman* was adamant about that since I was born, and my sister's obsessed with it. My dad's from Saskatchewan, so he had to learn as an adult. Technically French is my first language, but I grew up in Saskatoon. As soon as I got into kindergarten, I picked up English."

"Oh, ok. So, you're a Saskatchewanian?" My tongue stumbled over the difficult word, causing him to huff out a laugh.

"*Oui*," he said. "I consider myself a Canadian first, and Frenchman second."

I smiled. "And what about your sister? Are you two close?"

"Yeah," he said, grinning back. It was the first time I'd seen him grin. "She's the charismatic extrovert of the family. She's impossible not to love."

"That's good," I said. "Québec City, to Saskatoon, to here. That's quite the spread your family's had across the country."

"My parents work for Shane's," he said. "They saw a good opportunity here, and they took it. Believe it or not, Saskatoon isn't known for its high quality of life."

"Ah. So that's how you two met?"

He looked over at Shane, who was chatting with Avril, his chair turned in toward hers. "He was the first friend I made here."

"And what about Barrett?"

His expression darkened as he focused on Barrett. "I met him later, when my parents were doing well enough to send me to private school. We went there together. My sister went after. They weren't going to at first, but Shane's dad can be very convincing, and my parents took a massive financial hit to follow his advice." He chuckled before he brought down the axe on the next piece of wood. "I still remember the look on their faces when I told them I wanted to be a mechanic."

I thought about what Barrett had said about Kirk's successful business. "Joke's on them, right?"

He didn't say anything, but the look he gave me told me he appreciated it. "Anyway," he said, as he scooped up the wood and tossed it in the wheelbarrow. "We were fourteen when we met."

"That's a hell of a long friendship," I said, raising an eyebrow as I glanced back to the campsite. "Good for the three of you."

He snuffed as he set the next piece. "Yeah, well. It hasn't always been easy."

"Yeah, I know."

He scowled a little. Like someone had told me something they shouldn't have. "You know what?"

I was a little caught off guard but decided to answer honestly. "Um. Just that I can tell that there's tension between you two, Kirk. Between you and Barrett."

He slammed the axe down, and the wood burst like it had stepped on a land mine. When he turned toward me, his tone was as sharp as the tool that he held. "Listen. It hasn't exactly been easy for me. Being friends with him, I mean."

I threw up my hands. "Whoa. Okay. I'm not trying to insinuate anything, Kirk. I don't know anything about your past. I was just being honest about the energy I can feel."

And now I'd touched the nerves of both of Barrett's best friends. It was interesting, though, that both of those nerves *seemed* to be Barrett himself. What kind of hell had he put them through?

Then I thought back to the morning. After Barrett and I got back from the pictographs, Rebecca was annoyed that he'd gone off alone with me. He tried to explain that he was only trying to show me the wonders of the land, but they'd got into an argument that resulted in her storming off to the beach, and him storming into the tent. I'd seen the look that Kirk and Shane had shared—like they were suffering the same hidden anxiety—and Barrett came out of that tent as the other version of himself. The Bad-Roth. Pupils dilated and nose wiggling. He threw an arm around his two best friends and declared at the top of his voice how happy he was to be with his boys.

Shane and Kirk shot another look from across his chest, but I didn't have time to think about that, because not long after, Barrett was beside me, sipping coffee, and smirking. I'd apologized for being the cause of his fight, but he'd shushed me by telling me not to worry about it and then gave me a very, *very* unexpected kiss on the forehead.

My skin prickled from the contact with his lips.

He and Rebecca made up not long after.

Kirk jammed the axe into the chopping block, where it stood at an angle, before he picked up his bourbon from a nearby stump. He took a huge gulp, ice clinking against the glass. "I didn't mean to snap at you," he said as he swallowed. "I'm really sorry, Emily."

I was quiet as I picked up the wood and placed it into the wheelbarrow, thinking about how much he was echoing Shane's temper from yesterday. "It's okay," I said, trying to avoid the splinters and ignore the lump in my throat. I sighed and started again carefully. "You were fourteen. That means that Barrett's dad was still alive when you met."

"Yeah," he said, setting the glass back down and yanking the axe out of the chopping block. "His dad didn't die until we were sixteen."

Curiosity raised, I decided to test the waters again. The murder had risen to the forefront of my mind, and I didn't want to leave that weekend without finding out more. "What did you think of him? John, I mean."

He shrugged before he split the last piece of wood. "He was an asshole, and he didn't talk to me much. I think the only time he was nice to me was when I found the fucking cave that Barrett showed you this morning. There wasn't enough money in my family's bank accounts for us to be considered human." He took another sip of bourbon before his tone turned somber. "But his death put Barrett through hell, and he still struggles with it. Though he won't admit it."

I made sure that my next question came with a compassionate voice. "Do you know why he was murdered, Kirk?"

His stormy, blue eyes flicked to me before they moved to Barrett. "Joseph Mathis is a psycho, but I've never considered it any of my business." He swallowed, and his honey-blonde brows arched as he jerked his chin. "My business has always been to take care of *him*."

I followed his gaze to where Barrett and Rebecca were now taking a break from their make-out session. Her perfectly manicured nails were running through either side of his faux-brown hair, and his right hand was placed strategically on her ass.

"That *garce* isn't good for him." Kirk spoke like he was thinking out loud. "She's the same as all the other gold-digging whores he picks up. He doesn't deserve her toying with his heart."

I sighed as I brushed the dirt from my hands. "Yeah, but I think he needs to learn how horrible she is on his own, to be honest."

Kirk took a beat. Watching Barrett intensely. "He hides it, you know. He hides how big and fragile his heart is. I just hope he stops this rotating door of *putes* before it does any real damage."

Sympathetic, I stepped forward and touched his arm. The twitch of his skin made me drop it almost immediately.

The other side of the story was piecing together for me, and I was starting to see how broad the impact had been when Joseph Mathis had left Johnathan Roth to succumb to his bullet wounds in the street. There was pain and destruction on both sides—that much was clear—but the *reasoning* was what still eluded me. It was the *why*. The *why* was the big black hole that encompassed this whole story.

And how would I fit in with it?

I looked over at Barrett and wondered about us. What was going to happen. What it all meant. "I can't figure him out," I admitted to Kirk. "I've seen two very different versions of him."

"That's just Barrett," Kirk said. "Eventually you learn which one's real." He pulled his lips into something resembling a smile and tossed the axe into the wheelbarrow. It bounced and spun before settling atop the wood. "Come on. Let's get back."

Many glasses of alcohol and a game of strip poker later, the collective mood had raised—well before Shane had hopped up on the seat of the picnic table to prove that he was the loser. Plunging his thumbs into the waistband of his boxer-briefs—the only thing he had on—he threatened to drop them before Barrett cut in and called game over.

I was teetering on drunk by then, and I giggled to cover the fact that I'd been drinking in his body right before he jumped down. I had to hand it to Melissa; there was something about those aquamarine eyes and that bright blond hair that was really attractive. And it wasn't hard for *tipsy Emily* to notice the decent bulge that he had under those boxer-briefs.

Turning my lopsided grin toward her, I'd raised my glass and shot her a look that said, *Good for you.*

She grinned and flashed her eyebrows as we clinked our glasses.

Through my wine goggles, all three men were looking pretty damn good, and I played *single girl* as my eyes moved around the table greedily. Strip poker hadn't helped, but I didn't see the harm in looking when it served them up so easily. I was the she-wolf—hungry and hell-bent on my silent hunt—though two out of the three were men that I couldn't touch.

And it didn't stop me from turning Barrett into my main prey, of course. After seeing the version of himself that he'd shown me that morning, I just couldn't help it. And with his girlfriend sulking by the fire with Avril—Rebecca had refused to join the game because she thought it was "inappropriate"—I was free to take him in as much as I wanted. In the low light, the tiger stalked beautifully over his left shoulder, flowing in shades of watercoloured black like a Chinese painting.

Tiger spirited, I'd thought. *Come and get me, Barrett.*

Careless, I let him catch me looking. The delicate flare of firelight through his obsidian gaze, along with the tug of his smirk, told me that he liked it.

Then my favourite song came on, and I screeched in excitement, pulling myself out of the table to trot to the area meant for dancing. Melissa laughed and joined me. The two of us broke out some white-girl-wasted dance moves, wearing nothing but our bikinis and flipflops. Dixon was prancing on the ground between us.

The collective attention of the campsite turned, and I caught Rebecca's warning glare when I looked toward the fire. So, shifting my face into her man's defiant smirk, I took it up a notch by inviting Avril over. She grinned at me and rolled her eyes, but she hauled herself to her feet, giggling as she made her way to the makeshift dance floor. Then I pulled the elastic from my hair and tossed it free, throwing my arm around Avril as I reveled in the burn of a black gaze. Barrett's eyes were exactly where drunk-Emily wanted them. Locked on me.

Shane joined us soon after, bouncing around in his underwear as the bassline pulsed around us. We got immersed in the moment, and I was having so much fun that I didn't notice the burn of those black eyes fade until I looked back at the picnic table and found only Kirk standing there. He swayed where he leaned, arms crossed and staring at the ground with his expression strangely defeated. His eyelids were blinking at different times, like one was getting a delayed signal over the other, and I realized I wasn't the only one wearing a boozy lens.

Disappointed, I scanned the campsite for Mr. Roth, but he'd pulled another disappearing act and was nowhere to be found. I turned my attention to the group instead, and soon I was so filled with joy that I forgot I'd been looking for him.

He appeared a few moments later, shaking his head and rubbing his nose as he threw himself into our dance party at the last verse. Closing his eyes, he turned his head to the sky and moved like he was disassociating further from reality with every beat. Drunk Emily moved me toward him, and I drew in a shallow breath as we got closer. The wine was making my inhibitions melt away. It was making me forget to suppress my newfound hunger for him, and the fact that his girlfriend was sitting at the fire a few feet from us. I wanted to wrap my arms around his neck like she did. My skin simmered at the thought of what it would be like to kiss him. I wondered if bolts of electricity would go between our tongues when we tried to pull them out of their caress. Desire was overbearing and in control. I didn't know how to stop it, and part of me didn't want to.

Who are you supposed to be to me, Barrett Roth?

Sensing me next to him, he lowered his chin and opened his eyes. They bore into mine like he was reading my mind, flashing with risk and danger. There was something else swimming in the obsidian now. Something that told me he wanted to play the bigger predator. Something that told me he was hungrier than I was, and maybe even had less control. He slowed as he focused on me, and my heart skipped several beats when he reached for my hand.

I held my breath and prepared myself for the surge that shot through my body every time we touched.

But it never came. A set of perfectly manicured nails grabbed his hand instead. Rebecca turned him away.

He tried to distract her by running his lips up her neck in slow kisses, but it didn't faze her. Her stare was as cold as ice as it fixed on me from over his shoulder, and it only said one thing—*Back the fuck off.*

I released the breath I'd been holding and turned away, fighting drunken tears as I broke out of the group. The world was spinning around me, but I was desperate to focus on anything—anyone—else. I managed to stumble over to the picnic table, standing next to Kirk.

Bracing against it with white knuckles, I grabbed my wine glass and downed what was left. It slipped down my throat with a nice sting.

"Breathe," I told myself. "Just breathe."

But Kirk was watching me through bloodshot eyes. The stench of bourbon pierced the air when he lowered his lips to my ear and said, "I wouldn't."

Blinking, I looked at him. Though my mouth hung open, nothing came out. Turns out, I had no excuses to answer with.

"It's okay, Emily," Kirk said, but I didn't believe him.

Suddenly, I couldn't stand there anymore. Instead, I stumbled toward the blurred glow of the fire and collapsed in one of the Muskoka chairs, wrestling with dizziness. My mind was bombarding me with the shame of what I'd almost done, but my heart was pounding in longing. It felt cheated. And like it was going to break out of my chest before it let me forget it.

Pulling out my phone, I sifted through the blinding screen to find my messages.

David. I need David.

Even if he were too stoned to hold a decent conversation, I needed my other man to distract me. I was desperate for the familiar rumble of his voice.

But someone plopped into the chair beside me. I looked up to find Shane fully clothed and sitting with a bottle of wine in hand.

"Thank God." Huffing, I reached to snatch it, but he held it back, pulling out the cork and pouring me a controlled ration. Like a kid denied their favourite candy, I snorted.

"Hey," he said. "You're alright lass, okay? I ken you are. Everything's alright."

I squinted.

How would you know, Mr. Thomas?

Then he shot me a grin so adorable that it was almost Greggy-worthy and gave me a playful pinch on the cheek. "Come on, blondie.

We're having fun tonight, okay? You're making us look bad. 'Cus us blondes are supposed to have all the fun, right?" He glanced up at Barrett as he left Rebecca on the dancefloor, and I realized that my hunt hadn't gone unnoticed. Between Shane and Kirk, not much got past.

Shane nudged me. "Don't think what you're thinking, alright? Let's have a good time. Here. Have more of that."

I slurred out a whisper as I watched him pour more wine. "Thanks, Shay."

"Of course." He grinned but then caught me hiding my emotions behind my smile. "Do you want to hear a really lame joke? Would that cheer you up?"

"Uh huh." Soppy, yet grateful, I nodded.

"Alright." His eyes flew to the treetops as he muddled through his thoughts. "Ah! What do you call a cow with no legs?"

I couldn't do much but giggle at the way he'd pronounced the "o" in "cow." Elongated. Scottish.

He grinned. "Ground beef."

"*Seriously?*" I spit up some wine and slapped my knee. That's *awful*, Shay."

He winked again. "You're welcome."

Fuck, Melissa, you're so lucky.

But laughing made my bladder hurt. "Hold that thought," I said, pointing at Shane. "I gotta go to the little girl's room."

Following a fuzzy path of white lights that hung from the cedar trees, I made my way down the path to the fully plumbed washrooms that the Roths had installed for the campsites. The door was heavy under my boozy muscles, but I managed to push it aside, and the automatic lights blinked. Holding my head and pleading with vertigo, I made my way over to the toilet and dropped my ass with all the grace of an elephant falling.

"Break the seal," I mumbled to myself. "Is there anything better than—hic—breaking the seal?"

Not when I was breaking a whole bottle's worth, there wasn't.

I sighed in relief. Then decided to pull the white-girl-wasted move of texting a man from the toilet.

David...

Yeah, Em?

I chewed on my lip—my clumsy fingers barely able to type. *I think I might love you...* My thumb hovered over the *Send* button for a long time, but a long and painful history with Andy stopped it. So, I quickly erased every word and replaced it with, *I really want to fuck you...* Then I erased every word of that too.

"Fuck! Make up your *mind*, Em."

I felt helplessly tugged between two opposing men, and I didn't like it.

With an angry grunt, I locked my phone and pulled my shorts back over my ass, before I slipped it into the front pocket. Soon after, I fell back onto the seat, rubbing my head as I tried to soothe it.

Tomorrow's gonna be a long fuckin' day.

Suddenly, I heard the muttering of two voices from somewhere behind the bathrooms. Turning my ear to the open window, I quieted my breath as I tuned in on them. It sounded like Barrett and Kirk. Shane's lame joke combined with the waterfall of wine must have distracted me from realizing they'd left the campsite together.

Kirk was slurring—in as rough a shape as I was. "Tell me... Tell me what's going on, Bear. Tell me what's wrong with you."

"Ki, please. Why must you always be like this? Nothing's going on. I'm *fine*."

"You're *not* fine! Do you think I can't see what you're doing?"

"Kirk, I—"

"Don't you fucking lie to me, Roth. You're the king of liars, and you've got the crown to prove it, don't you? But I... I... see through it! I know you better than you know yourself. So don't fucking lie to me, *connard*."

Barrett sighed. "You don't have to worry. I have control."

Kirk spat sharp words at him. "I saw you after breakfast, and I saw you go off a few minutes ago. You are *not* in control, Bear. You're spiraling. Again. So, why? *Pourquoi?*"

"Shhh."

"Don't touch me! Don't you fuckin' touch me! I don't forgive you, remember? I don't *ever* forgive you! *Ever!*"

"Kirk, you're drunk, and getting aggressive. We can have this conversation when you're of better—"

"You're one to talk, you fuckin' hypocrite. We're having this conversation *now*. On *my* terms for once, Barrett Roth!"

Barrett's tone turned pleading in a way that I'd never heard before. "Kirk, please. I can't handle an altercation with you right now. I just can't."

I heard Kirk's feet shift on the forest floor. "It was your fault. When Shay put that gun to his head, it was your fault. I don't care that you deny it."

Barrett's voice swung the other way, and now he spoke like he had his teeth clenched. "You'd better back the fuck off me before you regret it, Kirk Richards."

Kirk sputtered through a laugh. "You think I don't know how to take a hit from you? I ain't scared, *espèce de tas de merde*."

"You're fucking cruel."

Kirk laughed. "Pot calling the kettle black. How can you live with yourself? How can you keep doing what you're fucking doing after what you did to him?"

Barrett paused for a long time before he spoke in a low growl. "How dare you accuse me—or even *speak* of—something you weren't around for. I *never* fucking denied it, and I live with that regret every single day. I'd take back every moment if I could. But I am *trapped*, Kirk Elliot. I am *trapped* and you have never tried to understand it. Don't fucking come at me when you're not willing to fight for me."

"I fought for you every fucking day for four years, *téteux!*"

"Then where were you, huh?" Barrett's voice warbled. "Where were you all the times that I needed you? That *he* needed you?"

Again, there was shuffling, and I imagined Kirk putting them nose-to-nose. "Protecting myself from the monster that you are, Barrett Nicholas Roth. You are—and always will be—a walking nightmare."

"Then why are you here?! Why come back?!"

Kirk lowered his voice, but the pitch stayed aggressive. "Because I will be *damned* if I let you drag him down with you. You can make your selfish choices, Bear. Day after day. But you don't fucking deserve him as your best friend. You don't deserve *anyone* as your best friend. Hell, you're barely worthy of love, but I can't stop him from giving it to you."

Barrett's voice was quiet but pained. "How could you say that to me...? You... Of all people..."

But Kirk ignored him. "I'm not gonna let Shane Thomas die by your hand. After all you've done. After all your *family* has done. All your *father* has done. Your father... You're *une merde* just like your father, Roth. You'll never change. I know that now."

Barrett choked on the next word: "Kirk..."

"Fuck you, Barrett. *Salaud.*" Staggering footsteps through the forest told me that Kirk had walked away.

There was silence before Barrett's breathing got louder. Like he was struggling to control increasing panic. I couldn't blame him. Their conversation had been fucking *brutal*.

The fuck was that about...?

It took everything I had to resist going out to comfort Barrett as I heard him collapse to the ground, wrestling with his breath as he tried to turn it rhythmic again. I mean, I could have. But I didn't want him to know that I'd heard every word they'd said. It seemed very much like a conversation that they'd meant to be private.

He started to whisper to himself in between his rapid gasps. "Five things... Four things... Three things..." Repeating it over and over, until his lungs started to slow and calm. "Fuck you, Kirk Richards... Fuck you..."

We sat in suspension—him using every ounce of strength to calm himself, and me using the same to keep myself quiet. Finally, his breath slowed, and I heard him pull himself from the forest floor. There was a dull thud like he'd hit something, followed by a grunt of frustration, and I didn't uncover my mouth until I was sure that he'd walked away.

My heart fell heavy for him, and I washed my hands while trying to wrangle the horrible energy that Kirk's words had left behind. Though drunk, I wondered what other excuse he'd had to be so cruel. What had he meant when said that Shane putting a gun to his head was Barrett's fault? How could that ever be true? And what would make a man as happy-go-lucky as Shane do something like that?

The summer night was warm, but I shivered when I walked back to the campsite. Kirk had now settled in the chair beside Shane, glaring at Barrett over a fresh glass of bourbon.

Barrett walked aimlessly over to the picnic table, leaning on it with his palms spread flat like he was under immense weight. He kept struggling with his breath and refused to look at anyone.

Concerned, Shane flicked his eyes between his best friends, before he stood and walked over to lay a hand on Barrett's shoulder.

And it was all too much for me now. This fucking horrible energy. So, I turned away and escaped into the tent, collapsing onto the air mattress, and letting the wine take me to sleep.

When I woke up a couple hours later, my head was pounding, and my eyelids fought to let me open them. Avril was curled up in her sleeping bag beside me, and I tried not to disturb her as I pulled myself up and fumbled for my water bottle. Finding it nearly empty, I groaned, not wanting to leave the comfort of my bed to go fill it up.

As I slipped on my windbreaker—muscles paining in protest—sounds from outside the tent started to come to me. Snoring told me that most of the people in the other tents were asleep, but sitting subtly under that were panting and low moans. Surprised, I shifted forward onto my knees and unzipped the tent enough to peer out without being seen.

Through the glow of the firelight, my fuzzy vision took a moment to focus, but then I saw Barrett lounging in one of the Muskoka chairs. His head was tilted back, and his left arm was hung lazily over the armrest. A cigarette was smoldering away in his hand, the smoke rising into the air to join with the mist of night. Then, I saw Rebecca. Down on her knees with her head buried in his lap. Her long red hair hanging toward the ground. They were the only two out there. Embers flared as Barrett drew a puff from the smoke, releasing while he sighed with pleasure.

Covering my mouth, I zipped the window closed and tried not to listen as I patted the darkness in search of Avril's water bottle. After I found it, I tipped it and drained all that I could, but it wasn't enough to distract me from the sound of Barrett's heavy breathing. My groin ached as I crawled back to the air mattress and started searching for my bag and headphones. In the space between plunging them into my ears and the start of the song that I used to drown him out, my brain had formed a full fantasy of him being on top of me. Making those sounds. Calling my name... I cranked the volume up as high as I could, before I curled back up.

Later, I woke up with my headphones still in. I was now *dying* for some water, so I pulled myself up and peered through the zipper again to check if it was safe to go out. I could see the back of Barrett's head still resting against the Muskoka chair, but Rebecca wasn't in his lap anymore. In fact, she wasn't there at all. He was alone.

I braved the outside, clearing my throat so that he'd hear me, but he didn't respond. I went to the kitchen, took a bottle of water from the fridge, and downed the whole thing before taking out another.

Curious about why Barrett was still sitting there, I moved around his chair to ask, but found him asleep. Blinking, I thought about what to do. Then tiptoed around him like a wolf in the snow and curled up in the chair next to him. The firelight flicking across his face revealed that his expression was peaceful in. I watched him and wondered about who he was. What he meant to me. What he was *going* to mean to me. I wished I could ask the Universe outright, but even if I could, I was sure that the answers wouldn't come back clear.

Sighing, I studied the silver crown on his right forearm as it rested on the chair. His palm was turned upward like he was holding something invisible, but valuable. I stared at it and imagined myself placing my hand there, longing for the moment that Rebecca had stolen from us on the dance floor. For some reason, I needed to feel him, and I wanted desperately to slip my fingers between his.

Kirk's wrong, I thought, as I reached out and took his hand, drawing his right arm closer. *You deserve love. No matter what you did, or what you're doing, you still deserve love...*

Soft tingling built when he retaliated—whether consciously or unconsciously—by running his thumb over the top of my hand in gentle strokes.

Smiling, I reveled in our secret interaction. I closed my eyes, not even bothering to think of my ability as I savoured the feeling of him. Then I fell asleep with his hand in mine.

CHAPTER 24
VOICES OF VIOLENCE

Barrett's lying on the floor of his room at the Roth Estate, with the imported rug soft beneath his stomach. From the full-length mirror that stands against one of the walls, I can see that he's a kid—eight or nine?—and his hair gleams in its natural red from the light of the mini-chandelier hanging above him. What he's doing is weird, and I don't understand it at first. There's a circular container of water in front of him with a cork bobbing in it, and he's running what looks like a magnet in short strokes along a sewing needle. He tests the needle against the magnet, but instead of sticking, they repulse. Satisfied, he takes the cork and plunges the needle through it, before he pops it back into the water, where the needle turns itself. He pushes it one way, then the other, but it returns to the same position each time, aligned with the Earth's magnetic field. I feel the joy of success as he grins. It's a compass, he tells me.

Oh my God, that's so adorable, I think.

But the sound of the front door opening downstairs extinguishes the feeling. He glances toward his bedroom door and hesitates, before pushing himself from the floor. John calls him before they can see each other, and he trots to the top of the master staircase, peering through the wrought iron.

John's now spitting some orders at the housekeeper while he hands her his things to put away. She scrambles to take them, and annoyance flashes through those black eyes before he watches her scoot to the closet in the foyer. By the time they turn up toward his son, Barrett's moved to the top of the staircase to make sure his father can see him. The corner of John's mouth twitches in what looks like satisfaction.

"Hi, Dad!" Barrett's voice is still so young and innocent. Casual and unbound by the private-school-proper way he speaks now.

John winces strangely at the sound. "Barrett. Come down at once. I'll take my decompression outside today, and I require some quality time with my son." Without waiting, he marches past the staircase and toward the back of the Estate, where I know that the kitchen leads to the patio, pool, and gardens.

Like a well-trained circus tiger following his master's commands, Barrett jogs down the stairs, stopping to greet the housekeeper at the bottom. She stands at the walk-in closet in the foyer, brushing off John's suit jacket with strong, sharp strokes like her life depends on it.

"Rose," he says. "Do you know what he wants of me?"

She shakes her head as she hangs John's jacket and shifts his briefcase into its spot. "I'm not sure, Barrett, but you'd best listen. You know not to keep your father waiting."

I feel his face drop, and he nods, turning away.

"Uh ah, Barrett! Here. Don't you dare get your socks dirty." Rose hands him his shoes from inside the closet, and he must be smiling at her, because she smiles back before she steps forward to kiss him on the forehead. "Off with you now," she says.

He turns and runs the length of the Estate in his socks, stopping at the French doors to slip on his shoes before he steps outside. Out on the massive patio, John's is lounging in one of the chairs, lighting up a cigarette. A bottle of rye and two glasses sit on the table in front of him.

"Is Uncle Mike coming over?" Barrett asks curiously when he walks over.

John exhales some smoke, picks up the rye, and pours two drinks. "No. The other glass is for you, son."

Barrett chuckles. "Dad, isn't that alcohol? I can't have alcohol. I just turned nine."

The annoyance returns to John's eye, and joy morphs into dread when Barrett realizes his father wasn't joking. "Your opinion is not warranted, Barrett."

He bites his lip as he steps to his father's side. "I'm sorry, Dad."

"Do you not remember what we talked about?" John's matching obsidian snaps toward him. "You are too old now to call me 'Dad.' You must address me as 'sir.' Just like your brother does."

Barrett swallows his guilt. "I am sorry, sir."

John smiles. "That's better. Now, that being said, I am still your father, and as your father it is my duty to guide you. In less than a decade, you will be a man, Barrett, so I must start preparing you for that. Men drink alcohol, and as such, it is best for you to get used to regulating it. The earlier you learn, the better. This is no different to what your brother learned when he was your age." He picks up his glass. "We're starting today. Sit down."

Barrett sinks into a chair and watches the amber liquid in front of him. Under the excitement of a new experience, I can feel apprehension. He knows how wrong this is. Pressured by the weight of his father's stare, he takes the glass, but the rye irritates his nostrils. He's only ever smelled the muted version on his father's breath before.

"Drink," John orders, and Barrett looks at him before looking back to the glass—swallowing fear this time.

He puts it to his lips, wondering what it will feel like, and what it'll do to him. He hopes it will feel good. He hopes that it will make him act silly like it does with Travis; not angry like it does with his father.

Bad things happen when he gets angry, he tells me. *Bad things happen to everyone.*

Aware that John's watching, Barrett braves the first sip and hopes for the best. The biting liquid burns his tongue like acid, before it punches the back of his throat, leaving a bitter aftertaste that's damn-near torturous. He shivers and screws up his face, squeezing it down his throat.

John chuckles. "You are a good boy, Barrett. You do what you're told."

I don't have a choice, Barrett thinks, but he tries to focus on how good it feels to receive praise. It is few and far between with his father, these days.

"Thank you, sir." He drops his attention to the glass and studies the acid that's left. He doesn't know how he's going to finish the rest. Or how anyone could drink it, let alone *want* to drink it.

John drains his own rye and sets his glass on the table. He jerks his chin at Barrett's. "Finish it."

And Barrett knows what to expect this time, so he braces himself, swallowing the rest in one painful gulp. The taste is still horrible, and it still burns, but he tries hard not to screw up his face. He'll do whatever it takes to make his father proud.

"There." John smiles as he takes the glass and pours them more. "Not so bad, is it?"

"How much do I have to drink, sir?" Barrett asks, trying to hide the anxiety behind his tone.

"Enough to get you exposed to the feeling of being drunk," John says. He takes a drag on his cigarette. The smoke escapes his mouth as he speaks. "Don't tell your mother."

I can feel the look that Barrett's giving him. One of muted horror and disbelief. He blinks to mask it and takes his second glass. "Fine," he says bravely.

John smirks, and there's an undeniable cruelty in those raven eyes. "Good boy." He flicks the ash into the ashtray, and some of it floats up into the air toward the mountains before going out. The two of them sit in silence. A gentle wind causes the pool next to them to ripple, and the birds chirp cheerfully in the western forests that rise above. If you don't consider the fucking patriarchal cruelty, it's a bright and cheery summer day.

Barrett watches his father and shifts to mirror some of his posture. He's taking mental notes on how he's supposed to act when he's older.

John ignores him and continues to smoke, crossing his right leg over his left. The friction causes his pant leg to shorten, exposing the plain black sock above his shiny tan dress shoes.

Melancholy washes over Barrett.

Is that all there is? he thinks.

"So, how was school today?" John asks suddenly.

"Fine." Barrett shrugs and swirls the rye. "We learned how to make a compass."

"Is that so? Well, that's a fine skill to have for going to the campground, but you are not going to need it when you grow up, are you? I'll have a word."

Barrett drops his gaze. "That was only geographical sciences, sir. We were learning about the Earth's magnetic field."

"Geographical sciences." John sighs before sipping more rye. "Why do we even have you in such a thing?"

Barrett looks up, fearful. "It is my favourite subject, sir."

"That does not matter, Barrett. It is a private school. Everything they teach you must be of use in your future."

"Why?" Barrett chokes down another sip.

"Well, your grandfather and I did not build a company from the ground up to have no one take over for me."

"But Travis is supposed to—"

"You *both* will," John says, sternly. "I've been thinking about it quite a bit lately. For some reason it has been at the forefront of my mind. Though I cannot put my finger on why." He pauses, drawing from the cigarette. "I need to set the two of you—and the company—up for success in the future. Maybe it's because you are getting older and I'm starting to get that vision. And visions do not turn into reality without hard work, son."

A flicker of anger rises from Barrett's chest. He's starting to feel funny from the alcohol, and it presses him to say what's on his mind. "What if I don't want to?"

John smiles, but I can see the irritation on the rest of his face. "Well, I wouldn't say that you have a choice." He twists the cork off the bottle and pours them a third glass. "You want to make me happy, don't you? You want to make me proud?"

Barrett glares—black challenging black—before he quickly remembers he'll lose. He backs down and nods.

"Then you're going to do as you're told, like a good son would. A good son listens to his father. He heeds every word, Barrett. Because his father knows best. It is that simple."

Barrett glances away. He studies the pool like he's desperate to concentrate on anything but this conversation.

"Right, Barrett?" John seems miffed by his silence.

He shoots his father a blank smile and answers with an absent mind. "Yes, sir."

"Good."

Barrett clears his throat and takes the first sip from his third drink. It hasn't gotten any better, but the burning seems to have singed his tongue, and at least he can't taste it as much. Tapping his foot on the stone, he notices the sudden dizziness, and wonders how much more of this he has to take. He's not confident about it, and he thinks about how his personal time with his father isn't fun these days. Maybe at some point it had been, but as he's starting to grow, it feels like bigger and better things are expected of him. And he doesn't know if he'll be able to deliver them.

"Now," John says. "Finish that third glass and then off with you. Let your father drink in peace."

Happy to be released from the suffering, Barrett downs most of the third glass in one gulp. He sets it on the table and tries to stand, but he instantly loses his balance and is forced to grab the top to steady himself. His head's swimming, his mouth's dry as a bone, and suddenly all he wants is to sleep.

"See?" John gives him a *well-done* pat on the shoulder. "That was the lesson. If you see your brother, send him out, will you?"

Barrett's eyes burn with frustration, but he doesn't say anything, and John doesn't seem to notice, or care. He turns away and goes back to the French doors, but the world is moving in slow circles around him, and he can't seem to walk straight. He stumbles into the kitchen and manages to pour himself some water. Then he drinks all of it to wash the taste of the rye from his mouth.

Leaving the glass on the counter, he goes back into the hallway, grabbing the wrought iron railing to haul himself up the marble stairs. Each step is careful and calculated, and the ruby-red carpet provides a bright path like the Estate's helping to guide him back to safety.

Then the click of the front door warns him that it's closing, and Barrett knows that Travis is likely the one that just stepped through. He freezes and swivels carefully to face his seventeen-year-old brother, struggling to look normal. It's imperative to hide what his father has done from his brother, he tells me. Knowing that he's been forced to drink will upset Travis, and it could cause a fight. And fights between his father and brother are a dangerous risk right now.

With every year, Travis is gaining strength. With every year, Travis is gaining wisdom. Soon he'll be able to overpower his father, but Barrett—even at nine—is conscious that he doesn't want to be the reason for that to happen. He tries to smile as he watches his brother toss his tie and briefcase into the closet, but he's sure the drunkenness has morphed it into a dopey grin.

A raise of one chestnut eyebrow tells me that Travis has recognized the odd behaviour right away. He walks over and takes each of Barrett's shoulders in hand. Barrett's raised up by two steps, which makes them level with each other, and Travis is too close to hide it now. His pale brown eyes are searching Barrett's face. "Bear? Are you alright?"

The alcohol causes a strange rearing of rage, and suddenly

Barrett's mad that he couldn't throw his brother off the trail. He pushes Travis away. "I'm fine!"

And now he's made it obvious that he's not.

Travis backs off. "What's happened?"

"None of your business," Barrett hisses. Fatigue worsens from his outburst, and he's desperate for bed. He points one wobbly finger back down the hallway. "H—He wants to, um... see you... by the way..."

Travis arches his brows, then sighs.

Barrett turns away and stumbles while he attempts to climb.

"Barrett?"

"What?" He spits the word and wheels back to his brother.

Travis responds calmly, stepping up to level them again. "Listen to me, brother. Go upstairs, force yourself to throw everything up, and then get into bed."

"Wha...? How do I...?"

"Stick your finger down your throat. It'll all come up. Trust me." He presses a heavy hand through his brother's hair, and Barrett stares back at him. Fear is clouding his mind like a midnight storm. "Close your door, go to sleep, and don't come out. I'll be up to check on you in a bit. Alright?"

Stunned and afraid of how little control he has over his body, Barrett gives him a disconnected nod.

"It'll be okay," Travis says, before he turns away and disappears down the hall.

Travis's absence causes dismay, but Barrett pushes himself up the staircase, trying not to lose his balance as he shifts his weight from one foot to the other. He goes into the nearest bathroom and follows his brother's instructions. Nausea pushes him to heave seconds after he gets to the toilet, so he doesn't need to use his finger, anyway. The rye scorches his throat when it comes back up, but he endures this because he's desperate to get it out of his body. He needs to feel normal again. Not weighed down by induced sickness.

Wiping his mouth with toilet paper, he flushes the alcohol away, and washes his hands before he leaves.

In his bedroom, he trips over the compass, and the water soaks his shoe.

Shit. I failed to take them off, he thinks.

The cork and needle bounce across the rug, but now he doesn't care. He uses all the energy that he has left to climb up onto his bed and pass out on his stomach.

Barrett startles awake to the sound of glass shattering downstairs. He feels sober now, but it's dark and a lot of time must have passed. He jumps out of bed and yanks his door open, bolting into the hallway and down the stairs to see what's going on. He can hear John and Travis screaming at each other from the kitchen, and he realizes that his earlier fear has come true. His body plagues him with more nausea and the start of a bad headache. He ignores it and creeps over to the kitchen doorway.

"Fuck you!" Travis is spitting when Barrett peeks in. "How could you do that?!"

"*Fuck you?*" John slurs, pointing into his own chest. "That's the way you speak to your father? With such disrespect? Huh?" He sneers with disgust. "Such a *brave* man now that you're seventeen."

"Yeah, well, you're a drunk, and a shit father!" Travis says. "You deserve it!"

Now John's ravenous. With a strange quickness for someone who's drunk, he snatches the largest butcher's knife from the counter and pushes forward. He grabs Travis by the throat and throws him against the wall of the doorway that Barrett's looking through. Barrett jumps from the closeness of the impact. He can tell by the horrifying choking noises coming from his brother that John's grip is tight and fueled by his anger. Travis struggles against him, but John's too strong, and he's fuming. Ignoring his son's wordless plea, John brings the knife to Travis's throat, where it threatens to cut through his perfect skin like butter. With his sinister smirk playing on his face, John whispers something that Barrett doesn't hear, because a hand has grabbed him.

It's Rose—trying to pull him away with one floral-scented hand across his mouth.

He flails, pushing against her.

"Shhh!" Rose hisses quietly. "Barrett, please. No. It's too dangerous! No. I have to get you out of here..."

On the other side of the doorway, his brother is still silently pleading with his father—his face and neck darkening into a reddish colour—but John looks like he's enjoying this too much to let Travis go. Drunk with power as much as with rye, he does the opposite and shifts his forearm so that it's pressing against his son's throat. He throws his weight into it and says something else that Barrett can't hear because Rose is yanking him away from the door.

"No!" Barrett manages to spit, after he drags her fingers from across his mouth. "Let me go! I must help him!"

"Shhh!" Rose warns in return, but on the other side, John and Travis are too wrapped up to notice.

Now Travis looks like he's starting to get desperate, and there's no noise coming from him at all. He claws at his father's forearm, leaving visible scratches down his skin, but John's too drunk to feel them. Their position leaves Travis no room to strike with any strength that would matter. But Barrett can tell that he's trying, and it makes anguish soak into his young soul.

Then, that signature smirk appears on John's face. His raven eyes are menacing and victorious. A bead of angry sweat runs down the side of his cheek, and his red hair falls out of its perfectly gelled position over his forehead. "You see, Travis Benjamin, you are forgetting one thing when you say these cruel words to me..." He presses his face close to Travis's, expression twisted in dark emotion.

And he spits the words like he can't stand the sight of him. "That you're also a *shit* son. And I *made* you, so I can *end* you, *motherfucker!*"

The statement sets off an explosion of panic inside Barrett, and he fights Rose harder.

"Barrett. There's nothing you can do. Please!"

"Let me go!"

"Please—"

"No!"

"Stop—"

"He'll kill him!"

The struggle has drawn his brother's weakened attention, and Travis catches Barrett's eye. Bright red lines are spreading through the white around his irises. A single tear runs down his cheek, glistening in the pot lights of the enormous kitchen. His face and neck are now turning purple, and Barrett can see the mixture of regret, shame, and fear in his brother's expression—along with a silent warning to stay away.

Barrett can't. He sees his older brother fading; his body slumping with weakness; his scratching and clawing slowing. In front of him, his father has a devilish expression on his face. John's enjoying the strangling. Like he's either a monster himself, or some monster has possessed him.

Oh my God... Barrett thinks. *This is it. He's going to fucking kill Travis.*

Fury rises from his core and mixes with the alarm. He starts screaming, "Noooo!" before he even hears himself, stomping backward on Rose's foot, causing her to yelp and let him go.

Free from her grip, he charges into the kitchen, throwing himself toward them. He grabs his father's scratched-up forearm, and with the strength of adrenaline, and all his weight, manages to yank it away from his brother's throat.

But in the shock of the moment, John loses control, and now Barrett's in harm's way. He forgets that the butcher's knife is in his hand when he pushes him away, and it catches Barrett on the right side of his neck, causing a cut long enough to span it. Young blood splatters everything—the counters, the knife, their dress shirts, the walls. Horrified, John drops the knife and his oldest son, turning his attention purely to his youngest. Too weak to hold himself, Travis slams to his knees, clutching his throat and gasping for air.

Barrett stumbles but doesn't fall. He holds the stinging part of his neck and stares at his father. He can already feel the blood seeping through his fingers.

"Barrett..." John chokes and reaches out to him, but Barrett recoils like a frightened cat faced with a threat.

His gaze flashes from his father to Travis, and he's confused about what to do. What to believe. He wants his older brother to give him some direction, but Travis is still frantically gasping in between the chokes and sputters. The sight pains Barrett viscerally, and tears push their way forward, blurring his vision. He wants to help Travis, but his father's now coming at him, and the fear of this looming monster paralyzes him. Sticks his feet to the Estate's marble, like glue.

Travis looks up with horror in his bloodshot eyes. He draws a big enough gasp to inhale once. Just once. And somehow, he screams. "Barrett, run!"

It takes a second for Barrett's brain to process, and I feel his jaw droop as his eyes flick between his brother and his father. The final movement lands them Travis, and Travis communicates the criticality through his terrified expression.

John's approaching like he's trying not to startle Barrett, but this only makes Barrett more aware of how close his father is. I feel him shoot a look of apology at his brother before he swivels on his left foot and bolts for the door. Something snags him. His father's caught his dress shirt, but he yanks himself free, leaving it ripped into John's hand.

"Barrett, no! Get back here!"

But he doesn't listen to the monster that his father has become. He runs from them like his life depends on it. Which—he realizes—it probably does.

Outside, the weather has changed, and the rain has turned everything slick, like oil. He slips on the deck, but catches himself and continues forward, leaping off and running through the extensive gardens. In the dark, they're like a maze to me, but Barrett knows them like the back of his hand and has no trouble navigating to an area of the back gate that leads out onto the mountainous forest beyond. He reaches a keypad, and with a shaky finger, punches in a code. His father's screams echo behind him.

A red light blares from the keypad, and he spits "Fuck!" when he realizes he's got the wrong code. A stickler for security, Barrett tells me, John changes them regularly. Hysteria shoots through him, and he shakes the bars as he thinks about what it could be. He tries again, and then again—red light blaring brighter as he hears his father nearing.

"Barrett! Please, son!" John's gaining ground, and in a matter of seconds he'll be able to catch him, but Barrett keeps trying.

It must work, he thinks. *It* must*! One of them* must *work!*

On his last try, the gate finally swings forward, but John's close enough to reach out and grab him. Highly aware of his father's position, Barrett surges forward. John catches his foot with the other hand. Barrett crashes to the ground and smacks his chin hard enough to make him "Oomph!" into the dirt. He sees stars, and John's crawling on top of him, rolling him onto his back as he blubbers from above. John tries to shush him, and he reaches out for the wound that Barrett's been too panicked to even remember is there.

"I'm sorry." John's sobs mix with the rain and the babbling spit that drips off him. "Barrett. Please, son! I'm so sorry." He touches the wound with a bloodied hand that's covered in dirt and wet grass. The jolt of pain—and having his father's hand against his throat—puts

Barrett in pure fight mode. He squirms, freeing his legs, curling up, and kicking John full force in the face. John grunts and falls to the side. Even in his drunkenness, he's stunned.

Then Barrett's free. He pulls himself to his feet and darts away. John tries to grab him again, but this time he's too fast. Barrett leaves his father gripping the air.

Knowing that, in his drunkenness, John will have trouble navigating the trail that runs along the base of their mountain, that's where Barrett heads. He ignores John's calls as the rain soaks him, and the thick forest plunges the path forward into darkness. It's hard to see, but these trails are his own, and they're familiar, so he lets his memory guide him.

Although it's terrifying to have his monster-of-a-father following him, he knows that the distraction will give his brother enough time to escape in his car, and he hopes that Travis will be okay. He hopes this will be what saves him. It's worth the pain from his sliced neck and his burning lungs.

A heavy fog winds through the trees around him, making the trail even harder to see. The rain weighs down his clothes as he runs, and his neck is searing, but he doesn't let up. He leads Johnathan Roth further into the woods, trying not to think of the other predators that might smell his blood.

By the time the lights at the back of the Thomas Estate come into view, he's weakened from blood loss and heavy breath, so he stops for a moment, panting into the night air. He removes the hand that's been holding his wound, and it comes back red; blood pooling in his palm before it drips onto the forest floor. He returns his hand and tries not to panic as he catches his breath.

Consciously, he slows it and listens, relieved to hear nothing but silence under the sound of pounding rain. But then, like an echo on the wind, he hears his father's voice from much further down the path —"Barrett!"—and he lets it drive him forward.

The Thomas Estate has a similar security system, with a keypad allowing access from the back gate. But unlike his paranoid best friend, Michael Thomas keeps the code standard, and Barrett knows it because he comes this way often. He punches it in and gets through on the first try, pulling the gate shut behind him, and hoping to keep his father out. If only temporarily. He runs around the Thomas' glowing pool and toward a sliding door that leads into their TV room. It's there that the nine-year-old Shane is distracted by ancient video games on the other side of the glass.

"Shane! Shane!" Barrett bangs on the door with the ghost of his father looming over his shoulder.

Shane jumps high enough to send the controller flying across the room, before he recognizes his best friend. In the space that it takes to get up and wrench the door open, his face turns from fearful to worried.

Barrett flies in through a flurry of cold and blood. "Lock it! Lock it!"

Shane watches him wide-eyed as he latches the door. "What the *bloody* hell—?"

"M. My. My Dad." Barrett huffs, and a wave of weakness hits him. The cut throbs beneath his hand.

"Wha—?"

"He's drunk. Got into a fight with Travis. Tried to kill him. I stopped him." Barrett coughs.

"He tried to *kill* Travis?!"

"Yeah." Another heavy exhale. "He. Strangled. Him."

"Oh my God. Barrett. And you're bleedin'!" Shane snatches Barrett's hand from his neck and covers it back up after getting a glimpse of the filthy wound below. He tries to act calm, but his bright blue eyes tell lies.

"He. Cut. Me." Barrett huffs. "But please! Shay. He followed me. He knows. I'd come. Here. Please. *Please!* You must. Hide me. Please, Shay. Please!"

"Yeah, yeah, of course," Shane sputters through his shock. "We have to tell my parents! Mum will know what to do." His accent is young and heavily influenced by his father, so "do" comes out really Scottish. Still holding Barrett's neck, he guides him out of the TV room and into a long hallway toward the lobby. "Come with me, brither."

The acoustics of the massive space cause his screams to bounce from the walls, so as soon as Shane starts calling for his mother—*Samantha,* Barrett tells me—she appears at the top of the stairs. Him and Barrett move toward the bottom, shifting in some strange, conjoined motion where Shane fools himself into thinking he's slowing the bleeding.

"Shane? What—" Samantha's struck speechless, and she rushes down the stairs in one flowing motion. Her floor-length nightgown trails softly behind her. "Barrett! What happened?"

Shane speaks on Barrett's behalf. "Mr. Roth. He's drunk and he tried to kill Travis! He hurt Barrett too! Please, Mum. We must hide him. He's coming—"

Insistent pounding on the front door causes them to collectively jump. Three sets of eyes shoot toward the door. It hammers in four loud beats—*Bang. Bang. Bang. Bang.*—along with the slurring voice of Johnathan Roth. "Mike! Mike! *Mikey!*"

"Barrett. Get upstairs," Samantha breathes. "Our walk-in closet. Hurry!"

Barrett nods gratefully and darts upstairs with as much strength as his bleeding wound allows. Shane stays behind to back the illusion that everything's normal.

"Don't come out," Barrett hears Samantha say; the end of her sentence muffled by his entrance to their bedroom.

He turns into a walk-in closet and—sheltered between what I'm sure is a million's worth of designer clothes and jewelry—pushes his back against one of the many mirrors to drop to the floor. He still has his hand on his neck, and he's trembling. His father is at the door, and if he finds him, Barrett's not sure what's going to happen.

Will he be apologetic? he wonders. *Will he be angry? Will I be safe? Did Travis escape?*

There's more pounding from downstairs, and he can hear John screaming Shane's name now.

"Oh, God," he hears Samantha breathe. "Okay. Act normal. Okay?"

"Aye," Shane bravely agrees.

"Okay," Samantha says again. Then, suddenly shouting: "Mike! Mike!" Quieter: "Stay close to me, Shane. Please. Get behind me. And clean your hand. Quick! The blood." Shouting again: "*Michael!*"

But Barrett doesn't hear Uncle Mike's response, and that scares him. His father's strong enough to overpower both Samantha and Shane and Barrett knows this. Plus, he's already proven himself dangerous tonight. The thought of them becoming some sort of fucked-up collateral damage in the Roth family drama makes him feel contrite and scared. It would be his fault. He led his father here.

"Wash your hands," Samantha says. "Quickly, Shane! In the bathroom there. Wash the blood off your hands. He'll see."

He catches the sound of urgent footsteps, the hiss off a tap being run for a moment or two before cutting off. John's still pounding on the front door.

"Okay." Samantha says, like she's trying to sound sure of herself. "Ready?" He can't hear Shane's answer, but his fear heightens when he hears the door open. "John?" Samantha plays. "What's going on? It's late—"

"Sam, Sam, please." His father's words are frantic, and they escape in short huffs like Barrett's were earlier. "Please help me. I'm looking for Barrett. Is he here?"

"What? No, I—"

"He must be. He ran this way. He must." John takes a couple breaths, causing a short silence. "Shane! Have you seen him? Tell me you've seen him."

"No, Uncle John. He's not here." Shane's calm innocence gives him away.

Fuck, he's never been a good liar, Barrett thinks.

"What? He *has* to be." John's voice comes out in a low growl. "You're lying to me. Give me my son."

"He's not here," Samantha repeats.

"Bullshit! You're a family of bad fucking liars! Give me my fucking son! He's hurt for fucksake!"

"John, please—" Samantha says.

"*Shane?*" John presses.

"He's not here!" Shane says.

"Barrett!" John says.

He flinches at the sound of his own name, curling himself deeper into a ball. Wanting to disappear. Wanting to be invisible. Wanting to merge with the wall.

"Barrett! Get the fuck down here!"

His breath is quickening.

Then the sound of footsteps come up the stairs to the lower level, and a deep Scottish voice follows. Relief spreads through Barrett's fading body. "What's all this about? John? What's going on?"

"Mike," John breathes. "Barrett ran away from me. I know he's here. I think—I mean—I injured him. So I must find him. It was an accident!"

"What do you mean, you *injured* him?" Michael asks, his voice raising in concern. "What did you do?"

John stammers. "I mean—He—I—He... got in the way..."

"Got in the way of *what?*" Time pulses by in a few tense seconds, where there's only John's rapid breath. Michael lowers his voice, his Scottish burr turned stone-cold and serious. "Johnathan Roth, what have you done?"

"I..." John can't say it. *I almost strangled my son to death.*

More silence passes before Michael icily says: "Get out."

"Fuck you," John growls back.

"You're drunk. Go home."

"I'm not leaving without him."

"Did you not hear my wife and son clearly? He *isnae* here!"

"Bullshit!" John says. Then there's a bunch of shifting, and Samantha shrieks. "Tell me the fucking truth, Shane!" The young Shane has obviously not kept himself out of the reach of his irate, drunken, so-called uncle.

"I dinna ken," Shane says, grunting. "I dinna ken where he is, Uncle John."

"Get yer damn hands off my son!" Michael's voice booms, and I imagine him lurching forward to pull Shane from John's grip. "You touch him again and I'll fecking kill you, Johnathan Roth! Get *the feck* out of my house, now!"

"How could you—?" John spits.

"I said *get out!*"

"I'll never forgive you for this, Michael Thomas. You're refusing to help me when my boy is at risk. Betrayal! Pure fucking betrayal!"

"*Get out!*"

There's pushing and grunting, and John is spitting insults at his best friend left, right, and center. Then, the sound of the door closing again lets Barrett release the breath that he doesn't realize he's been holding. Finally, he's safe.

Isn't he?

Travis... he thinks.

"Where is he?" Michael asks from downstairs. "Where's Barrett?"

"Upstairs," Samantha says. "The walk-in closet. He *is* hurt, but we couldn't let him... I mean, we just couldn't!"

Travis... Come for me, brother... Please...

"Of course, of course. Thank God. What the bloody *feck* has he done?"

"We need to find Travis. Or at least call him. Oh, Mike! I'm so worried about him! Barrett said John tried to kill him."

"*What?*"

"Yeah." Samantha's answer is more of a squeak than a word.

"I'm getting my coat and going out to find him. You get Barrett to the hospital."

"Oh, Mike!"

As Samantha sobs, young footsteps hammer up the stairs, and suddenly Shane's there with muted alarm behind his bright blue eyes. He drops to his knees beside Barrett, once again removing his best friend's hand and replacing it with his clean one. It doesn't take long for the blood to start dripping down his fingers.

Barrett won't look at him. I can feel the overwhelming embarrassment swelling within him as he tries to wrestle it down. To push it away. He wishes that he never brought this upon the Thomas family. And as much as he urges them not to, his tears break free. He tries to hide them from Shane, but then remembers that his best friend can practically read his mind.

"Everything's okay, Bear," Shane says, softly. "He's gone. Dad made him go."

Travis... Please... Come for me...

"I'm sorry," Barrett whispers. "I'm so sorry, Shay."

"Shhh." Shane tightens the grip of his hand and shifts closer. They're face-to-face with their noses almost touching. "It's not your fault."

"He would have killed me... I mean... He hurt me, Shay. How could he...?"

Shane swallows like he's not sure what to say. He wraps his free arm around Barrett's back and rests his forehead on Barrett's, holding him. Then he closes his eyes to hide the anguish that taints that night.

Barrett starts to cry, and Shane sighs with sadness. "Don't worry," he whispers back, wise even in his young age. "Everything's going to be okay. I promise, *ma brither*. I'll protect you. I will *always* protect you."

CHAPTER 25
ANIMAL I HAVE BECOME

"Barrett!" I shot up in the Muskoka chair, surrounded by the Roth Campground and the break of dawn.

"What?!" he said, jolting from beside me.

And I was fucking *mortified*. Not only had I screamed really loud, but I never imagined that he'd ever be beside me when I did.

"Emily, my God. What is it?" He got up and squatted at my feet. "What's wrong?"

I heaved. And heaved. And heaved. "I—uh— I—dunno— Animal. Thought I saw— An animal." I couldn't even use the nightmare excuse. If I did, I'd have to explain that I'd fallen asleep in the chair beside him. Which would be very fucking awkward.

Barrett took my hands. "You look like you've seen a ghost."

I tried to soothe the horror that was coursing through my veins. I'd never seen something that bad. Never. Even after David's torture memory. "Animal. Like I said. I wanted to warn you."

He looked around. His brow was furrowed. Concerned. Questioning. In the firelight, I saw the scar when he twisted his neck. It'd grown with him, and was white and stretched, but straight. Must have been a clean cut.

Oh, Barrett. I'm so sorry. That night must haunt you.

I realized that I'd only ever seen him in shirts with collars before. Shirts that would hide it. Tonight was the first time he'd ever worn a V-neck. And even so, the scar was barely noticeable if you didn't

311

know that it was there. I blinked at it several times. If there was any possible validation that I'd been seeing memories, that was it.

"Barrett..." I reached out and brushed it.

"What?" he said, glancing down at my hand. He'd lived with it for nearly twenty years. It must have been easy for him to forget.

"There's a scar—"

"Yes. I have many." He met my gaze with dark inquisition. Like he could tell that something was wrong here. There was something I wasn't telling him, and he knew it.

"I mean the one on your neck."

He pulled himself from my touch. "It's from long ago. Please don't ask about it."

Apologetic, I nodded. It made sense that he'd say that. If given the choice, I wouldn't wanna be reminded either.

"Barrett?" Rebecca was standing at the door to their tent, arms crossed and eyeing me suspiciously. "What are you two doing out here?"

"Nothing, babe." He stood to separate us. "We couldn't sleep, and Emily got frightened by an animal, that's all." The way he lied was flawless.

She twitched her nose. "It's four-thirty. Come to bed."

"Alright. I'll be in momentarily."

Rebecca huffed and turned back inside.

Barrett reached out and hauled me to my feet. As soon as I stood, my legs threatened to give out. "Are you quite sure you're alright?"

I really wasn't, so I reached out and pulled him into a tight hug. I could feel the lean runner's muscles of his back, and I wasn't sure how better to cleanse myself from the abhorrent energy than to put my heart close to his.

Oh my God... Poor Travis, as well... He must have been so scared...

Something in the way Barrett looked at me after I touched his scar told me this wasn't all of it. There had been more abuse than this. I was sure.

Johnathan Roth was a monster...

I squeezed Barrett tighter.

He rested his chin on the top of my head, and I thought about my own ancient scar that pulsed just below. "It's alright. This area of the property is gated. The bigger predators can't get through."

You sure about that, Bear?

"You likely saw a racoon, that's all."

I vibrated my head. It was close to a nod as I could do.

"You're safe, Em."

God, I liked it when he used my nickname. Especially when he was holding me. Especially while I was breathing him in.

Soothed by his touch, I finally began to settle. "I feel so stupid," I huffed into his chest.

He chuckled a little. "Think nothing of it," he said. "Now, let's get some more sleep, shall we?" I was very aware that he'd taken a few extra seconds after saying this to hug me.

"Yeah. Sorry." I sniffed as I stepped away from him. "Let's go to bed."

Later in the morning, the empty tent was bathed in a white glow. Avril must have already gone out. My head was killing me, and I felt like I hadn't drunk water for a thousand years. With hung-over determination, I stood and dressed while I was still alone. The smell of coffee was drawing me, and my only hope was that the caffeine would help to steady my shaken nerves.

Outside, Shane and Kirk were sitting at the picnic table. Barrett was beside the grill, stretching like a cat as he released a deep yawn into the morning air. He rubbed his eyes and reached for the coffee kettle, glancing over his shoulder at Kirk, whose mug was empty. He hesitated, and I wondered whether he was thinking about all the

THE VEIL OF OPPRESSION

cruel things Kirk had said to him last night. In the end, he stepped forward to fill it.

Kirk met Barrett's gaze and touched his arm in silent thanks. Barrett gave him a weak smile and an even weaker wink. From across the table, Shane glanced up from his phone and caught the exchange, but he didn't say anything. Instead, he pushed his mug forward. The coffee kettle froze in midair as Barrett looked at his best friend. It reminded him. I was sure of it. It reminded him of that night, and I could see it flashing through the obsidian like a real-life horror film.

Shane raised an eyebrow. "Anytime today, there, Roth."

Barrett cleared his throat, shook his head, and shot him a smile. "Sorry. I was miles away." He stretched his jaw in another yawn. "I didn't sleep well last night."

"I sleep like a baby after a good gammy," Shane said, smirking at him. "There must be something wrong with you."

Barrett's gaze flicked over to me. "Emily is present, Mr. Thomas."

"Not my fault," Shane said. "She probably heard. You could have a least gone into the woods."

"Shay..." Kirk furrowed his honey-blonde brows.

Shane pushed his mug further in reminder. "Yeah, I ken. Ladies present, and all." He pointed at Barrett. "I blame you, Roth. Gentleman that you are."

Barrett smirked as he stepped forward to fill Shane's mug. "I am no stronger than the next man when given the offer. Forgive me." His eyes flashed to Kirk, who rolled his in return. Barrett swallowed and handed Shane's mug to him.

"No man can blame you, brither," Shane said, taking it with one hand before he continued reading on his phone. "Cheers. And I love you, lad."

"I love you, too." Barrett smiled before turning to the grill to get another set of mugs.

The morning sun made Shane's hair shimmer like gold. After

seeing Barrett's memory, I had no doubt that he was an amazing person, and an even better friend. It was clear that he had done—and would still do—whatever it took to protect the people that he loved. And though the joker often came out of him, underneath was a loving, loyal, brave, and kind, Scottish-Canadian. He had a heart bigger than he liked to show. Just like his best friends around the table with him.

I broke out a somber smile as I approached him, winding my arms around his shoulders. "What does it mean?" I asked. "*Brither*."

Shane chuckled, rebalancing under my arms. "It simply means 'brother.'"

"Is it Gaelic then? That you know how to speak?" I asked. It was incredible how nice he smelled after two days of camping. The smell of his cologne was still there under the tinge of campfire.

He shook his head and drew a sip of coffee. "I wish, lass. Scottish Gaelic is a dying language, unfortunately, and it's really only spoken in the Highlands and North. My family comes from Aberdeen in the East. What we speak is a version of Scots called *Doric*."

I leaned my head against his. "That's beautiful."

"And for that, I'll thank ye, lass." He chuckled and pulled himself to the side to look at me. "Also—good morning—but what is this for?"

I sighed and squeezed him tighter. "I needed someone to hug."

"Ah, well. In that case, let's do it properly." He stood and pulled me into his arms, and I rested my head gratefully against his chest. Tears were starting to prick the back of my eyeballs.

You're an amazing friend, Shane Thomas, and you always will be.

"You alright, lassie? You seem a bit *doon aboot the moo*." He cleared his throat. "I mean, let me speak Canadian. You seem a bit depressed, eh?"

I giggled and shoved away my desire to cry. "It's the hangover, I guess."

"Ah, well. Barrett's breakfast will set you right. Come. Sit down and have a cuppa."

We let each other go, and I looked at Barrett's back as I made my way to the picnic table. "Honestly, when I saw his penthouse, my first thought is that he never uses that kitchen. But this weekend has proven me wrong."

Shane smirked as he slid back into the table. "If that man had time to cook, he'd do it every day. There's a good ol' housewife in him, for sure."

Barrett laughed but didn't give us the satisfaction of turning around.

I slid into the picnic table and raised a playful eyebrow at Shane. "I was also surprised that there isn't a hidden playroom up there."

This brought out Barrett's perfect grin as he turned. "In truth, I would love one. But *Fifty Shades of Roth* doesn't sound right, does it?"

I laughed, thankful that our playful banter was raising my mood.

Barrett poured me a cup of coffee and brought it to our side of the table. He served it to me with a spoon and a container of sugar, tussling my hair before he walked back to the grill. I hoped that he hadn't noticed my scar like I'd noticed his.

"Mr. Billionaire, serving everyone else," I toyed with him, as I spooned some sugar into my coffee. "Isn't that nice?"

He snuffed. "Don't get used to it, kid."

I let myself take in the movements of his body as the steam from the coffee tickled my nose.

Then, Avril and Rebecca came out from the trails with Dixon prancing ahead of them, and I knew my time to look had come to an end. Dixon ran up to greet Shane and then came between Kirk and me, propping himself up on the picnic table bench with his front paws. I rustled his fur and cuddled him. He rewarded me with kisses on my face.

Shane smiled as he watched us. "I think we're going to have to schedule dates for you two after this weekend. He really loves you, Em."

My cheeks flushed as I snuggled Dixon. "I know. I'm not going to be able to stay away from him after this."

And he's not the only one, I thought, glancing over at Barrett, who was busy preparing the plates for breakfast.

From out of nowhere, Rebecca's voice intruded. "Emily, can I talk to you in private for a second?" Shit. She'd caught me. I'd been careless.

"Sure..." I took a drawn-out sip of coffee before getting up.

Fuck, fuck, fuck!

Giving Dixon a pat, I tried to pretend I wasn't freaking out. Barrett turned from the grill, looking like he was thinking the same thing I was.

Rebecca shot me a forced smile and then stormed off across the campsite and back toward the bathrooms. I followed, glancing back at Barrett before I turned and took a deep breath. My tired feet trudged across the dirt until we were out of earshot of the campsite. Crossing her arms, Rebecca waited in the same area that Barrett and Kirk were in last night—the *confrontation* area, apparently—and then wrinkled her nose at me.

I cleared my throat and tried to keep calm, but I was aware of the trouble that I was in. "What's up?" I asked, shoving my hands into my pockets like I was totally innocent or something.

"Listen," she said. "I don't know how it works in the slums of the dirty city that you're from. But here, it's not alright fuck around with another woman's man."

"Rebecca, I'm not sure I—"

"I don't know if you even realize you're doing it, but you've been acting like a boyfriend-stealing *slut* all weekend."

"I'm sorry, Rebecca."

"Really?" she said, hands flying to her hips. "Then why were you out there with him this morning? Alone?" She raised her eyebrows in a silent, *Well?*

I tried to think of a good answer, but there wasn't one. "I'm sorry," I repeated, quietly. "I had a nightmare last night and I couldn't sleep.

He was still up, so I figured it was better than lying in bed." It was a weak excuse, and I knew it, but it was the only one I had.

She scoffed. "Yeah, right. I've seen the way you've been looking at him all weekend. Like you *desperately* want to fuck him. I'm not sure if you've realized this, but not only does he belong to me, but you don't exactly have the caliber, girl."

"What's that supposed to mean?"

She barked out a laugh. "Oh, come on, Emily. Why would he be interested in garbage when he owns gold?"

"Excuse me?" My hangover didn't help with my rising temper.

"Listen," she said, again. "I really wanted to like you, but I won't put up with this. I suggest you back off and you back off quick, bitch." She flashed her perfectly plucked eyebrows. "*Or else.*"

My jaw dropped. Never in my life had I been threatened by someone like that.

Done with her shameless bullying, she gave me a final glare before she started to storm off.

"Rebecca, I'm sorry," I said, giving it a last-ditch effort. "I didn't—"

"Don't ever fucking touch anything that belongs to me again!" She turned, pointing a finger at me, before she continued storming away.

Afterward, an unwelcome anger coursed through my veins, and all I could do was stand there in shock. It overwhelmed me, and I started to hyperventilate in the same way that Barrett had last night. I wanted to run at her and tackle her to the ground. I wanted to slap her and scratch her face. I wanted to do things that I've never wanted to do to someone before.

Oh my God...

This wasn't me. It was like the exposure to Barrett's memory had changed me. Like the violent rage of Johnathan Roth had been so intense that it had seeped into my system upon the mere exposure to him. Barrett's memory had injected me with something dark that shouldn't have been there.

I plummeted to the ground and curled myself in a ball, fighting it with my mum's breathing techniques. It worked for a little, but it wasn't enough.

Who the fuck is she to call me a boyfriend-stealing slut? She can't define me!

In truth, I knew I had overstepped, but I had a bond with Barrett that I couldn't ignore. My instinct flared when I was around him. I'd been screaming his name for years. And I wasn't about to let Rebecca take him away when I'd only *just* found him.

So, I drew a deep breath and told myself that I'd have to be more careful. That was all. And she hadn't *really* threatened me. She hadn't even touched me. There was nothing to get upset about.

I was lying to calm myself, and I knew it.

With weak determination, I stood and dusted the forest floor from my butt. And when I walked back to the campsite, I realized that nothing I'd told myself had worked. Rebecca had driven a theoretical wedge between us, and I would never be able to forget that it was there. But the truth was, I wanted it to be. I wanted a reason to hate her. She'd shown me her true colours, and we clearly weren't compatible as anything but enemies.

She was now standing with Barrett, cuddling into him with a coy smirk as she glared at me.

I rolled my eyes and turned down the path toward the lake.

Fuck this.

"Em?" Barrett questioned, as I passed. "Are you not going to sit down for breakfast?"

I couldn't look at him. I didn't want to give away the fact that his girlfriend had upset me to the point where I was on the verge of tears. "Thanks, but I'm not hungry," was all I managed to mutter.

Dixon got up and followed me down the path, annoyingly aware of my condition.

"What did you say to her?" I heard Barrett ask Rebecca as I walked away.

"Nothing, baby—"

"What the fuck did you say to her?" he repeated.

"Em, are you okay?" Avril called.

But I didn't stay in earshot for much longer. I was too mad to risk overhearing the verbal diarrhea that was sure to come from Rebecca's mouth next.

Inhaling the fresh air, I went down toward the beach with Dixon trotting at my side. The sight of the lake drew the allure of escape, along with the annoyingly happy memory of falling in with Barrett yesterday. I suddenly wanted to be in the middle; far from where anyone could reach me without significant effort. I trudged across the sand and yanked open the door to the boathouse, snatching a lifejacket and the keys to one of the many seadoos that were anchored on the long dock. I was so desperate. Desperate to feel anything but the unfamiliar rage that Rebecca and John had both triggered in me.

Ignoring Dixon's whining, I stormed up the dock, mounting the seadoo that matched the keys that I'd snatched. I didn't understand the gauges or controls in front of me, but the keyhole was clear enough, so I plunged the key into it. The thing beeped, switching into neutral. Then I pressed the red "Start" button to switch on the ignition, and the rest seemed easy enough. Squeeze the right trigger to go forward and speed up, squeeze the left for brake and reverse. Good to go. After playing with it a little, I unhooked myself from the anchor. That's when Dixon started to bark, and I heard footsteps pounding up the dock.

"Emily. What are you doing? Do you even know how to use that thing?" It was Kirk, annoyingly coming to check up on me.

"I've already figured it out. Just leave me alone, okay? I need to clear my head."

"What do you mean? What happened—?"

I squeezed the right trigger, taking off into the lake with a growl from the engine and a wave spouting from behind me.

"Emily, stop!"

Kirk's calls and Dixon's barking faded as the mountainous air began to whip past my face, and the sun warmed my skin. I took it in, allowing it to fill me with positivity. As the water splashed up around me, euphoria rose with it. I started to test the boundaries of my novice maneuvering and began to weave back and forth across the lake, squeezing the right trigger harder as I got used to driving it. Then I craved more speed. It was liberating, and I soon found myself laughing as I used the lake as my personal playground. The rage was no match for the beauty of nature.

It wasn't long until I heard the drone of the second seadoo, and I realized that Kirk had followed me across the lake. But the heat of the moment turned my mood, so I now welcomed his company. I started racing him as he tried to keep pace.

"Take it easy!" He said over the rushing air, but I wasn't in the mind to listen.

This was too good, and this was too much fun, so I sped away from him with: "No way! This is incredible!"

As we neared the middle of the lake, Ava falls came into sight, and drawn by my happy memories, I steered toward it, dismissing the whistle in the wind and Kirk yelling at me to stop. Through the rush of the wake, I escaped into those positive memories, and my mind flashed with images of Barrett. I pictured his perfect smile as I met him at the canoe; the shock in his expression as I tipped us overboard; the joy in his wild laughter afterward; the gleam of the red undertones of his hair; dark-chocolate eyes in the lantern light; the petroglyph under my finger as his hand clasped mine; the overwhelming desire to kiss him...

Then the reality of Kirk screaming and the impact on shallow rocks yanked me out of it. Before I knew it, I was thrown from the seadoo, and my body skipped across the lake like a stone. The cold water burned my nostrils and lungs. The world became a blur. Intense pain reared its ugly head, and for the second time in my life, there was nothing.

The memory comes into view more hazily than one ever has before. Barrett. Eighteen? Nineteen? The unfinished Chevelle. The driveway of the Roth Estate. They all melt into focus like some acid-fueled drug trip.

Whose is this?

But I can feel the rising warmth within the person's core as they glance up at Barrett from behind the hood of the car. They're yanking on something in the engine with some sort of tool, and it's clear that this memory belongs to Kirk. The feeling is strange, but it must be a form of love from their close friendship. Barrett stands from where he's been working on the back wheel well of the car and meets his eye, shooting him a smile. This intensifies the warmth, but something else appears under it. I can't sense what Kirk feels as easily as I would with the others whose memories I've seen, but I know these feelings are mixed. Happiness. Pride. Anxiety? Fear?

Then I pin it. He's nervous. He's nervous around Barrett, and he's trying to hide it.

The day is bathed in bright sunlight, and the black of the paint is turning the engine bay into an isolated sauna, but Kirk's focus is only partially there, anyway. He keeps glancing from the part to Barrett, to the part, back to Barrett, like he's trying to monitor his every move. The sweat from his brow forces him to wipe his face and look away, and when he looks back, his best friend hovering over the trunk.

"Not there!" Kirk's voice booms so loudly that it snatches Barrett's attention. "*Tabarnak*, Bear! Not there! What? Do you think I had Walker do the paint for nothing?"

Barrett shoots him an icy look but flashes his eyebrows. "You're right, Ki. Sorry." He moves to the other side of the car, where he's blocked from Kirk's view. "No matter. I'm a pro at the old-fashioned way."

Kirk's feelings intensify as he watches. Now the happiness and pride are gone, leaving behind a painful singe of anger, fear, and frustration. It leaves an awful taste in his mouth, like bile and acid after dry heaving on an empty stomach. Then, fear steps forward to take center stage, and Kirk doesn't want it there. He tries to usher it off to stop its performance, but no matter what he does, it's dancing away. Deafening. Refusing to be ignored. This is what it's like when instinct starts screaming at you.

I realize that he's scared to be robbed of a person who he loves.

Then I start to hear his jumbled thoughts: *Pourquoi lui? Pourquoi fallait-il que ce soit lui? Je sais qui tu es. Tu n'as pas à te cacher. Je te connais mieux que quiconque. S'il te plaît, arrête, Bear. S'il te plaît, bats-toi. Tu ne mérites pas ça. Comment je peux lui prendre ça? Comme j'aimerais pouvoir. On t'aime, Bear. S'il te plaît, ne part pas. Je t'aime...*

"So, where were we?" The slap of Barrett's hand on the edge of the engine bay makes Kirk jump like he's been jolted, and his sudden closeness causes nervousness to pitch fear from its place. Barrett's grinning at him with his pupils dilated, and there is something in that grin that Kirk hates because he knows that it's not real.

Kirk hesitates but pulls fourth bravery. "I wish you would stop... It's gonna kill you..."

S'il te plaît... Je t'en supplie.

Barrett chuckles and puts a heavy hand on Kirk's shoulder. "You don't have to worry about that, Ki. Nothing can kill me. I'm already dead."

I was on the dock, soaking wet, freezing, and in Kirk's arms. I couldn't scream because I was spitting up water, and a sharp pain was shooting across my head, reminding me horribly of my other accident. Beside us, Dixon was whimpering, his warm tongue lashing my cheek as he tried to help me regain consciousness.

Kirk's face came into view, and his dark blue eyes were burning. His mouth was moving, but all I heard was a dull ringing. Like a soldier, shell-shocked after an explosion. Only, the thing I was fighting against wasn't an enemy. It was common sense.

Kirk gave me a shake, trying to get me to stay conscious as his lips moved frantically, but all I could do was study his face. Wonder what language he was speaking. I hadn't ever been this face-to-face with him before, and I began to realize just how symmetrical it was. He had a dimple on the right side that appeared when he pulled his lip back. The blue of his eyes was like the colour of the mountains on a dark and cloudy day. Kindness radiated from him naturally.

Finally, his voice turned from ringing, to muffling, to words. "You're okay. Everything's going to be okay."

"Kirk..."

"Em, can you hear me? C–Can you hear me? *Merde.*" Then to someone down the dock: "Get the emergency kit! Hurry! She's bleeding."

"You were nervous..."

He shifted beneath me, and my head settled in the crook of his elbow with agony. "You're damn right I was nervous! You don't know that lake at all. You shouldn't have been driving like that."

"That's not what I mean..."

"Huh?"

"Barrett... You were nervous of him... Why?"

We shared a moment of austere energy, but the only response he gave me was a narrowing of those stormy eyes.

The multiple pairs of feet running up the dock robbed us of anymore private time. Someone dropped to their knees beside me, and from the sweet-musky scent surrounding us, I knew that the next pair of eyes that looked down on me would be black. "Fuck! What happened?"

"A rock," Kirk said. "She hit a rock. Really hard. I think she's concussed."

"Okay. Alright." Barrett propped me up into a sitting position, making my body scream in protest. "Em, can you hear us?"

"Yeah, Bear..."

"Good. Okay. Good. You're bleeding. I must bandage your head, alright? Then I'll get you to the hospital in Squamish."

"I'm sorry, Bear..."

"It's fine. You only scared the shit out of me. And—you know—*Kirk.*" Barrett started cleaning the wound with antiseptic and spoke to Kirk as he held me up. "You pulled her out of the water unconscious?"

"What else was I supposed to do?" Kirk said. "Let her drown?"

Barrett gave him a twitch of his smirk. "You're a hero, Kirk Richards. A fucking *hero.*"

Kirk gave him a half-smile but didn't say anything else.

The antiseptic was starting to sting, and I reached up to touch my head, but Kirk pulled my hand away and encouraged me to be still while Barrett worked. He was so close to me that I could smell the bacon and coffee on his breath, and his eyes gleamed in obsidian, which didn't hide the serious concern that he tried to hide behind them. I knew that concern was for me—the wound must have been worse than I thought—but I was so dopey that I couldn't feel it for myself. All I could seem to think about was Kirk's short memory. I racked my brain to try to bring meaning to it.

Good thing for high school French class.

I watched Barrett, then watched Kirk, and thought about the long history of their friendship. I thought about how this very trip had been the first time they'd seen each other for over a year.

What the fuck happened to them?

Suddenly, Shane was in front of me, shining his phone's flashlight at me before he held up a finger and asked me to follow it. I tried my best, but Shay pursed his lips and shot a look at Barrett. "You've gotta go, Bear."

"Okay. Grab me the keys to the Chev?" Shane nodded and then took off down the dock.

Avril's angelic voice cut in from somewhere to our right. "Barrett, I can take her. Then we can head straight home after."

"Are you sure?"

"Yeah. It makes more sense than you having to wait at the hospital."

"Alright. Pack your belongings and load it—fast. I'll bring her up to the car."

Avril nodded and then took off down the dock too.

By then, Barrett was finishing the dressing on my wound by winding the gauze around my head and holding it in place with a little clamp. "What the fuck were you thinking, kid?" he mumbled. "The area of the falls is not safe for seadoos. You should have listened to Kirk. Very few know this lake as well as he does."

My voice was sluggish. Like my tongue was numb. "I wasn't. I'm sorry."

"Well, make sure you *are* next time." He slipped an arm under my knees, and the other behind my back, before he hauled me up as he stood. Kirk asked if he needed help, but he grunted, "No, I'm alright," before he shifted me into a better position to carry me down the dock.

My head rested on his right shoulder, and I had a close-up view of his dismal childhood scar. But being in his arms made me comfortable and safe. I wrapped mine around his neck and curled so that I could be closer to his heart.

"It's going to be alright, kid," he said, as we left the dock and stepped on solid ground. "We're going to get you looked after."

I sighed. I wasn't afraid, but the fatigue was overwhelming. I could fall asleep at any moment and slip into another one of his horrible memories.

Maybe this bump will stop my ability?

Wishful thinking on my part.

"Bear?" I asked.

"Yeah, kid?"

"You're not dead."

He chuckled. "Well, of course not. I don't think I'd be carrying you if I was."

"No... I mean... you're *not* dead."

His tone dropped serious. "Not yet anyway."

"Please don't give up..."

He fell silent. Our combined weight made his footsteps fall heavily through the dirt. "You've a concussion," he finally said. "You're not making any sense."

Back at the campground, Shane was helping Avril load our bags into her Fit. She spotted us and jogged over to the passenger side door, opening it so that Barrett could usher me inside. I didn't see Rebecca, and I didn't want to. Especially since I'd found myself into her man's arms.

Barrett lowered and shifted me into the passenger seat before kneeling to my level. My eyelids drooped, and my consciousness threatened to fade away.

"Stay with us, kiddo," he said, with a soft hand on my cheek. "Don't close your eyes. That's the worst thing that you can do with a concussion."

I held my head. "I'm sorry, Bear. I didn't mean for the weekend to end like this."

"Shhh," he said. "Don't even worry about it. You merely need to get to the hospital so they can make sure everything is alright." He paused and smiled. "I mean, it's partly my fault. I shouldn't have left the keys *anywhere on this fucking land* where you could find them."

I giggled. "How could you be so foolish?"

"I guess I never thought that I'd encounter an amateur using a rock for a jump on my lake."

"There was your mistake," I said, with a snuff.

"Perhaps. But at least you've made it clear what's *not* going to happen next time."

I raised a sluggish eyebrow at him. "Me on a seadoo by myself?"

"You got it, kid," he said, giving my leg a nudge. "I mean—let's face it—you're no good at it, and I, quite frankly, don't want to be sued for that shit."

I laughed, then winced as I clutched my head. Even though I was injured, I didn't want to leave him so soon. The "thud" of the trunk closing and the shape of Avril on the driver side distracted us, and Barrett cleared his throat as she stepped inside.

"Call me tonight and let me know how you are, okay?" he said.

I nodded, looking up at him. "Okay."

"Alright. Get better." He closed the car door and gave the window a pat. Again, I thought about how this wasn't the man that strutted across the stage at the Roth Banquet.

Avril backed her car out of the campsite, and I waved to the entire group, holding my head as they watched us do a three-point turn and drive away through the forest. Everyone waved back except Rebecca, who kept her face stoic, like she didn't give a fuck less what was going to happen to me. And I couldn't give a *fuck less* that she didn't. If she hadn't threatened me like that, none of this would have happened.

We made our way across the property, out the gate, and onto the gravel road, following Barrett's path in reverse. Avril hadn't said anything to me. Her grip was tight on the steering wheel, and she stared through her windshield like she was afraid to blink. I couldn't tell whether she was mad at me or not.

I cleared my throat and flashed her a guilt-ridden face. "Avril, I'm sorry that I cut the weekend short. I didn't mean for that to happen—"

"Em, don't even worry about it," she said, continuing to move her car carefully over the gravel. "All I want is to make sure you're okay."

We drove through the roads that wound down the mountains wordlessly, and Squamish soon came sprawling within sight below. I looked like a prized idiot, and my head was killing me, but I figured I deserved it for being so stupid.

The only silver lining was that I'd had a great weekend—even with Rebecca's vicious attack and Barrett's awful memory—and I was happy that I'd been given the chance to spend more time with Barrett. The more I saw of him, the more I started to believe that he was *my* Barrett. The one I'd been calling for. All this time.

But what did that mean for the future? What did that mean for David and me? What did it mean for the Roth-Mathis feud and the motive behind it? What did it mean when his father had been murdered in cold blood for something he probably deserved?

I sighed and rested my head against the car window, trying not to think about it. Avril drove as quickly as she could toward the hospital.

CHAPTER 26
SOMEBODY'S KNOCKIN'

I spent the entire next day in bed, watching movies on my laptop. My head was still sore, and I was a little dizzy, so I decided to take a day off from school to rest. Avril and I had spent over six hours in the hospital the day before, but I'd been discharged after, so I considered myself lucky this time. I couldn't believe how stupid I'd been, just because I was upset. The reaction that I'd had to Rebecca's interrogation made me look like some silly, little girl that had to be pulled out a lake by some big, heroic man. And I couldn't believe that I'd let her do that to me. My emotional control had failed me in the worst way, and I needed to refresh my techniques, so I caved and called my mum for some advice.

After I told her about my meltdown—leaving out the seadoo accident because I didn't want her to freak out and tell me to come home—and we picked apart how I was feeling together. She reinforced the distancing technique that I already knew—getting the hell out of there when you're triggered—and taught me a couple of new breathing and meditation strategies.

Then, she dove into internal validation and how others have no right to define us. What did this woman really know about me, anyway? Barely anything if not nothing at all. She'd had no right to judge me. She was clearly thinking from a lens of fear and had taken it out on me when she was threatened. I cringed when she mentioned that I should give Rebecca grace, even in her bitchiest of times. That was going to be a hard one going forward and it wouldn't happen at the drop of a dime. But at the end of the day, I knew she was right.

When we'd talked about what happened with Barrett, Mum smiled through the screen and said whispy things like, "Whatever will be, will be," and, "The heart wants what it wants."

The problem was my heart wanted two things right now, and it would tear itself apart if I let it. So, I decided to just protect it for now. Besides, I wasn't ready to make any relationship decisions in Vancouver, and even if I was, I only had one logical choice. David was single. Barrett wasn't.

Talking it out with Mum made a world of difference, and by the time our call came to an end, I was glad I'd reached out to her. But my stomach hurt when she told me that she had to go. Despite my need for independence, I promised to call her more often, and we said "I love you" before saying goodbye. I smiled as our video call ended, but my face dropped like I'd peeled off a mask after. I put my phone aside, insides clenching as I thought about how much I missed my parents. The House-of-Wolves had helped make this move a successful one, but something deep within my heart told me that I still needed my mum and dad. And that I always would.

You're a master's student, Em, I told myself, gently. *You can do this.*

I pulled myself out of bed, holding my forehead to manage the vertigo. I looked out my window at the landscape beyond, which was still bathed in the summer evening. Far from the sunny and warm days that we seemed to be having, today had been cooler and overcast. The wind was moving through the trees and rocking the cattails in the marsh, and low clouds were sat on top of the mountains, hiding their top half. It'd been the perfect day to stay in, have a warm cup of coffee, and rest.

Then I stood there, watching the mountains, and thinking about the night before. At the hospital and on the drive home, Avril had asked me several times what Rebecca had said that upset me. I brushed it off, because even though Rebecca was a bitch with a capital B, I didn't want to be the reason their friendship drifted apart. And when we got home, David wouldn't leave me alone. Assisted by Greg, he nursed me like a dying patient; waiting on me hand and foot as he shuttled Gatorade, medication, snacks, and anything else that could help, in and out of the kitchen. When he'd finally plopped beside me on the couch, he'd clicked his tongue, looked at me like the whole thing was Barrett's fault, and said, "I knew I shouldn't have let you go."

"This was me," I reminded him. "He didn't do anything wrong. It was my own stupid fault."

David looked like he really didn't believe me.

Back in my bedroom on that Monday, my phone started vibrating from the nightstand where I'd set it. I glanced down and my heart skipped a beat. *Barrett Roth*, it told me, as it jingled away.

Pushing down my weird excitement, I cleared my throat and took a deep breath, letting it ring a couple more times before I picked up. "Hi, Barrett," I said, moving to my bed and sliding back into the pillows. High school nostalgia was hitting me like a brick.

"Hey, kiddo. How are you doing?" The sound of his voice sent coziness through my bones. Though he'd asked me to call yesterday, I'd only had the energy to text him and tell him I was okay. It was nice for him to call and check up on me. Really nice.

"My head's a bit sore, I've got a couple of stitches, and I'm tired. But I'll be fine," I told him.

"Sorry to hear that, kid. What did they say at the hospital?"

"That there's no serious damage and it's just a bump on the head. Luckily, no harm done."

"That's good, considering how much of a fall you took."

"Yeah, totally," I said. "But I'm a tough, nerdy chick. I can handle it."

Tough, nerdy chick?? Really??

He laughed. "More like a *clumsy*, nerdy chick." A moment passed where I just enjoyed being on the phone with him, before he said,

"Hey, listen. I don't want to keep you too long, but I was under the assumption that you'd want your car back."

"Right..." I hadn't even thought of my little Yaris cooped up in his massive condo building. "I'm *probably* gonna need that back, but it's no problem. I'll come get it when I get out of school tomorrow. It's easy to get down there by bus, right?"

"I am not the man to ask about such things. But you needn't worry. I've brought it to you."

"What?" My eyebrows shot into my hairline as I sat up. The dizziness roared in protest. "You did?"

"Well, of course. Did you think I was going to leave you without a vehicle? I'm outside your house right now."

I bolted to the window and kneeled below it, peering out. I didn't want him to see the God-awful state I was in.

He was in the driveway, standing beside the Yaris with a hand on his hip, dressed in a white dress shirt, black slacks, and dress shoes. Rocking a corporate kind of hot.

His driver was sitting in the black Mercedes that I'd seen in his garage. He must have come straight after work.

Catching a glimpse of my movement, he turned, and I dropped to my knees below the window.

Shit...

My hair was a natural disaster, I had no makeup on, and I was dressed in my pink, fuzzy pajama pants, slippers, and a bright-blue bra with a yellow tank top over it. Not exactly the look that I wanted him to catch me in.

"Em?" Barrett said.

"Uh... yeah?" I crawled under the window and grabbed the brush from my nightstand, trying not to hiss in pain as I began to gently pull it through my tangled waves. "That's super nice of you, Bear. You shouldn't have."

"Alright." His quiet laugh hid undertones of confusion. "Are you going to come down and get your keys, or shall I toss them through the window? Presuming your window is even at the front?"

"Right! Yeah, I'll be right down. One sec."

I hung up and tossed my phone onto the bed, running over to the mirror and brushing out as much of my hair as I could. I wiped my face with both hands like they'd magically take the fatigue away, but then I made eye contact with myself and stopped. It was my job to love myself no matter what, and at the end of the day, I had to protect my heart. Besides, I was being neurotic. The guy had seen me knocked out on the lake and bleeding from my head. I had nothing to worry about. It couldn't get worse than that. And *besides, besides*— he was *unavailable*. Why should I care how I look? I was recovering from a concussion, for godsake!

Sighing, I pushed my blonde waves forward to frame my face and snatched my cardigan from my bed. I rushed down the stairs, stopped at the front door, took a deep breath, and I reminded myself that the man on the other side was just a friend. That was it. Just a friend, coming to check up on me. That was all. No matter how I felt about him, or what I'd screamed for over a decade, it didn't change the fact that he was in a relationship. And (although it was toxic) I'd have to have *some* sort of respect for that. Any flirting that we did was harmless fun between friends, and it couldn't be any more than that. At least, for as long as that gold digger claimed to own him.

When I opened the door, he was grinning on the other side, leaning with his right arm on the frame like some male model. A really hot, CFO, male model. The dull light caught the copper that was growing out above his ears. "Hello," he said, coolly.

I swallowed. "Hi." His musky-sweetness caught my attention, and I broke out a nervous smile, trying hard to redirect it. "H—How did you know where to drop my car off? I mean, how did you know where I lived?"

"Emily, I'm one of the most powerful men in this city. I have connections." He winked.

"Oh..."

Something funny ran down his face as he pushed off the doorframe.

I blinked.

Oh my God—the haze!

Catching the look on my face, he frowned. "Are you quite sure you're alright?"

"I don't know, Barrett," I admitted, putting a hand to my head. "I feel like it's catching up on me, to be honest. My mind's... I dunno... foggy. Like it takes extra time to process everything."

"Well, you're looking much better today." He smiled. "You aren't bleeding."

"Yeah, at least there's that." I smiled back. He opened his palm, revealing my keys, and I took them from him with a dainty movement, careful to avoid brushing my fingertips against his skin. I didn't want to fight that electric spark that I got whenever we touched. "Thanks, Bear. Really. You shouldn't have."

"Tell me about it," he said, with a slight chuckle. "For the entirety of the drive, all that I could think about was how much I desired to buy you a *real* car."

"Hey," I said, glancing out at my little Yaris. She was the only car in the driveway. The rest of the House must have still been out. "Considering I'm not in the *one percent* of people on this planet with too much money—like you—she does just fine, thank you very much."

He laughed. "There is no such thing as too much money, kid." Then, he paused, and I studied those eyes again. I noticed that the shade of black seemed to change depending on what mood he was in. There were so many fascinating things about him. So much hidden. So much to learn. He raised an eyebrow, and I realized I'd been staring.

"So, how was work?" I blurted out.

"Satisfactory," he said.

"Oh, sorry to hear that."

He rubbed his brow. "It's fine."

As I stood there, I thought about our moment in the cave, and how he'd said that he was obligated to the family business. Then my pelvis throbbed when I thought about when I'd wanted to kiss him.

"I find it difficult to go back to work after a weekend out in nature," he added, luckily distracting me.

It was true. If you chopped out the bits about his fight with Kirk, *mine* with Rebecca, and my accident, it was an incredible weekend. I couldn't remember the last time I'd had that much fun dancing, and drinking... Being with him... I'd certainly needed it with the stress of starting school.

I grinned. "I loved it, Barrett. I really did. Your campground is incredible."

"Even with your accident?"

"Yes, even with, you know, *that*."

"Pleases me to hear it," he said. "But I *was* worried..." He cleared his throat. "Anyway. I'm glad to hear that the severity of your tumble wasn't as bad as we first thought."

Feathers of appreciation tickled my soul, and I focused on them to mask the guilt hidden below. "Me too. I'm sorry that I scared you, Bear. I'll be more careful next time."

"You're not driving next time," he pointed out. "And it was Kirk that you scared more than anyone. I'm merely thankful that he had the good sense to follow you down there." He studied me, before looking over my shoulder, eyes glazing. "He did what I *should* have. You were clearly upset, and I should have come to check on you." Then he twitched an eyebrow. "But then again, I didn't get the nickname The Bad-Roth for no reason. I'm sure you're aware of that by now."

I pulled my cardigan across my chest and crossed my arms as I leaned on the doorframe. It hadn't occurred to me that he'd also feel guilty about it. "Barrett, I—"

But then David's Mazda pulled into the driveway, and he and Greg got out. Barrett and I froze mid conversation, and all my fucking muscles tightened at once. I hadn't realized what time it was, and having Barrett Roth on our doorstep was not a good thing right now.

My heart started to pound.

Oh. My. God. What the fuck do I do?

My fuzz-brain was out of options. All I could do was stand there like an idiot and hope that this wouldn't explode.

David and Greg were joking around and laughing like they would on any other day, but then David noticed the *Roth* at our doorstep and stopped dead. He locked on Barrett with an energy so strong that it threatened to swallow the world, and I wished it would swallow me too. It was like working for National Geographic and watching a wolf and tiger a size each other up for the kill, knowing there was fucking *nothing* you could do about it.

Then Barrett put on his smirk like he enjoyed being in enemy territory. There was a power dynamic here that he seemed happy to challenge.

Finally, David found his words through a clenched jaw. And though he was talking to me, he didn't take his eyes off Barrett. "Emily. What the *fuck* is he doing here?"

"Nice to see you too, David," Barrett said.

"I—" I started.

"What do you want, Roth?" David growled. "You think you can jus' show up here, where I live, out of the blue? Like father, like son? Well, *fuck you*. You don't have anything on me. I'm compliant."

"Oh, I don't doubt that," Barrett said.

And I blinked at him before turning my attention back to David. "Okay, let's just *chill* here. It's not a big deal. I left my car downtown for the camping trip, and he brought it back to me. Simple as that. And anyway, what are you talking about? What do you mean, compliant?"

David's gaze flicked between mine and Barrett's. He was fuming, and Barrett looked like he thought it was funny. "Listen to me, Roth," David said, locking back on him. "This is my house, and it's the only place I'm safe from you. So, get the *fuck* off our doorstep. You're not welcome here. You're not *ever* welcome!"

Barrett straightened his glimmering wristwatch. "I was under the impression that more than one person resided here, David. So, I don't believe you get to dictate that." He paused. "Besides, what are you going to do about it? Shoot me? *Like father, like son?*"

"Barrett..." I warned.

Holy shit, this is bad.

"Fuck you, Devil's son," David spat.

Barrett tossed him a sarcastic laugh. "Catchy. Haven't heard that one before."

David sneered. "Believe me, if I could shoot you and get away with it, I would."

"David!" I cried.

Holy shit. This is really, really bad!

But Barrett's expression had settled back into his smirk. He was baiting David, and he looked like he was having fun with it. "You're lucky that no one's recording this conversation," he said. "With a family history like yours, they wouldn't hesitate to lock you up next to your father. Perhaps you could share a cell. Have a family reunion."

David's green eyes flared. "Get the fuck out of here, Roth."

"Don't worry, I will," Barrett said. "But speaking of your dear old dad, how is he, by the way? Still rotting away in said prison cell?"

I swallowed. The Bad-Roth had returned, and I wasn't happy to see him. "Barrett..." I tried.

David stepped forward. "How's *yours*? Still rotting away in the fucking *ground*?"

"David!" I barked again.

Then the humour dropped out of Barrett's face, and he didn't have anything witty to throw back this time. His skin dropped a few shades paler while he resized his enemy.

David, on the other hand, was done. "Go. Away. Before. I *make* you."

"Oooo," Barrett said, getting in his face and putting them nose-to-nose. "This, I would like to see."

David didn't shrink an inch, but Greg pushed between them. "What the hell is your problem, dude? He said, get out of here!"

"Awww," Barrett said. "You're *so* cute." The way he pressed forward made Greg shrink back, and Barrett's obsidian flashed like a cat toying with a mouse. "I can't imagine how anyone takes you seriously. You don't happen to bottom, do you?"

David snapped and shoved him away from the pup-of-the-House. I braved a bout of wooziness to jump off the doorstep and put myself between them. The flurry of testosterone was bound to explode if I let it.

"Alright, enough, enough!" I said, wedging myself in the middle and putting a gentle palm on Barrett's chest. "Please leave. Alright? Barrett? Please?"

He let my hand linger on his heart as he flicked his eyes between David and me. The tension was so thick that you could cut it like a cake. "Alright," he finally said. "If that's what you'd like, Emily, then I shall. But try to remember not to fuck with those above your caliber, David. I don't want to have to remind you again."

"Fuck off, Roth," David said, pushing past and storming into the House with Greg in tow.

Barrett turned the opposite way toward his driver.

I stood there like the John Travolta meme from Pulp Fiction, not quite knowing which way to go. Once again, I was feeling like a piece of meat being torn between two very opposing alpha males.

The door slammed behind David and Greg and snapped me out of it, so I took that as a sign to follow Barrett to the curb. "Oh my God. I'm really sorry, Bear. That was so *stupid* of me."

He adjusted his wristwatch again. The wind caught the wave in his brown-red hair. "No, Emily. It was my fault. You had told me before that David Mathis was your roommate. I blatantly ignored that and came here. Then, suffered the inherent risk."

"No, really. I should have thought of that well before you did. That wasn't fair to either of you." I touched my brow and sighed. "I blame the concussion." And I was relieved when he rewarded me with a half-smile. "Let me make it up to you. I'll take you out for coffee, instead."

I will?

He raised a curious, copper eyebrow. "*You* want to take *me* out for coffee?"

"Yeah?" I leaned on his Mercedes as casually as I could. Then felt like an idiot. "I—I mean! As a thank you for bringing my car back. And for the amazing weekend."

He watched me like he wasn't sure whether to humour me or say, *That's a good one!* "Alright," he said, instead. "Name the time and the place. I'll be there."

"Um. Great! I—I'll text you."

"Goodnight, Emily. And I'm happy to see that you're better today."

I watched him get into the Mercedes and slip out of sight, realizing that I was acting like that silly, little schoolgirl with a crush again... And for the wrong man, as well.

Barrett's driver took off down the street and I jolted myself out of it.

Oh my God! David!

"I'm *so*, so sorry."

"How could you do that to me? How could you let *him* come here?"

"I wasn't thinking. Y—You were at work and my-my head—"

"Do you have any idea what you jus' did?" David's eyes were brimming. He turned away with his hands on his hips.

I stepped forward and reached out. "David. Please. No—just look at me. Please."

He tried to hide how badly his hands were shaking by pulling them away. "Fuck... No..."

I took him in my arms and held his curls. "Shhh. I'm sorry. I'm so sorry."

"Fuck. I jus' *need* you to understand..."

Cupping his face in my hands, I guided his teary gaze to mine. "If you'd tell me, then I can help you. If there's something suspicious going on between you and Roth Pharma, then I want to know. Please. Let me *help* you."

"You can't fight them, Emily! Trust me, I've already tried!"

"Fight them about what? Please tell me."

He dropped his head and shook it again. "I can't..."

My voice was as gentle as a whisper. "Why?"

"Because I *can't*, Emily!"

He'd pulled himself away, so I latched back onto him. "Shhh. I'm sorry. I'm so sorry. That was thoughtless and stupid of me."

"You can't get in too deep," he choked. "You're too pure. They'll seduce you with their evil. I won't be able to protect you."

"Listen," I muttered, softly. "I know that this reaction you have to them is out of fear. That what your *father* did was out of fear. He's not the psycho that they say he is, David. I know that. You're safe with me, okay? You're safe... But what did Johnathan Roth do that made you both so afraid?"

He blinked away the tears and searched my face. In his eyes, I could see that he desperately wanted to speak, but he didn't.

"Tell me what he did to you... Tell me what they're *doing* to you... *Please*..." I ran my thumb along his black beard.

His jaw slacked and he watched me for several seconds, but then he shook his head a third time. And when he spoke, it was pained: "I can't."

CHAPTER 27
ENEMY

I still found myself sitting at the café on the corner of Georgia and Howe that Thursday evening. And though I regretted how I'd made David feel on Monday, I knew that I was never going to get answers to the Roth-Mathis feud without stepping outside the box a little. After that clash between the two of them, my intrigue went through the roof. What was David talking about when he said he was compliant? Compliant with *what?* His treatments? And if that was the case, then why couldn't he tell me? Was he afraid to reveal his illness because he worried that I'd think less of him if he did? And why would Roth Pharma be treating his illness, anyway? Wouldn't they just make the drugs and hand them off to the people that did?

Ugh! I didn't know. But something told me that I needed to get to the bottom of it. Especially if big pharma was breaking the morality code.

And spending more time with Barrett could only help give me some more breadcrumbs. Right?

(Plus... you know... I'd get to see Barrett...)

It was a sunny afternoon in mid-June, so I decided to take one of the small patio tables outside after I'd grabbed a latté and a muffin. I still had a couple minutes before Barrett was supposed to show, so I figured I'd grab a bite. The sun shone from between the skyscrapers, and I let it bathe my face as I scoffed down the muffin. Then, latté in hand, I sat back and watched the city.

It was the end of another workday, and the streets were bustling with people desperate to get back home. I watched a cyclist peddle past at hustling speed; his hoodie pulled up around his head as a pair of headphones cupped his ears. A woman pulled her Tesla up on Howe Street, pinned in place by the traffic as she started a very heated conversation in another language with someone on her Bluetooth. She didn't care that her windows were open, and the entire city could hear. She was more concerned that the person got the message. And I kind of admired it.

Wish I could stand up to someone like that....

Next, the traffic took her out of sight, revealing a group of young, corporate-looking men trying to flag a taxi from the other side of the street. Their suit jackets were unbuttoned, and the gentle Pacific breeze tossed their ties as they caught sight of me. An abundance of charming smiles wafted across the street and blushed, but I smiled back, cupping my latté in my hands. Despite all the weirdness over the past week, I must have been glowing. The slight trauma from my seadoo accident had definitely passed.

Then, like he was drawn by the threat of "lesser" males, the roar of the Ferrari echoed from the walls of the skyscrapers. And I heard Barrett well before he ever saw him, and the glimmering supercar came into sight from the west side of the Vancouver Art Gallery, coming north down Burrard Street. He turned onto Georgia, lurching into a quick sprint as he crossed in front of me. The Ferrari's rims blinded everyone with sunlight as he slowed to turn right onto Howe, bass booming. He finished by jumping ahead of the flow of traffic before he parked on the east side of the Art Gallery.

Across the intersection, the corporate men were watching with their jaws hanging open, as he stepped out of the Ferrari and went toward the crosswalk. They probably wanted to be him—this cocky billionaire driving around in his rare supercar, draped in his pristine suit, wearing thousand-dollar sunglasses—without ever considering what he'd had to go through to get here. They didn't know about the alcohol forced down his throat at nine. They didn't know about the scar that spanned his neck. The abuse. The trauma. Or, what the money meant for him in the long run. They didn't know that it had him trapped in a pre-determined fate, or that he couldn't follow his dreams...

But who was I to blame them? I was gawking at him too. Once he was there, I subconsciously pushed aside the weird interaction between him and David on Monday. I buried the horrid things that were likely going on under the surface. I forgot about the existence of other men in general. Every time Barrett Roth was around, I was cursed with the inability to peel my eyes off him.

My Barrett...

But what the fuck did it all *mean*?

The sunlight caught the red in his hair as he pressed the button for the crosswalk, and it turned him into an image of his father. It only lasted a split second, but it gave me a chill severe enough to tell me something was wrong. John was here. I could feel the energy of his ghost looming over my shoulder.

The light turned and Barrett smiled as he crossed the street, giving me a glimpse of those raven eyes. He seemed happy to see me at first, but when he got closer, I saw his face fall. Then he started looking *through* me instead of *at* me, and he threw a strange glance across up Georgia like he was expecting someone. "Hey, kid," he said, turning back to me like he was trying to hide it.

I stood and gave him a weird, friend-hug. Even after a full day at work, he smelled amazing, and I couldn't help but breathe him in during the short time I had to be in his arms. "Hey, Bear."

"How has the rest of your week fared?" he asked, letting me go and taking the chair across from me. He picked it up, moved it, and put it back down with noiseless perfection.

I settled back down. "Oh, you know. I've only had one day of school, but it felt like a lifetime. My unexpected sick day put me further behind than I thought."

It was true. I'd spent the entirety of Tuesday at the library, cramming for the Bioethics lecture that I was TA-ing for on Wednesday.

"The price of being a klutz." He grinned as he smoothed the collar of his shirt and unbuttoned his suit jacket. "You know, I've considered passing a law that you're not allowed on, in, or near, anything that floats ever again. It's just too much of a risk."

I snorted as I sipped my latté. "As much as I hate that, it's probably a good call."

He shot me something apologetic. "I'm only teasing, Em. And don't worry. You merely require practice. I'll turn you into a professional by the end of the summer."

My stomach flipped. That meant he *wanted* me to come back to the campground.

The barista stepped out and asked if she could get him anything. I thought about how she hadn't batted an eye at me when I was out here alone. She smiled sweetly as he ordered a dark roast with two sugars, and then broke out a flirtatious giggle. "Alright, I'll be back," she said, tossing her hair as she turned back to the shop.

"I'm paying for it," I called to her, but she shrugged me off, and Barrett chuckled.

"You're serious, aren't you?"

"Of course I am," I said. "A coffee is about the only thing I can afford to buy you, so please let me do it."

"Alright, big spender." He winked, before he threw a glance at the barista through the window, in that subtle-but-not-so-subtle manner that men do when they're trying to check out a woman's ass.

I wondered how many women threw themselves at him in a day. Then didn't want to think about it.

"Bear," I said, drawing his attention along with his *I'm innocent* grin.

"Yes, kiddo?"

"Do you think that next time we go up there, you can show me some of the trails?" It'd be nice to get another chance to be alone with him in the environment he loved. I wondered what else he could tell me about the land along the way.

"Of course. Any time you want."

"Okay." I dropped my attention into my coffee cup and studied the way it hit the cardboard when I swirled it. I really wanted to ask him about what David had said about being compliant yesterday, but I didn't know how to approach it without pissing him off. Awkwardness spread through me like an unwanted visitor.

Across the table, he didn't seem to notice. He started chewing on the thumb nail, ebony eyes glazed as he searched the corner of Georgia and Howe from over my shoulder. A flutter of nervousness warned me that I was close to losing him. And just as I was about to launch into a desperate conversation about the weather, he looked at me sharply. "Can I ask you a question?" he said.

"Only if I can ask you one after," I blurted.

"Alright then." He pointed to the sign above the café. "Why did you pick this place?"

"What? This coffee shop?"

He nodded and chewed on his nail again.

"Oh. I don't know. I mean, it seemed like a good location, and it caught my eye... It's across from the Art Gallery... It has a cute name... Convenient location... Close to your office. I guess it spoke to me." I sipped my latté and smiled. "Why do you ask?"

Dropping his arm, he looked at the street behind me and swallowed. It seemed very un-Barrett like. Something was definitely wrong.

"Bear? Did I do something wrong? I—I mean, you said 'okay' to this place in the text..."

He scrubbed his jaw, drew a shallow breath, and said, "No, Emily. It's not you."

"Then what is it?"

"This is where my father was killed."

My stomach turned into lead.

Oh. My. Fucking. God. I knew there was a reason this place looked familiar!

Dropping my cup, I covered my mouth. "Barrett... I am *so so* sorry."

Not just sorry. *Mortified.* Absolutely and completely *mortified.* This was where John was killed—right in this fucking spot—and I was making him sit here!

"It's alright, Em. You're not at fault. I said yes because I can handle it, and you clearly weren't aware." He was trying to console me, but the sorrow in his undertone worked against him.

Except you were *aware!*

"No, it's not," I breathed. "I'm so sorry. That was completely thoughtless of me. We can go somewhere else—"

"It's alright, Em, really." Then he told me something that the look on his face immediately credited as a lie. "It was twelve years ago. Really, it doesn't bother me anymore."

When I shook my head, my blonde waves hit the sides of my face like they wanted to smack some sense into me. "No, it is a big deal. It's a big, *big* deal, Bear." I started fumbling around for my keys and cardigan. "We need to leave. We should go."

But he sat back. "You're bordering on hysteria. Forget I said anything about it. I merely wanted you to know that, if I'm acting a little strange, that is why."

"I feel fucking awful," I admitted.

He pursed his lips and attempted at a smile. "I know it wasn't callous." Then, he looked at the café's sprawling header. "This place was one of his favourites, anyway. It's not necessarily a bad thing."

"I know— It's just— I—I mean, if you want to go..."

He raised an eyebrow. "I haven't yet received the coffee you promised me."

"Okay. I mean. If you're sure..."

He nodded sternly. "I'm sure." He turned his perfectly clean palm up to me. Rolex and all. "Now, your question?"

"What?"

"We agreed that if I asked you a question, you could ask one back."

"Uh, yeah. That was, uh, *the deal.*"

His smirk twitched. "So?"

I fanned my hands in front of my face.

I'm just gonna ask it.

"Uh."

Just gonna fuckin' ask it.

"You remember Monday? When you and David accidentally met, and he said that you had nothing on him because he was compliant?"

"Yes," he said slowly.

"Well, um, what did he mean by that? 'Cus it kinda seemed like you were on the inside on that one."

Again, he sat back. Took a gentle breath. Studied the people in the square across the street. Watched the sky. "I enjoy your company, Emily, so I feel that it's best I be honest with you. So, yes, I admit it. I am aware of what David meant. But unfortunately, it is no concern of yours and you need not be worried, anyway. Let's just say that there are things that you are not, well, *privy* to worry about."

Again with the private-school perfect cover up. Who the fuck used the word privy? I wasn't even a hundred percent sure what that meant!

My cheeks reddened. "Yeah, but Barrett, he's sick, and I *am* worried. I thought that maybe if you knew then it could help—"

"Medical Ethics, is it not?"

"Huh?"

He held that palm toward me again. "Medical Ethics. That's what you're researching for your master's?"

"Uh, yeah, but what does that have to do with anything?"

"Oh, Em. Your curiosity's going to be trouble, kid." He winked like there was something to fucking wink about.

Then the barista came back out with his coffee and the bill, holding the machine out for me to tap.

Barrett smiled and thanked her, but I couldn't take my eyes off him again. Although for a completely different reason now. He hadn't answered me, and I kinda knew he wouldn't. My intestines tied themselves in knots.

Barrett took his first sip and sighed happily. "Fear not, kiddo. If something pertains to you, David Mathis will be sure you. He's good at spreading lies."

I wrinkled my nose. "Huh?"

"Receipt?" the barista asked.

I'd almost forgotten she was there. "What? I mean, no. Thanks. I'm good."

She went back inside, and then Barrett spun the conversation like a dinner plate. "What are you up to this weekend?"

When is anyone going to tell me the truth?

I wanted to throw my arms up and slap my thighs. Instead, I stuffed my hands under them.

Patience, Em. You need a Roth in your back pocket, here.

"My roommate Greg has been trying to get the House to go to his family's ranch outside Kelowna," I said, with a shitload of patience. "A bunch of us took Monday off, so it seemed like a good time to go. Plus, I haven't seen any of the interior yet."

"Kelowna is a beautiful drive. You won't be disappointed."

"Nothing about this province has disappointed me so far."

Except the big pharma bigotry.

He shot me his perfect grin. "Pleased to hear it."

I tapped the table, pushing myself to play along. "Have you ever been there?"

"Many times. You know, Shane—before he decided to grace

350

this province with his presence—was born in a small town called Cochrane outside of Calgary in Alberta."

"Oh. He wasn't born here?"

"No," he said. "His family moved to Vancouver when he was very young. Maybe two or three? I can't remember. It's been so long since we've met. But if you ever meet Michael Thomas and want to hear something hilarious, then ask him to say it. Cochrane. It's one of the funniest words to hear a Scottish person say."

I laughed a little, but my skin crawled as I thought about Michael's accent from his memory: *Johnathan Roth! Get the feck out of my house, now!*

"Occasionally Shay will get an itch to go back there," Barrett said, pulling me out, "even though he has no memory of living there. We'll do the drive, all the way up and through the Rockies. That's an experience. Sometimes we stop in Kelowna on our way through."

"I'd love to do that," I said, pushing away the dread with a longing exhale.

"Well, don't mention it to him unless you mean it. He'll take you in a heartbeat, and that drive can top twelve hours easily."

"Yikes."

"And it's not *half* as bad as the drive out to Saskatoon, where Kirk's from. The three of us did that once and will probably never do it again." He chuckled and glanced away like he had a memory in mind. "By the time we got back, we were so sick of each other that none of us spoke for about a week and a half."

My smile filled up. "I can imagine."

"Yes. Well. Kirk. I mean, he talked about Saskatoon all the time when we were younger. You know, *Back in Toontown...* That's what he tends to call it. *Toontown...*" He paused and began to peel the paper sleeve on his cup. "If anything, it was nice to see where he was from."

I was happy to see some of his nostalgia. "It sounds like you've had a lot of adventures."

He nodded again, but I caught the sad jerk of his left eyebrow.

"Yes. We used to do things like that all the time when we were younger. Not so much anymore. All three of us now have businesses to run."

Across the street, a woman was strolling by in a baby blue dress. It was gliding on the breeze behind her, reminding me painfully of what Samantha Thomas was wearing on that night. That horrible night.

"It sounds like I need to give us all an excuse to go on a road trip," I said, trying—once again—not to think about Barrett Roth's horrible history. "Twelve hours packed in a car next to Shane. I'm not sure I'd mind that at all."

He smirked. "Is that so? Well, I must warn you that it's not as much fun as it sounds. And keep in mind that this is coming from the one who loves him the most."

I thought about how his expression lit up when he talked about his best friends. There had been pain. No doubt. But it was clear that he loved them. His dark chocolate eyes were warm again.

"How far is Kelowna?" I asked, iciness backing off. "Five hours?"

"Three, actually. It's a cakewalk. You'll be fine." He swallowed some coffee, and his expression darkened. "I imagine David's going with you?"

My toes wiggled. "Um, yeah, everyone in the House is."

"Hmmm." He glanced at Georgia and Howe over my shoulder again. Although this time, I knew why he was doing it. "You see, *that* I cannot picture doing."

Sighing, I wondered how I should start with this again. Was it better to go slow and honest, maybe? "Look, I know that you two have a bad history. F—For obvious reasons. But David's an amazing person, Bear." I paused, heart defrosting at the thought of him. "He has this incredible ability to make me happy, without even saying a word. He's kind and loving... I know it's not easy for you to understand, but I wish you two could... I dunno... Get to know each other. Then you'd see that he's not the man you think he is. Then you'd *both* see."

Barrett's irises plunged into pure obsidian and flared. I'd put us in a bad place again. "Emily. David Mathis and I have been locked in animosity since his father decided to take the life of mine. Right fucking *here*, in fact." He tapped the table with a rigid forefinger, and I got heartburn. "I'm aware of the murder's blood that runs in his veins, and I *always* will be. I'm acquainted with him on the level that I can tolerate, but I will take no more. And I recognize that it's not easy for *you* to understand. But I hope you can sympathize with how incredibly difficult it is to tolerate *any* presence from a man who shares blood with the one that murdered your father."

I dropped my gaze from the weight of his. "Sorry, Bear."

From across the table, he watched me spin my coffee cup a few times before his tone turned soft. "Regardless, I believe you."

"You do?"

"Yes."

"Why?"

Now he was wiggling his fingers sequentially across the table. "Because he couldn't have caught the eye of a woman as pure as you if it were not true." Then he looked away like he didn't want to see my reaction.

My nerves tingled, and I thought about how he'd caught something that I hadn't even fully admitted to myself. I was touched, and I watched him between fluttering lashes. Through his silver-tongued statements and Bad-Roth lies, he was giving me glimpses of the Real-Barrett again.

Bad-Roth, my ass.

Like he'd read my mind and was conscious to hide himself, Barrett crossed one leg over the other, which shortened his pant leg and turned him back into his father. And as he mirrored the stance that he'd studied years ago, I remembered his feeling of emptiness. His question of: *Is that all there is?*

He was still drumming his fingers on the table. Still refusing to look at me. I noticed he was much more fidgety than normal.

"I don't wanna talk about David anymore," I said, pulling those hardened, black eyes. "This is supposed to be my time with you."

To my relief, he loosened up. "Alright." But the street corner snagged him again before I could, and he watched it with despair.

I knew what he was seeing. Joseph. Over and over. Storming across Howe as he raised the gun.

"Barrett..." I tried softly.

He dropped his head to his hand and sighed in quiet distress. "I can't..."

I put my palm on the table, concerned. "Are you okay?"

He threw an anxious hand through his hair and looked at me with his eyes shimmering. "I'm going to be honest with you, Emily. I thought I could be here. But I cannot... It's too much... Far too much."

"Alright," I said. "That's completely understandable. Um. We could go for a walk instead?"

But he glanced across the street at his Ferrari, and a hint of excitement overshadowed the despair. "I have a better idea."

CHAPTER 28
EASY, TIGER

An hour later, we were pulling into the gravel parking lot at the Sea-to-Sky Gondola in Squamish. As Barrett brought the 812-horsepower engine to rest—he hadn't shied away from telling me *all* about it—I undid my fancy seatbelt and exited the haze of leather to be welcomed by the fresh mountain air. I shielded my eyes as I looked up the cliff face, trailing a string of gondolas that swung like Chinese lanterns.

"Where do they go?" I asked, as Barrett locked his car with a grin. After the dismal energy at the café, the Ferrari had brought him back to life. And as we drove, I'd realized again how easy it was for me to just *be* with him. It was hard to ignore the pinnacle of natural connection that was growing between us.

"Up," he said, throwing an arm around my shoulders and guiding me toward the buildings at the base. "You aren't afraid of heights, are you? This is the wrong province to live in if you're afraid of heights."

I shook my head. "Not necessarily, but I've never been in a gondola before?"

He looked at me, and I tried to ignore his intoxicating smell and the static tingle of his touch. "What? No one has taken you up Grouse yet? You don't even need to drive to Squamish for that one. It's practically part of the city."

"I heard it was expensive."

"Oh, kiddo," he huffed, as we moved toward the ticket booth. "You have much to see."

He paid for our tickets, and I thanked him—his response being something pretentious like, "I give no thought to the number unless there are at least five zeros following it"—before we went through to the boarding area. Here, the gondolas dipped into a semi-circle track and swung around for passengers to step on as their doors opened, their line carving a matching semi-circle through the roof above. And though they slowed, they didn't stop, so I hesitated as I watched Barrett step on as gracefully as a striding cat. Then, he offered his hand.

Afraid he'd leave me behind as the gondola slid toward the end of the loading platform, I grabbed his hand and let him pull me inside. It was evening, and they'd be closed in an hour or two, so we had the gondola to ourselves. There weren't many others forking over the money to go up that late.

Barrett settled on the left side of the cabin, and I took the right. The doors closed with a tight seal, and it went quiet. He exhaled peacefully, throwing an arm over the seat, and crossing his left leg over the right at his ankle. The gondola swung when it was freed from the track, and I sat up straight, gripping the bench. We rose swiftly up the side of Mt. Habrich, and the summer breeze made us sway more than I was comfortable with.

"Em," Barrett said, his voice soft over the whir of the gondola being powered. "Are you sure you're alright? I haven't made a drastic mistake with this decision, have I?"

The speed of my voice betrayed the words. "Yep. I'm good. Just a new experience is all. Blame the Ontarian in me."

He smirked. "Well, you'll be a British Columbian before long." He studied me, and I tried to ignore his penetrating gaze. "Try to remember that the swaying movement is normal. It's suspended and therefore bound by the laws of physics that this entails."

My hand slapped back to the seat as soon as I tried to let it go. "Do you ever talk like a normal person?"

He chuckled. "Only when I'm fucked up." Then, he glanced out the window, and his face fell like he realized that what he'd said wasn't as funny as he'd meant it to be. "Don't try to normalize me, kid. You'll only be disappointed, and I implore you not to hold me to that standard."

"I'm sorry, Bear. I meant that as more of a joke. Of course, I'll always take you as you are."

He raised an eyebrow but didn't expand. "Why don't you focus on the scenery in the distance? It will help to soothe your nervousness."

I nodded and turned my attention to the incredible nature outside. The view facing up the mountain that we were on was fascinating, but soon other mountains came within view; many of them snow-capped and looking like something straight out of a fantasy movie again. The forest sprawled in brilliant shades of green and blue on the jagged landscape around us, and the mountains and cliff faces rose from it like wide spearheads. It was awe-inspiring, and soon I was twisting in my seat, trying to take everything in. Below us, the Ferrari shrank until its glimmering red went completely out of sight.

"Wow..." I found myself breathing.

I could feel his black eyes watching me again. "Stunning, isn't it?"

"I never thought that this much natural beauty was possible before I moved to this province."

Then he shifted closer to me and started to explain the surrounding peaks. In the distance, and on our side of the Howe Fjord, stood the snow-peaked Mt. Garibaldi, Mamquam Mountain, and the Sky Pilot Mountain. Closer, and green with the summer heat, were the smaller peaks of Round Mountain, and Alpen Mountain. On the other side of the Fjord and across from us, the snow-peaked Mt. Sedgwick, Serratus Mountain, and Mt. Tantalus rose over the turquoise water. Barrett started telling me about the geographical significance of this area, and I studied him as he lost himself in it like no one had ever let him talk about what he loved before. By the time he'd finished, we were nearing the top, and I looked at him with pleasant surprise.

"You really do know a lot about this kind of thing, huh?"

He shrugged, glancing back out to the peaks in the north. "It's the geography freak in me."

"No, I mean, you're really passionate about it," I said. "I think you'd be amazing at environmental sciences, Bear. I mean, the way you explain things... The way you talk about it... I don't know. I feel like you're in the wrong business."

"I make money, Em," he said, shifting as he prepared to stand. "That's all I do."

At the top, we locked into another semi-circle track, and I took his hand as he helped me onto the solid ground. "But it's not enough, though, is it?" I said to him, before shooting a brief, "Hi!" at the attendant.

"Does that matter?" He walked off and led me toward the lodge.

"Of course, it does. We're talking about your *life*, Bear."

He shot me a divergent smirk. "You have the uncanny ability to unknowingly pry into places where you don't belong. Don't you, Emily?"

I stopped, thinking about how it was a different version of what David had said once.

"I, of course, meant no offense," he added quickly.

"It's fine, Bear," I said, shivering from the cooler air up here. "But I never meant for you to think that I was prying."

He took my shoulders and led me toward a viewing platform at the other side of the lodge. "Then, perhaps *pry* was the wrong word. I apologize. Anyway, I don't wish to talk about my life. It's sad—I'm aware—but as I've said before, I was born into an obligation that I have no choice but to meet. And, also, I didn't drag you up here to talk about it. I dragged you up here to show you this."

We stepped out onto the wide viewing platform, and the landscape sprawled around us in an indescribable beauty. The lodge of the Sea-to-Sky-Gondola sat high above the Howe Fjord; serving views of a two-toned aquamarine inlet, settled in a valley between the mountain ranges, with the town of Squamish nestled at its end. From here, the forests gleamed in a pallet of green, and the snow glowed at the tops of the higher mountains. Below us, the Sea-to-Sky highway wound around the base like a black-and-grey capillary, and the cars exploring it were coloured pinpricks. The gondolas were gliding along their cable, bobbing gently as they touched the top of the mountain before turning back down. A cool breeze tossed my hair, but it wasn't the only thing that took my breath away. I felt like I'd stepped straight into the frame of a painting, or onto the waxy page of a postcard. *Awe-inspiring* only scratched the surface of how amazing that view was.

Barrett watched me with a smile, before he turned to the view. "Squamish in its complete magnificence and glory," he said.

"Incredible..." It'd been my first time on the top of a mountain, and the unpolluted air was as fresh as a glacial spring. It carried the energizing scents of nature, and I inhaled them, wishing that I could stand there forever.

Barrett chuckled at me. I guess it wasn't as jaw-dropping to someone who'd been born among mountains. "They make astounding french fries here," he said. "I'll leave you in solace and go grab some for us."

I noticed that he'd moved away, but I was way too romanced by the view to do anything but nod. As I leaned on my elbows, I put my presence into the mountains and thought about how remarkable life can be. In the heart of the smoggy, concrete jungle that Toronto could be, I'd never pictured that my reality could be as invigorating as what BC had given me. I felt incredibly blessed to have such easy access to the best of nature; to have been introduced to a great group of new friends; and to be enrolled in a degree that challenged me. There were still many unknowns and mysteries that I was desperate to solve. But as I stood there, living in the moment with the mountains, I realized that this move had been the best decision of my life. I was right where I needed to be. Come what may. And that self-assurance was a Godsend.

Smiling at clouds that veiled the sinking sun, I pulled away to read the signs that were set along the railing. There was very little on them that Barrett hadn't—or couldn't—have told me, and again, I was sad that he had to bury his passion.

Shortly after, he came back with a cardboard basket of french fries and a side of ketchup, jogging down the short flight of stairs from the lodge. "Ladies first," he said, surrounding us with the mouth-watering smell as he rolled up.

I popped one into my mouth, finding it soft and delicious.

"Thank God," Barrett said, following my lead. "You have no idea of the level of self-restraint I just had to exercise. I am a complete sucker for french fries."

I tapped my temple and snatched another. "Mental note, Mr. Roth."

He grinned. "Ah. I'll have to make sure I don't give you too many of those going forward." Then, he jerked his chin over my shoulder. "Come on. Let's cross the bridge. The area over there is more private."

"What bridge?" I munched as I turned to look. I'd been too enthralled with the view to realize that there was a small suspension bridge that led to another platform, and to the trails beyond. The same fear that I'd had at Capilano swelled.

Another suspension bridge? What's with BC and suspension bridges?

"Come on," he said again, leading me toward it. Then, when we got there, he said again, "Ladies first."

I raised my chin, trying to make determination follow. I moved past and took a couple of steps, but my shitty balance instantly worked against me. The bridge threw me as he stepped on behind, and I fell against the right railing before bracing my hands between them.

I stumbled forward. "Bear...?"

"Yes, Miss Anderson?" His muffled voice told me that he was still eating. And how *the hell* was he still eating on this death trap?

"I—I think I need you."

"No, you don't. You're doing fine. One foot in front of the other. Don't look down."

Of course, I immediately did the opposite, and the canyon below gave me nausea. "No. I'm not fine. I need you."

"It's merely a bridge, Em. You don't need me to help you cross it. Press forward."

You should have a donkey tattooed over your shoulder instead of a tiger!

With an angry snort, I focused on the other side, adamant to not let frustration get the best of me. I was hoping he'd be a gentleman like David and give me a hand, but I didn't understand that you can't always expect generosity from a Roth. It was a road to quick disappointment when they purposely refused to give it to you.

Every step that he took made mine harder, and we worked against each other all the way to the other side. When my feet met land, I stormed over to the railing and leaned on it with a huff. Trying to draw some happiness from the view, I ignored him when he stepped beside me.

"See? That wasn't so bad, was it?" He set the basket of french fries on the railing between us.

I shot him a sharp look as I snatched a couple, dipping them aggressively in the ketchup before I popped them in my mouth and turned back to the view. Then I thought about how much I fucking missed my parents.

He nudged me. "Emily. Do not be indignant with me because I encouraged you to do something that you didn't want to do. You can do anything, Miss Anderson. I am aware of that. But you must try to remember it more often."

I softened my expression as his words did their work. He was good with them. I'd never deny that. "Don't you find that silver tongue gets you into trouble?" I mumbled.

"Mostly it gets me *out* of trouble. In more ways than one."

I rolled my eyes but couldn't help but laugh a little.

We sat in a comfortable silence as we munched, the french-fry basket gradually getting emptier. I skimmed the mountains, the sea, and the sky, which were starting to be filtered through a more golden light. Across the bridge, a few people were exploring the viewing platform, and I watched as a father picked up his young son, holding him high against his chest so he could get a better view.

"You're so lucky to have been born here," I finally said. "To have this as your home province."

"You seem to enjoy reminding me of how lucky I am," he said, swallowing as he watched the father and son.

I trembled and tried not to look at his scar.

"But it's not only *my* home province. It's yours as well. Don't you realize that?"

Straightening, I watched the evening sun glimmer off the mountain tops. "It's weird to think of it that way."

Warmth spread across my shoulder when he touched there. "It's true."

"Not for long," I said, sadly. "I'm just here for my master's. Maybe for two years, if I decide to change to thesis based. Then I've gotta go back to Toronto."

"But have you thought of staying?" he asked, gently.

I shrugged, crunching on a couple more fries. "I don't know... It's not like it hasn't crossed my mind... I mean, I've been so happy since I moved here."

"So, you *want* to stay, then?"

I threw in a couple more shrugs along with some ums and ahhhs.

"So, why don't you just... stay? As a born British Columbian, I'll even give you permission, if you like."

I giggled, then itched my nose from the tickle of the breeze. "I'm not sure I can. Being away from my parents is too hard. I miss them so much, and to be honest, I'm a bit lost without them."

Suddenly, I worried that I was being insensitive, because he had one parent that he'd never see again. But then he smiled. "They can always visit."

"Not everyone has money, Mr. Roth. Unfortunately, they can't afford to come out here very often."

He devoured a fry before he spoke. "That is a non-issue, Emily. I have a plane. I can fly them in if it would please you."

There was a tingle of excitement at his offer, but I pushed it down with reality. "There's no room at the House-of-Wolves."

"The House-of-What?"

I waved my hand. I'd almost forgotten who I'd been talking to. "The House-of-Wolves. It's what we call our house." My cheeks flushed, and I looked away from him. "We're kind of like a pack. I don't know..."

"Huh. Interesting. Well, there's plenty of space at mine. Or, as a better alternative, The Roth Estate. You know that Grandma would love to have guests to entertain, and I'm sure Travis wouldn't mind filling the plethora of empty rooms. And even if he did, I have honed my power as his younger brother. It's effortless for me to charm him."

You saved his life. Of course it'd be.

I gave him a sad smile. "I'm grateful, Bear. But... why would you offer something like that when we barely know each other?"

He acted all aloof. "I must kind of like you, or something."

The butterflies kicked up, and I begged them to calm down as I watched the view.

And when I looked back, he had those dark-chocolate eyes again. "We're friends, aren't we?"

A mixtape of David's warnings started up in my head, but I ignored them and answered from the heart. "I'd like to think so." I leaned my chin on my propped hand. "But I couldn't ask you to do that, Bear."

"Nonsense," he said. "You can ask me for anything you desire. But whether I'm willing to give it to you—well—that's a different story."

I eyed him. "That's *a lot* for me to ask of you."

"I assure you that it isn't. But if it eases your apprehension, let's call it a birthday gift. Wait. When's your birthday?"

"December fifth."

"Early birthday present."

I tapped my fingers along the railing. I couldn't help but think about how Rebecca would feel if she knew he was offering that to me. "Bear... You're being very sweet, and I appreciate it, but that's more than I'm comfortable accepting."

He crunched on a crispy fry before he raised his chin and looked at the mountains. "You know, kid, I have many theories on wealth. Naturally. But the one that pertains to this moment is that abundance is nigh useless if it's never shared. As a wealthy man, you must try to remember to use it to do something worthwhile, at least *once* in a while. And I consider that a worthwhile gift for a friend. Especially one who deserves it as much as you do."

My smile shifted sweet. "Really?"

"The offer's always on the table. Think about it. Seriously."

"Thanks, Bear." I thought again about how much he hid behind his Bad-Roth nickname.

He dipped his chin in a single nod and smiled, before he covered a long fry in ketchup. The tip of it bopped him on the nose when he put it in his mouth and left him looking like Rudolph. And I was *way* too happy to see him so imperfect.

"What?" he asked, munching.

I pulled a napkin from the basket. "You've got ketchup on your nose." Something inside prickled when I cleaned it off.

Still chewing, he grinned, and then gradually let his expression soften as we locked eyes. I held my breath, unable to control the flood of electric tension that fell over us as we watched each other. My skin sizzled, and I was consumed by his obsidian gaze, but my entire fucking *body* craved it. This was the same feeling I'd had when he'd taken my hand at the pictographs. The same feeling that told me that we were destined for something more. That this man was meant to be more than my friend…

Swallowing, he released me and focused on the view. But even when I took a breath, I wasn't free. Something told me that we weren't going to be able to contain this connection for much longer; despite what I'd told myself about just being friends. From that point on, I knew we were in trouble.

The sun sunk behind the mountains and shaded us. I pulled the sleeves of my cardigan down and wrapped my arms around my chest. I didn't want the cooler air to drive me away from the majestic view, or the man next to me. Barrett stepped away from the railing and shrugged off his suit jacket.

"You don't have to—"

"It's alright, Em," he said, draping it over my shoulders, where it bathed me with his scent. Adjusting the cuffs on his dress shirt, he stepped back to the railing. "I didn't prepare you for an evening on a mountaintop."

I snuggled his jacket as I held it tighter. "Um. Okay. Thanks."

Again, he nodded as he leaned his elbows on the railing, and I watched him clasp his fingers as he sighed calmly. On the middle finger of his left hand, he was wearing a gold ring set with rubies, and I was surprised that I'd never noticed it before.

*Man, he'd have nailed it if this were a date…*my stupid thoughts added.

Rebecca popped into mind immediately after, and envy reared its ugly head. How could she not see that *he* was worth much more than money?

Disturbed by the reminder of her, I cleared my throat. "Um, Bear? This is going to sound a little funny, but can you maybe *not* tell Rebecca that we spent time together?"

He looked at me and raised a dark red eyebrow.

"It's just…" I sighed. "She gave me a pretty strong warning about being alone with you…"

"Ah, so that's what it was. That's what made you so upset."

My cheeks burned.

"I'm very sorry about that, Emily. And I would kindly ask that you ignore what she said."

"Uh. Are you sure?" I asked.

He gave me a smile and nodded. "The thing that she still fails to realize is that she can't control me. I'm like a wild stallion. I refuse to be controlled."

"Like a tiger," I corrected him.

"That's right." He grinned. "So, standing strong in my stubbornness, I act to remind her of this. Hopeful that she'll one day figure it out. And—as bad as it sounds—unless your name is Kirk Richards, Shane Thomas, or Travis Roth, your opinion is not of higher value than my own. If I enjoy spending time with someone, I will simply spend time with them. I don't think this is of relevance to our relationship the way that she does, and I consider what she told you to be unjustified jealousy. Give it no more thought."

"Okay. Um. Fair enough."

"In *normal-people* words: Don't worry. She doesn't have to know."

"Right." I let his *normal-people words* comfort me while I traced a line in the wood with my finger. "I mean, I think she loves you. So, it probably makes her a little defensive."

He spat out a humourless laugh. "She loves me," he echoed. "She doesn't love me. She loves my money." Then we shared a weird look, and he cleared his throat. "I apologize, Em. I shouldn't be expressing things like that to you. It's merely... There's a fraction of me that knows it's true."

"Then why are you—Actually. Never mind. It's none of my business."

"I know what you are about to ask me," he said, tone shifting serious. "*Why are we together?* And the only answer I can give you is that I have needs. Needs that cannot be met at this time by the people in my life that love me."

"Bear..." My vibe pulsed with sadness for him.

He pivoted toward me with his left elbow resting on the railing. "Let me ask you a question, because I believe you'll answer it honestly." This made me apprehensive from the get-go. "When you look at me, do you see me? Or do you see my money?"

Oh God.

"Um. You sure you want me to answer honestly?"

"Of course."

"Well..." I sighed, wondering how to word this. "Okay. Um. Well... Honesty. Here we go. It's kind of hard to see past your money when we're driving up here in a Ferrari, you're giving me a tour of your multi-million-dollar condo in Coal Harbour, and you're offering to fly my parents out in your private jet. But I think it depends on the environment, and whether you're allowing yourself to be *you*."

I shifted on the railing. "Right now, I see two different versions of you. There's your *billionaire* side, where you're dressed up in your suit, you're showing off your cars, and you're playing CFO. And then there's the *Real-Barrett*, who's singing to the radio of a car he brought back to life with his best friend... Who's laughing freely because I tipped a canoe and forced us to go for a swim... Who's teaching me about pictographs, and every single mountain that's surrounding us, wherever we happen to be..."

I glanced over at him, but he was wearing a look that was hard to place. Like he wasn't sure whether to be happy or hurt.

Turning up my palm, I continued gently. "I mean, you change, and you adapt, but so does everyone, Bear. It's called *survival*, and you don't need me to tell you that. What you really need to figure out is if you want someone that loves your *money* side or your *real* side. Then your life will follow that path naturally."

God, I really sounded like my mum.

He watched the mountains, and when he spoke, his voice was quiet and rough. "I wasn't expecting a response so profound."

"You asked me to be honest."

"I suppose I did."

After that, I questioned whether I'd upset him or not. He'd gone back to studying the view in silence, his fingers clasping and unclasping. The sun broke between the peaks of the mountains and fell over us in a soft glow. It caught the undertones of red in the hair above his ear and made it glimmer like a flickering flame.

Intrigued, I reached out before I could stop myself and ran my fingertips through the softness of his natural colour. A delicate arch above his ear. His obsidian turned questioning, yet gentle, and he didn't stop me.

"Why do you dye it?" I asked. "It's so beautiful."

He hesitated. "Would you like *my* honest answer this time?"

"Of course."

Jaw tensing, he looked back over the railing. "Because I resemble my father too much if I don't." He flashed his eyebrows. "No. *Too much* is an understatement. I've grown into an *exact* replica of him, and people remind me enough as it is. Especially those that knew him. I get it constantly."

"And you hate that." It was more of a statement than a question. I knew how much of a monster John was now, so I really didn't blame him.

"Very much so. It's frustrating when the thing that people find most interesting about you is how much you look like someone else." He rubbed his brow. "I'm sorry. I don't tell people that. I mean, I've never told anyone that. I'm not sure why I just told you."

I wasn't sure whether he was apologizing to himself or to me.

"It's okay," I said, finding the skin under his dress shirt cold when I rubbed his shoulder. "I'll keep your honesty safe, Bear. You don't have to worry."

Appreciative of his vulnerability, I pulled his jacket tighter around myself, shifting closer to him as we listened to the birds singing through the trees. He made a similar move, but was careful again, and I could feel him holding back. There was a part of him that wanted to trust me, but a stronger part made him hesitant about it. And I was gaining a better understanding of who he was in the process, but I wondered how much he'd actually tell me if I asked.

"Bear?"

"Em?"

"Um. In the spirit of honesty, I have another question."

His gentle laughter lifted my soul. "Then I shall do my best to answer."

I hesitated, before I manifested all my fucking bravery. This was a big question, and I wasn't sure how he'd take it. "Why did you and Kirk not speak for over a year? I could feel the tension last weekend. There seemed to be... I dunno... Resentment? Sometimes? When you spoke to each other."

Something strange ran across his face, before he masked it with irritation. I'd touched that nerve again—same one that I'd touched for Shane and Kirk—and I found myself wondering if the cause of that pain was the same for all three men.

"I don't know," I continued. "Is there something... you need to get off your chest?"

He held me in a suffocating moment before dropping his eyes to the railing. They twitched back and forth like he was searching for an answer in the wood. Then he looked at the mountains, and I saw the line between his copper brows, the slight reddening of his skin, and the pulse of his temple. "Emily, I very much appreciate the time and connection we've shared this evening. It was lovely to spend some time with you, away from the influence of everyone else. And to be frank, I've enjoyed it. So, I urge you to not think of my next statement as rude. Nevertheless..." He paused and gave me a serious look. "You *don't know me well enough* to ask something like that." The tone of his voice was like the growl of a crouching tiger.

Once again, I'd overstepped. Just like my curiosity had made do many times since I'd made this move. Barrett was right. It was gonna be trouble.

"I'm sorry," I said.

He swallowed. "The three of us, along with others that love me, are struggling against something that I can't contain. That I am *deplorably pathetic* for not being able to contain. Something that drowns me, day after day, in a sea of blame." He paused. "You don't need to know more than that." I thought I caught a shimmer in his eye, but he turned his head to hide it from me.

Desperate to make amends, I startled stumbling over my words. "Okay. That's fair. I'm sorry. I'm really sorry. Forget I said anything about it."

His back expanded in three deep breaths.

"I'm so sorry, Bear."

"It's fine, Emily."

"No! I mean. I didn't mean to offend you. I swear. I've had a lovely time too. Fuck. I really didn't want to fuck this up. Oh... I'm so sorry, Bear."

But then he laughed quietly and shot me an appreciative look while he hid his emotions. "You're..."

"What?" I said, way too quickly. "What? I'm what?"

He smiled as he studied my face. It took him several seconds to add, "Righteously endearing."

I swallowed. Hard.

Oh God.

He looked away and shook his head. "Also, I'm a Roth, kid. We have thick skin. You'll have to try harder if your goal is to offend me."

You're lying, Barrett. I know I just hit you straight in the feels.

"Anyway." He pinched the bridge of his nose and ran his thumb and forefinger down the sides. "Have you had enough? It's getting late, and we should have dinner at the lodge. We can return another time if you want to explore the trails. And plus, I'm fucking cold."

I laughed as I squeezed his biceps. "Okay. And thank you so much, Barrett. This was really nice." I started to shrug off his jacket.

"Keep it," he said. "Just until we get to the car. The past couple of days have been unseasonably cool in the evening."

I plunged my arms back into the sleeves, grateful for his warmth in more ways than one. "Okay. Shall we *take our leave* to dinner, then?" I said, trying to lighten the vibe again.

He chuckled, took the empty french-fry basket, and offered his arm. "Yes. Let's take our leave."

This time, he gave me his arm as we crossed the bridge. And side-by-side, and with my arm looped in his, the journey was a lot easier.

CHAPTER 29
HERE FOR YOU

The weekend in Kelowna came quickly, and the drive alone was worth raving about. We'd taken David's car, and Greg and Avril rode in the back while I took shotgun upfront. I'd taken over David's aux cord and was enthusiastically pumping my nineties-pop playlist through his crackling speakers as we wound through the mountain valleys. About an hour into the drive, Greg couldn't stop talking about a girl from his soil sciences class that he had an obvious crush on.

I turned and gave him an encouraging smile. "If you like her so much, Greggy, then why don't you ask her out?"

Even shaded in the backseat, his blush was obvious. "She probably has a partner, Em."

My heart sank a little, and I scrolled through the songs on my phone to distract myself from fantasizing about Barrett. "Maybe best to move on then," I mumbled.

Look who's talking.

"No," Avril said. "You should totally ask her out!"

"Nah... I dunno," Greg said.

"Come on, Greggy!" she said, jostling him. "You're cute, and funny, and handsome, *and* a cowboy. What's not to love? Even if there's a chance she has a partner, you should totally go for it." She gripped Greg's arm and shook. "Because what if she doesn't? And what if she says *yes?*"

"I dunno," I said. "It's a risky one."

"No! Go for it!" Avril said.

"You two are making this unnecessarily hard," Greg said.

Avril and I broke into a contrasting duet of her saying, "Do it! Do it! Do it!" and me saying, "She might have a partner! It's best to move on to someone else," while Greg chuckled nervously in the throes.

"Alright!" David hissed; Eastern accent strengthening like it did when he was irritated. "Can everyone jus' be quieter for a bit? This is a long car ride, and I need the children to calm down." He glanced over into the next lane, checking for space to pass as he dropped his voice. "Holy fuckin' mackerel."

I stifled a laugh at his Nova Scotia-ism, but he didn't seem to share the humour.

"Something funny?"

I grabbed my Timmies from the cup holder, shook my head, and took a big gulp to drown the giggling. "Nope, nothing." I nudged him, trying to turn his mood. It didn't work, and instead he sighed. I reached over and ran a hand through his curls. "Everything okay?"

"Fine," he said, rubbing his brow. "I jus' have a huge headache, and you three aren't helping."

I frowned. "Do you want me to drive?"

"No," he said. "I want you to be *quiet*."

"Dave, are you sure?" Greggy asked. "You've got three other people that can drive, here. You don't always have to push through the pain, you know. You don't always have to suffer... just to feel alpha."

David silenced him with one stern glare through the rearview. "If I said I'm fine, I'm fine." He dropped his attention back to the road. "And how far is the next gas station, Greggy? I need some drugs and could use a fill up."

Greg perked up like he was happy to be of service. "We'll have to get off and stop in Chilliwack. So, not far."

"Sounds like a good idea," I said. A cramp in my knee told me that my legs agreed.

A few clicks later, we pulled into a gas station in the valley town of Chilliwack. Here, the great mountains of the Fraser Valley surrounded us, with the Fraser River still flowing wide along the base of those in the north.

David shifted his Mazda into park and squinted into the sun, running a hand through his curls. Then he promptly turned to the three of us and told us to cough up some gas money.

I pulled my purse onto my lap and fished for a ten-dollar bill as I tried not to picture the number in my draining bank account. My savings had gotten me through to this point, but I wouldn't get much further without a job. My free Tuesdays and Thursdays had been nice, but they'd soon have to be sacrificed in the name of making a living.

Thanking us, David stepped out of the car, and Greg followed, leaving Avril and me behind. Through the window, I watched Greggy step around the hood and raise his arms behind his head in an adorable stretch. His cowboy hat was tilted on his faux hawk.

David latched the nozzle to his tank with a dull thud and broke into a stretch as well. His white t-shirt slid up enough to give me a glimpse of the black hair that ran down his stomach and into his shorts.

I gulped at the craving that followed. "Looks like a good idea," I said to Avril. "I'm gonna get out and stretch too."

I left the car and started up some ad hoc yoga moves so I didn't have to look at David's sexiness. In Barrett's absence, my lust had swung right back to my Nova Scotian roommate, and I couldn't make up my mind which man I wanted more. After I finished stretching, I sat on the hood and crossed my legs at the ankles, trying to pretend that this inner complex didn't annoy me. I was here to obtain a master's degree, not to be stretched in a romantic tug-of-war between two enemies.

Oh My God, Em. Just stop fucking thinking about it.

Turning my mind to money again, I pulled out my phone and

found Barrett's name in my messages. *Hey*, I text him, *I have a bit of an odd question for you…*

A half-moment later, my phone buzzed with his answer. *What kind of odd?*

Reading it in his voice, I laughed. *Well. I'm kind of looking for work and I was wondering if you knew if you were hiring? I need something part time (obviously), but I'm at a loss on where to start.*

If anything, working at Roth Pharmaceuticals would let me get my foot in the door of the industry. And David had said he understood why I'd networked at the Roth Banquet to advance my career, so surely, he'd be okay with it, right? Plus, having a budding friendship with the CFO would make getting a job there easier. Plus, plus, I'd be on the inside, so I'd be able to peek into anything fishy going on. Maybe it would help me nail down what was happening with David?

Oh God.

Who was I kidding? He'd totally be pissed if he found out what I was doing. But I couldn't help it. If there was some sort of tyrannical injustice going on with his treatments, then I needed to dig it up and make big pharma accountable.

That's a very disappointing odd question, Miss Anderson, Barrett replied, causing me to smile again. *But I will enquire for you.*

Thanks, Bear.

"Em?" A loud click that spread across the Mazda told me David had finished filling it.

I instinctively pulled my phone into my chest.

"I'm going in. I need some water and drugs. You want anything?"

I smiled, shook my head, and turned back to my phone.

"Okay," David said.

Then, as he walked around the hood and came close to me, I did a mental 180. "David?" My thoughts plummeted into a fantasy world where I grabbed him by the collar and pulled his mouth to mine.

"Yeah?" His voice brought me back to reality, where he was very much standing there with his eyebrows raised.

I fought the hunger in my lady parts. "Um. I changed my mind. Can you get me a pack of cherry candies?"

"Sure, princess," David said.

"I'll come with you and carry the snacks!" Greg offered, following David toward the store.

I watched them go. Then ran a hand of frustration through my hair and turned to the back window that Avril had rolled down.

"What's up Em?" she said, craning her neck to look at me. "You seem tense. I can tell that something's on your mind."

Sighing, I kneeled to her level, and crossed my arms over the open window. "I think I have feelings for David."

She blinked. "Romantic ones?"

"Yeah." My chin pinched the skin on my arm as I nodded. "I can't stop thinking about how much I want to kiss him. And... *other* things."

"Oooo, girl. I've been there before."

"I know. So, like, what do you think about it?"

She paused, starting her sentence at a higher pitch. "Well... Okay. Here's the thing. If you have those feelings for him, then they're probably never going to go away. At least, not without a lot of conscious work. And the only way to find out if it's going to go somewhere is to try. But keep in mind that you're roommates, so—speaking from personal experience—if things go south, then it's not going to be easy to deal with."

"Right," I mumbled. "That's part of what I'm worried about."

She shrugged. "At the end of the day, every relationship comes with some sort of risk. You just need to decide whether to take it or not. And if you don't, then you have to force yourself to stop imagining him as a romantic option. You know, set your sights on another man."

Hmmm. It didn't help that said *other man* had a toxic gold-digging girlfriend, and a morally questionable pharma-giant-of-a-company.

"And if I did take the risk?" I asked. "That wouldn't bug you?"

She tilted her head for a second. "I mean, he's not mine, so I don't really have a leg to stand on, do I? Plus, I've got someone else in mind now."

I grinned. "Really? Who?"

She gave me nothing but a coy smile.

David and Greg were now finished in the store and coming back to the car.

"Put some thought in before you go for it," Avril said. "And keep in mind that he's romantically intoxicating to a frustrating degree. That part's not your fault."

I nodded and tried to ignore David's invisible pull as he neared the Mazda.

After we got back in the car, he offered me my bag of candies, but I couldn't help but think about how it wasn't what I'd *actually* wanted from him. He opened the water and pulled out a bottle of painkillers, popping the lid open and tossing a couple back. The bottle was labelled with Barrett's last name, because of course it was. As he swallowed, I tried not to focus on the movement in the middle of his neck and how much I wanted to put my lips there. Finally, David set the water aside, and shifted the Mazda into drive, putting us on the road again.

My phone pinged with a text from Avril. *I see those looks, Em. If you go off alone with him this weekend, I'll cover for you.*

I turned and shot her a furtive eye.

Shortly after we got back on the road, Greg and Avril fell asleep in the backseat, and I dug into my packet of candies as I chatted with David. They gave me a sugar high, but it didn't last long, and about half an hour later my eyelids were heavy. As the movement of the car rocked me, I lulled in and out of a light snooze where I thought I heard David singing to himself. His voice was as soft and fluid as a wolf howl, and even in my grogginess, my lust flared at the sound.

Hours later, we were pulling down the long gravel drive to the sprawling Oliver Ranch, which was nestled at the foot of the dusty mountains on the edge of Kelowna. Here, a large farmhouse and three extensive stables stood amongst patches of paddocks and fields. The Oliver's had over thirty horses boarded, and many of them were peppered throughout the grass as we drove past, grazing in the evening sun. It was a beautiful and welcoming sight.

As the House-of-Wolves got out of the Mazda—each with a variation of a groaning stretch—I couldn't help but notice how much hotter it was in the interior. There was something about it that reminded me of Ontario.

Greg's parents, Tim and Sandy, welcomed us with a barbeque dinner and drinks. They were friendly and charismatic people, and after a few moments of chatting, it was obvious where Greg inherited all his adorable charm from.

Sandy showed us our rooms—I was staying with Avril—and then we met on the Olivers' deck to eat too much meat, and down a lot of beer and wine. Many hilarious and embarrassing stories about Greg and his brother, Scotty, were shared, but Greg was a good sport and sat there quietly, rolling his eyes, and smiling as he sipped his beer. Good laughs were had, but the sun soon retreated behind the dusty mountains, turning the desert-like landscape colder. Feeling the collective pull to our beds, the group of us said goodnight and staggered up to our rooms, happy to be tipsy and tired.

It's the middle of the night, and the crickets are chirping in the midnight air. I'm sitting awake, staring at the ceiling of my room at the Oliver Ranch. Beside me Avril is quietly snoring, deep in her dreams of what I imagine are about rainbows and bunnies and all manners of innocent beauty. I watch her shoulder rise and fall with each breath. Her golden hair is draped over it like a silk blanket.

I can't sleep. I'm restless, and I huff as I slip out of the bed and move with care across the aged hardwood of the farmhouse. I go to the door and draw it open before stepping into the hall, graceful and silent, like a stalking she-wolf. My movements draw no more than a "mew" from one of the Oliver farm-cats, and before I know it, I'm at his door. I want him, and I can't wait anymore. Without hesitation, I open it and slip inside, closing it behind me before I move to his bedside.

Just like me, he can't sleep, and he props himself up against the headboard. "Em?"

"Shhh," I say, pulling back the duvet and climbing on top of him. "Don't speak."

Then I savor the softness of his curls in my fingers and guide his mouth to mine. Like I imagined, his kiss is tender and passionate, so I enjoy it. I caress his tongue with mine, wrapping my arms around his neck and pulling him closer as he retaliates, kissing me deeper before he starts to move down my neck. I sigh, enjoying every moment that he's touching my body before I reach down to take him into my hand. He's already hard, so I tease him for a moment, which deepens his hunger.

"Stay quiet," he breathes, before gliding his hands down my body and shifting me onto him.

I inhale sharply and start to move against him, connecting us in a way that we've never been before. Every thrust is better than the last, and my breath quickens as he kisses my chest. I raise my chin to the ceiling and moan. "David—"

"Wake up, wake up, wake up!" Avril's voice couldn't have been *more* intruding first thing. "Good morning, Emily!"

I groaned, turned over in the bed, and pulled the duvet over my head.

"Nope!" she said, pulling it back down. "Breakfast is almost ready, so get up, you lazy bones!"

I grunted. "You just interrupted a really good dream."

"Oh, I'm sorry," she said, tossing a pillow at me. "Are we here to sleep, or are we here to have fun? Carpe diem, girl."

I watched her disappear behind the door before burying my face in the pillow.

Fucking hell, that was good, though...

Pushing back my disappointment at being slung so rudely back into reality, I dressed myself in a pair of jean shorts and a tank top. But I couldn't push the erotic dream from my thoughts.

It seemed so real.

I decided that the best way to distract myself was to force myself to be social, even before my first coffee. So, I made my way out into the hall, where the curious "mew" of a farm-cat brought me right back. I ignored it and trotted down the creaky stairs.

At the bottom, everyone was sitting around the Olivers' table with Sandy winding between them, pouring coffee and tea. From the bottom stair, I caught sight of David flashing his white smile before he brushed the raven curls from his eyes, laughing and chatting with Greggy. Like I'd done with Barrett many times before, I held my breath and stood there like a stunned zombie, until someone snapped their fingers in my face.

"Wake up," Avril said, flashing me a covert smile.

I dropped from the last stair and followed her to the other end of the table, where Sandy poured me my much-needed coffee. From across the table, David met my gaze and grinned; almost like he could read my thoughts.

Later, we met Greg's brother, Scotty, who was an older and darker-haired version of Greg. The two of them decided to show off their riding talents by starting up an ad hoc barrel-race as the rest of us propped ourselves on the fence. Trying to ignore the pull of David's hand beside mine, I focused on how impressed I was with

Greg, as I watched him wind around the barrels with blinding speed on his favourite stallion, Captain. The speed of rider and horse in perfect connection turned Captain into a flash of white, tossing our hair as they thundered past. They were so fast that Greg couldn't keep his hat on, and he let it fly behind him as he focused on the finish line. I stopped the timer on my phone.

Scotty teased him with some brotherly jostling, before he took to the course to show off his own talents on his bay mare, Gypsy. He was faster than Greg by mere milliseconds, so in the spirit of fairness, I called it a tie. But neither of the brothers were happy about that, so after a bout of playful arguing, I crowned Scotty the winner based solely on the fact that he'd kept his hat on.

For lunch, Sandy packed us a picnic, and the Oliver brothers led us on a trail ride into the low mountains of their property. As an unexperienced rider, I was given a tame buckskin gelding named Spirit, and though I struggled to balance myself every time we moved, I couldn't stop petting and praising him.

David rode beside me, looking very much at home on the back of a black horse named Sparrow.

It was a slow climb—made even slower by us amateurs—and it took us over an hour. As we neared the flat plain that would serve as the stage for lunch, I saw light at the end of the tunnel.

That was until everything went wrong.

The sun in the interior was relentless, especially without the cover of the coniferous forests on the coast. It bombarded us with heat, and I watched it drain the energy from the whole group, but it seemed to hit David worse than anyone. Concerned, I watched as he rubbed his brow and started to sway a little too much for the movement on the back of a horse. The Olivers kept telling us that there would be shade from the sparse trees at the top, but our collective attention turned to David as he progressively got worse.

Somewhere near the end, he started slumping in his seat, and my heart started to race when Greggy called out: "Dave? You okay?"

"I'm fine..." David breathed. But right after, he went limp and slid to the side, thumping to the ground below.

There was a symphony of screams, but none were louder than mine when I jumped from Spirit and landed in a painful crash. Ignoring the pulsing from my legs, I tore toward him, sliding onto my knees beside him. I took him into my arms and rested his lolling head on my thighs. The Oliver brothers thundered forward on their horses, and they leapt down with Scotty joining me at the other side.

"Greg, get him some water! Now!" he said, as he started to fan David's face with his cowboy hat.

I brushed the curls from David's forehead.

"Oh, God. He's out cold. But he ain't hot," Scotty said.

He was right. David's skin was cooler to the touch. Like he hadn't been warmed by the sun as much as the rest of us.

I started to tremble as I tapped his face. "Come on David. Wake up. Come on. Come on."

Greg bolted back with the water. We ran some of it through his hair, but all it did was bead within the black, before it trickled like sparkling diamonds to quench the dusty ground below. Greg knelt at his head and provided the cover of more shade, but all we could do was keep him protected from the sun and wait for him to wake up. From somewhere on the outside of our little circle, I heard Avril whimpering.

"Come on. Please, David. *Please.* Wake up. Come on." All I could do was beg as I held him.

Finally, his eyelids fluttered, and he stirred as he started to regain consciousness.

"Oh my God," I said. "Thank God!"

Thank the Source, the Universe, and anyone else that could be thanked!

"David? Can you hear us, bud?" Scotty asked.

David moaned and started to move.

"Alright. Sit up," Scotty said, as we helped him upright. "Have some water. There we go."

I shifted forward to support him, stroking his head. "David, we were so worried!"

He sipped the water that Scotty held for him, and then bent his knees into his chest. "What happened?"

Holding a frivolous hand to his forehead, I raised an eyebrow. "You don't remember? You fainted."

"And took quite the fall from a horse while you were at it," Greg added.

With a soft sigh, David crossed his arms over his knees and rested forward. "I'm fine."

"No, you are *not* fine," I said. "You just fucking fainted!"

"We'd better get him checked out at the hospital," Scotty said. "Greggy, stay with this lot. I'll take him back."

"No," David said, his voice muffled by his forearms. "I'm fine. Jus' a little dizzy is all."

With tears streaming dusty patterns down her cheeks, Avril stepped forward. "David, please listen to them. You need to go—"

"No!" David swayed from raising his head in the protest. "I don't need to go to the fuckin' hospital! I jus' need you guys to give me some space!"

Like a shameful pack lashed by their alpha, Greg and Avril stepped back and widened the circle. But I wasn't going *anywhere*.

I dropped my voice and cradled him. "Hospital or not, Scotty needs to take you back to the house. This is serious, David. You need to stop lying to yourself."

He blinked before he weakly turned his green eyes to mine, and we shared several seconds of austerity before he dropped his head and nodded.

"Good man," Scotty said, hooking an elbow under his. "Alright. Up you come."

We hauled him up, but when he stood, he swayed like a newborn foal. It took both Oliver brothers to support him as Scotty whistled for Gypsy. Sensing urgency, the mare obeyed and trotted over. Greg went to her other side, and Scotty helped David to load his foot in the stirrup and mount her. He shook when he grabbed the horn of the saddle and swayed in the seat after he'd pulled himself up, but he stayed up there as Scotty mounted behind him. Taking the reins in his right hand, Scotty held David with his left arm and told him to keep holding the horn. Then, as the others cleared their horses from the path behind us, he urged the mare into a full gallop.

"Gypsy. Fast, girl. Hup! Hup!" They rumbled away in a cloud of hooves and dust, but my concern didn't go with them.

When we got back to the Oliver ranch later in the afternoon, I went straight to David's room—although, under a very different premise than the fantasy I'd had the night before. Sandy was sitting with him, running her fingers through his curls like a nursing mum. She smiled and laid a warm hand on my shoulder after she got up to leave, but it didn't stop the mutual exchange of anxiety that flowed between us.

Swallowing, I closed the door behind her, and brushed my shorts of horse dander, before sliding into the bed beside him. "How are you doing?"

He sighed, shifting toward me. "Tired. And sore."

"Hmmm. Yeah. I can imagine." I resumed the stroking of his curls. "Take the remainder of today to rest. I can drive home tomorrow."

"Em, please don't baby me."

"No, I *will* baby you," I said. "I'm worried about you, David. In fact, you're scaring the *shit* out of me."

He took a beat. "I'm fine."

"There you go with that bullshit again. You're *not* fine. Do you think I haven't noticed that you're getting sick all the time? That

I haven't noticed the wide variety of symptoms you seem to suffer from every time you do?"

His gaze met mine in a sharp warning. "What about it?"

"What about it?" I echoed, notably. "You're my friend, and I'm scared for you, David."

He paused, then looked away. "I can handle it, Em. Believe me. I've tried to fight, and I lost, okay? So I have no choice."

"Yeah, well, you shouldn't have to!" The creaky walls of the old farmhouse echoed a voice that was louder than I'd meant it to be. The memory of his burning veins was on my mind, and again, it brought a rage that shouldn't have been there.

He looked at me again. This time with sadness.

I took a deep breath and exhaled through my mouth before I lowered my voice. "If you can't be honest with anyone else, then at least be honest with me, David. Please. What is this? What's wrong? A—Are you sick? With something... serious?"

He bit the inside of his lip and thought for a minute. But then he turned his back to me. "I can't tell you, Em. I'm sorry."

He settled in silence, and I battled some very intense frustration.

"I can see it in your eyes, bu'y. There's something bothering you," Joseph says.

Panic and hopelessness are mixing in a toxic concoction through David's veins. He taps the cold table of the visiting room as he tries to suppress it, but it's bubbling up like a combative chemical reaction. Like a high school chemistry teacher is trying to get gasps from the class. It overwhelms him, and he bursts into tears. Immediate embarrassment rises after.

Joseph glances around to check who's seen.

"I can't, Dad," David says, behind a flood of tears. "I can't do it anymore. I can't handle the RAP."

Reaching forward, Joseph takes his son's hand, but it's not enough to ease his dread. "Oh, my boy. I'm so sorry."

David releases a shuddering breath and wipes his face. "I'd rather die... then do this anymore... It's so painful... It makes life so painful..."

Joseph shifts forward and winds his son's fingers through both of his hands. "Shhh. I know. But please, son." His eyes are darting around the room, and David's follow before he pulls his hands free to wipe his face again.

"I know. Ugh. I'm sorry, Dad." The ominous attention of three prisoners is on him now. Maybe four, he thinks, but the one in the back is hidden by their visitor.

"It's alright. Jus' get them tears away."

David draws a deep breath and holds it, but it comes back out in three sharp stutters. The tears are stinging as they fight to be released. Microscopic, caged wolves, lashing between the bars. He palms his eyes and begs it to stop as he tries to get a hold of his lungs. A headache is starting to pulse from somewhere in the depths of his brain. "I can't do this anymore," he repeats.

"You have to, son. You are strong. And you'll get through it." Joseph squeezes his forearm.

David shakes his head as he drops his hands. "You think they're gonna let me go after what you did? No. The'll never do that. They're angry."

Josephs arches his brows. He sits back and drops his gaze.

Stinging pierces David's nose as he sniffs and looks around the room again. He's fighting desperately to contain himself. "I have to run, Dad. I gotta get outta this place. Maybe I'll go home and—"

"No!" Though Joseph's voice is muted, his words are stern. "They'll find you, son. They won't stop 'till they find you. You're right. They're angry, and the reach of their evil has no boundaries."

"Then, what? Huh? What?"

His father swallows and falls silent, with no good suggestions to give. "I'm sorry you're still suffering for my mistake."

David scoffs. "What good's sorry gonna do?" He taps the table so hard that his index finger curls at the tip. "My only choices now are to kill myself quick or let them kill me slow."

"Don't talk like that, David."

"It's the truth! Those are my choices, Dad!" He sits back and lets his words hover in the air. His father's lip quivers, and it makes David feel guilty. Sniffing, he wipes his cheekbones and starts quieter. "Are you ever gonna fix what you did to me?"

Joseph blinks like it hurts and leans on the table. "David, I love you. I only wanted to save—"

But then his memory cuts.

CHAPTER 30
THE KING MUST DIE

The day after we got back from Kelowna, there was an e-mail from the HR department at Roth Pharmaceuticals in my inbox. There was an assistant receptionist position at their head office downtown, which, I'd learned, was also called the Roth Tower. It wasn't *exactly* what I'd been hoping for when I asked Barrett if they were hiring, but it was an easy foot in the door. David's memories were steering me to believe things about Roth Pharma that I didn't want to believe, and if I worked there, it would be easier for me to sniff around and get to the bottom of it. Plus, the position was simple, part time, and I, uh, needed the money.

It was Tuesday, and the members of the House had returned to work, so I sat alone in my room, staring at my laptop as I contemplated whether this was a good idea. Tapping my finger on the mouse pad, I thought about Barrett, and what he could have been hiding from me. Whether it was the same thing that David was hiding.

"I'm compliant," David had said as they came face to face on our doorstep. And Barrett had smirked and said, "Oh, I don't doubt that."

Whatever this was—whatever John did—I was sure that his sons were now involved in it. Or, at the very least, *aware* of it.

Who are you, Barrett Roth? And what are you and your brother doing?

I looked at the application and started to fill it out.

By Thursday, I was pulling up on Burrard Street for my interview.

Looming above me in sleek steel and dark glass, the Roth Tower was a forty-story monster-of-a-building, with their name in bold red letters at the top. For some reason, I was sure that the harsh style of lettering was handpicked by Johnathan Roth when he built it. Like a beacon of ownership over the city itself, the Tower stood tall among the rest of the buildings downtown, forever marking the skyline with their name. I squinted as I parked my Yaris and stepped out into the summer rain. At its base, I felt small and insignificant. Unworthy to be approaching its three sets of double doors.

Outside, five wide steps led to a large platform at the bottom of the building. Where the steps ended, a rectangular fountain was built into the shallow wall that ran further down Burrard. The water fell continuously from the top, like the edge of an infinity pool. There was a tall curb at the bottom of the fountain, where people could sit and enjoy their time outside. The platform itself was shared with another skyscraper next to the Tower, and outdoor seating was set up between the two.

Inside, the lobby reminded me a lot of Barrett's condo building. Massive and expensive looking, with the air as clean as a valley breeze between the mountains. The décor matched that of the building itself. Everything was grey, white, or stainless steel, with hints of gold spread out in all the right places. My heels clicked on the marble as I approached the security gates.

After a couple of awkward moments of me trying to get the attention of the receptionist, they swung forward for me, and I approached the desk where I'd be working if I got the job. Behind it was a man who looked at me like I was going to be a pain-in-the-ass. And it only intensified when I told him what I was interviewing for. With an impatient sigh, he signed me in on the iPad and then told me to have a seat. The glass tables that sat in the middle of some oversized white-leather chairs didn't have anything more interesting to read than *Pharma on the Inside* or *Canadian Business Insights*.

Just over ten minutes went by before the HR manager came out, and my heart started to pound, despite her welcoming smile.

Interviews had never been my favourite, and every time I went through one, I'd barely squeeze by. I was led across the marble and past the set of three stainless-steel elevators, to an area of the first floor that housed some polished meeting rooms. We had a forty-five-minute interview that took me fifteen minutes to relax into, but by the time we were wrapping up, I felt more like I was chatting with a coworker than a hiring manager. All-in-all, it was easy, went well, and by the next day, I got a job offer.

Thank you, Mr. Roth.

By Sunday, I knew I'd have to bite the massive bullet of telling David. I put it off all weekend—first hours, then days—but my first shift was scheduled for the next Tuesday, and I didn't want to lie to him about it. We got all the way to the end of Sunday night, before my guilt didn't let me go any further. I invited him up to my room and closed the door behind him.

With a sluggish sigh, he collapsed onto my bed and cuddled into my pillows. I was sure that I wouldn't have the heart to kick him out afterward. "You've got an *awesome* bed," he said, as he hugged my accent pillow to his chest. "I've always been jealous of your room."

I laid my head beside him and smiled. I could smell the weed smoke on his breath, and that wasn't ideal, but I couldn't wait anymore. Stoned or not, I had to tell him. "It gets too cold for you. You know you'd hate it."

He curled out a dopey grin. "Not with you next to me."

I snuffed, before I reached out and cupped a hand to his face, running my thumb along the trimmed jawline of his beard.

He closed his bloodshot eyes at my touch, and then blinked a couple times before he settled them on my lips. "If you don't kiss me someday soon, I'm gonna go insane."

Blushing, I pulled my hand away. The weed was making him fearless, and that wasn't what I needed right now. "I have to tell you something first," I said.

He yawned, and his eyelids drooped. I was worried that he'd fall asleep before I could get the words out.

"David?"

He smiled. "Em?" He'd already forgotten that I'd called him in to talk.

I shifted the pillow beneath my head. "I got a job."

"You did? That's awesome. Good for you."

I chuckled. When David was high, everything was "awesome." It was his favourite word when he'd had a lot to smoke.

"Yeah. I'm going to be a part-time receptionist on Tuesdays and Thursdays."

He nudged my shoulder. "Amazing. And see? You were worried. Everything is going to be A-Okay..." He made the gesture to match before letting his hand fall on the bed below. "You're great... You can do anything, Em."

"Um. Well. Here's the thing. It's kind of..." I hesitated, "at Roth Pharmaceuticals?"

His brow slowly pinched. "Okay?"

"Um. The receptionist position is at their head office."

Being stoned didn't stop him from scowling. "But you're jus' being strategic, right? Jus' for your master's?"

"Exactly. It's a foot in the door to gaining insights about the pharma industry. That's all."

With a harsh sigh, he rolled onto his back and stared at the ceiling. "Still... I don't know how to feel about you working for the goddamn *devil brothers*."

I bit my lip. "It's a good opportunity, and I took it. That's it."

"Maybe you can catch them..."

"Catch them doing what?" Suddenly, I'd perked up like a squirrel after a peanut.

David shook his head like a sloth. "Jus' please don't let it happen..."

Knowing that he was already onto something else, I sunk back down in disappointment. Would he ever tell me? "Let what happen?" I asked, gently.

"The thing I said would happen. They turn you against me."

With a gentle hum, I shifted forward and cuddled his shoulder. Beneath the weed, I could still smell his tropical essence. "I promise, I won't let that happen," I reassured him. "It's a job. That's it. I need money and experience. It's nothing more than that."

"Except you don't know, Em," he said, throwing his arm behind his head. "You don't know what you're getting yourself into. You don't know what they do."

"Then *tell* me."

"I don't like it," he said, shaking his head. "He's reeling you in."

I put my arm across his chest and gave him a squeeze. "This has nothing to do with Barrett," I whispered. "It's a means to an end. I promise."

He groaned, and his muscles started to melt beneath me. "He's a professional predator... The son of the devil..."

"David." But when I propped myself up to look at him, he'd already drifted off.

From what I can tell, it's winter. The skies are dark and overcast, which is made more ominous by the fact that it's evening. A gentle rain is falling, and the droplets settle on David's black curls as he walks the streets of Vancouver, breath condensing. He shivers, pulling his worn coat tighter to his frame. He starts to walk quicker, dodging the pools of cold water sure to soak through his aging sneakers. Through his reflection in the windows, I can see he's a teenager—Sixteen? Seventeen? Eighteen?—and he's at a stage in his life where he's still unsure of himself. His body is growing, and it's left him with a thin and lanky frame, far from the toned man that he is today. The wind picks up and blows a sheet of rain in a steep angle toward his face, but he wipes it away. It coats his lips, and he spits it vehemently onto the sidewalk.

Ahead of him, a crowd of bundled-up people are in line for a local bar, faces illuminated by the neon lights as bursts of cigarette smoke rise to meet the winter air. David doesn't want to meet anyone's gaze, so he drops his eyes. The rain runs off his curls to stream down his face. He speeds up to pass quickly, but the movement of three teenage boys up the line draws his attention. Resentment pulses through him like a shockwave.

The sixteen—Seventeen? Eighteen?—year-old Barrett, Shane, and Kirk are greeting the bouncer, all dressed in slick peacoats that are probably worth more than I paid for my car. The rain is repelled to their surface, causing them to glisten in the dark like David's hair. Not surprisingly, the teenage Barrett is quick to sweet-talk the bouncer, flashing his perfect grin and joking around with the guy like they're old friends. There's no doubt that they'll be let in with minimal effort on his end. Like usual, he's exuding confidence, and his copper hair glows at the top from the neon lights. David grinds his teeth while he watches.

Then Barrett notices him, and his expression shifts into an odd empathy, before he replaces it with disgust.

David puts his head down and walks quicker.

"Mathis! Hey, Mathis!"

Aware that nothing good will follow, David ignores him and passes.

"I'm speaking to you!" Barrett calls.

"If you're gonna fight, do it away from the fucking line," the bouncer says after.

David's breath quickens, and adrenaline surges. Footsteps follow, and he can feel Barrett behind him.

"Bear, come on," he hears Shane say. "Let's not do this, brither. Just leave him alone."

"Not a fucking chance," Barrett answers. Then, to David: "Don't you dare ignore me when I'm speaking to you!" He grabs David's shoulder, and David knows that he's gonna snap.

"What do you want, huh?" he says, wheeling around and shoving Barrett off. "You wanna fuckin' fight me?"

"More than *anything*," Barrett answers, sneering.

"Well, go on then, Devil's son!" David says.

Barrett charges him and, unable to wrangle his fury, David punches him right in his perfect teeth. A wave of gasps runs down the line for the club. Right-hand throbbing, David recovers from delivering the blow and steadies himself.

Barrett's bleeding, and there's mania in his raven eyes. The burn of his hatred is terrifying, and I can't tell whether David's holding his breath or I am. Barrett lurches forward with a rush of testosterone.

Still guarded, David backs away and leads them further down the street, before he plants himself firmly. Barrett's now laser-focused, and David prepares himself for the pain.

But then Shane and Kirk jump into action, catching Barrett by his shoulders before anything else can happen. Enraged, and hungry for blood, he uses all his strength to struggle against them, but the two make a good team.

Confident that his enemy is under control, David starts on the verbal. "My father was sent to fucking prison 'cus of your family, Roth!"

"Yeah?" Barrett spits back. "And mine is *dead* because of yours! Which one of us do you think should be more upset?" He grunts, fighting the boys. "You can still see his face, you fucking piece of shit!"

Shane resorts to talking him down, quietly murmuring in Barrett's ear as he holds him.

"We had nothing, and you still took it from us!" David says. "Tell your boys to let you go so I can knock you out, Devil's son!"

"Oh, with *pleasure*," Barrett says. He surges forward, but the boys are prepared, and they hold him.

Shane's now muttering in low increments: "Bear, Bear, Bear."

"David!" Kirk says, grappling with Barrett. "What the hell do you think you're doing, man? There's three of us and one of you. Do you want to fucking die?" He grunts, pushing his best friend. "He'll put you in the hospital if we let him go."

"You're fucking right!" Barrett lashes out like a tiger between the bars of a cage.

"Seriously," Kirk says, with another grunt. "Back off before you get yourself killed."

On the other arm, Shane continues to mutter. "Bear, calm down, mate, calm down. Dinna let him get to you. He isnae worth it."

Barrett cries out in anguish: "Joseph killed my father, Shay! I want to rip him apart in revenge!"

"I ken," Shane says. "But that's what he wants you to feel, brither. Are you going to let him get control of you that easily?"

Barrett draws a deep inhale and lessens his struggle. Shane's words are working.

"Seriously, do you want to go to jail?" Shane says. "He isnae worth it. And you're Barrett Roth." He gives him an encouraging pat on the chest. "You're Barrett Roth, mate. You're better than this."

Then Barrett calms enough that his two best friends can loosen their grip.

"Alright?" Shane continues. "He isnae worth it."

Though it's clear that Barrett's listening, his burning gaze is still focused on David. "How are you staying so calm right now?" he growls at Shane without looking at him. "If anything, *you* should be just as enraged."

What does he mean by that? I think.

Shane takes a deep breath. "He isnae worth it," he repeats.

Barrett stays silent, but he's unable to hide the hatred in his ebony glare.

"Seriously," Kirk says, again. "You two are in the most fucked up situation right now. How is this supposed to help?"

"It's not," David spits. "But I needed him to know that now I have nothing."

"And I want *you* to know how little I care," Barrett says, finally wrenching himself from the grip of his friends.

Shane and Kirk stay in his way, watching him like a wildcat on a chain.

Barrett starts to pace behind them, wiping the blood from his mouth before he spits some on the sidewalk. "Your father took *everything* from me when he pulled that trigger, Mathis. My *father* was everything to me. So don't sit there and whine about what you've lost, because you've lost jack-shit." He pauses, face twisting as he throws an index finger at David. "And let me tell you something else—you will *always* have nothing. You came from nothing, and you'll always *be* nothing. Just like your dad. The apple doesn't fall far from the tree, and you are pure shit, David Mathis. You're so poor that you couldn't pay for my breakfast."

"Bear..." Shane says, but his warning goes ignored.

"As for me," Barrett says, shifting into a bloodied grin. "I'm going to *be* everything. I'm going straight to the top, because that's the vision that my father had in mind for me, and I plan to see it through. He wanted me to be a fat cat with a glimmering crown, and I'm aligned with that idea. I'm going to be King; you'd better believe that, Mathis." He points at the surrounding streets. "Look around, because this city is going to belong to me—my kingdom— and if you are going to survive here, you need to play by the rules. I could effortlessly make your life a living hell. Could effortlessly *crush* you, even now, so get that straight in your fucking head. And if you don't step in line, before long, you'll need *my* benevolence to continue your pathetic existence." He wrinkles his nose in disgust, before he turns and heads back to the line. The neon colours move through his dark copper hair.

Shane shoots David an uncertain look, then nods at Kirk before turning to follow Barrett.

But Kirk's stormy blue stays fixed on David. He takes a deep breath before he speaks. "Listen, I know you're angry about your dad, but if you know what's good for you, you should lay low and remember every word he said. Because it's true. Believe me, David. 'Cus you're already in trouble. Big trouble... You've made an enemy out of a Roth."

CHAPTER 31
READY TO START

It was the Tuesday morning of my first day of work, and I didn't see David because he'd left early. I had a good breakfast and then put on a pink blouse, black pencil skirt, and the nude heels that I'd picked up on the weekend. The summer day was overcast, but it was warm, and the streets of downtown Vancouver smelled fresh from the overnight rain. It took me two circles around the Roth Tower—and a glimpse at the e-mail the HR manager had sent me—to find the parking garage. But once I did, the attendants were friendly and helpful. I was given a pass to hang on my rearview mirror, and as I squeezed my Yaris into the only spot left—marked appropriately as *Small Car*—I felt a little, well, giddy.

What was I going to find when I walked through those doors? And would it lead me to the purpose that the Universe had in mind when They made me move here?

The parking spots next to the elevator were reserved for the company's senior leadership team, and the lineup of luxury cars made my Yaris look like a glorified golf-cart. A white Tesla with matching leather seats was parked in Travis's spot. Which was first in line, obviously. Barrett's glimmering, blue GranTurismo was second, and I rolled my eyes as I passed.

Rich people.

After I took the elevator up to the lobby, I got stuck at the gate again and was forced to wait for my new coworker to let me through. I saw the looks he gave me, but he let me wait a good thirty seconds before he opened them, and I was far too uncomfortable to call it out to him. He watched me with a strange coldness in his brown eyes as I rolled up.

I stuck a hand over the counter and gave him a warm smile. "I should reintroduce myself. I'm Emily."

He raised an eyebrow and took my hand like it was diseased. "Adam."

"Adam. Right. You're going to be the one that I'm working with, mostly."

"Lucky me. And technically you're my assistant," he said, as he clicked away at his computer apathetically. "So, let me guess, *Emily*. You're friends with the CFO?"

I shrugged, shifting my purse. I wasn't sure what to do next. "Uh, yeah. How'd you know?"

With a heavy sigh, he reached to the other side of the desk and plopped a circular vase of sunflowers on the counter. There was a card inside that said, *Happy First Day, kiddo! B.N.R.*

I smiled as I touched one of the petals.

"Also, how else would you have gotten this job with only one interview?" Adam said, with a condescending snort. "I had candidates lined up, but he had other ideas. And, you know..." he looked me up and down, "he's the boss."

Yikes. Okay. I get why he's being a dick.

"Um. Yeah. I guess he is."

Adam rolled his eyes and turned back to the computer without giving me directions, but the sound of heels on marble instantly relieved the awkwardness. The HR manager had come down at the right time.

Three hours passed before I returned to the front desk, and I'd spent the first two sipping coffee and watching overproduced orientation videos. I spent the last with an excitable Health and Safety Manager that was way too into his role.

My attention was waning by that time—I'd done easier jobs in my sleep—so I tried to listen. But I couldn't help but make up my own fake warnings, just to entertain myself.

Do not stick your finger in the stapler. Beware of the inevitable bitch-slap from your new diva of a coworker. Avoid death by GranTurismo and/or Ferrari in the parking garage. Do not jump from the upper balconies of the Tower.

Afterward, the HR manager took me back to the front desk, and my heart sank at the sight of Adam. My right shoe was already starting to wear a blister into the back of my heel.

"She's all yours," the HR manager said to him, as I drifted to her side. "Spend the next two weeks really showing her the ropes."

He flashed his eyebrows, then looked back to his computer.

"And Adam?" she said. "Be nice."

"Of course," he said, dropping his smile after she'd turned her back, and pulling his mouth tightly to one side. He looked at me, raised his chin, and said, "Well? What are you waiting for?" He jerked his head toward the chair and computer beside him. "That's your desk. Make yourself at home and then we can get started on your training."

I inhaled patience and exhaled negativity. "Thank you." Moving past, I sat in a chair that was way too comfortable to be for work, before I searched through the drawers to find somewhere to put my purse.

"Listen," Adam said, drawing me back. "I apologize if I seem harsh at first glance. I'm going to try to be tolerable to work with."

Sounds great...

"But I need you to understand that I've been working alone for a long time, and this is my territory. So, what I say goes, alright? You're only here to help me out."

I raised an eyebrow, but swiftly dropped it. "Uh. Okay."

And what's the animal form of your spirit? A honey badger?

"Good." He gave me the worst fake smile ever, before he dropped it and rolled over to my side.

I tried to soothe my tension as he invaded my personal space and started to take me through the first steps of my new job. He spent some time showing me around our work area and helping me navigate the computer system, and I tried to draw it all in like a sponge. He acted like what he did was complicated, but I was mastering in what I considered one of the most complex areas of the ethics community, and I'd done stuff at my job in Social Services that was ten times as hard. But I kept those thoughts to myself. If anything, I needed to be grateful for the simplicity. It was two days a week of easy money, an opportunity to poke around a little, and a chance to see more of Barrett. (Although I'd yet to catch a glimpse of him in his own Tower.)

After that, Adam told me to start cleaning out our desks because he hadn't had time to do it before I started. I groaned on the inside but kept quiet. Sifting through all manner of things—hair ties, paperweights, broken cords, old Halloween candy from several years before—I filled up an entire garbage can by the time I had the paperclips and pens organized. Then I came upon some old visitors' logs and asked him what to do with them.

"You can—" His phone rang, and I saw his face light up. "Hold on. It's my boyfriend."

Grateful that he was distracted, I turned toward my sunflowers and ran my thumb along Barrett's writing.

The Real-Barrett; shining through once more.

"Emily?" Adam was now holding the heel of his palm against his phone and eyeing me expectantly. "You can take those down to the library. It's in the basement. Level marked with a B. Look for the file in the Security records." He swiftly turned back to his loved one on the phone.

Ok. Cheers for showing me there, Adam.

With a muted sigh, I grabbed the folder and ignored my stinging heel as I went back to the elevators. The overzealous air-conditioning pricked my skin, and I shivered as I pressed the button and stepped inside. The Tower elevator was quick, and soon I'd dropped into the level that housed the documents protected by the Roth Corporate structure.

When I stepped out, the silence was deafening, and everything was incredibly still. Like I'd stepped into a room suspended in time. It was oddly peaceful, so I decided to reframe my visit there as a welcomed break.

Ahead of the elevators, there was an open space filled with plain tables and chairs, but on either side of that, broad filing cabinets ran up to the ceiling in six distinct rows. Ladders slid along tracks that let you access the upper cabinets, and signs hung from the ceiling that marked the category of files in each row. But I was in no hurry to follow them. The longer I stayed down here, the less time I had to spend with Adam.

I wandered to the second last row on the right side and walked with my heels snapping in slow thuds to the carpet. I read the labels on each of the cabinets as I held the old file to my chest and started humming. It was a song I heard on David's radio. The one he was singing to himself on the drive to Kelowna. *Find Your Love*, by Drake.

I frowned at the thought.

God, I miss Toronto.

As I wandered and entered the last row, I broke out the song, voice muffled by the stuffy library. In the last row, the ladder had been left in the middle of the cabinets, and I grinned as I stepped onto it, sliding myself along with a giggle. Feeling like the keeper in some ancient bookstore, I held out my arm. But somewhere along the back of the row, the file slipped from my hand and the papers fluttered to the floor.

"*Goddamnit.* I mean, sorry." I flicked my eyes up to the *Source* for good measure.

Huffing, I stepped from the ladder and dropped to my knees to clean them up. And when I looked back at the cabinets, a label on the lower half caught my eye.

RAP, it said.

Stunned, I thought back to David's memory at the prison.

"I can't handle the RAP," he'd said.

I repeated it in a whisper, staring at the label like an apparition. And when it was still there a few seconds after, the realization hit me like a Mack truck. It felt like all the evidence about Roth Pharma that I'd ignored up until this point was being shoved violently in my face. This was the cause of David's suffering. Hidden in plain sight at the back of the Roth's library. It was too much of a synchronicity to be a coincidence.

I thought of Joseph, and why he'd murder a man like Johnathan Roth. My understanding of it was pixilated and full of holes. An unfocused image. A puzzle left undone. The only pieces that I'd gathered told me that a desperate man was fighting for something. But what that *something* was, I had no clue.

That was until now.

Was this it?

Setting the old file aside, I tried to twist the three-pronged handle that sat in the middle of each cabinet, but it didn't budge. It was locked.

Fuck.

I reached out and brushed the keyhole. The matching key would be small. Like something you'd use for an apartment mailbox.

Suddenly, the ding of the elevator made me jump, and I backed away from the cabinet, scooping my file from the floor. The sound of footsteps across the carpet told me that I was no longer alone, and then a man came into view, setting his things at the table lined up with the end of the row.

Straightening the waist of my skirt, I took a few heavy steps toward him. "Barrett?"

He jumped like a cat with its hair standing on edge and almost dropped his iPad. Then he saw me and grinned. "Emily! Welcome to the family, kid!" He set it down and then spread his arms for a hug.

I stepped into him and wrapped my free arm around his waist. Inhaling, I tried to soothe myself with his musky-sweet scent, but something was off with his energy. I could sense it.

Or maybe it's mine?

After all, I *had* just discovered a suspicious filing cabinet in his library. Did he really have something to do with this? Did he really know?

"Oh, I'm so happy to have you here!" Barrett held my shoulders as we separated, and I noticed that his pupils were so dilated that his eyes were pure black.

"Thanks, Bear," I said, giving him a feigned smile. "I'm, um, *really happy* to be here. And very grateful for your help, of course."

"Always, kiddo." He jerked his chin toward the row of cabinets that I'd come from. "Meddling in our confidential section already? You're going to be trouble, Em. I can already tell."

"Oh," I glanced back, "ha ha. That. Well. Um. Actually. I was just looking for the security documents?" I hadn't meant for it to come out like a question. "Adam told me to file these old visitors' logs."

He pointed to a row on the other side. "Aisle three, I believe. Should be next to the Quality Assurance records."

"Thanks." I held the file to my chest and looked at his iPad. It was displaying a plethora of graphs and information that I didn't understand. "What about you? I didn't expect to find the CFO meandering in the library on my first day."

He put his hands on his hips. "Ah, yes. Well. Our glorious leader has tasked me with digging up some figures that I won't find at my fingertips." He dropped one hand to the table and scrolled through the iPad with the other. "No matter. The library is a great place to gain some seclusion. I enjoy the occasional visit here."

I watched as he clicked through the screen with his left index finger. "I never realized that you were a southpaw before," I said.

"The only left-handed Roth there ever was." He smirked as

he brought his dilated pupils to meet mine. "I merely had to be different."

I thought about all the things I didn't know about him again.

Then we fell into a brief silence where I racked my brain for what to say. I desperately wanted to ask about the cabinet in the back, but something told me that this was a bad idea. I needed more time to strategize. I was dealing with a Roth, after all. "Thanks for the flowers, by the way. They're lovely."

"I'll have to tell Natalie that you were pleased with them. She has a keen eye for such things, don't you think?" Upon seeing my weird face, he clarified. "My assistant."

"Oh." My stomach dropped. Of course he wouldn't have had time to send the flowers himself. He was the CFO of North America's largest—and apparently, *most evil*—Pharma company. How could I expect any different?

He smiled when he caught the shift in my mood. "But you know what? I did write the card myself, if that makes it any better."

"I appreciate it, Bear," I said flatly.

He ignored it and winked. "I know you do, kiddo." Then he went back to his scrolling, and I watched a slow line of blood start to run from his right nostril. It trickled down his face like a river of rubies and caught on his top lip before dripping on the screen below. He recoiled, hand flying to his face.

"Bear?" I slammed the file on the table and started patting my pockets for the Kleenex that I'd stuffed in there earlier.

He shot me a look somewhere between embarrassment and horror. "Em. Have you a tissue?"

"Yeah. Right here."

"Thank you." He held it to his nose and tilted his chin to the floor. A puddle of red spread through the white.

"A—Are you okay?"

"Yes. Everything's alright." Behind the cloud of fluff, he tried on a smile. "*Dinna fash.* I've been prone to nosebleeds for many years now. I'm quite seasoned at handling them."

I stepped forward, hands hovering. "D—Do you need me to do anything?"

"Cease acting like I'm going to die, for starters."

Snuffing, I stepped back.

"Trust me, Em. If anything is going to kill me, it won't be a nosebleed. Even so. Cats have nine lives, you see."

I wasn't convinced. There was something in that look he'd given me that told me he was playing off something bigger. Something that told me he was sorry that I'd seen this.

After a few tense moments of him holding his face and me frozen in worry, the bleeding stopped, and he used the rest of the clean tissue to clean the blood off his lip. It left his nose raw and red, like he'd walked through a blizzard in the middle of Winnipeg.

"See? Everything's fine."

I decided it was a good idea to be super awkward and tell a bad joke to disperse the negative energy. "A hundred bucks and I won't tell anyone upstairs about this."

He pouted and pulled out his wallet, handing me five $100 bills instead.

"Um. No, Bear. I was only joking." I offered them back like they were cursed.

He settled into his smirk. "I'm aware. But the look on your face was priceless." I shook my hand insistently, but he just kept fucking smirking at me. "Keep it. And never tell me that I don't uphold my end of bargains."

I tossed it on the table and shook my head. "I can't keep that. It's too much money."

"Do you not remember my rule around zeros? *That* is mere pocket change." He scooped it up and shoved it back in my hand. "Keep it. Consider it a welcome gift."

Swallowing, I backed down and nodded. That black gaze told

me he was serious, but it didn't stop me from feeling like I'd taken blood money. "Thank you, Mr. Roth."

Pleasure flared in his eyes. "You're welcome, Miss Anderson."

I folded the bills and stuffed them in my pocket, before I nodded and turned to walk away.

His rushed tone turned me back halfway to the aisle. "Hey. I was planning on taking you out for lunch today, but my schedule is relentless. So, instead I'm hosting some friends tomorrow night, and I'd love for you to join us. We can celebrate your conversion to the dark side."

I blinked. "Okay. Sure. What time?"

"Seven o'clock."

"I'll be there." And for the first time since we'd met, I shuddered from the way his eyes grazed my skin.

"I look forward to it."

Nodding, I turned away, pushing back the coldness that ran through my veins.

The dark side, I thought to myself, when I got to the security cabinet.

Something told me that it was a very appropriate ruse for what I'd just joined.

"Emily," Dr. Tsuyuki said. "Something's wrong. I can see it on your face."

It was our end of the month check in. Two weeks since we'd last met.

"Um. No. Everything's fine."

Everything was *not* fine. I was still having some serious doubts about the topic of my thesis, and I hadn't even started my research yet.

"Well, tell me how your research is going so far?" he said.

Shit...

"Uh. It's been slow. But fine."

Dr. Tsuyuki raised both eyebrows. He wasn't buying it. "Have you even structured your hypothesis?"

Double shit...

I dropped my head into my hands.

My TA sessions—along with my ad hoc inquisitions about the Roth-Mathis history—had kept my attention very much occupied over the last few weeks. How was I supposed to balance all this *and* craft a thesis paper? And crafting said thesis paper was what I'd apparently come all the way out here to do!

No matter how much I'd tried, the she-wolf in my spirit wouldn't bite on the topic of *analyzing the quality assurance strategies utilized by global pharma companies* that I'd thrown out before. It wasn't baiting me in the way that it should.

"Can I be honest?" I asked.

"I hope you feel you wouldn't need to be any other way," Dr. Tsuyuki said.

"Um. Okay. Well... M—My spirit's, uh, not in the topic I chose."

He looked at me from over his glasses. "Your *spirit's* not in it?"

"Yeah?" I cleared my throat. "So, is it too late to choose something else?"

The *disappointed parent* energy that he'd started radiating was a lot right now. "No, however, we're a month into the semester and we're quickly approaching the time when starting your research is imperative."

I swallowed.

"I'll tell you what," he said, gently. "We'll meet again in exactly one week's time. Take that week to dive deep into the topic you want. But I want you to have it written in stone by next Friday. Deal?"

It wasn't one I liked, but I'd take it. "Deal."

CHAPTER 32
WOLVES

On Friday evening, I found myself sitting on one of the sunbeds on Barrett's patio, surrounded by a group of other women, and trying not to think about my thesis. The sinking sun was bathing everything in the hue of golden hour. The North Shore Mountains stood a bright green against a cloudless sky, and multiple seaplanes circled the city from above, taking the tourists for their over-priced sunset tours. There were a lot of people there that I didn't know—Barrett didn't seem to have any issues making friends—and everyone had clustered into small groups throughout his extensive outdoor space. A few service people wound through them, and though Avril and I weren't used to having a personal waitstaff at our fingertips, we took advantage as we sprawled there.

"Another glass, miss?" A server hinged at the hips, offering a platter of champagne. The bottle balanced there was wrapped in gold and was marked in the middle with a spade.

"Thank you." I took one and moved aside for Avril to follow suit.

"I had him break out the good stuff for us, ladies," Rebecca purred from the other sunbed, glancing over her shoulder at Barrett. "No more of those cheap $1000 bottles. Tonight, we drink like the worthy women we are." I caught the flare in her eyes as she looked over, like she didn't consider me part of that statement.

Pulling my knees to my chest, I clicked through my phone to find the price of the bottle, nudging Avril. *$7000.*

Seven thousand? she mouthed.

I thought about the crushing weight of my student loans. Then about the blood money that probably paid for what I was drinking.

Rebecca raised her new glass, as Melissa thanked the server from beside her. "To my billionaire boy," she said. "May his bank accounts, and his dick, remain ever large!"

It was the weirdest thing that I'd ever given cheers to, and I put the glass aside without drinking soon after.

Following the clinking, Melissa scrunched her nose like she was struggling with Rebecca's presence too. But she was the only one who could wear it on her face and get away with it.

Rebecca hummed after she drew her first sip. "Also, congratulations, Av."

Avril, who was starting to get quite tipsy, turned her attention. "For what, Beck?"

Rebecca's bright-red lipstick framed her grin. "I heard that you've caught the eye of the notorious bachelor, Kirk Richards." She glanced back over at the group of guys.

Barrett, Kirk, and Shane were standing among a couple of other men, nursing glasses of hard liquor as they laughed. I watched as Shane put an arm around Kirk's shoulders, almost like he was congratulating him with the same. They looked over at us, and Kirk shot Avril his half-smile.

"You sly little fox," Rebecca said, flashing her brows as she turned back. "Well done."

Avril pursed her lips. "We went on one date, Beck. He's nice, and I like him a lot. But we'll see where it goes." A very level-headed response, despite how much champagne she'd had. I was proud of her.

"I'm only saying," Rebecca said, shifting toward us. "The guy has a luxury car collection that makes our two men look like pussies." She nudged Melissa, who scoffed.

"Speak for yourself," Melissa said. "I don't measure my man by his car collection."

Rebecca ignored her. "*And* he hasn't been in a relationship for over seven years. Think about that. No woman has caught his eye for *seven* years."

Avril sighed. "Beck, please—"

"Spend that time on your knees, girl. It will be worth it. He's a big catch." Rebecca drew a prissy sip of champagne from a glass balanced at the tips of her pointed, red fingernails. She might as well have extended her pinky, for fucksake.

I caught the look on Avril's face as she glanced over at Kirk, along with the uncomfortable way she swallowed. It was *one date*, and she was already being given advice on how to be a gold-digger.

I put a hand on her leg and drew her gaze. "He *is* nice," I said, thinking back to our wood-chopping session and they way he'd saved me at the campground. "I think you two will be great together. But there's no pressure at this stage. You're just getting to know each other."

She smiled gratefully. "Thanks, Em."

"Yeah, he *is* nice," Rebecca said, mocking me with a childish tone. "Nice and *loaded*. Tick, tock, girl."

We locked in stare-down from across the sunbeds, and the blue of my eyes burned before Avril drained her glass and broke it. "Let's go swimming," she suggested. "Anyone else want to go swimming?"

Melissa took her up on the offer, but I wasn't in the mood. Then I instantly regretted it because I'd accidentally left myself with Rebecca. After they left us, we re-locked in our glare.

"You know, she's not you," I said, with a warning growl. "She doesn't need advice like that."

She snorted, turned onto her back, and adjusted her sunglasses. "I have nothing to say to you, Torontonian *slut*."

Taking out my phone, I ignored her as I turned the other way. My heart sank as I clicked into my messages and looked for someone to text.

David hadn't spoken to me much all week, and it'd made me

horribly cold. Like a windswept beach that had been robbed of its tropical sun. I missed him, but I wasn't sure how to reconcile things this time. Or even *if* I needed to reconcile things? The pain and suffering of his memories—and the cabinet in the basement of the Tower—told me that I'd made another mistake in messing with the "dark side." He was acting all cool about it, but would he really understand my reasoning for accepting a job from his enemies? And how could he be so understanding when the murder that imprisoned his father was probably caused by my new employer?

I *had* to get into that cabinet. Even if I was fired long before my first paycheque, I *had* to. If the only thing I walked away with after accepting this job was the knowledge of what they were doing to him, then so be it. I'd take that chance a hundred times if it would help me uncover the injustices of a pharma giant and bring me closer to him. I was sure that the answers could be found between the cabinet's hanging files, but I wouldn't bring anything up to David until I was positive. Hopefully by then I'd have a solid plan, and we could nail down how I could help him with all this. *If* I could even help him with this...

Swallowing my remorse, I brought up our last text conversation. *Hey. Can we talk?*

I'm a little busy, Em.

I know... Avril told me you were meeting a friend downtown for drinks. But I mean after. Can we meet? I'm downtown too. Several minutes passed with no response. *David, please. I really want to make sure we're okay. Please, please, talk to me.*

I could almost hear the heavy sigh that came with his next text. *Meet me at Jack Poole Plaza in an hour.*

It's a date. I smacked my forehead. Why the fuck would I add that?!

With our conversation at a natural, awkward end, I shivered and put my phone away. Rebecca was still ignoring me, and I didn't want to hear anything she had to say anyway, so I pulled myself from the sunbed and went over to join the guys.

When I came up, "I'm Gonna Be (500 miles)" by the Scottish band *The Proclaimers* came on, and Barrett grinned at Shane. "Ah! I was hoping this would play. Hey, Thomas. Remember the dance that your *da* used to do to this song when he was smashed?" He broke into a makeshift Scottish jig, and Shane shook his head.

"Yeah, dinna remind me," he said. But Barrett continued, so he joined him for a moment, mirroring his best friend. Then he laughed, throwing a dismissive arm. "So cringy."

Kirk laughed like it came to mind for him too, but the reminder of Michael Thomas brought Barrett's deplorable memory like a slap to the face. Again, a booming Scottish voice ran wild through my thoughts: *Get your damn hands off my son! You touch him again and I'll fecking kill you, Johnathan Roth!*

It stunned me to the point that I didn't feel Shane's arm until it was around my shoulders. "Hey, lassie! Thank God. You're just in time to rescue me."

I smiled as he welcomed me into their circle. "Hey, Shay."

Barrett's grin was now directed at me. "Hey, kiddo."

I suppressed how much that new nickname intoxicated my spirit.

Shane jostled me. "I heard congratulations are in order. But, you know, if you needed a job, you should have asked. I'd have given you a chance to work for the good guys."

My stomach plummeted into a deep pit at the reminder, and I looked away from Barrett.

"Too late," I heard him say, with what I was sure was his smirk playing on his face. "She's part of the family now."

The guilt seeped from my heart. Stinging like the venom from a snake.

Kirk nudged me. "Don't listen, Em. It's not too late to leave him. I'd also kill for a good receptionist."

I smiled again. "Thanks, Kirk. I'll have to keep that in mind if he ever pisses me off."

Or horrifies me with what I find in that cabinet.

Barrett chuckled. "I've never been made to be at such mercy from you, Miss Anderson."

Clearing my throat—and desperate to change the subject—I stepped out of Shane's arms and closer to Kirk. "Hey, how much have you had to drink?"

His brow furrowed, but his tone stayed kind. "Only the one. I'm trying to cut back, and I drove tonight. Why?"

I glanced toward the pool, where Avril and Melissa were giggling as they splashed each other. Their champagne glasses were bobbing in the water beside them, long since spilled and turned over. I snuffed. "Avril's a bit tipsy, and we came on the SkyTrain together, but I'm leaving earlier than her." I eyed him suggestively. "I was thinking that maybe you could take her for something sugary after, and then take her home?"

He set his scotch on the tray of a passing server. "Can I get some water, please? *Merci beaucoup.*" Then he gave me his half smile when he turned back. "You sure you don't want to come with us?"

I shook my head. "I've got other plans."

From the other side of the circle, Mr. Roth raised his chin. "What *other plans* would summon you to leave me so soon?"

Biting my lip from the inside, I dropped my gaze. "I have a commitment to someone." To divert the attention, I turned back to Kirk and gave him a playful pat on his muscular chest. "But can you promise me something? Don't break her heart, okay? She means a lot to me, and she really likes you. Even if she hasn't said it yet."

He nodded, but then looked at Shane for backup.

Shane raised an eyebrow and laughed. "You've been told, lad," he said.

"Yes," Barrett added. "It appears that I'm not the only one at mercy." Until now, I hadn't looked at him long enough to realize that he was watching Kirk with a strange sense of displeasure.

It wiped off as Rebecca cooed for him from the sunbeds. She'd realized that I was with him, and had stripped herself down to her skimpy, red bikini, posing as he drank in her form.

"Come here, babe," she said, curling a long finger at him. "I'm lonely."

The corner of his mouth twitched in the threat of his smirk. If he was one of those cartoon dogs, his jaw would have probably hit the floor, his eyes would have popped out, and he'd be howling. "That woman is a thorn in my side," he muttered. "But sometimes I enjoy the pain. Excuse me, gentlemen. Miss Anderson."

We pulled into a curved line, with me between the boys as we turned to watch.

"More of a fucking psycho than a thorn, I think," Shane said, with a bitter twang.

Kirk sighed. "I hear you, brither." The server returned with his water, and he thanked him before he drew a long sip. "Tell Emily about last weekend."

"Ah!" Shane spat. "Brutal, mate! So, Em, last weekend was the first we'd had to spend together in a very long time. So, Barrett naturally suggests that we go out and have some fun at the strip club."

I raised an eyebrow.

"No. Just hear me out. We get a VIP room. You know, we pay a lot of money for it. We support the workers there. Sex work is real work, and all that. And Mel's okay with it, by the way. I checked with her beforehand, and she always gives me hall passes on boys' nights. Anyway, this bitch *finds out* that we're there, breaks into the VIP room and starts harassing the strippers, and then *him*."

"Woe is you, Mr. Thomas," I said.

"Well, wait, lass, wait. That isnae all." Shane sighed. "It was amateur night, so they were inviting girls from the audience up on stage. Anyway. After she busts us, she climbs up and starts to get her tits out for him. Then, guess what? He forgets all about his boys to go drool in pervert's row and stuff some bills in her panty line. Bloody brutal."

Kirk shook his head. "Fucking *trou de cul*."

"Mmmm, that's right, brither." Shane caught his breath at the end of a sip of scotch, tipping his glass to Kirk before he turned to me. "Do you know what it's like to have a fucking *arsehole* for a best friend?"

I shrugged. "You two are the ones that choose to love him."

"It isnae always a choice, lass," Shane pointed out.

Acrimony flared in Kirk's stormy blue when he looked at Barrett. "It's unconditional."

"Fecking *one* way to put it, brither," Shane said. "Anyway. She *kens* that's our place. And she definitely has eyes on it. Now we need to find another strip club."

"Well," I said, throwing him a *I-can't-relate* shrug. "My condolences on your guys' night, you two."

But if anything had come to the surface after hearing that story, it was that Rebecca was willing to do anything—*anything*—to keep Barrett's attention on her. She was a touch crazier than even *I'd* thought.

I glanced at my phone and sighed. It'd only been fifteen minutes, but I was coming to the end of my rope. "Um. I think I'm going to get going. Can you say goodbye to Barrett for me? He looks a little..." I watched him and Rebecca fall into one of their make-out sessions, and nausea rose, "occupied."

"Oh, trust me," Shane said. "I'll have plenty of words for him when he's done."

I stepped in front of him, drawing his bright-blue gaze. "Try to be nice."

He shot me an adorable grin. "Always, lass."

Then I gave each of them a warm hug, before I warned Kirk to get Avril home safe and said goodbye.

When I stepped over the threshold into Barrett's condo, I found it cold and quiet, because everyone else was enjoying the summer night outside. My bare feet threatened to freeze as I walked across the dark hardwood and started to search through the lines of shoes in the closet near the front door. I found my sandals and started to slip them on, bracing myself against the wall of his powder room.

And it was there that I discovered a custom key rack that I hadn't seen before. Multiple sets hung from hooks that sat below the silver-plated logos for each car—Porsche, Chevy, Benz, Maserati, Ferrari—but below that was another rack for miscellaneous keys. His badge for the Roth Tower was hanging there, connected by a single ring to a set of keys. From the middle of the set, a little gold one glimmered in the pot lights. Flashing at me. Daring me to take them. I blinked but didn't hesitate.

Bingo.

Jack Poole Plaza was right next to Barrett's condo, and when I walked out, the Olympic cauldron stood like a silver pinnacle from its fountain; three arms sprouting from the bubbling water below. It was lit up in purple, and behind it, the North Shore Mountains were framed in a sky streaked with orange, red, and pink, beneath a navy blanket of stars. It was so picturesque that I moved past the fountain and walked to the end of the plaza to lean on the railings that hovered above the SeaWall. Though the sun was setting, the city was alive. Many people strolled along the SeaWall, and the boats were coming in to stop at the floating gas station before making their way into Coal Harbour. The seaplanes were still taking off and landing, but they were beginning to slow for the night, docking at the seaport to let their passengers back onto land.

Bubbly and romantic, I watched all of it with my chin leaned on my hand, smiling while I thought about how awe-inspiring Vancouver is and how lucky I was to live here now. Time passed without me noticing, and soon the navy disappeared behind the mountains, leaving them twinkling with the neighbourhoods of

West and North Van. The Lions Gate Bridge blinked into a string of lights that connected Downtown with West Van in two tented peaks. Across the harbour, the nine o'clock gun boomed from Stanley Park, exploding with firelight as it signaled the end of another day in our city.

I felt David's warmth—and caught his tropical scent—before I realized he was there. And when I turned to my left, he was smiling, dressed in a t-shirt with short sleeves that showed off his wolf portrait.

My body started to glow from the inside out. "Hello, stranger."

He looked out into the night. "Rough party, there, princess?"

Brave, I shifted toward him and looped my elbow with his, leaning onto his shoulder. "Not necessarily. Just not in the mood anymore."

"Okay." He touched his lips to my head in one of his signature ghost kisses. I waved away the butterflies that tickled my gut. "Where's Avril? She was out with you."

"Don't worry," I said, softly. "She's in good hands."

"Mmmkay."

Listening to the soft sound of his heartbeat, I closed my eyes and savoured him. But my nervousness was killing off the butterflies one-by-one in short, sharp bites. "David?"

"Yeah, Em?"

"About my job at Roth Pharma—"

"Don't wanna talk about it."

"But, I mean, I know you've been avoiding me this whole week—"

"I haven't been *avoiding* you. I've jus' been, I dunno, keeping a little distance while I figure it out in my head." He shrugged. "I know it's strategic. And I get it, okay? But that doesn't mean I wanna talk about it. Believe me, the less I gotta talk about *them*, the better."

I pulled away to look at him. "Are you sure? Because I really don't want to make you feel some kind of way..."

He watched me before drawing his lips into a thin line and looking at the SeaWall below. "Em, I wanna tell you something."

Brushing my fingers through his curls, I asked, "What, David?"

With one blink, he looked back at me and smiled. "Over the past two months, I realized that my life is much happier with you in it. So, I'd rather have you around—even working for the *devil brothers*—than not." He swallowed as he looked back to the sea. "And I know that you wanna know what's going on. With me. With my illness and all that. But I can't tell you, Em. I wish I could, because then you'd understand. But I can't. So it's not fair for me to be mad about you taking a job for money and experience when you don't know."

I stepped forward and cupped my hand on his face. "I'm not doing this to hurt you. The last thing I want is to cause you more pain than you're already in. But I wish I could help. I wish I could take it all away."

He squeezed his green eyes shut, and when he opened them, they glimmered with hopelessness. "I'm paying for what I owe. Okay? I know you're worried about me, but it's been a long time... And they won't listen. They won't change anything. It is what it is... And I need you to trust me. But you can't fall prey to their lies. Don't believe anything you see in there."

I nodded, trying not to think of the collection of keys that were burning a hole in the pocket of my jean shorts.

He took my head in his hands and gave me a soft kiss on the forehead. "So, can we jus'... go back to normal now? Our normal is kinda helping me stay afloat, here."

Smiling, I took him into my arms and squeezed tight. "Yes. I'd love nothing more."

"Okay," he said.

We cuddled and fell into a comfortable silence. The wind picked up and knocked the seaplanes against the dock, making them sound like wooden wind chimes. I focused on the darkening peaks and valleys of the mountains ahead. Skimming the view for the Two Sisters.

"It's so beautiful," I whispered.

His soft chuckle was comforting. "Yeah, I knew you'd like this view."

I lifted my head to look at him. "It's one of my favourites."

He returned my smile but didn't respond.

Running my gaze down his neck and across his shoulder, I focused on the intricate beauty of his wolf portrait. Each stroke of fur was a perfect blend of black and grey, but the eyes and nose were so sharp that they twinkled like it was alive on his arm. I traced them with my fingertips, making his skin rise in goosebumps from under them.

"Why a wolf?" I asked, breathlessly. "I don't think you've ever told me."

He raised a black eyebrow. "You really wanna know?"

"Of course." My lust was rising again. Crawling from my core like the tickling flames of a slow burn. The amount of champagne that I'd had (before realizing it was probably tainted by blood money) was encouraging it.

"Well," David said, "when I came to Vancouver, my whole world changed. It was hard, Em. Everything was hard to adjust to. Everything was different, and everyone looked at me and Dad like we were nothing. Because we were poor..."

I cuddled into his arm again, thinking of the memory I'd seen last week where Barrett had spat cruel insults at him.

"At first, I was moved by nothing, but as I adjusted to life here, I drew strength from the wolf. It's a symbol of fearlessness and beauty, with such dedication to preserving family, yet surviving on your own when you need to." He paused. "And I know it's silly. But I feel... I dunno. Like it's a part of me."

"That's because it is," I pointed out. "You're wolf spirited. It's the animal form of your spirit."

Luckily, he'd heard too much about Mum, and the mood was too romantic, for him to think I was crazy for preaching my inherited spiritual beliefs. "Wolf spirited," he echoed. "Huh. Makes sense. But see, I don't think I needed you to tell me. I think I knew all along."

Mesmerized by the reflection of the city lights in his eyes, I watched him as my heart started to pound. Desire pulsed from deep within me, and overwhelmed by the scene, it was all too much. The sea. The mountains. The smell of him. The beauty of his words. They had me hooked like an awestruck mermaid, and I couldn't wrestle with the pull any longer.

Then his gaze brushed my lips like he was giving me silent permission, and I stepped forward, pressing them softly into his.

For a millisecond, I thought I'd made a mistake, but then he placed a gentle hand behind my neck and drew me closer. Suddenly, David Mathis was kissing me, and it was *wonderful*. Soft. Passionate. Tender. Flourished with the heat of a thousand suns. His lips felt like sinking into a cushiony bed after a hard day's work. Familiar. Comforting. *True.* Just like I'd imagined them to be when I'd dreamed about him...

He caressed me, asking wordless permission to brush his tongue against mine, and I met him halfway, encouraging him to come closer with every stroke. The seconds that passed allowed us to sink deeper into each other until time sat suspended, and I never wanted it to start again.

"Wow," I breathed, after we'd managed to separate.

He scraped his teeth over his bottom lip like he was trying to hold the imprint of my kiss. Then he grinned as he turned back to the railing. "Jus' don't say anything for a bit. Let it be. Jus' like this..."

I leaned beside him, taking his hand, and lacing our fingers together as we looked back into the night. I'd never been so amazed by anyone in my entire life, and I took those moments to sit with it. Revel in it. *Live* in it. This was my new reality, blooming into life right before me, and I never imagined that a move across the country would change it so viscerally. I was so different from the woman I'd been two months ago...

"Em, no matter what happens, it's gonna be okay, alright?" David marked my forehead with a delicate kiss. "I promise. Everything's gonna be okay."

"Of course, it is," I said, squeezing his hand. "As long as I have my new family—as long as I have *you*—I know it will be."

We turned inwards, and he let go of my hand so he could step behind me and wrap me in his arms. I wasn't sure how long we'd held each other, but it was long enough for me to tune into the rhythm of his heartbeat. Within his embrace, I felt safe. Welcomed. Supported. Like I was finally home...

"Do you want me to take you back to the House?" he eventually asked.

I turned, peeled away a tad, and then kissed him. Again. And again. Discovering that each time was better than the last. "Actually, David Mathis, I think I'd like to take you for a drink," I said, fiddling with the collar of his t-shirt and finding the skin beneath flushed. Full of *him*. Full of life. "How about Cactus Club?"

"Cactus Club?" he said, glancing over his shoulder at the bougie restaurant beside the Olympic Cauldron with a laugh. "Em, you and Avril have been hanging around with those rich bitches too much."

I grinned. "Don't worry, it's on me. Lucky for us, I happen to have five hundred dollars cash on me."

"Wha...? *Five hundred?*"

"Yeah, don't ask."

CHAPTER 33
CASTLE OF GLASS

On any other day, taking the elevator from the parking garage to the lobby of the Roth Tower would have been a normal thing. But that Sunday at the end of June, I was there alone and on a mission. The air conditioning smacked me in the face like a tidal wave of the purest ventilation, and I raised my chin as I stepped out of the elevator. Pulling my own badge from my pocket, I let myself through and pleaded with my heart to stop pounding as I tucked it away and watched the security guards pop their heads up from their station. I smiled as I rolled up, but the two of them looked at each other, each trying to gauge the other's reaction.

I yanked my best acting voice from the depths of my bravery and leaned on the counter. "Hi. I'm Emily. The new receptionist."

"Emily." One of them chewed on my name like he was trying to draw out the taste. "Hi. What are you doing here on a Sunday?"

Pouting, I sighed. "Oh, well, I got the strangest call from Barrett Roth earlier. He told me that he urgently needed some documents scanned from the library, but that he couldn't get a hold of Adam. So, here I am. Up for the task as the newbie."

"What a dick," the other one said. "You'd think he could come in and do it himself."

I shrugged. "He said something about being up at his *Whistler* property. I dunno. Plus, I don't think he'd lower himself to that level, anyway. That's what us normal people are for, eh?" The two of them mumbled in agreement, so I decided to play into it further. "I mean,

I was just about to crack open my last beer of the weekend and enjoy some sunshine, but here I am. At the mercy of his beck and call."

"Asshole," the first security guard said, with a short laugh. "He can't do anything for himself, can he?"

I shook my head. "Anyway, the sooner I get this done, the sooner I can make that beer a reality. I'll be down in the library for a bit, okay?"

"Have fun," one of them said, sarcastically.

"You know I only live to serve *his majesty*."

Okay. So that last bit might've been too much. But as I moved toward the elevator and glanced back at them, they seemed none the wiser. They'd gone back to fooling around with the staplers, and I'd gotten away with Barrett Roth's keys in my back pocket. All I had to do now was brave the library and hope that, out of the collection of small keys that I'd stolen, one had been what I was looking for.

The Tower elevator was quick, and soon I'd dropped back into the eeriness of the library. This time, only the emergency lights were on, and it was a cavern of darkness. I'd learned during orientation that this was part of the Roths' sustainability strategy, and a great majority of the lights in the Tower were on motion sensors or timers. Stepping out of the elevator, I rocked from one foot to the other, and discovered that this was the latter. I had my phone, but I knew the flashlight wouldn't be enough, so I started to search the wall for the emergency station that I knew was on each level. As my fingers brushed it, I found the latch, and it opened with a squeak. Then, squinting in the low light, I searched for the flashlight and grabbed it. Who knew that the health and safety training would come in handy?

Clicking the flashlight on, I began to follow its spotlight to the back of the library, where I knew the cabinet labelled *RAP* was hidden in plain sight. I propped it to point at the ceiling, and the light fell like an umbrella, illuminating the keyhole like some horrid, little portal. I dropped to my knees beside the second cabinet from the bottom. Then I pulled Barrett's keys from my pocket and started with the gold one. It slipped in but didn't move. Sighing with frustration, I tried the others one by one, but they refused to budge or even enter the keyhole. There'd only been four on his set that looked like they could fit a filing cabinet, so I'd burned through them in a matter of seconds; failure throbbing between my temples when I sat back on my knees.

No. Work! One of them has gotta work!

Gritting my teeth, I shoved the gold key in again and jiggled it back and forth. Like it was determined to cover for its owner, it refused to budge.

"Fuck!" The library stifled my scream, which made it unsatisfying.

Well, that was it. At least I could take comfort in the fact that Barrett didn't have the key. Maybe he wasn't involved with what was behind that cabinet. Maybe he didn't know about David's suffering. Maybe he was innocent in all this. Maybe I *could* justify the contrasting feelings I'd had for him... Because I would never let myself be seduced by the bad guy, right? Surely the good energy of the Real-Barrett was true...

Then I remembered he'd told me he was aware what David had meant when he said, "I'm compliant," and it made me mad. I slammed the side of my fist against the cabinet, and a quiet click responded. The gold key shifted, and I stared at it in several seconds as it sparkled in the low light. My fingers seemed to move in slow motion, as I reached out and wrapped them around its circular base. I twisted and the key finally turned, unlocking not only that cabinet, but the ones above and below it as well.

I plunged, cold and gasping, into the depths of reality, as I rotated the cabinet's prongs. "You motherfucker!" Pulling the key out, I chucked the set down the length of the aisle before I could stop myself. "Fuck you!"

Then I wrenched the cabinet out to its full extent. Even with its weight, it glided effortlessly, braced on the custom supports that ran from the floor-to-ceiling. Fingers fiddling through the alphabetically ordered names, I skipped forward to M. It was somewhere in the middle, and the hanging folders screeched on the metal bars as I shot them forward. Many of them were filled with documents.

Maalouf, Mabel, Macallister, Madoff—in my flurry I almost missed it, but it stuck out like a flashing alarm—*Mathis*. My breath ran ragged, and I brushed my fingertips over the two files inside. One was much thicker than the other. I pulled them both, sitting back on my knees as I flipped the thicker one forward.

David—99856, it said. Because that's all he was to them. A subject number. Just like his father was at the prison.

I found myself gripping the file so tight, that it was a miracle I didn't give myself paper cuts. For several moments, I battled for control of my emotions, sitting in silence as my knees threatened to put my calves to sleep. I didn't want to open it. It alone had put me into enough shock, let alone the horrors that I'd find inside.

But again, Mum's breathing techniques worked, and I pulled myself to my feet shortly after, snatching the flashlight as I made my way to the same table that Barrett had bled at days ago. I spread out the files and shone the light on the one labelled with David's name. It illuminated like a spotlight of the youngest Roth's red-handed guilt. Drawing a deep breath, I flipped it open.

What are you fucking doing to him?

The first thing was a copy of a contract for something called the "Research Acceleration Program," and this ancient version was signed and dated by Joseph in Halifax. And the witness signature was none other than Johnathan Roth himself. It was ten pages long, and full of legal conditions that I was way too emotional to read. *Subject—company—conditional—agreement;* The words kept scrambling in my brain, so I ignored them for now. I flipped forward to the second thing, which was an updated contract signed by David seven years later when he'd turned sixteen. My jaw clenched when I thought about the tyrannical collateral that they must have used to get him to scrawl his name on that page.

Then, the real terrors began. The pages were filled with details about "products" that they'd administered and their subsequent reactions. Every "appointment," every drug, every side-effect, every awful-fucking-detail was printed out over dozens upon dozens of pages. I pushed back tears as I read through what could have been the life of a lab rat instead of a human being.

Days enrolled: Sixty-five.

Subject administered 600mg of product 0000346 and experienced bleeding through the nose, followed by a migraine headache and nausea including sensitivity to light. Will administer product again in seven days to confirm reaction to product.

I flipped forward.

Days enrolled: 1526.

Subject administered 3cc of product 0006787 and reported no side-effects. Subject returned fourteen days later and administered 5cc of product and after three minutes experienced allergic reaction including minor swelling of throat and tongue. Immediately administered product 0000931 to counter allergic reaction and subject monitored for ninety minutes to ensure reaction under control. Subject instructed to return in seven days to receive 4cc of product to determine reaction threshold.

Trembling, I flipped through what seemed like a novel to more recent appointments, and a familiar event caught my eye:

Days enrolled: 6985.

Subject administered 12mL or product 0075438 intravenously under normal clinical conditions. Subject experienced previously un-seen symptom of "burning veins" before symptoms of severe muscle seizure arose. Subject immediately taken to the emergency room and hospitalized for two days until residue of product was removed. Side-effects previously unobserved with this product, and reaction attributed to possible subject sensitivity to component L-00345 present in product recipe. Made note that subject can never be exposed to product going forward. No other corrective actions required. Product integrity still sound.

A handwritten note was scrawled at the bottom of the page:

Note: Similar reaction seen in subject 021322 at 487 days in enrollment when administered product 0075438.

My breath hitched. I'd watched him go through that. *Felt* him go through that. On paper it seemed so nonchalant and factual, but I'd experienced the pain and the panic. The dread and the hopelessness. The way that it'd made him wish for death.

My God...

They were using him. And for what? Pharmaceutical companies were held to certain standards and liabilities when it came to clinical trials on humans. How were the Roths getting away with this? And what was the benefit to them? What made modern-day torture worth it? Surely it couldn't have just been *profit*.

I thought of the three cabinets in the haunted aisle behind me and all the names that they held. It wasn't just David that they had enrolled in this "RAP." There must have been hundreds of folders in there. John's death *wasn't* the reason they were doing this to him. It was bigger than that. A more horrid nightmare than I could have ever imagined.

A wave of nausea hit, but I grappled with it, pushing myself to flip forward to David's most recent entry.

Days enrolled: 7210.

Subject administered 180mg of product 0098564 and had an immediate seizure. Five days later, subject returned for another administration. Seizure happened again, and four days later subject reported symptoms of dizziness and vertigo—one event causing fainting. Adjustment of the recipe needed? Component N4550? Subject must be exposed to a lower dose to determine probable cause. Will continue to monitor for signs of this reaction in other subjects.

With a frustrated scream, I slammed the folder shut and put my head in my hands. I couldn't read any more. I'd seen enough to know what was happening. They had him trapped. A wolf in the excruciating pain of a leg-hold as a corporate giant crossed his arms and loomed over him. Laughing and laughing. Revelling in his agony as he watches the money pile up.

My body shuddered, begging me to release the tears as I fought for control. I wouldn't let it.

This is it, I thought, staring at the file. This *is what I should do my thesis on. The moral infringements of drug trials, and how big pharma can be held accountable.*

My spirit latched onto the idea, and I finally knew what the Universe had planned for me when I moved here. And I had work to do if I wanted to help David, so I couldn't let my emotions derail that now. Plus, the Roths' library was *not* the place that I was going to release the anguish I held for him.

Determined, I focused on my breath as I took the files of father and son to the copier, punching the buttons as it groaned and lit up in response. I copied everything that I thought could be evidence and tucked the warm papers in a fresh file before I began to scan them to my e-mail. I didn't know what I was going to do with them yet, but I knew that I needed the information if I was going to pursue change. This had gone on long enough, and it had to stop. They were killing David slowly, and he had no power to stop them.

I paused for a sec.

The problem was, neither did I. How was I—a piddly little she-wolf—going to take on two tigers that sat high in their crowns? How would I ever get power or leverage over them?

I didn't know. But I knew who to ask for help.

Wiping the tears that'd leaked through, I packed everything up and returned the files. Then I searched for the glimmering keys as I wound down the aisle with the flashlight, snatching them before I struggled to lock the heavy cabinet.

As I grabbed my copies and returned the flashlight, I thought about David and what he meant to me. Since my move, he'd been a loving and supportive ally—a glowing beacon of hope in my new life—and he made the dark days bearable. He'd been there for me, whether I was missing my parents, or protecting me from the things that I shouldn't know. This entire time, he'd been trying to guide me away from the seduction of evil, and I felt like an idiot for not listening.

Although, if I hadn't been hooked by a Roth, I would've never found any of this out.

It didn't matter. All I knew now was that I was ready to fight for him. I'd do whatever it took. Anything to save him.

When I pulled my Yaris into the driveway at the House-of-Wolves, the frogs and the crickets were chirping cheerfully in a stark contrast to my mood. I spent most of my drive home trying not to be furious with Barrett, and then my emotions had gone into a horrible ebb and flow. They'd push forward to the point that I'd feel like an over-stuffed pillow bursting at the seams, before they'd back off and leave me empty.

And when I stepped across the threshold, I was on that empty side. But then they swelled again when I caught sight of David in the kitchen, popping open a couple of cans of beer with a sizable joint smoldering from between his lips. The sound of laughter from the basement told me that Greg and Avril were down there.

Frozen in dismay, I watched David before he knew I was there, as he hummed to himself. Again. "Find Your Love," by Drake. His curls spread across his forehead when he reached in the fridge for a third can.

Years, I thought, with my skin growing paler. *Almost twenty years of pain and suffering.*

My purse and coat dropped to the floor like heavy burdens that I'd no energy to hold. And I'd left the evidence of his suffering tucked in the back seat pocket of my car. I wasn't going to let it cross our threshold like I'd almost done with Barrett Roth.

The sound drew David's attention along with his beautiful smile. "Hey, you, princess. You're home late." His East-Coast accent was muffled by the joint. "I was startin' to get worried."

Barely breathing, I trudged across our aged hardwood and threw myself into his arms so hard that I almost knocked him off balance.

He set the beer on the counter so he could return it. "Hey, hey. What's wrong, Em?"

My voice wavered when he pulled himself to meet my pained gaze. "I had a really bad day..."

"Ah, princess." He took the un-lit joint between his fingers, kissed me softly, and tucked a wavy strand behind my ear. I rested my head against his chest. "We're playing some right good pool downstairs. Come'n have a drink. And j'eat yet?"

With my cheek rubbing against the soft cotton of his t-shirt, I shook my head. "No, David. I know it sounds bad, but I don't want to see them. Only you. I just want to be with you."

He held me tight and kissed the top of my head—very much un-ghost like now. "Okay. Do you wanna watch TV in my room?"

I nodded like I needed an oil change.

"Okay," he said again, separating us and handing me the joint. "Here. Take that. The lighter's in the nightstand. Let me take these beers down to those guys, and I'll be right up."

Then he left me cold as he disappeared into the basement, and I turned to make my way upstairs. Each step poignant and pained. The faded hardwood creaked in all the familiar spots, and I burst into the room at the top. It comforted me with how warm it was, and how much it smelled like him.

My butt sank onto the edge of his bed, and I dug through the nightstand to find the lighter, hoping to draw some relief from the end of the joint. But my shaking thumb slipped on the trigger when I tried to light it. Once. Twice. Three times. I couldn't get it. I screamed and threw it away as David came up.

Closing his bedroom door, he snatched it and knelt in front of me, lighting the joint with effortless ease. "Em, here. Jus' breathe, okay? Breathe." With a quiet laugh, he began to walk me through a drag like I'd never done one before. "In. Hold, hold, hold. Okay. Now, out."

I listened, letting the weed gift me with relief as I took three more drags.

"There you go." He swiveled to sit on the bed beside me. "Holy mackerel. How bad a day didja have?"

I choked on a laugh as I looked at him, but then I thought about all the pain that those beautiful, green eyes had been forced to see. The tears started rolling down my cheeks.

He wiped them with his thumbs, and then asked me something that men didn't really seem to ever ask me: "Are you gonna talk to me about it?"

My blonde waves flowed from side to side as I shook my head.

He clicked his tongue. "C'mere," he said, pulling me onto his lap.

I set the joint in the ashtray and buried my face in his neck. My arms wrapped around him. Shaking with sobs.

"Ah, princess," he breathed, rubbing my back. "I can't help you if you don't tell me what's wrong."

"I don't need you to help me," I sputtered. "I need you to let me cry."

He nodded and started running his fingers tenderly through my hair.

Gasping from my sadness, I let him hold me as my thoughts sifted through the years of undeserved torture that he'd suffered. "David..."

Why are you stuck in it? And how have you survived them? How've you gotten through this? You incredible man...

"It's okay, Em," he whispered, stroking my head before he kissed me there. "Jus' cry, okay? Jus' cry."

And I listened. Because there was no one that I would have rather been with as I cried louder. As I released all my pain for him. As I let him see a part of me that he'd never seen before. As I fell apart.

CHAPTER 34
THE MAN WHO SOLD THE WORLD

The next day, I pulled into the visitor's parking lot of the Correctional Center in Mission. I was still shaken from my discovery at the Roth Tower—and the intimidating prison guards at the gate hadn't helped—but I was determined. I had to know more about this program, and for that, I'd need to brave those walls again.

Without David, the woman at the front desk asked more questions, but she was kind and she believed me when I told her that I was visiting my boyfriend's father. Subduing my nervousness, I tried to remember the steps that we'd followed before and found that my feet had remembered them better than my brain. After I set off the metal detector and explained myself, they directed me through the double doors to the visiting area, but this time I was told to go to the right. They refused to let me have a contact visit, but *any* face time that I could get with Joseph would help.

Settling myself at a booth that was near the end, I took a deep breath and prepared myself to hear some things that I didn't want to hear. Was I really ready to take action on this? Me? The girl that could barely make breakfast without my parents?

I rubbed my arms and studied the scratches in the plexiglass in front of me as the cold, metal chair bit through the back of my dress. The booths were quieter than I'd expected, and the tapping of my foot soon became annoying enough for me to consciously stop it. I looked around the empty, black booth on the other side, before settling on the pair of matching receivers. One for him. One for me. There was something creepy about the way they hung there. Like some sort of weak defense against the "monster" caged on the other side.

The hair on my arms stood up, and the click of the door made my heart skip a beat. Joseph shot me a look of pleasant surprise as he was escorted through, and he rubbed his wrists again after the guard released him and closed the door. The way he smiled turned the scar on the right side of his face into a deep ridge across his cheekbone. He sat down and picked up the receiver. I followed.

"Emily." His heavy, Eastern accent was muffled by the static of the receiver. "It's a pleasure to look upon such beauty on a Monday night."

I felt a smile tug at my lips. "I was about to say the same to you, Joseph."

He laughed, glancing over his shoulder before he leaned forward. "How'd you manage to get in by yourself?"

"Easy," I said, channeling Barrett-Roth-level confidence. "I'm your common-law daughter-in-law, right?" I even winked like he would. Then cringed inside.

Joseph sat back with a smile. "'Magine. How silly of me to forget. But what brings you to visit a worn-out, old man on a weeknight?"

"Well. Uh. I'm afraid it's not actually *social*, Joseph." I brushed my fingers over a scratch in the metal counter below my elbows. "I came here because I need your help."

His tone turned soft. Not out of character for the loving father that he was. "Emily. Anything I can help you with from behind prison bars, I will."

I dipped my head in thanks. "David's become so important to me. We're close now, as you know... But I'm worried about him, Joseph. Over the past few months, I noticed that he gets sick often. He suffers, and his symptoms are often serious. He even fainted when we went to our roommate's ranch. Fell right off a horse. Did he tell you that?"

A glimmer of anguish ran across his face, before he shook his head. "Ah, Emily. I know what you're gonna ask me. But it en' that simple." He chewed on his bottom lip. Then shook his head again. "I can't tell you."

"Um. Well. I don't need you to tell me. I already know."

He narrowed his eyes a little.

"Did David tell you that I started working at Roth Pharmaceuticals? Did he tell you that Barrett Roth is a friend of mine?" The admission made me shiver on the inside, but I kept still.

Joseph paused carefully. "Yes, me love. He did."

I drummed my fingers on the counter and crossed one leg over the other, foot bouncing. "Um. Well. David tells me things in his sleep sometimes." Technically, not a lie. "And one night he told me that he couldn't deal with the RAP anymore. I figured it had something to do with his condition, so I mentally filed it away. And then I saw a cabinet in the library at work that was marked with the same acronym."

My jittering was starting to bother me. I leaned forward, tucked my foot behind my ankle, and shoved my fingers under my elbow. The pain of David's revelation pulsed in my gut, but I pushed myself to open my mouth and talk to his father about it. "Anyway. I got into the cabinet and found his file. And inside, I found the most horrible things, Joseph. I read the most disgusting details about what they've been doing to him."

I thought I saw Joseph's lip tremble like it had in David's memory.

"I'm not an idiot," I said, with my voice barely above a whisper. "I know you signed a contract that stuck him in that program, and there's a reason why. I wanna help him, Joseph. And I wanna use what little leverage I have to get him out. But I can't do that unless you tell me what I need to know. Right here. Right now." We watched each other, and the tension threatened to snap me like a twig. But my love for David made me brave and fearless, so I didn't back down. I challenged his father; my blue gaze as strong as the she-wolf that had risen within. "Tell me why you killed Johnathan Roth."

I can picture it as he tells me:

A young Joseph is sitting alone at a plain desk in a plain office. It has white walls and bright florescent lights. As he sits, he picks at the corner of the pamphlet that sits in front of him. It's a collection of pages with a laminated cover, and on the front in bold black letters, it says: The Research Acceleration Program. Below that is the red, four-lettered logo of the company: ROTH. He picks it up and lets the pages fall over each other, but he can barely look at it anymore. He's already sifted through it with a fine-tooth comb. Read it cover to cover.

A gentle knock at the door makes him jump, and a blonde woman with a tight bun pokes her head around the corner. "Mr. Mathis? Mr. Roth will see you now."

Joseph nods and makes to stand.

"No, it's quite alright," she says. "You can stay seated here. He's coming in now."

Joseph lowers himself but stays as tense as a targeted wolf. His eyes focus unblinking on the door.

The Devil steps around it, dressed in a sharp, black suit with a leather-clad notebook under his arm. He thanks the woman, and she closes the door, leaving Joseph paralyzed under that black gaze. John gives him a sardonic smile—a motion that resembles his youngest son down to every detail—before he steps toward the table and pulls out the chair.

"Mr. Mathis." He extends his right hand, and Joseph pops up to shake it. "Pleasure to meet you. Johnathan Roth."

"Please, sir," Joseph says, clearing his throat as he sinks back down. "Call me Joseph."

"Very well." John settles himself across the table. He opens his notebook and glances over the notes that he has about the man on the other side. The same one that'll later take his life. "I suppose you're probably wondering why you're seeing the CEO today."

Joseph blinks. He hasn't been wondering that. He's been wondering how the hell he's going to keep himself and his son alive. "Uh."

"This program is an exciting nuance in the industry, so I'd like to be its spearhead," John explains. "Now. I understand that you have some questions you would like to ask me about the program. Are you apprehensive?"

Joseph shifts. "Forgive me, sir. I en' sure what you mean."

With a gentle nod that doesn't mask his impatient obsidian, John rephrases the question. "Are you unsure?"

"Yeah. I'm not sure if this is what I want."

John sits back against his chair. "Alright. Then let me ask you something, if I may." Joseph nods, and he continues. "What drew you to inquire about the program in the first place?"

"My family."

"Your wife?"

Joseph's whole body tenses, and he shakes his head. It's like someone has their hand around his heart and is digging their nails in deep. "No, she passed away. It's jus' me and my son now."

"I'm very sorry to hear that." John's forced sympathy doesn't seem right on him. "How old is your son?"

"Turning nine."

"Do you have a photo?"

Joseph pulls out his wallet and a faded picture of him holding David. They're on a fishing boat, beaming at the camera with nets and lobster traps surrounding them. It was taken a couple years earlier when things weren't so difficult. He passes it to John, who studies it like he's trying to find an angle to wrench. "He's David."

"A handsome young man," John says, passing back the picture. "You must be very proud."

"Thank you, sir," he says. "I am."

"You know, I don't think there can ever be anything more important in a man's life than his son. I should know. I have two of my own." He points forward with his pen. "My youngest is the same age as yours, in fact. Such an enjoyable time, isn't it?"

"Oh, sure is." Joseph laughs a little, but John's expression falls.

"It's an age where he'll listen. Where he still respects every word and heeds you well. So, enjoy it while it lasts." He runs a hand through his dark copper hair, and sighs. "My oldest is a teenager, and I must admit, that's much more of a challenge."

Joseph shakes his head. "Yeah, I'm not lookin' forward to that."

"It requires a lot of standing your ground," John says. "And it will be worth it in the end, but it doesn't make it any less frustrating at the time." He glances at the wall on the other side of the room, and his eyes go all fuzzy before he snaps them back to Joseph. "In any case, there's nothing more important to me than the two of them. My boys. I would do anything for them. Anything to protect them. Anything to give them the best. You know, even as a man who built his company from the ground up, they are still the pride and joy of my existence. Nothing makes a man worthier. It's hard to understand until he is in your arms for the first time. I'm sure you would agree."

"Yes, sir. David is everything to me."

"I understand." John pauses. His raven gaze scans Joseph like he's calculating his next move. "You may correct me if I'm wrong, but it seems to me that you are stuck in an unfortunate situation where there is nothing left for you here. Where there is nothing left for *David* here."

Joseph ignores the twinge of embarrassment. Instead, he nods.

Then John taps on the pamphlet with his pen. "This program, Joseph, opens up a world of possibility, and opportunity. Not only for your son but also for yourself. Think about it. What I'm offering here is a chance for you to start over in the most beautiful city in the country. Where the possibilities are endless, and you have the chance to improve both of your lives drastically. I'm sure you've read the section on life in Vancouver?"

Joseph swallows. "It looks like a beautiful place. Different. But beautiful."

"It is an *incredible* place." John breaks out his perfect grin. "The most amazing city in the world, in fact. And I'm not just saying that because I was born and raised there." The quick wink that he gives Joseph makes him look too much like Barrett. "There is nothing you can't do—that *David* can't do—after you move out. He will have access to the best. The best education, the best careers, the best quality of life. I'm sure that you want nothing less for him. And I can help you give that to him, Joseph. Father to father. You don't need to do this alone anymore."

Joseph hesitates before he braves John's face. "Mr. Roth, the program says that, as long as we're enrolled, you'll cover the relocation and housing costs."

"Correct. Pending the housing is approved under the program."

"And in return?"

"And in return, you actively participate in our ongoing research program," John says, spreading his hands. "At intervals and times that are convenient for you. When it doesn't interfere with your new life."

"I'm not sure I like the sound of 'research program' when what you make is drugs."

"I assure you, it is perfectly safe," John says. "You will only be exposed to products that are in the final stage of development, and we are open to negotiation on anything you have concerns with. I know it may sound frightening, but it isn't. We will do everything it takes to make you comfortable, because the simple fact is, we need help from people like you."

"Yeah?" Joseph says, defiantly. "Then why don't you offer it to people that live there?"

John chuckles like he's about to explain something simple to a kid. "Well, we do, however, it isn't as practical as you'd think it would be. Vancouverites have comfortable lives and can be quite greedy, and I have a business to run, Joseph. Contemporary technical advances—although significant—haven't allowed us to extend this program beyond our city. We need our subjects close. So, it made a lot more sense to extend the offer to people that deserve the opportunity to move there. People like yourself and David, who would like a second chance. Who would like to start over. Somewhere new."

Joseph drops his eyes and flips through the pamphlet again. He can feel John watching. "What if I don't want David enrolled? Jus' me?"

"I'm afraid that's not possible. We need both of you. And let me stress that, as long as he's enrolled, his housing costs in Vancouver will be covered, even after he's on his own."

"But this contract says that he'll be enrolled until he's forty, Mr. Roth," Joseph says, flipping to the page that says it. "That's a *right* long time."

"I agree. It is. But think of the financial stability he'll have if he doesn't need to worry about housing costs until then. He'll be able to save up enough money to build the life that he wants. To build the life that he's going to want for his own family someday. You're giving him that peace of mind."

Joseph skims the pamphlet, but he's not really reading it. He starts to run through the scenarios in his head. It's a lot to risk...

"Joseph." John's quiet tone pulls him from his thoughts. "You don't have to sign today. You have the freedom to think about it and ask as many questions as you'd like. I will be here for the week." He falls into a pregnant pause, waiting for Joseph's reaction. "But, sitting here, I get the distinct sense that you've already been considering it. Haven't you?"

Joseph looks up and thinks about how unsettling this man is. Big pharma CEO. Devil in disguise.

Does he really want to sell their souls?

John leans forward, palm flat on the table. The rubies in his gold wedding band sparkle in the florescent light. "As one man to another, I implore you to make your decision, Joseph. Because it will eat you alive if you don't. And all you need to do is ask yourself one question: What kind of future do you want for David?"

Joseph looks, studying Johnathan Roth as he repeats the question to himself. He already knows the answer, even if he's scared to admit it. Where he's from, opportunities like this are rare, and he can think of many people that would've jumped at the chance to give their children the life that they deserve. Whatever the cost.

He swallows and asks the next question feebly. "How soon can we leave?"

John breaks out his smirk, and I know that look. I've seen it many times on his son. It's the one that says he knows he's got him. "As soon as you'd like. We can have you and David on a plane to Vancouver as early as tomorrow morning." Then he has the audacity to smile while he offers Joseph the pen. "All you need to do is sign."

Joseph watches it like a viper about to strike, before he takes it with dainty fingers. He winds it through them, back and forth. The contract seems to exude urgency, and he can feel the opportunity slipping away with every tick of the clock on the wall. He doesn't know how dangerous it is yet. He doesn't know that it will trap him and his son in something he'll regret later. All he thinks about is how he can do the best with what he has. With what he's been given.

He holds his breath and asks David to forgive him. "Okay," he says, exhaling. And he signs both copies without looking back.

"So, this program," I asked, from the other side of the plexiglass. "It pays for your housing costs as long as you agree to be tested on like a lab rat?"

Joseph nodded, solemnly. "What they do is they 'recruit' people that're desperate, so they can trick them into a program that's torturous. The RAP pays for housing costs—that much is true—but what they fail to mention is that it's low-cost housing in the pits of Vancouver."

I looked away, calculating how to word my response. "Forgive me, Joseph. But, even in desperation, how could you think that was a good idea?"

He frowned. "David don't ever talk about his life in Dartmouth, does he?"

I shook my head. He didn't, really. Other than teaching me Eastern slang. All I knew about his life there was what I'd seen in his memory.

"That's because we were in a bad place," he said. "Especially 'round the time I decided to make that horrible decision." He looked pained. "I was having a hard time after my wife died. I struggled to provide alone. And my poor boy... He was starving, Emily. I was starving. I couldn't afford to renew my trapping license, so I took some risks and made some bad decisions. Did some bad things to feed him and keep a roof over his head. By the time I met Johnathan Roth, I was in deep, and I owed a lot of money to some very dangerous men." Tears shimmered in his eyes. "I was so scared, Emily. So afraid. I couldn't even sleep, because I thought they'd come slit my son's throat in the night."

I covered my mouth.

Joseph wiped his face with his thumbs. "And Johnathan Roth... he had himself a silver tongue."

"Yeah." I swallowed. "I can think of someone else like that."

He took a deep breath and looked at the wall over my shoulder. "David," he said, more to himself than me. "I made a bad call to save his life, but what life did I give him in return?"

I leaned forward, adopting a sympathetic tone. "You were only trying to do what little you could to protect him," I said. "And I understand now. You just made a mistake."

"A mistake that my son still lives with today..."

Sitting back, I searched for meaning in the patterns etched into the metal. Finally, I sighed. "So, that's why the illness. It's a side effect of whatever they choose to test on him. But why won't he talk to me about it?"

"He's under a non-disclosure-agreement, Emily," Joseph said. "He *can't* talk about it. I am too, but for me, it don't matter. What're they gonna do? Put me in a worse prison?"

Right. Because this "program" that the Roths are running is full of moral wrongdoings. We wouldn't want people having the right to talk about that now, would we?

But one critical piece was missing. "Why did you shoot him, then? Did you think his death would null your contract or something?"

He looked at me for several seconds; grazing parts of my face like he was trying to decide what to tell me. "I thought we could run. I thought if he was dead, then we could escape. But it didn't work that way."

I coiled the cord and searched him back. There was something about his answer that didn't add up, but I'd have to leave it for now. I had more important things to deal with first. "They're killing him, Joseph. So, we have to get him out. Maybe, if I could talk to Travis then—"

"No." The way he cut me off was sharp and firm. "*Barrett*," he said. "It's Barrett that you need to go after, Emily. You say you're good friends with him, so maybe he'll listen. People think he's like his father because of how he looks, but what if he isn't? What if he wouldn't be, for you?" He tapped on the counter. "If we're gonna win this fight, you need to keep him in your back pocket. Stay in his good books, ya know? 'Cus Barrett's the one, me love."

Barrett's the one... It echoed in my thoughts. *Is that why I've been calling for him? So I can stand up and make him accountable for the injustices his father created? Is that what the Source wants?*

I remembered the collection of keys hidden in my purse, and my anger threatened to rise. "Maybe he will."

Then, I met Joseph's gaze through the scratched plexiglass. "The first time I got into the cabinet, I copied a bunch of stuff. But I was emotional and neurotic. I think I need to go back there. Gather more evidence."

He nodded. "Be careful, though, sweetheart."

"Don't worry. I have my tactics." It just needed to be soon. It wouldn't be long until Barrett noticed that some of his keys were missing. If he hadn't already.

Joseph looked like he was swallowing all his life mistakes at once. "Emily—"

Three loud bangs from his side made us jump. "Wrap it up in there, Mathis! Visiting time was over ten minutes ago!"

Joseph sneered before turning back to me. He softened and started again. "Emily. I'm so sorry that you have to fix my fuck up. But I've never known anyone that cares about David like you do. If anyone can help him, I trust you to."

I wiggled my toes.

"But be careful and be cautious, me love. Because playing with Roths is a dangerous game. You already know that."

Huffing out my emotion, I nodded.

"And listen to me. Don't you *ever* forget these words." Joseph leaned forward. "Never trust a man with the last name Roth. *Never.*"

"Okay," I agreed, in a soppy whisper. "And thank you, Joseph. Your vulnerability has helped me in ways that you can never imagine."

"I jus' hope it's enough to save him," he said, miserably.

I put my palm flat against the plexiglass, and smiling, he did the same. But then our improvised connection was cut short.

The guard came in to take him away.

CHAPTER 35
BURN THE EVIDENCE

The next Tuesday at work had me pushing my emotional self-control to the limit. As I walked across the marble and through the gates, all I could think of was David and what he'd said before I started: *You don't know what they do.* And now that I knew the truth, I was horrified to be there.

The first thing that I wanted to do was quit so that I could stop supporting a company that profited from oppression, but I knew that was a stupid move. If I was here, I could gather evidence and listen for new information. I could get closer to Barrett and determine the best angle at which to pull on his heart strings. As long as I was here, David had a chance, and so did my thesis. So, I grinned and bared it, now painfully aware that knowledge was much more traumatic than ignorance.

But I couldn't get David's suffering out of my head. It was all I could think about, and his cries of agony echoed in my mind like they were bouncing from the walls of the Roth Tower.

About an hour into my shift, Barrett was in the lobby chatting with a couple other members of the senior leadership team, and I tried my hardest not to glare at him from behind the desk. He was dressed in black slacks, and a maroon jacket over a cream-coloured dress shirt that was open to the top of his chest. His brown-red hair was swept back in its signature wave, and the maroon complemented the red undertones perfectly, making him look straight off the cover of *GQ*. This didn't go unnoticed by Adam, who sat there watching with his chin rested in the palm of his right hand, and a dreamy smile spread across his face.

Almost like clockwork—or a deliberately typed DM—our coworker Katie appeared, leaning against the counter beside Adam as she pretended that she had a reason to be there. The two of them were regular "Barrett-admirers," I'd learned. Big fans of The Bad-Roth. And they spent their downtime watching him from a distance—especially on days when he looked good enough to surpass his brother on their "gorgeous meter." It was an odd hobby of theirs. A tidbit of excitement to brighten up a mediocre day.

And I couldn't blame them. I used to do the same thing before I found out what his set of keys unlocked.

"Check him out today, Kate," Adam said, like it wasn't the reason that she was there in the first place. "God, he looks good enough to eat."

"Love the jacket," she said, with a less-than-subtle glance over her shoulder. "Very sophisticated and sexy."

"Doesn't he pull it off flawlessly?" Adam added.

"Sure does," she agreed.

Adam sighed longingly. "God, I wish he was gay."

"God, I wish he'd notice me," she said. Then they shared in some awkward laughter, while I rolled my eyes.

"Um, isn't there some sort of HR policy against this?" I couldn't help but ask.

Katie shrugged. "I won't tell if you won't."

I sighed.

Right. I forgot for a sec that the rules don't matter here. That's just how things work at Roth Pharmaceuticals, *isn't it?*

I stood up.

"Where do you think you're going?" Adam said, turning a burning gaze at me.

"Coffee." I pointed to the elevators.

"Good." He looked me up and down. "You look like you need one."

I shook it off, but my feet fell heavily across the floor. It was a beautiful summer day, so I'd worn a flowy dress with a black cardigan and had replaced my regular set of heels with flats. I noticed that the marble was colder than usual today.

As I passed, Barrett offered some handshakes to those around him, and my heart started to pound when he called me.

Don't scream at him. Do not *scream at him.*

It took everything I fucking *had* to turn and throw him a smile. I took a deep breath, shielding myself from his intoxicating smell as he trotted over.

"Morning, kiddo!"

"Uh. Morning, Bear."

Across the lobby, Adam and Katie looked really jealous.

"Where are you headed?" he asked.

I shrugged. "Going to get coffee."

"Perfect! So was I. Jerry's outside today. Would you care to join me?"

"Who's Jerry?"

He chuckled, and my skin tingled uncomfortably as he placed a hand on the small of my back. "Who's Jerry? Only the best coffee truck owner in Vancouver. Trust me, you won't be disappointed."

I gave him another forced smile. "Um. Okay."

Outside, the gentle breeze was refreshing, and the sun shone like it was trying to pull me out of my gloom. I followed Barrett down the steps and to the street side, where a small coffee van was parked at the curb. He made his way over to order, and I drifted toward the fountain, dropping myself to sit on the raised edge. Then I studied the curve of his shoulder blades through the jacket. The way the sun caught the glimmers of red through his hair. How the tip of his ancient scar was visible above his collar. I studied his every move like prey.

How many wolves does it take to bring down a tiger?

Maybe just one, but I had to be smart about it.

He smiled and handed me my coffee as he sat down beside me, angling himself in a position that was (presently) too close for comfort.

I thanked him and drew a sip. It was hot-but-not-scorching, so I sipped a little more. Across Burrard, a man hobbled his way north up the perfectly manicured streets. He looked out of place. Like the city was shining a spotlight on his poverty. I shivered despite the heat.

"Hey, question for you," Barrett said. "During my party on Friday, did you happen to see a set of keys laying somewhere odd?"

My hands turned clammy. Not able to meet his eye, I shook my head.

"And nowhere on the first floor of the Tower? Sitting off to the side of the counter, perhaps?"

I shook my head again.

He patted his suit jacket. "Huh. I have the whole team upstairs on the lookout for them. I haven't the foggiest what I've done with them."

Oh God...

"Sorry to hear that," I said, like we were standing over an open casket at a wake.

"What ails you today, kid? You don't seem yourself." Barrett's enquiry was gentle, and I was glad he'd turned the topic. He couldn't see me as a suspect of key theft. It would fuck everything up.

I set my cup on the platform between us and ran my fingers through the cool water of the fountain. I was doing anything I could to avoid looking at him. "I guess I have a lot on my mind."

"Yeah?" After a sip of coffee, he released a small, satisfied sigh. "Well, talk to me."

Crossing my legs and smoothing out my dress, I cradled my

coffee back in hand. And when I finally looked at him, I focused on the sound of the bubbling fountain to stop myself from getting lost in that obsidian. "Bear, if I had a problem, would you help me with it?" It was an honest question, but I didn't know if I could believe his answer.

He twitched a copper eyebrow. "Of course. Without hesitation, Em."

I looked back across the street and watched the man inch his way toward the coast in quiet determination. One painful step after another, he was still going.

I drew another sip of my coffee. When I looked at Barrett again, the weight of his father's gaze was heavy. "I want to trust you..." My whisper amplified the thought before I could stop it.

He shifted closer. "Em, when have I ever given you a reason not to trust me?"

I couldn't think of a lie to cover it, so I didn't say anything. Then I thought about his keys and felt *extra* awful.

He put a hand on my shoulder and spoke softly. "What's on your mind, kiddo?"

Shuddering internally, I looked at him again. I was desperate to talk to him about the RAP, but something was off with the timing. If I brought it up, I'd have to know how to cover my bases, and I'd need to be prepared for any outcome. After all, I was dealing with a Roth. Sitting there on the fountain, I felt far too "unguarded" to go for it. I needed something more. A heavier dose of leverage, in case he started to push back.

So, I lied and gave him a small smile. "Guess I'm just stressed out about school."

He chuckled. "Well. I'm afraid I can't help you there. Geography nerd, remember? Ethics was never my strong suit."

His last sentence was so ironic.

"It's a little overwhelming," I said.

He rubbed my shoulder. "Yes, but you'll get through it. You're one of the strongest people I know, Em. You can handle it."

This pulled on something inside me, and I ended up saying, "Really?"

He nudged me. "Hey. Would I lie to you?"

That was loaded—coming from a Roth.

Then, Travis rounded the corner and went up the coffee cart. It was the first time I'd seen him since finding the file, and my she-wolf growled a little. Surely as CEO, he knew about his immoral research program. I mean, so did Barrett, but I had to keep Barrett on my side, so I'd have to at least *pretend* to like him.

In the warmer weather, Travis had slipped off his jacket and was in his dress shirt. The white was clean in a blinding kind of way.

"How's business today, Mr. Roth?" Jerry's voice was muffled from inside the van.

"Business is fantastic, Jerry," Travis said.

Fantastic when you run it on oppression.

I thought back to the Roth Banquet and all the achievements the brothers had presented. They'd flourished their company like some golden beacon of sustainability and progress— Which, in some sense, it actually was. But underneath it all lay this horrid cesspit of immorality.

Why?

They both seemed so authentic in their efforts to run a respectful company. (Well, as respectful as a big pharma company could be.) What would make both Travis and Barrett okay with having a program like the RAP at their foundation? Did they inherit it from John and not think anything of it? Were they aware of its horrors, but were consciously hiding the bad and the ugly by spotlighting the good? And if so, what the fuck? Was that just a Roth thing, or...?

Travis handed Jerry a ten-dollar bill, and Jerry gave him his coffee. "I'm telling you though, my life would be a lot easier if I didn't have an atrociously *useless* CFO. What a pain in the ass that is." He shot an amused glance at Barrett. "Oh, sorry. I didn't see you there, brother."

Barrett pinched his lips to one side.

Grinning, Travis raised his coffee cup to the truck owner. "Thanks, Jer."

"Anytime, Mr. Roth," Jerry said, before phasing inside.

Sighing, Barrett leaned on his knee. "You know how I can tell you're getting old, brother? You're making dad jokes, and you're not even a dad yet. That's how old you are, Trav."

"That's uncalled for," Travis said. "Don't be envious that I'm turning into a silver fox."

Barrett huffed out a laugh and looked at me. "Someday he's going to get over himself, right? I am praying *to God*. Either that, or I'm going to have to fork over a bunch of money to have the research and development team make a cure for *I'm-sexy-and-I-know-it* syndrome."

Travis put a hand to his chest. "Emily, do I look like a man that suffers from such a thing?"

The way he'd included me made me stifle a jump, so I was glad when Barrett answered. "You were born suffering from it, Travis Benjamin."

Travis downed some coffee before checking his watch. "Anyway, Bear. On a more serious note, I'm aware that it's beautiful out, but you're going to have to wrap it up. I need your advice on a couple of things. My office. Five minutes."

"Alright," Barrett groaned.

"Emily." Travis nodded before heading back to his Tower.

Barrett watched him go. "They really need to add 'slave to the CEO' to my job title, because half of the time, that is what I am. That, or 'my brother's bitch.' Either would suffice." He stood and stretched his back.

Despite how I was feeling, I giggled. "Thanks for the coffee, Bear."

"Anytime." He pinched my chin and raised it before he left. "Keep your chin up, kiddo."

The next Sunday, I snuck back into the library to continue my research. I didn't want to risk going down there during the week in case it raised suspicion. Especially with everyone and their mother asking about Barrett's keys.

The security guards were easier to fool that weekend. I spun a story about how I was voluntold to do overtime filing, and we joked around for a minute before their guard dropped completely. Having a badge assigned by their company helped, but as I walked off to the elevator, I thought about how they should probably hire better security.

Knowing the tricks also helped, and down in the library I opened the cabinet with a sure pound of my fist. My anger reared as I slid it open, and once again I swore at Barrett before I chucked his keys down the length of the aisle. Huh. I'd have to be careful with that. The last thing I wanted was to lose them.

Running my fingers along the tabs inside, I thought about how I should probably copy some of the documents in the other folders, but my emotions took me straight back to the one labelled *Mathis*. I pulled it out, clamping down on my tongue to stifle the squeak. His file was heaping with horrors, so maybe it would be better to dig out some of his other high-impact events first?

Huh. Either way, it was gonna suck to read that shit.

Suddenly, a dark figure at the end of the aisle caught my attention, and I froze like a deer in headlights. The library plunged into a deep freeze, and my veins filled with ice. I watched wide-eyed as it glided toward me, morphing into the ghostly shape of a man. And as the shadows moved across its form, I recognized Johnathan Roth.

My breath hitched.

Oh my God, oh my God, oh my God!

The silence made my heartbeat pound between my ears. I started to hyperventilate, and I wanted to bolt, but I couldn't move. It was like his ghost had me stupefied, and I couldn't do anything but watch as the spirit came closer.

What's gonna happen? What's he gonna do to me??

The flashlight picked up the shimmer of red in his hair. A glimmer of black velvet played through his eyes. "Emily," he said.

Shaking, I backed into a kneeling position, trying to gather the strength to get up and run to the door. My legs and lungs burned, but he kept coming. I was on the verge of screaming for my life when he stepped into the light—

"B—Barrett?"

Of course, it was fucking *Barrett.* What the hell was I thinking? John was *dead!*

My guard dropped like someone had turned gravity back on, and I exhaled. But then I had another problem.

Shit.

If this was Barrett, then he'd caught me red-handed. And suddenly, the ghost option was much more preferable.

I dropped to my knees. "I—I'm sorry. I thought you were..."

"You thought I was *who,* Emily?"

I swallowed. "Doesn't matter."

In the dark of the library, his black eyes burned like coal. "It seems you forgot to ask me if you could borrow these." He held up his keys. They jingled from the tip of his finger like a tattletale. "Then also forgot to mention you had them when I asked you."

"Bear..."

"Emily," he said, his jaw tensing. "What the fuck do you think you're doing?"

I stammered again, and he moved forward, snatching the folder. He read David's name and hit me with a look of accusation. "Of course," he said to himself.

"Bear, please. Let me explain."

"Alright then, give it your best shot." He stuffed David's folder back and slammed the drawer shut. Then he pounded on it, jiggling the key in the stubborn lock. "Fucking cabinet!"

I backed off, gut ringing in alarm. His energy was off again, and I realized that this was the other version of him. The one I hated and feared. The Hyde to his Jekyll. The Bad-Roth come to life on a whole other level. I had to tread lightly.

"Go on!" he said, his obsidian flaring as he wheeled around to face me. "Give me one good reason why I shouldn't fire you. Right now."

I took another step back, trying to think about where to start. Joseph was right. I needed him on my side, and I couldn't fuck this up. Already, my chances weren't looking great.

If only I'd gotten the Real-Barrett...

"Bear, please listen. I can explain." I paused to do a mini breathwork session. "Since I got here, I've noticed David getting sick. At first, I didn't think anything of it, but lately his symptoms have been getting worse, and I was worried, so I started to investigate—"

"Right," he cut in. "So then, he told you all about the RAP, did he? Because how else could you know?"

"No, he didn't tell me—"

"Of course," he said to himself. "*Of course!* That's why you asked me to hire you. So you could gain my trust, and then break into the library behind my back, for what? To quench your *Medical Ethics* thirst? To gain leverage against my brother and I for a program that David is enrolled in, completely legally and at his own will?" He scoffed. "How could I be so fucking foolish?"

"No," I rebutted. "Me working here had nothing to do with it, I swear! I didn't find out until after—"

"How, then?" His tone was as sharp as a razor blade.

"Um. Well. Uh. Here's the thing, Bear." He put his hands on his hips expectantly, and I blurted, "David didn't tell me. Joseph did."

Silence smothered us as he glared at me in the dark. I'd never told him that I had met Joseph before, and I caught the betrayal that flicked across his features. Then he tried to mask it by taking a sharp breath and looking away. "I get it."

"Bear, please," I said, again. "This has nothing to do with me picking sides, alright? My friend is suffering, and I was desperate to find out why! He doesn't talk about it—never said a word—because he can't. You have him under an NDA."

He fanned a finger at me. "That's right. And guess what, Em? That's *exactly* what you're going to sign. Right now." Turning, he stormed back down the aisle. "Come with me," he shot, over his shoulder. "We're going to my office."

I was just about to tell him to go fuck himself, but then I remembered that I needed him. There was still room to fix this if I was smart. I followed him to the elevator, tearing my brain apart in search of my next move. I'd have to be submissive and apologetic. He was angry and high-strung right now. If I went on the offense, that would only make things worse.

He grabbed my arm and wrenched me into the elevator, and I tried not to gasp. Once I was inside, he pressed the button for the top of the Tower so hard that it made a sound.

I side-stepped to distance myself from him. "H—How'd you know I was down there?"

"I was in my office," he growled, "so your unanticipated presence on the security cameras was of great interest to me." He gripped his right wrist with the left and the skin below turned white.

"Bear, okay. Look. Please. David's my friend, and I can't watch him suffer anymore. It's as simple as that."

The elevator broke through the underground, raising us into the late afternoon light. He didn't answer.

"And all I want is to learn more about this program so I can influence positive change and get him out. I promise that I'm not being vindictive. The only reason I broke into the library is because

I'm desperate." We rose higher, and my ears popped. I braved a gentle touch to his arm. "Please, Barrett. I really need your help."

He shrugged it off and moved forward as the elevator opened. "I cannot help you."

The top floor was open in the middle, with the offices around the outside. They were separated with a special kind of glass that could be frosted for privacy. This was where all the bigwigs sat, and I'd never been up here before. I followed him to the left side, where the two biggest offices were marked with gold name plates that said: *Travis Roth, CEO and President of Roth Pharmaceuticals, Barrett Roth, CFO and Senior Vice-President of Roth Pharmaceuticals.*

As we stepped inside the giant office "worthy" of a pharma giant executive, my temper flared. It was so big that he had his own fucking boardroom at the front.

"*Can't* help? Or *won't* help, Barrett?"

He stepped behind his massive desk, and in the light of the top floor, I caught how dilated his pupils were. His degrees and achievements were framed on the solid wall beside it, and sticking out among them was a side-profile of a tiger's head, wearing a glimmering gold crown set with rubies. It reminded me of the one that Kirk had tattooed on his left forearm.

"You own half of this company," I said, as I stood by the leather chairs that sat on the other side of his desk. "Don't tell me that you can't help me."

"I don't, actually. Publicly traded company and all. It's a little more complicated than that." He plopped into his billionaire's office chair and ran his hand through his hair three times. Then he started speaking so fast that I had trouble catching the words. "I do, in fact, own a significant portion, but my brother owns more. That asset difference gives him a lot of power over me, Em. The RAP is managed by him, and I have little to no involvement. He calls the shots. I'm not responsible for it."

"*What?*"

A framed portrait of John on the opposite wall caught my eye. He sat regal in suit and tie, with his expression stern and intimidating. His hands were folded on the desk in front of him, and I saw the golden wedding band that Joseph had described, glistening from his ring finger. His obsidian gaze followed me. I glared back.

"How are you not responsible?" I spat at Barrett. "This is *your* company, Bear! You can't just sit here and do nothing! And this program that you *two* are running is completely immoral, cruel, and wrong. You're violating basic human rights and taking advantage of people, for your own profit. You've gotta take accountability!"

He clicked through his laptop with lightning speed. His hand vibrated as it curved over the mouse. "Emily. You'd be foolish to think that profit is made from honesty. There isn't a billionaire on this Earth that doesn't break the moral code on a daily basis. You should expect no less from us.

"And, in addition, business is complex, and this program is *not*, in fact, immoral. It is a matter of goods and services. I don't expect *you* to understand this, however, if you need someone to listen to your concerns, our legal team would be able to assist you with obtaining the understanding that you require."

My temples bulged. "You sound like your fucking father."

"And you would know, would you?" He snatched the NDA from the printer and put it in front of me, raising an expectant eyebrow as he offered me a pen. Now he *really* looked like his dad.

"Fuck you, Barrett." Furious tears burned the back of my eyes. "You're supposed to be my friend. You're supposed to understand and sympathize with my point of view. You're supposed to help me when I need it!"

"Yeah? Then don't give me a reason to go after you with everything I have. Trust me, I don't want to have to do that. I can crush anyone in this town, but I'd rather it not be you." He clicked the pen and offered it again. "Sign."

I snatched it from him, but my vision blurred so fast that I couldn't read what I was signing. It was probably stupid for me to find the line at the bottom and scroll my name without reading it, but I was so emotional that all I wanted was to get out of there. I'd fucked up so bad by turning him against me, and the anger at myself was almost as intense as what I was directing at him. How was I going to get David out without his help? And how could he do this to me? I thought we had a connection... I thought he'd understand... Why would I have screamed his name all this time if he was the bad guy?

Wiping my face, I tried to ignore how both him and his father were watching me. I couldn't stand this Hyde version of him. This Bad-Roth—who he turned into when he wanted to mask himself. In fact, I fucking *despised* him.

If only he'd come to me as himself and not the monster that he morphs himself into...

Knowing I'd already ruined my chances, I set my fury on him. And I decided that I was going to hit him with some of the biggest lies that I've ever told to someone, just because I knew it would hurt.

"You were right, by the way. This whole time. It turns out that you know yourself a hell of a lot better than I do." I shrugged. "You're a pathetic, coward-of-a-man that hides behind his money and revels in playing the bad guy. You dye your hair to stop yourself from looking like your father, but you are *exactly* like him, anyway! True Devil's son, aren't you?" Choking back tears, I threw the pen onto the desk. "And I fucking hate you, Barrett Roth."

After I said it, I couldn't look at him. I turned and ran from his office, desperate to be anywhere but there.

CHAPTER 36
WHAT'S UP, DANGER?

The streetlights on Highway Ninety-Nine passed in a rhythmic whoosh.

One. Two. Three. Four.

I was counting them so I wouldn't run my car off the road. Every muscle in my body was sore from being clenched too tight, and my head threatened to explode into a ball of outraged confetti. My throat ran dry from all the ragged breathing I'd done. I was sure the chakra was straining to be released.

One. One. One.

I clutched my steering wheel, thinking about my move to Vancouver and how it was supposed to change my life. My idea had been simple. I was supposed to come here, get my master's, and dip my toe in independence before flying back home to tuck under the covers of my childhood bedroom knowing that's where I belonged.

But now I knew I didn't. Now my life was so wildly complex. Now I was intertwined with the messiness of two opposing men, a murder, and a tyrannical drug trial program that I just couldn't ignore. I'd had my own plans, but the Universe had taken over, and Their plans had turned out to be so much bigger. The signs had been followed and the path had been forged, but I had no idea where else to go. It was like being led straight to a cliff face overlooking a storm-ridden sea—the only choices being to jump or turn back.

What was I supposed to do?

Which one was I supposed to choose?

I glanced into the rearview, hoping to find the answers bobbing along in between the other cars. But in life, there was no rearview. There was only the road ahead. And I knew that road would be wrought with reckless idiots, and potholes, and cars driving the other way. Maybe even a sign crashing down, or two. But if I was going to make it to the other side and into a brighter future, I'd need to be strong. I'd need to be fearless. I'd need to use the whole pallet of the newfound confidence that I'd gained from being a whole country away from my parents. Away from where I felt safe.

I couldn't lapse back into that older Emily—trembling on the plane to Vancouver. Pining for Mum and Dad like a wayward pup. I'd have to embrace my independence to be strong enough to stand up for others. Wasn't that the whole reason I got into ethics in the first place?

My knuckles turned white.

Now that I knew about the RAP and the true nature of the Roths, I wouldn't turn away. I was the new Emily; armed with the weapons to survive and no longer afraid to venture out on my own. I was a Valkyrie; strapping on some shiny new armour as I stepped into the battle against injustice. A she-wolf; teeth bared against a couple of oversized fat-cats that stuffed themselves while starving others.

The fight had only begun, and I couldn't shy away. Here, I was needed. Here, I'd have to stay. Here, I'd have to stand. I'd have to run toward the danger, because it was my only way forward. My reason for jumping into that stormy sea. My true purpose here.

For David and the others, that battle was worth it. For David and the others, I'd have to stand my ground and fight.

I dropped my things in the general direction of the closet at the House-of-Wolves, then made my way to the kitchen to grab a beer from the fridge. Popping the top from the bottle, I tossed it into the garbage and glanced out the window before taking a deep swig. Outside, the weather had turned, and heavy rain was starting to fall along with the gentle rumblings of thunder.

Storm's coming, Em. You'd better be ready.

The quiet drone of the TV in the living room drew my attention, and I followed it with heavy feet, finding Avril curled up in the armchair and David lying on the couch. Avril greeted me with her normal cheeriness, but my horrible mood wouldn't let me do more than give a mumbled, "Hey."

David smiled at me, but I couldn't meet his eye. I knew that I was going to have to explain everything, and after Barrett's cruel lashings, I wasn't sure how much negativity I could take. But it couldn't wait. Again and again, I'd need to be brave.

I set my beer on the table. "Avril, could I please have some alone time with David? I'm sorry, but... would you mind?"

"Of course," she said, wiggling out of the chair. "Gives me an excuse to go upstairs and call Kirk."

I watched her go before I dropped my gaze to David. He'd propped himself up on his elbow, one eyebrow raised in subtle concern. With a shuddering sigh, I grabbed the remote and turned off the TV, which left us with the sound of muted thunder. The storm was still coming, whether we liked it or not.

I took a swig of beer, which made my voice husky and heavy. "I need to talk to you. But just listen, okay?"

"Yeah. Okay." He pursed his lips but agreed.

"And I can't look at you while I do this," I added, snatching a pillow, and throwing it on the floor in front of the couch. I plunked myself down, facing the blank TV as I brought my knees to my chest. I snatched the beer bottle and cupped it with both hands, focusing on the cold. Trying to draw courage like I could absorb it straight through the glass.

Then, with a sharp inhale, I began. "David, I want you to know that I know everything." I paused and took a sip. "I know about the RAP, I know what happened between your dad and Johnathan Roth, and I know about your dark history in Dartmouth."

From behind me, he drew a controlled breath but didn't say anything.

Dismally, I continued. "And I want you to know that none of this knowledge was gained with malicious intent. I dug it up because... I care about you..." My emotions swelled as I forced myself to continue. "And you matter to me... So much..."

"Likewise, Em," he said.

A silent tear ran down my cheek, and he shifted forward, wrapping his arm around my collarbone. He kissed my neck three times before resting his chin on my shoulder. I gripped his forearm with a contrasting, cold hand.

"Shortly after I got here, I started to notice you getting sick," I continued, quietly. "I didn't think anything of it at first, but it got to the point where you started scaring me. After you fainted in Kelowna, I was so desperate that I drove up to Mission after work one day and saw your dad on my own. I explained to him what happened and asked for his help, so he told me everything. He told me about your old life and about the program. Why he signed the contract, and later shot and killed Johnathan Roth.

"Then, as the two of us tried to come up with an escape plan for you, he suggested I win over Barrett's trust, because he seemed like the only avenue we had left. So, that's what I tried to do." I took another swig, swirling the liquid in the bottle. "I studied him, continuously weighing out my options, while having to watch you suffer this week. Which is more difficult now because I *know* the fucking reason." Dropping my lips to his arm, I left a tender kiss there.

"Oh, Em," he breathed.

"Wait," I said. "There's more. Before I visited your dad, I managed to get my hands on Barrett's keys—don't ask how—and I used them to break into the cabinet in their library. Then I found your file."

My heart filled with acid and threatened to burst. "I found your file, and I forced myself to read about the horrible things they've done to you... And they're so awful... so fucking awful, David... They've been torturing you... For almost *twenty years*, they've been torturing you..."

I wasn't sure if I could continue.

His chin massaged my shoulder when he nodded. "Yeah... That's why I smoke so much... Weed, I mean. It's the only thing that helps with the pain."

"And I understand that now," I managed. "And I'm so fucking sorry, David."

"It's not your fault, princess."

Silence. Then thunder.

"I've tried to fight it in the past," he finally continued. "Filed complaint after complaint. Crafted a petition signed by hundreds of other people in the program and submitted it to them on their behalf. Called and e-mailed, day after day. Raised it to the program managers every fuckin' time. I fought tooth and nail with what little power I have, but nothing changed. They don't listen, and I'm not even sure they documented any of that. If I took it public, they'd jus' fuckin' crush me. I had no choice but to give up and take it or... die."

I buried my face into his forearm and breathed in his familiar scent, taking comfort from it. "I believe you, I really do," I said. "And I didn't find any of that in your file, so I really don't fucking doubt it." I paused, letting the heaviness linger in the air. "Today, I went back to the library to read it again. I wanted to use your history as leverage, but Barrett caught me before I could. I begged for his help, but it turns out that he's not who I thought he was. He refused to help me. I can't believe he refused."

David nuzzled me, before he spoke in a whisper. "He'll never let me go anyway, Em. It's not your fault."

"I know." My tone bordered on hopelessness. "He's a bad man...

Joseph told me to never trust a man with the last name Roth, and he was right... You were right... This entire time... I should've listened."

"Em, I don't want you getting dragged into this. I can handle it until it's over."

"Is it ever going to be over?" I heaved. "Do you really believe that?"

His lips were a welcome feeling in the area below my ear. "I don't need you to save me, princess."

I twisted, finally meeting his gaze. The trimmed beard on his jawline was soft when I ran my thumb across it. "I know how strong you are. You've proven it time and time again. But we *can* change this and it's our only option. So let me help you."

We kissed deeply, then again, and I revelled in every second that his lips were on mine. I couldn't take David Mathis for granted now. The Roths could rob me of him at any second.

"I can't let them to keep you trapped like a wolf in a cage."

And though my next sentence scared me, I pulled all my bravery forward. Because that's who I was now. Brave. Independent. A woman, fearless in her dedication to stand up for her man.

"We have to get you out. Whatever it takes. There must be another way, David. There's gotta be another way..."

Sneak peek of Part Two
The Snare of Addiction:

PROLOGUE
ARROW

In my dreams, I'm walking barefoot through a forest, with the pine needles creating a comfortable cushion under my feet. The forest is silent; submerged in dusk with the light fighting through the softness of the branches. It catches the debris floating in the air, causing it to twinkle around me. Stars that brush my skin with delicate kisses. I can smell the cedar and pine, as the warmth of the setting sun falls on my face. The beauty of the scene is intoxicating, and I'm enthralled as I move across the dirt.

Then I hear a rustling in the trees to my right, and I'm curious, but not afraid. The branches begin to shift. Out of the darkness a lone wolf comes, his footsteps soft and silent. Upon discovering me, he stops at the edge of the trees and watches. With delicate expressions, we study each other, and the warm air touches his fur, causing it to move like a wheat field. Blinking from between tender lashes, I lower myself onto one knee and spread my arms to welcome him, as the pine needles envelop my skin in coolness. He tilts his head and stands still. His green eyes glimmer in question, but doubt passes quickly, and he lowers his head as he starts toward me.

As he comes out from the cover of the trees, I realize that he can't walk properly. He shuffles with a limp, and my heart grows heavy when I see the trap that's clamped around one of his front legs. Behind him, a trail of bright blood follows, which turns into a line of rubies as it falls on the forest floor.

We meet, and I reach out a sympathetic hand. He steps into my touch, gifting me with his soft fur through my fingers.

Resolute to ease his suffering, I grasp the trap with vehement fingers, but it's bound by a lock whose key I don't have. My head swivels as I search for it, but the forest returns no answers. I have no choice but to feel the rippled energy of his pain as I bring one hand to the side of his neck and touch it there. The physical contact soothes my troubled mind, and soon I start to feel the love instead.

Watching the reflection of the forest stars in his deep green eyes, I smile. "You are such a beautiful soul."

He sits and brushes his tail across the dirt.

For a little while, we bask in our presence together, and I think about how happy I would be to have him by my side for the rest of my life. The love flows freely between our heart centers, and I want this friend to come with me to the edge of the forest, where I know I'm going to leave this Earth. I have a resounding sense that he'll protect me, and that I'll protect him, too. If only I could find the key that frees him. Once I do, everything will be good. As long as we have each other, we can face any enemy that presents itself.

Stifling a whimper, my wolf rises to his three good legs and stumbles down the path before us, stopping only once to glance back. I rise—pine needles falling from my skin—and pick my way carefully around the trail of rubies that shadow him. The glimmering gems are tempting, but I don't pick them up. Doing so would see his blood on my hands, and I love him now.

We walk down the path for a while, coming to a shallow river that flows in a bubbling brook. He steps fearlessly into the water and turns to follow it, checking again that I'm with him. Enjoying the cool embrace of the river around my ankles, I reach out to touch his shoulder. Soft splashes follow each of our footsteps.

Up ahead is a wide lake, its water as still as a mirror. The trees around its banks tower above us before they rise into the surrounding mountains. As we near, I hear the deep moan of another being in pain, and I gasp. I stop on the rounded stones of the riverbed. Undeterred, my wolf nudges my thigh with his muzzle and urges me forward. With each step, the sounds of suffering grow louder, and I swallow my fear. No matter what this other being presents itself as, my wolf is with me.

Soon after, we come to the mouth of the river, and as we round the corner, I see a black and orange figure sprawled across the bank. Curious, I narrow my eyes to bring this other being into focus, but he's not made clear until I gather the courage to step closer. Beneath four massive paws, the water runs red, and I recognize the distinct feathering of an arrow impaled in the tiger's shoulder. Though he raises his head and reaches for it with his glimmering white teeth, he can't remove it. This isn't an arrow that he can dislodge by himself.

Cautiously, I lower myself at his side and reach for it, but he growls and lashes out before I can grab it. The wolf tenses and returns a warning rumble, but I've backed away. I'm too far from the tiger's reach for him to be a threat.

Then, a glint of silver from between the tiger's teeth draws my eye, and I realize that he's holding a filigreed key in his mouth. My heart leaps, and I turn to my wolf to find that the shape matches the lock on his trap. The tiger holds the key to his freedom. All I have to do is convince him to give it up. But how can I do that when he won't let me save him from the arrow in his side?

"I can help you," I tell him. "I have enough love in my heart for you both. Please. Let me help you so that you can free him."

The tiger's heavy breath clouds in the twilit air, and he looks at me with skeptical, obsidian eyes. They paralyze me with a strange and foreign feeling, but suddenly it becomes clear that I must gather the strength to solve this.

If I don't, I'll surely lose them both.

CHAPTER 1
THE DEVIL INSIDE

I pulled my knees to my chest, as I stared at my phone and snuggled my duvet. It was draped over my legs in a comforting warmth, which was made even warmer by the Nova Scotian man that was asleep in the bed next to me. Biting my lip, I stared at the text conversation for an unknown amount of time.

Please talk to me, I typed out, hitting the send button.

No response.

Barrett. I need you.

Still, no response.

Tapping my phone with restless fingers, I swallowed my fear and pushed myself to call.

"Hello. You've reached the voicemail of Barrett Roth—"

I hung up and called again.

"Hello. You've reached the voicemail of Barrett Roth—"

I hung up again. "*Fuck.*" Frustration left my lips in a whisper. I didn't want to wake my roommate-slash-friend, David Mathis.

Please, Barrett... Please...

I was hoping that my nudges would remind Barrett Roth of the deep connection that we once had. Maybe if I pulled on that particular heart string, I'd draw the Real-Barrett back out. I *had* to reconcile with him.

But what the fuck are we gonna do if he refuses to speak to me? I wondered.

After fifteen minutes of waiting, I gave up. I snapped my laptop shut from where it was sitting between David and me, stopping the movie that neither of us was watching, anyway. I set it on my nightstand, before I turned to look at him. In sleep, his face was tranquil and calm, and I watched him smile in his dreams. I smiled back, brushing the curls from his forehead and kissing it. I hoped he was in a peaceful place, for once.

Don't worry, I thought. *I'm gonna find a way to reel him back in. I'm gonna find out what he wants. I'll get you out, David. This, I promise.*

Reaching across my nightstand, I clicked off the light.

The next morning, I was sitting in my Yaris trying not to cry before heading to work at Roth Pharmaceuticals. I was thinking about David and his suffering, and my mind bubbled like a pot about to boil over. I wanted to help him, but he was entangled in a plot so much bigger than me. I still couldn't believe it. How could his father, Joseph Mathis, sign him up for a thirty-year, top-secret pharmaceutical trial at only nine years old?

I felt powerless.

Somehow, I'd need to use my connection to Barrett Roth, co-owner, and CFO of Roth Pharmaceuticals (and my former friend), if I wanted to help David. But I'd pissed him off by uncovering the confidential Research Acceleration Program—or RAP for short—that held David captive and exploited him. I'd also accused Barrett of being unaccountable for the atrocities of said program, which made him even angrier with me. He claimed that he knew little about it, and that it was managed by his brother, the CEO, Travis Roth. Shortly after, he'd forced me to sign a non-disclosure agreement for the RAP.

Now I was afraid that, in the game of conflict between these two men, there was no winning. If I failed to reconcile things between Barrett and me, David would have no chance in hell of being freed from the RAP. I was also afraid I'd lose Barrett completely, and despite how much of a dick he could be, I valued the friendship we'd built together. I'd also been screaming his name after waking up from my strange ability to see other people's memories in my sleep. For over a fucking decade. And I still believed we were fated in some way. So, I wasn't sure which loss scared me more. In the grand scheme of *me*, both men were heavily weighted.

If David wasn't able to see the light at the end of the torture, then I knew his future would be in question; especially since I'd seen a memory where he'd told his father that he couldn't handle the RAP anymore. And if I lost Barrett, then I'd be losing a powerful friend, along with any clues about how we were spiritually connected. I couldn't let either one happen. But right now, I didn't have any other plan than getting up and going into work.

No one had called me to tell me that I'd been fired, so I figured that I might as well suck up the pain of stepping into my tyrannical workplace. Besides, some time there would help me gather my thoughts on what to do next. Now that I was locked in an NDA for the RAP, any evidence that I'd gathered was meaningless, and there was no point in re-targeting the library at the Roth Tower to gather more. As long as the NDA stood, Barrett had me within his power, and I was no longer a threat to him. All I could do was show up and do what I was being paid to do. And try to repair our friendship. Which was something I still had hope for.

Though I'd been livid with him after he refused to help me, I knew that the man that I'd grappled with wasn't him. Not really. Not the real him, anyway. That indifferent monster was another cruelty-crafted veil that he used to hide himself, and I tried to think about the man camouflaged behind. I'd seen him a few times now, and that masked man—the Real-Barrett—was the one that I needed to reach. He was the one I genuinely cared about and was afraid to lose. But I was also terrified to face the Bad-Roth that stood in between us, and I wasn't sure how to get through to him when he had himself encased like that.

Pull on his heart strings, I told myself, as I took a deep breath and looked at myself in the rearview. *Or, at least, avoid him until you can. Maybe he'll be different today. Maybe he'll be more like himself.*

I hadn't read *The Strange Case of Dr. Jekyll and Mr. Hyde* since high school, but there was nothing like Barrett Roth's mood swings to remind you.

Maybe he'll be more Jekyll and less Hyde.

I exhaled.

You can't shy away from this. David needs you. All you can do is try.

Nodding, I swiped my fingers in a semi-circle across my cheekbones. "Yeah," I said, gripping my aged doorhandle. "Okay. Let's fucking do this."

Ignoring the torment from my lack-of-a-plan, I grabbed my purse and my overly sweetened coffee, and made my way to the elevators that went from the garage to the ground floor. Barrett's empty spot gave me hope. There was no fucking *supercar* there yet, which told me I'd have time to gather my wits before I was forced to face him.

The air conditioning hit me like a wave when I came out the elevator. Reluctance flared in my veins. As my shallow heels clicked over the marble floor, I tried not to think about the portion of my paycheque that came from the exploitation of marginalized communities, but it was really fucking difficult. I was doing a master's degree in Medical Ethics at the UBC, so I couldn't avoid latching onto it and analyzing it from all angles. Before Barrett had forced me to sign an NDA for the RAP, I'd been planning on spearheading it for my thesis. Now, I couldn't use any of the research I'd done on the RAP or Roth Pharma specifically, but I'd still decided that my research would be on the ethics—*or lack there of*—in pharmaceutical trials. I was sure there was more to uncover in the industry as a whole, and it was a topic that clearly excited me.

But none of that changed the fact that I was trapped working for a company that profited from injustice. At least, until I could free my friend from it. I raised my chin and breathed through the thought, shrugging my purse onto my shoulder, and drawing a sip of coffee before I scanned my badge at the gates.

On the other side, my coworker Adam was watching me from the reception counter. I said nothing as I walked around him and sat down in a huff.

"Good morning, sunshine," he said, mockingly. "Who pissed in your cornflakes?"

I rolled my eyes and tucked my purse into the drawer. "No one. I just didn't sleep well last night."

He snorted, turning back to his computer screen. "Yeah, you look like it too. You know, concealer does exist. You should try it sometime."

"Piss off, Adam." I wasn't a fan of the snappy tone that'd recently made a home in my voice.

"*Excuse me?*" He swiveled back.

Dropping my head between my hands, I rubbed my temples. "Oh my God, I'm so sorry. That was really bitchy, and I didn't mean it. I'm going through a rough patch right now."

He snorted again. "Looks like it. Jesus." I pierced him with a look, and he threw up his hands. "Alright. Okay. Truce. I'll let you off."

Sighing, I ran both hands through my hair. "Thank you. I'm sorry. And thank you."

He eyed me before he flashed his eyebrows. "But you'd better get your PMS under control, or this is going to be a very long day for both of us."

"I'll do my best," I said, throwing back some coffee. Then I clicked through my computer and browsed aimlessly through my e-mails. "Do you know if Barrett's going to be in today?"

"What do I look like? His assistant? I fucking *wish*. I'd need to grow some tits and a tight ass for that."

Wrestling my frustration, I slammed both elbows down on the desk and threw my head back into my hands. "Right. Sorry. How silly of me."

Adam's coffee-breath was *a lot* when he leaned in. "Get it together, girl." And when I didn't respond, he continued with, "Unless he *died* on the way into work, I would assume there's a ninety-nine-point-nine percent chance he's gonna be here. He's always here, Em. Sick or well, he's always here."

I rubbed my brow again.

"Plus, it's not a good day unless I get to check out his ass as he walks to the elevators. You know that. So what are you complaining about?"

I sat up straight. "Nothing," I mumbled, before I began to pull my hair back in a tight ponytail. "I just... I don't know... need to talk to him..."

"That'd be ill advised," he said. "There's no way he's going to have time for whatever mediocre thing you're going to tell him."

I took a calculated ten-second breath in. As much as I hated to admit it, Adam was right. I'd have to re-strategize if David and I were going to survive this fight.

Get it together, Em.

Then, the clicking of high heels drew my gaze as Barrett's assistant, Natalie, made her way across the foyer on the other side. She was dressed in a black, pin-striped, skirt suit, with her brown hair tied back in her signature bun. I swallowed the stomach acid that rose into my throat. She stopped at the security gates, pulled her iPad to her chest, and straightened her spine. The ding of the parking garage elevator made my insides do a somersault, and I inhaled sharply when I realized that it was too late to avoid Barrett. As soon as he caught sight of me, I was sure that he'd have me paralyzed.

On any other day, there would have been butterflies running through me as I watched him. Especially—as frustrating as it fucking was—as hot as he looked in a full suit and tie. But today was different. Today I was fearful, and everything was cold. Like the entire Tower had turned to ice from the moment he stepped out of the elevator. I curled my fingers into my palms as he walked through the gates, and greeted his assistant with a frank, "Good morning."

She fell in stride with him as they passed. His obsidian eyes flashed to mine, and he started to crush me like a pop can under a tire. And that's when I learned what it was like to have Barrett Roth look at me like he hated me. With one piercing glance, he turned me into nothing. He made me worthless. He squashed me like a bug. I arched my brows and silently pleaded with him to stop. Merciless, he narrowed his gaze and intensified it. Time slowed down to a grinding halt. My heart drummed on my ribcage like it wanted out.

Please, Bear. Please. Let me go. I'm begging you.

Finally, he snapped it away as they moved toward the other set of elevators that rose to the top of the Tower. I exhaled; muscles liquifying as I watched his back. Natalie—unaware of all that—was still briefing him as they walked. Adam—also clueless—rested his chin on his propped hand and grinned. "I'll never get tired of that view," he said.

Pick up your copy of *The Snare of Addiction* to continue...

AUTHOR'S NOTE:

Dear Reader,

I recognize that there are dark elements to my writing, and that they may have had an effect on you. I'm deeply sorry if my writing triggered you in a negative way. This is why I took the time to include the reader advisory at the beginning of the book; to warn anyone that could be affected that these novels may not be the right fit for them. I believe that going through a traumatic childhood comes out in my writing, and I recognize that I do put my characters through some horrible things. Please understand that I take the heavy themes like suicide, parental abuse, and drug addiction very seriously, and I know they can be difficult to read—especially if you've suffered with experiences like this before.

If you're struggling, please know that you're not alone. Even in the darkest of places, there is hope. You bring so much love and light to this world, and your life and wellbeing matter. You are so loved, and even if you don't feel this way, the Universe, and the Source love you like no other. You have a purpose on this planet, and though you may not know what it is right now, that's okay. Trust that the world needs you, and that you'll find out in time. Life on this planet can be so, so, *so* tough sometimes, but we're in this together! And if you can't find the strength to believe anything else, please know that _you are worthy_.

If you want to, you can take this as a sign that it's your time to get help. A pure expression of love, from my heart to yours. You *matter*, and taking care of yourself trumps any to-do list or external commitment. I wholeheartedly believe that we are on this Earth to *be*; not to produce. You deserve your Earthy experience, and you deserve to have it be the best it can be. You're only one step away from brighter days, and I'm so proud of you!

I love you, my Reader. Thank you for being a critical part of my "why" and allowing me to share my world with you. I see you. I appreciate you. I value you like no other.

Thank you. Thank you. *Thank you.* I cannot say it enough.

Remember: you're worthy, and you matter.

xoxo

- Kaylee

Support in Canada (and for my international readers, a quick Google search does wonders):

Suicide prevention:

- Suicide Crisis Helpline – Call or text 9-8-8

- Canadian Association for Suicide Prevention – Search online

- Canada.ca – Suicide prevention – Search online

Domestic Abuse:

- Canada.ca – Stop Family Violence – Search online

- Canadian Association of Social Workers – Search online

- DomesticShelters.org – Search online

Substance Abuse/Addiction Support:

- Mental Health and Addictions Phone Line – 1-833-553-6983

- Addiction Services – 1-888-299-8399

- Canada.ca – Substance use – Search online

- Canadian Centre on Substance Use and Addiction – Search online

ACKNOWLEDGMENTS:

First of all, I'd like to thank my editor for her unwavering dedication and incredible hard work in helping me make this series the best it could be. I wouldn't even be a quarter of the writer I am today without her, and I'm endlessly grateful for the support, resources, and advice that she's provided me with on this project.

On the same wavelength, I'd like to thank my sensitivity reader for helping me create the right narrative for my characters, guiding me with the hard choices, and for keeping me honest with the internal biases that have come out in my writing. What an eye-opening experience!

I'd like to thank Jessie Cunniffe for her expert advice on crafting great book blurbs, because I'd never be able to condense such a series into kickass hooks without her!

I'd like to thank my coaches and support team, Barbara Hartzler, Dakota Jackson, Cassandra Choflet, Ramy Vance, Chandler Bolt, and everyone at Self-Publishing School for helping me turn this dream into reality.

Thank you to Alex Pinto for being my very first reader when I started writing this thing back in 2017, and kindly telling me, "I'm enjoying it so far," even though it was definitely not so good. Those words kept me going! And I love you endlessly.

I'd like to thank my family and friends for listening to me drone on and on about this series for years and providing loving support for my dream. Ditto to everyone at Orangetheory Fitness on Davie

Street in Vancouver. Special thanks go out to Sally Scott, Gaëlle Birolini, Joyce Collardé, Radz Lal, and James Tallosi for being my relentless cheerleaders throughout this whole crazy process, encouraging me during the hard times, becoming my chosen family in Vancouver, and reminding me what love looks like.

Special thanks to my Mum for all the support over the last seven years!

Thank you to my amazing designers and the team Miblart for being so patient with the perfectionist, control freak author that I can be. You're the whole reason that I'm so in love with my covers!

Thank you to my launch team for their awesome, selfless support. I couldn't have done any of this without you.

And last, but not least, I'd like to thank you, my reader, for allowing me to share the world inside my head, giving my series a chance, enduring my growing pains as an author, and believing in me enough to read my work.

Lots of love to you all!

Connect with me:

Website: www.kayleemillerwriter.com

Instagram: @kayleemiller_author

Facebook: @Kaylee.Miller.Author

Thank you so much for reading Mum's book!

She really appreciates your opinion and would love to hear what you think. She needs your input to help make her books better.

Could you please help her out by leaving a rating and review on Amazon, Goodreads, and BookBub? Your feedback is valued.

Lots of love!

www.ingramcontent.com/pod-product-compliance
Lightning Source LLC
Chambersburg PA
CBHW020146090426
42734CB00008B/717